To Sasha, Michèle, and Marc

THE INDIVIDUAL
IN A SOCIAL WORLD

Essays and Experiments

THE INDIVIDUAL IN A SOCIAL WORLD

Essays and Experiments

Stanley Milgram
The City University of New York

Addison-Wesley Publishing Company
Reading, Massachusetts
Menlo Park, California
London · Amsterdam · Don Mills, Ontario · Sydney

This book is in the

ADDISON-WESLEY SERIES IN SOCIAL PSYCHOLOGY

Preface and Acknowledgments

The late Gordon W. Allport taught that social psychology examined how the thought, action, and feelings of the individual were affected by the implied, actual, or imagined presence of others. At the center of his definition was the individual; the individual remains at the center of my own conception of the field. Thus, I have loosely structured this volume in terms of four domains of social facts confronted by the individual: the city, authority, groups, and media.

The volume describes research I have carried out over a period of twenty years, and it is impossible to thank here all those who helped me in carrying out particular studies. But I wish to indicate a general intellectual debt to a few people who have been especially important to my professional development: first, to the late Gordon W. Allport, who always encouraged me to think I could contribute something useful to social psychology, and to three inspiring teachers: Solomon E. Asch, Roger Brown, and Jerome S. Bruner.

Many of the experiments reported here were carried out in the context of my courses in social psychology at Harvard, Yale, and The City University of New York. The many students who participated in these projects were true partners in research, and I wish to express my appreciation to each of them.

Alice B. Kornblith and Alexandra Milgram provided helpful editorial and secretarial assistance in the preparation of this volume and Joan Gerver prepared the index.

Finally, I wish to acknowledge my appreciation to the several publishers who allowed me to reprint my articles, which first appeared in their journals and books.

New York City
February 1977

S.M.

Contents

INTRODUCTION

Part 1 THE INDIVIDUAL IN THE CITY

Introduction	16
1. The experience of living in cities	24
2. The urban bystander	42
3. The idea of neighborhood	47
4. The familiar stranger	51
5. A psychological map of New York City	54
6. Psychological maps of Paris	68

Part 2 THE INDIVIDUAL AND AUTHORITY

Introduction	92
7. Some conditions of obedience and disobedience to authority	102
8. Interpreting obedience: error and evidence	124
9. Ethical issues in the study of obedience	139
10. Disobedience in the sixties	147

Part 3 THE INDIVIDUAL AND THE GROUP

Introduction	152
11. Nationality and conformity	159
12. Conformity and Norwegian life	171
13. Ethics in the conformity experiment	174
14. Group pressure and action against a person	178

15. Liberating effects of group pressure   188

16. The drawing power of crowds of different size   200

17. Crowds   206

Part 4   THE INDIVIDUAL IN A COMMUNICATIVE WEB

    Introduction   276

18. The small world problem   281

19. The lost letter technique   296

20. Television and antisocial behavior   306

21. The image freezing machine   339

INDEX   351

INTRODUCTION

As a social psychologist, I look at the world not to master it in any practical sense, but to understand it and to communicate that understanding to others. Social psychologists are part of the very social matrix they have chosen to analyze, and thus they can use their own experience as a source of insight. The difficulty is to do this in a way that does not drain life of its spontaneity and pleasure.

A wish to understand social behavior is not, of course, unique to psychologists; it is part of normal human curiosity. But for social psychologists, this need is more central, more compelling, and thus they go a step further and make it their life's work.

The studies in this collection, carried out over a period of twenty years, examine the way in which the social world impinges on individual action and experience. The implicit model for the experimental work is that of the person influenced by social forces while often believing in his or her own independence of them. It is thus a social psychology of the reactive individual, the recipient of forces and pressures emanating from outside oneself. This represents, of course, only one side of the coin of social life, for we as individuals also initiate action out of internal needs and actively construct the social world we inhabit. But I have left to other investigators the task of examining the complementary side of our social natures.

The social world does not impinge on us as a set of discrete variables, but as a vibrant, continuous stream of events whose constituent parts can be dissected only through analysis, and whose effects can be most compellingly demonstrated through the logic of experiments. Indeed, the creative claim of social psychology lies in its capacity to reconstruct varied types of social experience in an experimental format, to clarify and make visible the operation of obscure social forces so that they may be explored in terms of the language of cause and effect.

The source for the experiments in this volume is neither textbooks nor abstract theory, but the texture of everyday life. They are imbued with a phenomenological outlook. Even so apparently technical a study as "The Lost Letter Technique" begins with the imagined experience of encountering such a missive, the consciousness of choice which the letter stimulates, and the ultimate resolution of conflicting tendencies in a decisive and measurable act.

Every experiment is a situation in which the end is unknown; it is tentative, indeterminate, something that may fail. An experiment may produce only a restatement of the obvious or yield unexpected insights. The indeterminacy of its outcome is part of its excitement.

Although experiments may be objective, they are rarely entirely neutral. There is a certain viewpoint that is implicit in the experiments that were carried out. Thus, in my studies of conformity and obedience, the moral value always rests with the person who rejects the group or authority. Going it alone seems to be the preferred value. But of course the experimenter himself set up the situation in a way in which only such rejection could constitute a morally adequate choice. The pervasive effects of such implicit values do not in themselves undermine the validity of the experiments; they do, however, give them a specific coloration that is not scientifically derived.

I do not mean thereby to reduce experimental social psychology to an emotional catharsis in which the feelings and needs of the investigator are paramount. Far from it! Even if a study originates in a personal interest, problem, or bias, it cannot long remain at this level. Emotional factors are severely disciplined by the experimental method and the ideal of scientific objectivity.

The most interesting experiments in social psychology are produced by the interplay of naivete and skepticism. The experimenter must be sufficiently naive to question what everyone thinks is a certainty. Yet he must be skeptical at every point—in his interpretation of data, and in the too hasty assimilation of a discovery to a preexisting framework of thought.

Although most of the papers in this volume deal with the presentation of experimental ideas, several represent attempts to justify or defend those ideas in the face of criticisms. Or they apply the experimental conclusions to issues of larger scope. Thus, in the section on "The Individual and Authority," I include a defense of the ethics of the obedience experiment. Another paper defends its methodological suppositions. Papers such as these, however necessary a part of the social psychologist's work, have always seemed to me a deflection from the more pleasurable activity of experimental invention.

The following interview, conducted by Carol Tavris for *Psychology Today*, expands on the remarks in this introduction and touches on a broad range of my substantive and methodological concerns.

Carol Tavris: Much of your work is directed toward the experience of living in cities, isolating the intangibles that make Oslo different from Paris, Topeka different from Denver, and New York different from anything. How do you go about defining those intangibles?

Stanley Milgram: First, you keep your eyes open; you generalize on the basis of numerous specific incidents; you try to determine whether particular incidents lead up to a definable pattern; you attempt to find an underlying coherence beneath the myriad surface phenomena in a particular city. You generalize from your own experience and formulate a hypothesis.

Then you become systematic about it. You ask people what specific incidents seem to them to characterize a particular urban setting, and you see whether any patterns or dimensions emerge. When you ask Americans to cite specific incidents they think typical of London, for example, they often center on the civility of the Londoner. Typical comments about New York focus on its pace of activity, and diversity. The psychologist differs from the novelist or travel writer in that he tries to measure whether these features—pace, friendliness, diversity—actually correspond to what is out there, and differ from one urban setting to the next. *Measurement* of ambience, then, is the special contribution that social psychology makes to centuries of travelogues.

Tavris: What features of urban life have interested you most recently?

Milgram: For years I've taken a commuter train to work. I noticed that there were people at my station whom I had seen for many years but never spoken to, people I came to think of as *familiar strangers*. I found a peculiar tension in this situation, when people treat each other as properties of the environment rather than as individuals to deal with. It happens frequently. Yet there remains a poignancy and discomfort, particularly when there are only two of you at the station: you and someone you have seen daily but never met. A barrier has developed that is not readily broken.

Tavris: How can you study the phenomenon of the familiar stranger?

Milgram: Students in my research seminar took pictures of the waiting passengers at one station. They made duplicates of the photographs, numbered each of the faces, then distributed the group photographs the following week to all the passengers at the station. We asked the commuters to indicate those people whom they knew and spoke to, those whom they did not recognize, and those whom they recognized but had never spoken to. The commuters filled out the questionnaires on the train and turned them in at Grand Central Station.

Well, we found that the commuters knew an average of 4.5 familiar strangers, and the commuters often had many fantasies about these people. Moreover, there are sociometric stars among familiar strangers. Eighty percent of the commuters recognized one person, although very few had ever spoken to her. She was the visual high point of the station crowd, perhaps because she wore a miniskirt constantly, even in the coldest months.

Tavris: How do our dealings with familiar strangers differ from those with total strangers?

Milgram: The familiar-stranger phenomenon is not the absence of a relationship but a special kind of frozen relationship. For example, if you wanted to make a trivial request or get the time of day, you are more likely to ask a total stranger, rather than a person you had seen for many years but had never spoken to. Each of you is aware that a history of noncommunication exists between you, and you both have accepted this as the normal state.

But the relationship between familiar strangers has a latent quality to it that becomes overt on specific occasions. I heard of a case in which a woman fainted in front of her apartment building. Her neighbor, who had seen her for 17 years and never spoken to her, immediately went into action. She felt a special responsibility; she called the ambulance, even went to the hospital with her. The likelihood of speaking to a familiar stranger also increases as you are removed from the scene of routine meeting. If I were out strolling in Paris and ran into one of my commuter strangers from Riverdale, we would undoubtedly greet each other for the first time.

And the fact that familiar strangers often talk to each other in times of crisis or emergency raises an interesting question: is there any way to promote solidarity without having to rely on emergencies and crises?

Tavrls: To study the familiar stranger, your students directly confronted commuters for information. Is this typical of your experimental style?

Milgram: Methods of inquiry must always be adapted to the problem at hand, and not all of life's phenomena can be assembled in a laboratory. You must often go out to meet the problem, and it doesn't require a license to ask someone a question. My experimental style aims to make visible the social pressures that operate on us unnoticed.

And an experiment has a tangible quality to it; you see people really behaving in front of you, which stimulates insight. It is a matter of bringing issues down to a level where you can see them clearly, rendering processes visible. Social life is highly complex. We are all fragile creatures entwined in a cobweb of social constraints. Experiments often serve as a beam that helps clarify the murky aspects of experience. And I do believe that a Pandora's box lies just beneath the surface of everyday life, so it is often worthwhile to challenge what you most take for granted. You are often surprised at what you find.

Tavrls: For example?

Milgram: We've recently looked at the subway experience which is so characteristic of New York life. If you consider that at rush hour total strangers are pressed against each other in a noisy hot car, surrounded by poking elbows, it is astonishing how little aggression this produces. It is a remarkably regulated situation, and we tried to probe the norms that keep it manageable. The best way to start was to be simple-minded and not too sophisticated, since sophistication assumes too much about the structure you wish to illuminate.

Tavrls: What did you do?

Milgram: I suggested to the class that we each go up to someone on the subway and simply ask for his seat. The immediate reaction of the class was exactly the same as yours—laughter. But anxious laughter is often a sign that you are on to something important. Many members of the class felt that no one in New York would give up his seat simply because a stranger asked him to. My students did a second thing that uncovered their prejudices. They said that the person would have to justify his request by asserting illness, nausea, dizziness; they assumed that the request itself would not gain the seat. A third clue: I asked for volunteers from a class of graduate students, but they recoiled *en masse*. That's very revealing. After all, they merely had to make a trivial request. Why was it so frightening a project? In other words, the very formulation of the research question began to generate emotional clues to its answer. Finally, one brave soul, Ira Goodman, took on the heroic assignment, accompanied by a student observer. Goodman was asked to make the request courteously, and without initial justification, to 20 passengers.

Tavris: What happened?

Milgram: Within a week, rumors started to circulate at the Graduate Center. "They're getting up! They're getting up!" The news provoked astonishment, delight, wonder. Students made pilgrimages to Goodman as if he had uncovered a profound secret of survival in the New York subway, and at the next session of the seminar, he announced that about half of those he had asked had gotten up. He didn't even have to give a reason.

But one discrepancy struck me in Goodman's report. He had only approached 14 people instead of the hoped-for 20. Since he was normally quite conscientious, I asked why. He said: "I just couldn't go on. It was one of the most difficult things I ever did in my life." Was there something idiosyncratic about Goodman, or was he telling us something profoundly revealing about social behavior generally? There was only one way to find out. Each of us would repeat the experiment, and neither I nor my colleague, Professor Irwin Katz, would be exempted.

Frankly, despite Goodman's initial experience, I assumed it would be easy. I approached a seated passenger and was about to utter the magical phrase. But the words seemed lodged in my trachea and would simply not emerge. I stood there frozen, then retreated, the mission unfulfilled. My student observer urged me to try again, but I was overwhelmed by paralyzing inhibition. I argued to myself: "What kind of craven coward are you? You told your class to do it. How can you go back to them without carrying out your own assignment?" Finally, after several unsuccessful tries, I went up to a passenger and choked out the request, "Excuse me, sir, may I have your seat?" A moment of stark anomic panic overcame me. But the man got right up and gave me the seat. A second blow was yet to come. Taking the man's seat, I was overwhelmed by the need to behave in a way that would justify my request. My head sank between my knees, and I could feel my face blanching. I was not role-playing. I actually felt as if I were going to perish. Then the third discovery: as soon as I got off the train, at the next station, all of the tension disappeared.

Tavris: What underlying social principles does such an experiment reveal?

Milgram: First, it points up the enormous inhibitory anxiety that ordinarily prevents us from breaching social norms. Asking a person for his seat is a trivial matter, yet it was extremely difficult to make the request. Second, it highlights the powerful need to justify one's request by appearing sick or exhausted. I must stress that this is not acting, but a compelled playing out of the logic of social relations. Finally, the fact that all of these intense feelings were synthesized in, and were limited to the particular situation, shows the power of immediate circumstances on feelings and behavior. I was relieved and back to normal the instant I was off the train.

Tavris: Your reaction sounds typical of the subjects in the obedience experiment. Many of them felt obliged to follow the experimenter's orders to shock an innocent victim, even though they felt great anxiety.

Milgram: Yes. The subway experience gave me a better understanding of why some subjects obeyed. I experienced the anxiety they felt as they considered repudiating the experimenter. That anxiety forms a powerful barrier that must be surmounted, whether one's action is consequential—disobeying an authority—or trivial—asking for a seat on the subway.

Do you know there are people who choose to die in a burning building rather than run outside with their pants off? Embarrassment and the fear of violating apparently trivial norms often lock us into intolerable predicaments. And these are not minor regulatory forces in social life, but basic ones.

Tavris: Can you recommend a similar experiment for those of us in cities without subways?

Milgram: If you think it is easy to violate social constraints, get onto a bus and sing out loud. Full-throated song now, no humming. Many people will say it is easy to carry out this act, but not one in a hundred will be able to do it.

The point is not to *think* about singing, but to try to *do* it. Only in action can you fully realize the forces operative in social behavior. That is why I am an experimentalist.

Tavris: It seems to me, though, that many experiments, while entertaining, do not take one beyond what sensitive perception and feeling would. Some people criticized the obedience work by saying, "I knew that." After all, centuries of human history amply document the excesses of following orders. What advantage derives from an experiment that confirms history?

Milgram: The purpose of the obedience experiment was neither to confirm nor disconfirm history, but to study the psychological function of obedience; the conditions under which it occurs, the defense mechanisms it entails, the emotional forces that keep the person obeying. The criticism you cite is akin to saying that we know people die of cancer, so why study it?

Further, it is difficult for people to sort out what they know from what they only think they know. The clearest indication of ignorance about obedience is that when psychiatrists, psychologists and others were asked to predict the performance of subjects in the experiment, they failed totally. The psychiatrists said, for example, that only one person in a thousand would administer the highest shock on the board, and they were off by a factor of 500.

Moreover, we must ask whether people really do learn the lessons of history. Isn't it always the "other guy" who shamelessly submits to authority, even in violation of elementary morality? I think it is hard for many people to accept that they themselves have the potential to yield without limit to authority. All the pedagogic means at our disposal, whether in the form of history, literature, or experiments, need to be called into service to heighten awareness of this issue.

Finally, if one group criticizes the experiments because they merely confirm history, an equally vociferous group vehemently denies that Americans are capable of the degree of obedience demonstrated in my experiment, and they consequently repudiate me and the experiment. I suggest people read my book and draw their own conclusions.

Tavris: Your obedience work and city work both consider the network of social rules that constrain us. In the galaxy of factors that make up a city's atmosphere, for example, which do you think are the most important?

Milgram: Clearly, the degree of moral and social involvement people have with each other, and the way this is limited by the objective circumstances of city life. There are so many people and events to cope with that you must simply disregard many possible inputs, just to get on. If you live on a country road you can say hello to each of the occasional persons who passes by; but obviously you can't do this on Fifth Avenue.

As a measure of social involvement for instance, we are now studying the response to a lost child in big city and small town. A child of nine asks people to help him call his home. The graduate students report a strong difference between city and town dwellers; in the city, many more people refused to extend help to the nine-year-old. I like the problem because there is no more meaningful measure of the quality of a culture than the manner in which it treats its children.

Tavris: But is it inevitable that big cities breed impersonal treatment of others? You don't find drunks or beggars on the streets in Chinese cities, but if you did it would be everyone's responsibility to help. The moral norms are to aid the other guy, so no one person must play lone Samaritan.

Milgram: I would be reluctant to compare a city such as Peking, in which the atmosphere is permeated with political doctrines and imperatives, to Western cities. Beyond that, it is true that not all large cities are alike. But the most general movement is toward an adaptation common to all cities. Paris today seems more like New York than it did 20 years ago, and 50 years from now they will be even more alike, as adaptive needs come to dominate local color. There will be some cultural differences, but these will fade, and I regard this as most unfortunate.

Tavris: You have just spent a year in Paris studying mental maps of the city. What are they?

Milgram: A mental map is the picture of the city that a person carries in his mind: the streets, neighborhoods, squares that are important to him, the way they are linked together, and the emotional charge attached to each element. The initial idea came from Kevin Lynch's book *The Image of the City*. The external city is encoded in the brain: you could say there is a city inside the mind. Even if the external city were destroyed, it could be reconstructed by reference to the mind's model of the city.

Tavris: What did you find out about Paris?

Milgram: First, that reality and mental maps are imperfectly linked. For example, the Seine may course a great arc through Paris, almost forming a half circle, but Parisians imagine it a much gentler curve, and some think the river a straight line as it flows through the city. And the pattern of known to unknown parts of the city is fascinating: there are large areas of eastern Paris that are not known to anyone but the residents of those particular neighborhoods. Old people tend to retain the map of an earlier Paris and find it hard to include newer elements, however monumental.

Tavris: Don't people have different maps, depending on their experience and economic status?

Milgram: There is both a universal mental map of Paris which all Parisians share, and there are specialized maps depending on one's personal biography and social class. We interviewed more than 200 Parisians, workers and professionals, and there were striking differences along class lines. For example, 63 percent of the professionals recognized a slide of the Place Furstenberg, an unexceptional square that professionals infuse with a kind of bourgeois sentimentality; only 15 percent of the workers could recognize it. And 84 percent of the professionals could identify the UNESCO complex at Place de Fontenoy; only 24 percent of the workers did. So there is an important class basis to the mental map.

On the other hand, as many workers as professionals recognized the Place St. Martin. And Notre Dame still represents the psychological core of the city to everyone, as it did a thousand years ago. So the maps have both universal and idiosyncratic components to them.

Tavris: What are mental maps good for?

Milgram: People make many important decisions based on their conception of a city, rather than the reality of it. That's been well demonstrated. So it is important for planners to know how the city sits in the mind. And wouldn't it be enlightening to have such mental maps for Periclean Athens, for Dickensian London? Unfortunately, there were no social psychologists to construct such maps systematically at the time, but we know better and will do our duty.

Tavris: I'd like to turn to another of your real-world explorations, the effects of TV violence. In eight elaborate studies you found no differences between the people who watched the antisocial show and the controls. Has the effect of television on behavior been overrated?

Milgram: I don't know if it's overrated, but neither I nor my colleagues were able to establish a causal relationship. My ideal experiment would have been to divide the country in half, remove all violence on television west of the Mississippi and include it east of the Mississippi, enforce laws so that no one could move from one part of the country to the other, and then see what happens over a five or ten-year period. It turned out not to be practical, so I had to work with what I had.

The approach was to take an antisocial act, write it into a real TV program (*Medical Center*), show some cities the program containing it and others the same program without it, then give everyone an opportunity to imitate the antisocial act. I thought we would detect imitation, but we didn't. You can control everything about an experiment but the outcome.

Tavris: But why didn't you find the link?

Milgram: Perhaps the antisocial act—breaking into charity boxes and stealing money—was not dramatic enough. Perhaps people have been so sated with violence in the media that one show doesn't make a difference. Perhaps there is no such link. This experiment, like most, is a chip in a complex mosaic. No one study can tell the whole story. We have not established that the portrayal of violence leads to violence, but we cannot discard that hypothesis either.

Tavris: Do you plan to do more research on the effects of television?

Milgram: I don't know. Actually, it occurs to me that perhaps it is not the content of TV but its form that constitutes the real affront to human sensibilities: I mean the constant interruption of cognitive processes every 12 minutes by irrelevant material—commercials. I wonder what decrement in appreciation and understanding comes about when children watch a show with such interruptions. I think this will be an important problem.

Tavris: Let's back up a moment if we may. How did you get into the field of psychology?

Milgram: My boyhood interests were scientific. I edited the high-school science magazine, and my first article in 1949 was on the effects of radiation on the incidence of leukemia in the Hiroshima and Nagasaki survivors. I was always doing experiments; it was as natural as breathing, and I tried to understand how everything worked.

I fell away from science in college to pursue courses in political philosophy, music and art. But I finally came to the realization that although I was interested in the questions raised by Plato, Thomas Hobbes and John Locke, I was unwilling to accept their mode of arriving at answers. I was interested in human questions that could be answered by objective methods. In the '50s the Ford Foundation had a program to move people into the behavioral sciences. It seemed like a perfect opportunity, and I shifted into social psychology at the Department of Social Relations at Harvard. Men of uncommon wisdom ran things at the time, and created a climate in which ideas and excellence found ready support and encouragement.

Tavris: Who were your most important influences at Harvard?

Milgram: Gordon Allport was my long-time mentor and friend. He was a modest man with a pink face; you felt an intense loving quality about him. Since I wasn't interested in personality theory, he did not provide a specific intellectual input, but he gave me a strong sense of my own potential. Allport was my spiritual and emotional support. He cared for people deeply.

Tavris: If Gordon Allport was your spiritual adviser, who was your most important intellectual influence as a student?

Milgram: Solomon Asch, a brilliant, creative man, who possessed great philosophic depth. He is certainly the most impressive social psychologist I have known. I was his teaching assistant when he visited Harvard, and later worked for him at the Institute for Advanced Study in Princeton. He was always very independent. I recall the day when the U.S. launched a successful space probe, after some early failures. The scientists at the Institute were visibly excited—as I was—at the prospects for space exploration. But Asch was uniquely calm, pointing out that we had enough problems on earth to solve, and he questioned the wisdom of deflecting attention to space. Of course there was enormous prescience in that view, but it wasn't recognized at the time.

Tavris: What about Henry Murray?

Milgram: A highly original man who abhorred unnecessary academic rules and regulations. But my most indelible memory of him concerns a song. In my early 20s I wrote songs as a hobby. I wrote a song for Murray that he claims got him a psychology building. They had torn down the historic old psychological clinic on Plimpton Street, and naturally everyone connected with it was very sad. Murray wanted me to write a song about it for a big dinner with President Nathan M. Pusey. At first I said no, since I was up to my ears in work. But the song more or less spontaneously materialized. After I gave Murray the song, I went off to Europe to collect data for my thesis. I didn't even turn in the paper I owed him for his course. So it was two years before I knew what had happened with the song.

Tavris: Which was...

Milgram: I went to find Murray to give him that long overdue paper. I was feeling enormously contrite, but the first thing he said to me was: "Stanley Milgram! You should have seen how well it went over! It was because of your song that we got this building, you know!" My song was more important to him than the late paper.

Harvard was full of lively souls like Henry Murray; some are still there. Roger Brown was a brilliant assistant professor 20 years ago and remains an inspiring scholar; Jerome Bruner was a vital and dynamic force, though he's now settled at Oxford.

Tavris: What would you say are the ingredients that make for a creative social psychologist?

Milgram: It's complicated. On the one hand, he needs to be detached and objective. On the other hand, he will never discover anything if he lacks feeling for the pulse and emotionality of social life. You know, social life is a nexus of emotional attachments that constrain, guide and support the individual. To understand why people behave as they do you have to be aware of the feelings aroused in everyday social situations.

Tavris: And beyond that?

Milgram: Out of your perception of such feelings, insights may arise. They may take the form of explicit principles of social behavior. But, more often, they express themselves in symbolic form, and the experiment is the symbol. I mean, just as a playwright's understanding of the human situation reveals itself in his own mind in dramaturgical form, so for the creative investigator, intuition translates directly into an experimental format that permits him both to express his intuition and critically examine it.

Tavris: Are there any ideas you had that you now especially wish you had carried out?

Milgram: Only one, really. The idea started in the summer of 1960, when some friends and I decided to improvise some street-theater scenes. We stopped at restaurants along the Massachusetts Turnpike, and enacted common human situations: irate wife discovers her husband with another woman and rages at him in an incomprehensible mock-foreign language. What impressed me was that despite the extreme emotion in the encounter, onlookers conspicuously avoided involvement, even when the husband shook and slapped his "wife" in retaliation.

When I returned to my room at Harvard, I reviewed the reaction of the patrons, and wrote out a set of experiments in which the subjects were to be exposed to people who needed help. Subjects would sit in a waiting room; through a closed door they overhear an argument between a man and a woman; the man would become increasingly aggressive, in gradual steps, and finally the woman would cry out for help. I planned to study when people would intervene, and under what conditions. I designed a timer into the connecting door, so I'd know exactly how long people delayed before helping.

Tavris: The bystander problem.

Milgram: Yes, although then I called it the problem of "social intrusion." A month after sketching out those experiments, I began to teach at Yale and work on the obedience experiments. I didn't have time to study social intrusion too, but once a year I issued to each class a solemn prophesy that if they worked on the bystander problem they would be making an important contribution to social psychology. Every year highly intelligent graduate students would listen with interest, and every year they would go off and study attitude change, which was fashionable at Yale then.

Tavris: When did they begin to see the error of their ways?

Milgram: With the Kitty Genovese murder, and the 38 silent witnesses. The matter attracted nationwide interest and finally social scientists attempted experimental formulations of the problem. My graduate students carried out an unpublished field study in which a supposed drunk abused a woman in a laundromat. She called for help, and the question was how long it would bo before she got it. The class found the experiment fascinating. But the *Zeitgeist* was about to catch up with us. Soon many other studies of this sort were being carried out. The best work was done by Bibb Latané and John M. Darley, then at Columbia and New York University. They chose the right variables, related them to the Genovese case, applied technical ingenuity, and reported their work in clear English. Appropriately, they won the AAS prize. And the field of bystander research is still blooming.

Tavris: How did that make you feel?

Milgram: The only satisfactions I derived from all this were of two sorts: first, what I regarded as a highly important sociopsychological question was now coming under examination; and second, a kind of prophetic function was fulfilled by my own experimental analysis of this type of situation, an analysis that preceded the Kitty Genovese case by three years, yet prophesied it in many ways.

The common view is that social psychologists derive their experiments from life, and there is an important measure of truth in this. But it's also true that events, such as the Genovese case, are the inevitable unfolding of forces that experimental analysis will frequently pinpoint first. Underlying the silly incident in the restaurant was an important principle of social behavior; by focusing on that latent principle, and extending it through to a concrete dramatized experiment, one could foresee certain inevitable results of such a principle. The Genovese case was merely one publicized expression of that principle. So analysis, combined with a certain imagined dramatic extension, will often prefigure events by years and decades.

Tavris: You generate a lot of ideas. What happens to them?

Milgram: Some of these ideas are realized; others filter into the atmosphere and they stimulate others to carry them out. Some are expressed through students. Some just fade. But Leo Szilard was certainly right when he said it is not the ideas you have, but those you act on that determine your character as a scientist. Every imaginative scientist dies with a host of good ideas that never make it into print.

Tavris: How did you come up with the idea for the obedience experiment?

Milgram: I was trying to think of a way to make Asch's conformity experiment more humanly significant. I was dissatisfied that the test of conformity was judgments about *lines*. I wondered whether groups could pressure a person into performing an act whose human import was more readily apparent, perhaps behaving agressively toward another person, say by administering increasingly severe shocks to him. But to study the group effect you would also need an experimental control; you'd have to know how the subject performed without any group pressure. At that instant, my thought shifted, zeroing in on this experimental control. Just how far *would* a person go under the experimenter's orders? It was an incandescent moment, the fusion of a general idea on obedience with a specific technical procedure. Within a few minutes, dozens of ideas on relevant variables emerged, and the only problem was to get them all down on paper.

But many years after I had completed the obedience experiments, I realized that my concerns about submission to authority had been incubating since I was a first-year graduate student.

Tavris: How so?

Milgram: For one, the central issues were symbolically expressed in a story I had concocted. Briefly, the story was about two men who agreed to accompany a clerk into an old shabby office. One of the men was informed by the clerk that his death had been scheduled for that day and that he had a choice of two possible methods of execution. The man immediately objected that neither method was suitable in his case, and after a lot of bickering, persuaded the clerk to execute him more humanely. And he was done in.

The second person, however, who was also brought into this bizarre situation, had quietly left the room. Nothing happened to him. When the clerk noticed he had gone, he simply closed the office, glad he could quit work early that day.

The story was quite macabre, but gave me insight into certain extraordinary features of social behavior. And it contains many of the elements that later appear in the obedience experiment, in particular the way the man accepted the alternatives that were presented to him. He failed to question the legitimacy of the entire context; he became preoccupied with choices as defined by the clerk and not with the larger issue of whether he should be there at all. He forgot that he could simply leave, as his friend did.

In just this way, our experimental subjects would temporize or get too technical or worry about details, trying to find the formula that would end their conflict. They did not see the larger framework of the situation, and consequently they couldn't see how to break out of it. The ability to see the larger context is precisely what we need to liberate ourselves.

Tavris: What then is the solution to the problem of the good man who is "only following orders?"

Milgram: The first thing to realize is that there are no easy solutions. In order to have civilization you must have some degree of authority. Once that authority is established, it doesn't matter much whether the system is called a democracy or a dictatorship: the common man responds to governmental policies with expected obedience, whether in Nazi Germany or democratic America.

Tavris: Then you do not think there is much variation in the extent of obedience that governments demand, or rather in the extent of disobedience they tolerate?

Milgram: Every society must have a structure of authority but this doesn't mean that the range of freedom is the same in every country. And of course it is true that Germany's destruction of millions of innocent men, women and children in concentration camps demonstrated the worst excess of obedience we've seen. But American democracy also has instituted policies that were severe and inhumane: the destruction of American Indians, the enslavement of blacks, the incarceration of the Japanese during the Second World War, Vietnam. There are always people who obey, who carry out the policies. When authority goes awry, individuals do not seem to have enough resources to put on the brakes.

But the problem is complicated. Individual standards of conscience are themselves generated from a matrix of authority relationships. Morality, as well as blind obedience, comes from authority. For every person who performs an immoral act on account of authority there is another who is restrained from doing so.

Travis: Then how do we guard against authority's excesses?

Milgram: First, we need to be aware of the problem of indiscriminate submission to authority. And I have tried to foster that awareness with my work. It is a first step. Second, since we know men will comply, even with the most malevolent authorities, we have a special obligation to place in positions of authority those most likely to be humane and wise. But there is a long-range source of hope, too. People are inventive, and the variety of political forms we have seen in the last 5000 years does not exhaust all possibilities. Perhaps the challenge is to invent the political structure that will give conscience a better chance against errant authority.

THE INDIVIDUAL IN THE CITY

Part 1

Introduction

The argument for studying the effect of the city on the individual seems self-evident: It is the fate of many of us to live in cities, and we ought to understand how this social fact shapes feeling, action, and thought. By the mid-sixties, social psychology had studied interaction within smaller units, but it had not yet examined how the person is affected by the extended urban environment. Urban questions had a well-entrenched tradition in sociology, but for some reason the social psychologist had preferred to examine small-scale social relationships—the dyad, the small group, or in his most expansive moments, intergroup relations. Yet the city itself remained immune to sociopsychological inquiry.

Many sides to the psychological effect of city life awaited examination. There was, first, the texture of everyday experience in the urban setting. How could it be described, and what precise features contribute to the differing tone of life in cities and small towns? Everyone who visits New York City feels its frenetic pace, and some complain of the abrasiveness of its inhabitants, but it remains for the social psychologist to determine if these constitute actual or merely alleged features of the social environment, and to demonstrate this by applying objective techniques of measurement. Would it be possible to measure the "ambience" of a city as we measure the temperature of the ocean with a thermometer? The purpose of such measurement is, first, to sift objective fact from prevailing fiction, second, to allow for more sensitive and valid comparisons among different settings, and finally, to stimulate us to explain such differences that we find.

An interest in such questions is most likely to arise in people who have not only felt the quality of city life, but who have a number of contrasting experiences which show them that the frenetic pace and the abrasiveness are not as invariable features of life as the law of gravity, but are variables which alter in strength in different settings.

For many years I lived in New York, Boston, and Paris. The contrast between life in these cities and my experiences in small towns doubtless stimulated my interest in this topic. This biographic accident provided a rich background of detail and experience from which a scientific exploration could be safely launched. The subjective emphasis is reflected in the first article, "The Experience of Living in Cities." The article does not start from very abstract considerations, but from the predicament of the single individual and the way in which the city constitutes a set of social facts that continuously impinge on him.

Beneath the questions raised in "The Experience of Living in Cities" is a deeper skepticism of whether differences between urban and rural persons exist at all, or whether they simply reflect prejudices and social myths. Sometimes in the midst of a lecture on urban differences I am afflicted with the painful thought that I am talking nonsense, simply perpetuating prejudices of rural folk against the city. In such moments, it is best to withdraw from academic abstraction and try to imagine the implications of such statements in concrete and measurable terms.

The required strategy is to find some simple act, embedded in the flux of daily life, that will tap a significant feature of the urban milieu. For example, in one seminar we discussed the presumed indifference of the urban dweller to the problems of his coinhabitants. Then the students and I devised a concrete situation in which children who claimed to be lost asked pedestrians for aid in downtown areas of New York City and several small towns. The initial results showed a higher likelihood of aid in the small towns. The students, David Lucido and Harold Takooshian, subsequently carried the experiments to Boston and Philadelphia and invariably found that a "lost child" is more likely to be helped in a small town than in a large city.

In all cases, the findings are actuarial. That is, the proportion of individuals who help changes from town to city, but there are always people in both settings who deny or extend help to the children. But this shift in proportion is sufficient to establish the tone of different communities, to create a distinctive ambience.

Experiments in social psychology often arise out of personal experiences. On a recent trip to Amherst, Massachusetts, I walked into a stationery store. The clerk beamed a broad smile, which immediately prompted me to believe that we were acquaintances. I rummaged my mind for the person's name, but finally apologized that I had forgotten it. The situation rapidly deteriorated into general confusion, since the clerk was perplexed by my apology. He could not understand why I assumed that we knew each other.

The misunderstanding arose because in the urban milieu in which I live, people do not smile at one another unless they are acquainted. For the rural clerk it was natural to smile at everyone, even a stranger. Once again, the reality of rural–urban differences was asserted. I related this incident to students in my seminar. But of course, the anecdotal method rarely proves anything. Members of the class contributed countervailing anecdotes of their own implying opposite conclusions.

It was clear that only a *systematic* examination of the issue would advance us beyond an exchange of anecdotes. To carry out a systematic study we would need, at the very least, a clearly measurable act that would in some sense signify a readiness to be friendly, at least superficially friendly. I suggested we approach strangers on the street and, without explanation, extend our hands in a friendly manner, as if to shake. Would the person reciprocate and shake hands? What could be a simpler or more symbolically pregnant measure of "friendliness" than this unreflective response?

Thirteen student experimenters went into the streets of mid-town New York City, hands outstretched, then into small towns in New Jersey, Long Island, and Westchester County, forever extending their hands. The results showed a highly significant difference in the readiness of town and city dwellers to reciprocate the gesture (see Table 1). Of the city dwellers, 38.5 percent reciprocated, but 66.7 percent of the town dwellers consumated the handshake. Although the behavior in question is simple, it is symbolically rich, and it is highly responsive to such variables as age, sex, and race. Table 2 shows that almost three times as many women shook hands in the small towns as in the city. This is a small fact, but it is reliably gleaned and gives us a further measure of the reality of urban–town differences.

Table 1   Incidence of reciprocated handshaking in towns and city (all subjects).

	Towns	City	
Yes	62 66.7%	40 38.5%	102
No	31 33.3%	64 61.5%	95
	93	104	197

Table 2   Incidence of reciprocated handshaking by women subjects in towns and city.

	Towns	City	
Yes	25 56.8%	8 19.0%	33
No	19 43.2%	34 80.1%	53
	44	42	86

Chi-square = 11.415
$p < 0.001$

The myriad details which distinguish cities from small towns need to be brought under the discipline of a theoretical framework. I attempted to do this in "The Experience of Living in Cities" by invoking the concept of "overload," and showing how it is produced by the demographic exigencies of urban life.

In addition to all the phenomena of the large city, resulting from density, homogeneity, and large numbers, there is a stage beyond: *the great city effect*. This refers to the special excitement of New York, Paris, London, and a few other urban agglomerations whose spirit and excitement seem to transcend the negative effects of overload.

BYSTANDER INTERVENTION

Sometimes a dramatic event will jolt ordinary people into thinking about the deeper issues of social life. It was not the murder of Kitty Genovese, but the failure of numerous neighbors to come to her aid while she was being killed that aroused consternation. Is indifference an inevitable consequence of urban life? Carey McWilliams, editor of *The Nation*, asked me to write an article about the incident. I

Studies in Social Intrusion

Experiments in Social Psychology: Other People's Business.

Social Involvement

The Problem: Under what circumstances do other peoples business become our own. Under what conditions do we implicate ourselves in it.

Every group of two people, circulating in the larger society, have a a kind of protective social membrane around them that isolates them from the larger society. Thus, others will not interfere with their discussion, if they donot know xxxxxxxx the two.

But, under certain circumstances, the general outsider will intrude. If for example, a man is beating his girl friend, their will be intrusion. If a person in harming another, there will be intrusion.

To undertake a series of experiments, ina naturalistic social settings, to understand some of the bases of social intrusion.

Very interesting theoretical concepts. Social privacy. Acceptable intrusions. Inviolable social fields. There are definitely forces that keep people from interfering or becoming implicated in the discussion of others. Might work with a standard intrusion situation.

Some questions: Will people more likely intrude when women are the insiders, when me are the insiders, or when insiders are mixed. 2)Relationship between side of insider group and xxxxxx tendency for intrusion. etc.

Aug 20 1960

Social Intrusion

The experiments could be undertaken first in a laboratory setting, and with relative ease. One could announce an experiment in perception. Several subjects would be seated in a dim room for dark adaptation to occur. It would be in that setting that the eliciting predicament would be staged. (Eventually, some of the predicaments could be moved to a more naturalistic setting).

Eliciting progression and response progression.

Eliciting progression: The staged scene could be carefully rehearsed and preplanned so that it induces more and more the liklihood of intrusion. It could go through carefully shaped stages. For example:
    joking stage
    light argument stage
    heavier argument
    girl slaps man
    man slaps girl
    man twist, s arm of girl
    girl calls for help (or simply shrieks, then calls for help).

On the response progression, we can measure various degrees of intrusion. Remarks to someone else; light remarks to social couple; admonition; threat; physical intervention.

Question: why use this particular model for intrusion. Wouldn't simple joking also elicit it? Yes, in the laboratory, but certainly not in the field situation.

Devices to prevent intrusion upon first intrusion--if man speaks to neighbor--xxxx about it, neighbor says: why don't you mind your own business? Might reinforce this with others.

Fig. I.1 *The author's notes for studies in "social intrusion" presaged the Kitty Genovese incident by several years.*

agreed without hesitation because the Genovese case had given me an uncanny sensation of *déjà vu*. A few years earlier, in 1960, I had devised an experiment which prefigured the Genovese case in its essential details. In this experiment, a man appeared to assault a woman in the presence of a group of casual bystanders. I suspected that there would be strong inhibitions against bystander intervention: I wanted to study the exact conditions that would determine whether or not people would be motivated to intervene. I did not carry out the experiment at the time, and soon, in the Genovese affair, urban reality was to catch up and overtake experimental imagination. And in the Genovese case, a true-to-life incident rather than an experimentally contrived situation needed to be analyzed. My friend Paul Hollander, the sociologist, collaborated with me in an analysis written for *The Nation* (p. 42). A fundamental viewpoint is expressed in the article: The question of bystander intervention has a moral component to it—that is what makes it interesting. But the social psychologist needs to see beyond the moral judgment to the analyzable causes of bystander response. Whether a person intervened or not is not only an expression of personal morality, but also depends on the exact way in which numerous variables of the situation fall into place.

Generally, we think about the Genovese case from the morally superior assumption that we would do better. Here we confuse our self-perception, generally skewed in a favorable direction, with an understanding of the actual causes of behavior. We may think ill of the Kew Gardens residents, but how often has each of us averted our eyes or walked away from the scene of a confrontation where one individual was obviously in need of help?

Social psychology has no monopoly in the understanding of bystander behavior. Startling insights into the bystander phenomenon are provided by anthropological examination of life in circumstances different from our own. Colin Turnbull's monograph, *The Mountain People*, describes the life of the Ik, an African tribe which lives under such impoverished conditions that it has turned into a society where every person is concerned only with personal survival. The uniform response to another person's distress is amusement or indifference. The picture portrayed by Turnbull is dreadful and depressing, but it serves to remind us that social behavior is always responsive to the material conditions of our existence, and that social norms will change in response to altered circumstances. Even the degree of helpfulness and compassion we now display to one another is precarious, dependent upon the larger social and environmental structures that support our present mode of life.

MENTAL REPRESENTATION OF THE CITY

If the individual is to function in the city, he must have some mental representation of it, and this phenomenon is addressed in the papers on mental maps. The work was stimulated by the thinking of Kevin Lynch. His 1960 book, *The Image of the City*, sparked research on urban imagability, which by now must contain a bibliography of several hundred contributions. Parallel developments were underway in departments of geography, where cartography had long been an established specialty, and which has recently extended its mapmaking to include not merely what the geographic environment is like, but what people *think* it is like.

We can assume that individuals have at least fragmentary mental maps of the city; the scientific problem is to learn how to measure the maps and how to express generalizations on the basis of the maps of many individuals. The methods used in this type of research were quite variable, and my hope was to give it a precision, and perhaps elegance, beyond existing studies. In "A Psychological Map of New York City" (p. 54), my collaborators and I conceived of the city as an infinite number of viewing points, and we wondered to what extent each of these points communicates a sense of location to the inhabitants.

But for all of its rigor, this study was too limited in scope. The effort to photograph the 150 viewing points and to obtain recognition judgments for each of them was substantial, but the resultant findings were thin and barely scratched the surface of how individuals mentally encode a city. Recognition of scenes, after all, is but a small part of the process. I wanted a set of maps—perhaps an Atlas—that captured richer aspects of the individual's mental map of a city. A Guggenheim Fellowship in 1972–1973 permitted me to go to Paris to extend the work on psychological representation.

"Psychological Maps of Paris" represents a multidimensional approach to cognitive mapping. Of all the studies reported in this book, it was the most difficult to carry out. This may seem surprising in view of its modest scope, particularly in comparision with the complex logistics of, say, the study of television violence (p. 306). But the difficulty of carrying out a study is not a fixed quantity, but a relationship between the work to be done and the resources available to do the job. In Paris I had the generous cooperation of Professor Serge Moscovici, Director of the Laboratory of Social Psychology, and the expert collaboration of Mme. Denise Jodelet. But there were almost no funds, and French subjects are more difficult to obtain than Americans, especially when their selection must conform to rigid constraints of sampling.

As I went on, the task became virtually a cottage industry, with my children pasting stamps on envelopes, my wife typing names and addresses from French phone books, and I assuming the lowly task of errand boy, messenger, and general factotum. The environment cannot help but influence the style and texture of the actual execution of research: About one-quarter of the subjects were interviewed in a Parisian restaurant. In the end, a useful surprise: The French government gave the project a grant of 35,000 francs, permitting me to employ a French survey organization to reach incompleted cells in our sample, particularly among lower-class Parisians. The analysis of data was substantially accomplished in France, and I was impressed by the extent to which computer technology is readily available in western Europe. The results of the inquiry were summarized in "Psychological Maps of Paris"; a more extensive exhibit on the work was displayed in the Piltzer Gallery in Paris, where it appears that materials I assumed to be social psychology were construed by others as a species of conceptual art.

Space limitations in the Paris article did not then permit me to cite a 1973 study written by Pailhous describing the manner in which French taxi drivers learn to orient themselves in the city. Pailhous points out that drivers first develop a knowledge of a

Fig. I.2   *"… materials I assumed to be social psychology were construed by others as a species of conceptual art." (Poster designed by conceptual artist Roger Welch.)*

primary network of streets. This network is almost universally known. They then develop secondary networks of a more idiosyncratic nature that are linked to the primary network. The street patterns of Parisian *patés* (blocks) are highly irregular, often forming irregular polygons. But Pailhous notes that when taxi drivers are asked to draw them, they often regularize the patterns, turning a trapezoid, for instance, into a rectangle and following other gestalt principles of good form.

"Paris is a non-Euclidean city." This remark was first made by my nephew, Dr. Joseph Gerver, who was completing his dissertation in mathematics and was visiting us in Paris. His observation corresponded to my own experience. Streets one assumes to be parallel may eventually intersect. If you miss an intersection and attempt to loop back at the next, you may find yourself in a completely unfamiliar neighborhood, unable to return to your starting point. Parisian street patterns defy the Euclidean mind; they are best embodied in some abstruse Riemannian geometry.

A pleasant career could be made of mapping the world's great capitals. But I am sure the next important step is to develop an adequate theory of mental maps, one that cogently accounts for the transformation of geographic information into its psychological form. The mental map is different from the geographic reality, yet it is sufficiently veridical to be useful. What set of transforms is needed to convert the geographic city into a city of the mind?

REFERENCES

Lynch, K., 1960. *The Image of the City.* Cambridge, Mass.: MIT and Harvard University Press.

Pailhous, J., 1970. *La Representation de l'Espace Urbain: L'Exemple du Chauffeur de Taxi.* Paris: Presses Universitaires de France.

Turnbull, C., 1973. *The Mountain People.* New York: Simon & Schuster.

The Experience of Living in Cities ___1

When I first came to New York it seemed like a nightmare. As soon as I got off the train at Grand Central I was caught up in pushing, shoving crowds on 42nd Street. Sometimes people bumped into me without apology; what really frightened me was to see two people literally engaged in combat for possession of a cab. Why were they so rushed? Even drunks on the street were bypassed without a glance. People didn't seem to care about each other at all.

This statement represents a common reaction to a great city, but it does not tell the whole story. Obviously, cities have great appeal because of their variety, eventfulness, possibility of choice, and the stimulation of an intense atmosphere that many individuals find a desirable background to their lives. Where face-to-face contacts are important, the city offers unparalleled possibilities. It has been calculated by the Regional Plan Association[1] that in Nassau County, a suburb of New York City, an individual can meet 11,000 others within a 10-minute radius of his office by foot or car. In Newark, a moderate-sized city, he can meet more than 20,000 persons within this radius. But in midtown Manhattan he can meet fully 220,000. So there is an order-of-magnitude increment in the communication possibilities offered by a great city. That is one of the bases of its appeal and, indeed, of its functional necessity. The city provides options that no other social arrangement permits. But there is a negative side also, as we shall see.

Granted that cities are indispensable in complex society, we may still ask what contribution psychology can make to understanding the experience of living in them. What theories are relevant? How can we extend our knowledge of the psychological aspects of life in cities through empirical inquiry? If empirical inquiry is possible, along what lines should it proceed? In short, where do we start in constructing urban theory and in laying out lines of research?

Observation is the indispensable starting point. Any observer in the streets of midtown Manhattan will see (1) large numbers of people, (2) a high population density, and (3) heterogeneity of population. These three factors need to be at the root of any sociopsychological theory of city life, for they condition all aspects of our experience in the metropolis. Louis Wirth,[2] if not the first to point to these factors, is nonetheless the sociologist who relied most heavily on them in his analysis of the city. Yet, for a psychologist, there is something unsatisfactory

This paper was first published in *Science*, Vol. 167 (March 13, 1970), pp. 1461–1468. The paper was based on an address given by the author on September 2, 1969 at the 77th annual meeting of the American Psychological Association in Washington, D.C. Copyright © 1970 by the American Association for the Advancement of Science.

about Wirth's theoretical variables. Numbers, density, and heterogeneity are demographic facts but they are not yet psychological facts. They are external to the individual. Psychology needs an idea that links the individual's *experience* to the demographic circumstances of urban life.

One link is provided by the concept of overload. This term, drawn from systems analysis, refers to a system's inability to process inputs from the environment because there are too many inputs for the system to cope with, or because successive inputs come so fast that input *A* cannot be processed when input *B* is presented. When overload is present, adaptations occur. The system must set priorities and make choices. *A* may be processed first while *B* is kept in abeyance, or one input may be sacrificed altogether. City life, as we experience it, constitutes a continuous set of encounters with overload, and of resultant adaptations. Overload characteristically deforms daily life on several levels, impinging on role performance, the evolution of social norms, cognitive functioning, and the use of facilities.

The concept has been implicit in several theories of urban experience. In 1903 George Simmel[3] pointed out that, since urban dwellers come into contact with vast numbers of people each day, they conserve psychic energy by becoming acquainted with a far smaller proportion of people than their rural counterparts do, and by maintaining more superficial relationships even with these acquaintances. Wirth[2] points specifically to "the superficiality, the anonymity, and the transitory character of urban social relations."

One adaptive response to overload, therefore, is the allocation of less time to each input. A second adaptive mechanism is disregard of low-priority inputs. Principles of selectivity are formulated such that investment of time and energy are reserved for carefully defined inputs (the urbanite disregards the drunk sick on the street as he purposefully navigates through the crowd). Third, boundaries are redrawn in certain social transactions so that the overloaded system can shift the burden to the other party in the exchange; thus, harried New York bus drivers once made change for customers, but now this responsibility has been shifted to the client, who must have the exact fare ready. Fourth, reception is blocked off prior to entrance into a system; city dwellers increasingly use unlisted telephone numbers to prevent individuals from calling them, and a small but growing number resort to keeping the telephone off the hook to prevent incoming calls. More subtly, a city dweller blocks inputs by assuming an unfriendly countenance, which discourages others from initiating contact. Additionally, social screening devices are interposed between the individual and environmental inputs (in a town of 5000 anyone can drop in to chat with the mayor, but in the metropolis organizational screening devices deflect inputs to other destinations). Fifth, the intensity of inputs is diminished by filtering devices, so that only weak and relatively superficial forms of involvement with others are allowed. Sixth, specialized institutions are created to absorb inputs that would otherwise swamp the individual (welfare departments handle the financial needs of a million individuals in New York City, who would otherwise create an army of mendicants continuously importuning the pedestrian). The interposition of institutions between the individual and the social world, a characteristic of all modern society, and most notably of the large metropolis, has its negative side. It deprives the individual of a sense of direct contact and spontaneous integration in the life around him. It simultaneously protects and estranges the individual from his social environment.

Many of these adaptive mechanisms apply not only to individuals but to institutional systems as well, as Meier[4] has so brilliantly shown in connection with the library and the stock exchange.

In sum, the observed behavior of the urbanite in a wide range of situations appears to be determined largely by a variety of adaptations to overload. I now deal with several specific consequences of responses to overload, which make for differences in the tone of city and town.

SOCIAL RESPONSIBILITY

The principal point of interest for a social psychology of the city is that moral and social involvement with individuals is necessarily restricted. This is a direct and necessary function of excess of input over capacity to process. Such restriction of involvement runs a broad spectrum from refusal to become involved in the needs of another person, even when the person desperately needs assistance, through refusal to do favors, to the simple withdrawal of courtesies (such as offering a lady a seat, or saying "sorry" when a pedestrian collision occurs). In any transaction more and more details need to be dropped as the total number of units to be processed increases and assaults an instrument of limited processing capacity.

The ultimate adaptation to an overloaded social environment is to totally disregard the needs, interests, and demands of those whom one does not define as relevant to the satisfaction of personal needs, and to develop highly efficient perceptual means of determining whether an individual falls into the category of friend or stranger. The disparity in the treatment of friends and strangers ought to be greater in cities than in towns; the time allotment and willingness to become involved with those who have no personal claim on one's time is likely to be less in cities than in towns.

Bystander Intervention in Crises

The most striking deficiencies in social responsibility in cities occur in crisis situations, such as the Genovese murder in Queens. In 1964, Catherine Genovese, coming home from a night job in the early hours of an April morning, was stabbed repeatedly, over an extended period of time. Thirty-eight residents of a respectable New York City neighborhood admit to having witnessed at least a part of the attack, but none went to her aid or called the police until after she was dead. Milgram and Hollander, writing in *The Nation*,[5] analyzed the event in these terms:

> Urban friendships and associations are not primarily formed on the basis
> of physical proximity. A person with numerous close friends in different
> parts of the city may not know the occupant of an adjacent apartment. This
> does not mean that a city dweller has fewer friends than does a villager, or

knows fewer persons who will come to his aid; however, it does mean that his allies are not constantly at hand. Miss Genovese required immediate aid from those physically present. There is no evidence that the city had deprived Miss Genovese of human associations, but the friends who might have rushed to her side were miles from the scene of her tragedy.

Further, it is known that her cries for help were not directed to a specific person; they were general. But only individuals can act, and as the cries were not specifically directed, no particular person felt a special responsibility. The crime and the failure of community response seem absurd to us. At the time, it may well have seemed equally absurd to the Kew Gardens residents that not one of the neighbors would have called the police. A collective paralysis may have developed from the belief of each of the witnesses that someone else must surely have taken that obvious step.

Latané and Darley[6] have reported laboratory approaches to the study of bystander intervention and have established experimentally the following principle: the larger the number of bystanders, the less the likelihood that any one of them will intervene in an emergency. Gaertner and Bickman[7] of The City University of New York have extended the bystander studies to an examination of help across ethnic lines. Blacks and whites, with clearly identifiable accents, called strangers (through what the caller represented as an error in telephone dialing), gave them a plausible story of being stranded on an outlying highway without more dimes, and asked the stranger to call a garage. The experimenters found that the white callers had a significantly better chance of obtaining assistance than the black callers. This suggests that ethnic allegiance may well be another means of coping with overload: the city dweller can reduce excessive demands and screen out urban heterogeneity by responding along ethnic lines; overload is made more manageable by limiting the "span of sympathy."

In any quantitative characterization of the social texture of city life, a necessary first step is the application of such experimental methods as these to field situations in large cities and small towns. Theorists argue that the indifference shown in the Genovese case would not be found in a small town, but in the absence of solid experimental evidence the question remains an open one.

More than just callousness prevents bystanders from participating in altercations between people. A rule of urban life is respect for other people's emotional and social privacy, perhaps because physical privacy is so hard to achieve. And in situations for which the standards are heterogeneous, it is much harder to know whether taking an active role is unwarranted meddling or an appropriate response to a critical situation. If a husband and wife are quarreling in public, at what point should a bystander step in? On the one hand, the heterogeneity of the city produces substantially greater tolerance about behavior, dress, and codes of ethics than is generally found in the small town, but this diversity also encourages people to withhold aid for fear of antagonizing the participants or crossing an inappropriate and difficult-to-define line.

Moreover, the frequency of demands present in the city gives rise to norms of noninvolvement. There are practical limitations to the Samaritan impulse in a major city. If a citizen attended to every needy person, if he were sensitive to

and acted on every altruistic impulse that was evoked in the city, he could
scarely keep his own affairs in order.

Willingness to Trust and Assist Strangers

We now move away from crisis situations to less urgent examples of social
responsibility. For it is not only in situations of dramatic need but in the
ordinary, everyday willingness to lend a hand that the city dweller is said to be
deficient relative to his small-town cousin. The comparative method must be
used in any empirical examination of this question. A commonplace social
situation is staged in an urban setting and in a small town—a situation to which
a subject can respond by either extending help or withholding it. The responses
in town and city are compared.

One factor in the purported unwillingness of urbanites to be helpful to
strangers may well be their heightened sense of physical (and emotional)
vulnerability—a feeling that is supported by urban crime statistics. A key test for
distinguishing between city and town behavior, therefore, is determining how
city dwellers compare with town dwellers in offering aid that increases their
personal vulnerability and requires some trust of strangers. Altman, Levine,
Nadien, and Villena[8] of The City University of New York devised a study to
compare the behaviors of city and town dwellers in this respect. The criterion
used in this study was the willingness of householders to allow strangers to enter
their home to use the telephone. The student investigators individually rang
doorbells, explained that they had misplaced the address of a friend nearby, and
asked to use the phone. The investigators (two males and two females) made 100
requests for entry into homes in the city and 60 requests in the small towns. The
results for middle-income housing developments in Manhattan were compared
with data for several small towns (Stony Point, Spring Valley, Ramapo, Nyack,
New City, and West Clarkstown) in Rockland County, outside of New York
City. As Table 1.1 shows, in all cases there was a sharp increase in the
proportion of entries achieved by an experimenter when he moved from the city
to a small town. In the most extreme case the experimenter was five times as

Table 1.1   Percents of entries achieved by
investigators for city and town dwellings (see
text).

Experimenter	Entries achieved (%)	
	City*	Small town†
Male		
No. 1	16	40
No. 2	12	60
Female		
No. 3	40	87
No. 4	40	100

*Number of requests for entry, 100.
†Number of requests for entry, 60.

likely to gain admission to homes in a small town as to homes in Manhattan. Although the female experimenters had notably greater success both in cities and in towns than the male experimenters had, each of the four students did at least twice as well in towns as in cities. This suggests that the city-town distinction overrides even the predictably greater fear of male strangers than of female ones.

The lower level of helpfulness by city dwellers seems due in part to recognition of the dangers of living in Manhattan, rather than to mere indifference or coldness. It is significant that 75 percent of all the city respondents received and answered messages by shouting through closed doors and by peering out through peepholes; in the towns, by contrast, about 75 percent of the respondents opened the door.

Supporting the experimenters' quantitative results was their general observation that the town dwellers were noticeably more friendly and less suspicious than the city dwellers. In seeking to explain the reasons for the greater sense of psychological vulnerability city dwellers feel, above and beyond the differences in crime statistics, Villena[8] points out that, if a crime is committed in a village, a resident of a neighboring village may not perceive the crime as personally relevant, though the geographic distance may be small, whereas a criminal act committed anywhere in the city, though miles from the city dweller's home is still verbally located within the city; thus, Villena says, "the inhabitant of the city possesses a larger vulnerable space."

Civilities

Even at the most superficial level of involvement—the exercise of everyday civilities—urbanites are reputedly deficient. People bump into each other and often do not apologize. They knock over another person's packages and, as often as not, proceed on their way with a grumpy exclamation instead of an offer of assistance. Such behavior, which many visitors to great cities find distasteful, is less common, we are told, in smaller communities, where traditional courtesies are more likely to be observed.

In some instances it is not simply that, in the city, traditional courtesies are violated; rather, the cities develop new norms of noninvolvement. These are so well defined and so deeply a part of city life that *they* constitute the norms people are reluctant to violate. Men are actually embarrassed to give up a seat on the subway to an old woman; they mumble "I was getting off anyway," instead of making the gesture in a straightforward and gracious way. These norms develop because everyone realizes that, in situations of high population density, people cannot implicate themselves in each others' affairs, for to do so would create conditions of continual distraction which would frustrate purposeful action.

In discussing the effects of overload I do not imply that at every instant the city dweller is bombarded with an unmanageable number of inputs, and that his responses are determined by the excess of input at any given instant. Rather, adaptation occurs in the form of gradual evolution of norms of behavior. Norms are evolved in response to frequent discrete experiences of overload; they persist and become generalized modes of responding.

Overload on Cognitive Capacities: Anonymity

That we respond differently toward those whom we know and those who are strangers to us is a truism. An eager patron aggressively cuts in front of someone in a long movie line to save time only to confront a friend; he then behaves sheepishly. A man is involved in an automobile accident caused by another driver, emerges from his car shouting in rage, then moderates his behavior on discovering a friend driving the other car. The city dweller, when walking through the midtown streets, is in a state of continual anonymity vis-à-vis the other pedestrians.

Anonymity is part of a continuous spectrum ranging from total anonymity to full acquaintance, and it may well be that measurement of the precise degrees of anonymity in cities and towns would help to explain important distinctions between the quality of life in each. Conditions of full acquaintance, for example, offer security and familiarity, but they may also be stifling, because the individual is caught in a web of established relationships. Conditions of complete anonymity, by contrast, provide freedom from routinized social ties, but they may also create feelings of alienation and detachment.

Empirically one could investigate the proportion of activities in which the city dweller or the town dweller is known by others at given times in his daily life, and the proportion of activities in the course of which he interacts with individuals who know him. At his job, for instance, the city dweller may be known to as many people as his rural counterpart. However, when he is not fulfilling his occupational role—say, when merely traveling about the city—the urbanite is doubtless more anonymous than his rural counterpart.

Limited empirical work on anonymity has begun. Zimbardo[9] has tested whether the social anonymity and impersonality of the big city encourage greater vandalism than do small towns. Zimbardo arranged for one automobile to be left for 64 hours near the Bronx campus of New York University and for a counterpart to be left for the same number of hours near Stanford University in Palo Alto. The license plates on the two cars were removed and the hoods were opened, to provide "releaser cues" for potential vandals. The New York car was stripped of all movable parts within the first 24 hours, and by the end of 3 days was only a hunk of metal rubble. Unexpectedly, however, most of the destruction occurred during daylight hours, usually under the scrutiny of observers, and the leaders in the vandalism were well-dressed, white adults. The Palo Alto car was left untouched.

Zimbardo attributes the difference in the treatment accorded the two cars to the "acquired feelings of social anonymity provided by life in a city like New York," and he supports his conclusions with several other anecdotes illustrating casual, wanton vandalism in the city. In any comparative study of the effects of anonymity in city and town, however, there must be satisfactory control for other confounding factors: the large number of drug addicts in a city like New York; the higher proportion of slum-dwellers in the city; and so on.

Another direction for empirical study is investigation of the beneficial effects of anonymity. The impersonality of city life breeds its own tolerance for the private lives of the inhabitants. Individuality and even eccentricity, we may assume, can flourish more readily in the metropolis than in the small town.

Stigmatized persons may find it easier to lead comfortable lives in the city, free of the constant scrutiny of neighbors. To what degree can this assumed difference between city and town be shown empirically? Judith Waters,[10] at The City University of New York, hypothesized that avowed homosexuals would be more likely to be accepted as tenants in a large city than in small towns, and she dispatched letters from homosexuals and from normal individuals to real estate agents in cities and towns across the country. The results of her study were inconclusive. But the general idea of examining the protective benefits of city life to the stigmatized ought to be pursued.

Role Behavior in Cities and Towns

Another product of urban overload is the adjustment in roles made by urbanites in daily interactions. As Wirth[2] has said: "Urbanites meet one another in highly segmental roles. ... They are less dependent upon particular persons, and their dependence upon others is confined to a highly fractionalized aspect of the other's round of activity." This tendency is particularly noticeable in transactions between customers and individuals offering professional or sales services. The owner of a country store has time to become well acquainted with his dozen-or-so daily customers, but the girl at the checkout counter of a busy A & P, serving hundreds of customers a day, barely has time to toss the plaid stamps into one customer's shopping bag before the next customer confronts her with his pile of groceries.

Meier, in his stimulating analysis of the city,[4] discusses several adaptations a system may make when confronted by inputs that exceed its capacity to process them. Meier argues that, according to the principle of competition for scarce resources, the scope and time of the transaction shrink as customer volume and daily turnover rise. This, in fact, is what is meant by the "brusque" quality of city life. New standards have developed in cities concerning what levels of services are appropriate in business transactions (see Fig. 1.1).

McKenna and Morgenthau,[11] in a seminar at The City University of New York, devised a study (1) to compare the willingness of city dwellers and small-town dwellers to do favors for strangers that entailed expenditure of a small amount of time and slight inconvenience but no personal vulnerability, and (2) to determine whether the more compartmentalized, transitory relationships of the city would make urban salesgirls less likely than small-town salesgirls to carry out, for strangers, tasks not related to their customary roles.

To test for differences between city dwellers and small-town dwellers, a simple experiment was devised in which persons from both settings were asked (by telephone) to perform increasingly onerous favors for anonymous strangers. Within the cities (Chicago, New York, and Philadelphia), half the calls were to housewives and the other half to salesgirls in women's apparel shops; the division was the same for the 37 small towns of the study, which were in the same states as the cities. Each experimenter represented herself as a long-distance caller who had, through error, been connected with the respondent by the operator. The experimenter began by asking for simple information about the

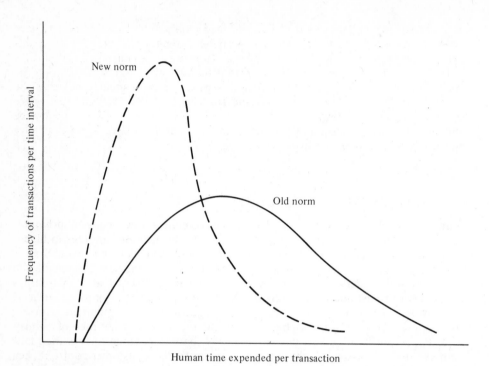

Fig. 1.1 *Changes in the demand for time for a given task when the overall transaction frequency increases in a social system. (Reprinted with permission from R. L. Meier, A Communications Theory of Urban Growth, 1962. Copyrighted by MIT Press, 1962.)*

weather for purposes of travel. Next the experimenter excused herself on some pretext (asking the respondent to "please hold on"), put the phone down for almost a full minute, and then picked it up again and asked the respondent to provide the phone number of a hotel or motel in her vicinity at which the experimenter might stay during a forthcoming visit. Scores were assigned the subjects on the basis of how helpful they had been. McKenna summarizes her results in this manner:

> People in the city, whether they are engaged in a specific job or not, are less helpful and informative than people in small towns;... People at home, regardless of where they live, are less helpful and informative than people working in shops.

However, the absolute level of cooperativeness for urban subjects was found to be quite high, and does not accord with the stereotype of the urbanite as aloof, self-centered, and unwilling to help strangers. The quantitative differences obtained by McKenna and Morgenthau are less great than one might have expected. This again points up the need for extensive empirical research in rural-urban differences, research that goes far beyond that provided in the few illustrative pilot studies presented here. At this point we have very limited objective evidence on differences in the quality of social encounters in city and small town.

But the research needs to be guided by unifying theoretical concepts. As I have tried to demonstrate, the concept of overload helps to explain a wide variety of contrasts between city behavior and town behavior: (1) the differences in role enactment (the tendency of urban dwellers to deal with one another in highly segmented, functional terms, and of urban sales personnel to devote limited time and attention to their customers); (2) the evolution of urban norms quite different from traditional town values (such as the acceptance of noninvolvement, impersonality, and aloofness in urban life); (3) the adaptation of the urban dweller's cognitive processes (his inability to identify most of the people he sees daily, his screening of sensory stimuli, his development of blasé attitudes toward deviant or bizarre behavior, and his selectivity in responding to human demands); and (4) the competition for scarce facilities in the city (the subway rush; the fight for taxis; traffic jams; standing in line to await services). I suggest that contrasts between city and rural behavior probably relect the responses of similar people to very different situations, rather than intrinsic differences in the personalities of rural and city dwellers. The city is a situation to which individuals respond adaptively.

FURTHER ASPECTS OF URBAN EXPERIENCE

Some features of urban experience do not fit neatly into the system of analysis presented thus far. They are no less important for that reason. The issues raised next are difficult to treat in quantitative fashion. Yet I prefer discussing them in a loose way to excluding them because appropriate language and data have not yet been developed. My aim is to suggest how phenomena such as "urban atmosphere" can be pinned down through techniques of measurement.

The "Atmosphere" of Great Cities

The contrast in the behavior of city and town dwellers has been a natural starting point for urban social scientists. But even among great cities there are marked differences in "atmosphere." The tone, pacing, and texture of social encounters are different in London and New York, and many persons willingly make financial sacrifices for the privilege of living within a specific urban atmosphere which they find pleasing or stimulating. A second perspective in the study of cities, therefore, is to define exactly what is meant by the atmosphere of a city and to pinpoint the factors that give rise to it. It may seem that urban atmosphere is too evanescent a quality to be reduced to a set of measurable variables, but I do not believe the matter can be judged before substantial effort has been made in this direction. It is obvious that any such approach must be comparative. It makes no sense at all to say that New York is "vibrant" and "frenetic" unless one has some specific city in mind as a basis of comparison.

In an undergraduate tutorial that I conducted at Harvard University some years ago, New York, London, and Paris were selected as reference points for attempts to measure urban atmosphere. We began with a simple question: Does any consensus exist about the qualities that typify given cities? To answer this question one could undertake a content analysis of travelbook, literary, and journalistic accounts of cities. A second approach, which we adopted, is to ask people to characterize (with descriptive terms and accounts of typical experiences) cities they have lived in or visited. In advertisements placed in the *New York Times* and the *Harvard Crimson* we asked people to give us accounts of specific incidents in London, Paris, or New York that best illuminated the character of that particular city. Questionnaires were then developed, and administered to persons who were familiar with at least two of the three cities.

Some distinctive patterns emerged.[12] The distinguishing themes concerning New York, for example, dealt with its diversity, its great size, its pace and level of activity, its cultural and entertainment opportunities, and the heterogeneity and segmentation ("ghettoization") of its population. New York elicited more descriptions in terms of physical qualities, pace, and emotional impact than Paris or London did, a fact which suggests that these are particularly important aspects of New York's ambience.

A contrasting profile emerges for London; in this case respondents placed far greater emphasis on their interactions with the inhabitants than on physical surroundings. There was near unanimity on certain themes: those dealing with the tolerance and courtesy of London's inhabitants. One respondent said:

When I was 12, my grandfather took me to the British Museum...one day by tube and recited the *Aeneid* in Latin for my benefit. ... He is rather deaf, speaks very loudly and it embarrassed the hell out of me, until I realized that nobody was paying any attention. Londoners are extremely worldly and tolerant.

In contrast, respondents who described New Yorkers as aloof, cold, and rude referred to such incidents as the following:

I saw a boy of 19 passing out anti-war leaflets to passersby. When he stopped at a corner, a man dressed in a business suit walked by him at a brisk pace, hit the boy's arm, and scattered the leaflets all over the street. The man kept walking at the same pace down the block.

We need to obtain many more such descriptions of incidents, using careful methods of sampling. By the application of factor-analytic techniques, relevant dimensions for each city can be discerned.

The responses for Paris were about equally divided between responses concerning its inhabitants and those regarding its physical and sensory attributes. Cafès and parks were often mentioned as contributing to the sense that Paris is a city of amenities, but many respondents complained that Parisians were inhospitable, nasty, and cold.

We cannot be certain, of course, to what degree these statements reflect actual characteristics of the cities in question and to what degree they simply tap the respondents' knowledge of widely held preconceptions. Indeed, one may point to three factors, apart from the actual atmospheres of the cities, that determine the subjects' responses.

1. A person's impression of a given city depends on his implicit standard of comparison. A New Yorker who visits Paris may well describe that city as "leisurely," whereas a compatriot from Richmond, Virginia, may consider Paris too "hectic." Obtaining reciprocal judgment, in which New Yorkers judge Londoners, and Londoners judge New Yorkers, seems a useful way to take into account not only the city being judged but also the home city that serves as the visitor's base line.

2. Perceptions of a city are also affected by whether the observer is a tourist, a newcomer, or a longer-term resident. First, a tourist will be exposed to features of the city different from those familiar to a long-time resident. Second, a prerequisite for adapting to continuing life in a given city seems to be the filtering out of many observations about the city that the newcomer or tourist finds particularly arresting; this selective process seems to be part of the long-term resident's mechanism for coping with overload. In the interest of psychic economy, the resident simply learns to tune out many aspects of daily life. One method for studying the specific impact of adaptation on perception of the city is to ask several pairs of newcomers and old-timers (one newcomer and one old-timer to a pair) to walk down certain city blocks and then report separately what each has observed.

Additionally, many persons have noted that when travelers return to New York from an extended sojourn abroad they often feel themselves confronted with "brutal ugliness"[13] and a distinctive, frenetic atmosphere whose contributing details are, for a few hours or days, remarkably sharp and clear. This period of fresh perception should receive special attention in the study of city atmosphere. For, in a few days, details which are initially arresting become less easy to specify. They are assimilated into an increasingly familiar background atmosphere which, though important in setting the tone of things, is difficult to analyze. There is no better point at which to begin the study of city atmosphere than at the moment when a traveler returns from abroad.

3. The popular myths and expectations each visitor brings to the city will also affect the way in which he perceives it.[14] Sometimes a person's preconceptions about a city are relatively accurate distillations of its character, but preconceptions may also reinforce myths by filtering the visitor's perceptions to conform with his expectations. Preconceptions affect not only a person's perceptions of a city but what he reports about it.

The influence of a person's urban base line on his perceptions of a given city, the differences between the observations of the long-time inhabitant and those of the newcomer, and the filtering effect of personal expectations and stereotypes raise serious questions about the validity of travelers' reports. Moreover, no social psychologist wants to rely exclusively on verbal accounts if he is attempting to obtain an accurate and objective description of the cities' social texture, pace, and general atmosphere. What he needs to do is to devise means of embedding objective experimental measures in the daily flux of city life, measures that can accurately index the qualities of a given urban atmosphere.

EXPERIMENTAL COMPARISONS OF BEHAVIOR

Roy Feldman[15] incorporated these principles in a comparative study of behavior toward compatriots and foreigners in Paris, Athens, and Boston. Feldman wanted to see (1) whether absolute levels and patterns of helpfulness varied significantly from city to city, and (2) whether inhabitants in each city tended to treat compatriots differently from foreigners. He examined five concrete behavioral episodes, each carried out by a team of native experimenters and a team of American experimenters in the three cities. The episodes involved (1) asking natives of the city for street directions; (2) asking natives to mail a letter for the experimenter; (3) asking natives if they had just dropped a dollar bill (or the Greek or French equivalent) when the money actually belonged to the experimenter himself; (4) deliberately overpaying for goods in a store to see if the cashier would correct the mistake and return the excess money; and (5) determining whether taxicab drivers overcharged strangers and whether they took the most direct route available.

Feldman's results suggest some interesting contrasts in the profiles of the three cities. In Paris, for instance, certain stereotypes were borne out. Parisian cab drivers overcharged foreigners significantly more often then they overcharged compatriots. But other aspects of the Parisians' behavior were not in accord with American preconceptions: in mailing a letter for a stranger, Parisians treated foreigners significantly better than Athenians or Bostonians did, and, when asked to mail letters that were already stamped, Parisians actually treated foreigners better than they treated compatriots. Similarly, Parisians were significantly more honest than Athenians or Bostonians in resisting the temptation to claim money that was not theirs, and Parisians were the only citizens who were more honest with foreigners than with compatriots in this experiment.

Feldman's studies not only begin to quantify some of the variables that give a city its distinctive texture but they also provide a methodological model for other comparative research. His most important contribution is his successful application of objective, experimental measures to everyday situations, a mode of study which provides conclusions about urban life that are more pertinent than those achieved through laboratory experiments.

TEMPO AND PACE

Another important component of a city's atmosphere is its tempo or pace, an attribute frequently remarked on but less often studied. Does a city have a frenetic, hectic quality, or is it easygoing and leisurely? In any empirical treatment of this question, it is best to start in a very simple way. Walking speeds of pedestrians in different cities and in cities and towns should be measured and compared. William Berkowitz[16] of Lafayette College has undertaken an extensive series of studies of walking speeds in Philadelphia, New York, and Boston, as well as in small and moderate-sized towns. Berkowitz writes that "there does appear to be a significant linear relation between walking speed and size of municipality, but the absolute size of the difference varies by less than ten percent."

Perhaps the feeling of rapid tempo is due not so much to absolute pedestrian speeds as to the constant need to dodge others in a large city to avoid collisions with other pedestrians. (One basis for computing the adjustments needed to avoid collisions is to hypothesize a set of mechanical manikins sent walking along a city street and to calculate the number of collisions when no adjustments are made. Clearly, the higher the density of manikins the greater the number of collisions per unit of time, or, conversely, the greater the frequency of adjustments needed in higher population densities to avoid collisions.)

Patterns of automobile traffic contribute to a city's tempo. Driving an automobile provides a direct means of translating feelings about tempo into measurable acceleration, and a city's pace should be particularly evident in vehicular velocities, patterns of acceleration, and latency of response to traffic signals. The inexorable tempo of New York is expressed, further, in the manner in which pedestrians stand at busy intersections, impatiently awaiting a change in traffic light, making tentative excursions into the intersection, and frequently surging into the street even before the green light appears.

VISUAL COMPONENTS

Hall has remarked[17] that the physical layout of the city also affects its atmosphere. A gridiron pattern of streets gives the visitor a feeling of rationality, orderliness, and predictability but is sometimes monotonous. Winding lanes or streets branching off at strange angles, with many forks (as in Paris or Greenwich Village), create feelings of surprise and esthetic pleasure, while forcing greater decision-making in plotting one's course. Some would argue that the visual component is all-important—that the "look" of Paris or New York can almost be equated with its atmosphere. To investigate this hypothesis, we might conduct studies in which only blind, or at least blindfolded, respondents were used. We would no doubt discover that each city has a distinctive texture even when the visual component is eliminated.

SOURCES OF AMBIENCE

Thus far we have tried to pinpoint and measure some of the factors that contribute to the distinctive atmosphere of a great city. But we may also ask, Why do differences in urban atmosphere exist? How did they come about, and are they in any way related to the factors of density, large numbers, and heterogeneity discussed above?

First, there is the obvious factor that, even among great cities, populations and densities differ. The metropolitan areas of New York, London, and Paris, for example, contain 15 million, 12 million, and 8 million persons, respectively. London has average densities of 43 persons per acre, while Paris is more congested, with average densities of 114 persons per acre.[18] Whatever characteristics are specifically attributable to density are more likely to be pronounced in Paris than in London.

A second factor affecting the atmosphere of cities is the source from which the populations are drawn.[19] It is a characteristic of great cities that they do not reproduce their own populations, but that their numbers are constantly maintained and augmented by the influx of residents from other parts of the country.

This can have a determining effect on the city's atmosphere. For example, Oslo is a city in which almost all of the residents are only one or two generations removed from a purely rural existence, and this contributes to its almost agricultural norms.

A third source of atmosphere is the general national culture. Paris combines adaptations to the demography of cities *and* certain values specific to French culture. New York is an admixture of American values and values that arise as a result of extraordinarily high density and large population.

Finally, one could speculate that the atmosphere of a great city is traceable to the specific historical conditions under which adaptations to urban overload occurred. For example, a city which acquired its mass and density during a period of commercial expansion will respond to new demographic conditions by adaptations designed to serve purely commercial needs. Thus, Chicago, which grew and became a great city under a purely commercial stimulus, adapted in a manner that emphasizes business needs. European capitals, on the other hand, incorporate many of the adaptations which were appropriate to the period of their increasing numbers and density. Because aristocratic values were prevalent at the time of the growth of these cities. the mechanisms developed for coping with overload were based on considerations other than pure efficiency. Thus, the manners, norms, and facilities of Paris and Vienna continue to reflect esthetic values and the idealization of leisure.

COGNITIVE MAPS OF CITIES

When we speak of "behavioral comparisons" among cities, we must specify which parts of the city are most relevant for sampling purposes. In a sampling of "New Yorkers," should we include residents of Bay Ridge or Flatbush as well as inhabitants of Manhattan? And, if so, how should we weight our sample distribution? One approach to defining relevant boundaries in sampling is to determine which areas form the psychological or cognitive core of the city. We weight our samples most heavily in the areas considered by most people to represent the "essence" of the city.

The psychologist is less interested in the geographic layout of a city or in its political boundaries than in the cognitive representation of the city. Hans Blumenfeld[20] points out that the perceptual structure of a modern city can be expressed by the "silhouette" of the group of skyscrapers at its center and that of smaller groups of office buildings at its "subcenters" but that urban areas can no longer, because of their vast extent, be experienced as fully articulated sets of streets, squares, and space.

In *The Image of the City*,[21] Kevin Lynch created a cognitive map of Boston by interviewing Bostonians. Perhaps his most significant finding was that, while certain landmarks, such as Paul Revere's house and the Boston Common, as well as the paths linking them, are known to almost all Bostonians, vast areas of the city are simply unknown to its inhabitants.

Using Lynch's technique, Donald Hooper[22] created a psychological map of New York from the answers to the study questionnaire on Paris, London, and New York. Hooper's results were similar to those of Lynch: New York appears to have a dense core of well-known landmarks in midtown Manhattan, surrounded by the vast unknown reaches of Queens, Brooklyn, and the Bronx.

Times Square, Rockefeller Center, and the Fifth Avenue department stores alone comprise half the places specifically cited by respondents as the haunts in which they spent most of their time. However, outside the midtown area, only scattered landmarks were recognized. Another interesting pattern is evident: even the best-known symbols of New York are relatively self-contained, and the pathways joining them appear to be insignificant on the map.

The psychological map can be used for more than just sampling techniques. Lynch[21] argues, for instance, that a good city is highly "imageable," having many known symbols joined by widely known pathways, whereas dull cities are gray and nondescript. We might test the relative "imagibility" of several cities by determining the proportion of residents who recognize sampled geographic points and their accompanying pathways.

If we wanted to be even more precise we could construct a cognitive map that would not only show the symbols of the city but would measure the precise degree of cognitive significance of any given point in the city relative to any other. By applying a pattern of points to a map of New York City, for example, and taking photographs from each point, we could determine what proportion of a sample of the city's inhabitants could identify the locale specified by each point (see Fig. 1.2). We might even take the subjects blindfolded to a point represented on the map, then remove the blindfold and ask them to identify their location from the view around them.

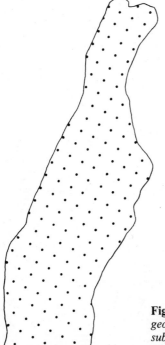

Fig. 1.2 *To create a psychological map of Manhattan, geographic points are sampled, and, from photographs, the subjects attempt to identify the location of each point. To each point a numerical index is assigned indicating the proportion of persons able to identify its location.*

One might also use psychological maps to gain insight into the differing perceptions of a given city that are held by members of its cultural subgroups, and into the manner in which their perceptions may change. In the earlier stages of life, whites and blacks alike probably have only a limited view of the city, centering on the immediate neighborhood in which they are raised. In adolescence, however, the field of knowledge of the white teen-ager probably undergoes rapid enlargement; he learns of opportunities in midtown and outlying sections and comes to see himself as functioning in a larger urban field. But the process of ghettoization, to which the black teen-ager is subjected, may well hamper the expansion of his sense of the city. These are speculative notions, but they are readily subject to precise test.

CONCLUSION

I have tried to indicate some organizing theory that starts with the basic facts of city life: large numbers, density, and heterogeneity. These are external to the individual. He experiences these factors as overloads at the level of roles, norms, cognitive functions, and facilities. These overloads lead to adaptive mechanisms which create the distinctive tone and behaviors of city life. These notions, of course, need to be examined by objective comparative studies of cities and towns.

A second perspective concerns the differing atmospheres of great cities, such as Paris, London, and New York. Each has a distinctive flavor, offering a differentiable quality of experience. More precise knowledge of urban atmosphere seems attainable through application of the tools of experimental inquiry.

NOTES

1. *New York Times* (15 June 1969).

2. L. Wirth, *Amer. J. Soc.* **44**, 1 (1938). Wirth's ideas have come under heavy criticism by contemporary city planners, who point out that the city is broken down into neighborhoods, which fulfill many of the functions of small towns. See, for example, H. J. Gans, *People and Plans: Essays on Urban Problems and Solutions* (Basic Books, New York, 1968); J. Jacobs, *The Death and Life of Great American Cities* (Random House, New York, 1961); G. D. Suttles, *The Social Order of the Slum* (Univ. of Chicago Press, Chicago, 1968).

3. G. Simmel, *The Sociology of Georg Simmel*, K. H. Wolff, ed. (Macmillan, New York, 1950) [English translation of G. Simmel, *Die Grosstadte und das Geistesleben Die Grosstadt* (Jansch, Dresden, 1903)].

4. R. L. Meier, *A Communications Theory of Urban Growth* (MIT Press, Cambridge, Mass., 1962).

5. S. Milgram and P. Hollander, *Nation* **25**, 602 (1964).

6. B. Latané and J. Darley, *Amer. Sci.* **57**, 244 (1969).

7. S. Gaertner and L. Bickman (Graduate Center, The City University of New York), unpublished research.

8. D. Altman, M. Levine, M. Nadien, J. Villena (Graduate Center, The City University of New York), unpublished research.

9. P. G. Zimbardo, paper presented at the Nebraska Symposium on Motivation (1969).

10. J. Waters (Graduate Center, The City University of New York), unpublished research.

11. W. McKenna and S. Morgenthau (Graduate Center, The City University of New York), unpublished research.

12. N. Abuza (Harvard University), "The Paris-London-New York Questionnaires," unpublished.

13. P. Abelson, *Science* **165**, 853 (1969).

14. A. L. Strauss, ed., *The American City: A Sourcebook of Urban Imagery* (Aldine, Chicago, 1968).

15. R. E. Feldman, *J. Personality Soc. Psychol.* **10**, 202 (1968).

16. W. Berkowitz, personal communication.

17. E. T. Hall, *The Hidden Dimension* (Doubleday, New York, 1966).

18. P. Hall, *The World Cities* (McGraw-Hill, New York, 1966).

19. R. E. Park, E. W. Burgess, R. D. McKenzie, *The City* (Univ. of Chicago Press, Chicago, 1967), pp. 1–45.

20. H. Blumenfeld, in *The Quality of Urban Life* (Sage, Beverly Hills, Calif., 1969).

21. K. Lynch, *The Image of the City* (MIT and Harvard Univ. Press, Cambridge, Mass., 1960).

22. D. Hooper (Harvard University), unpublished.

23. Barbara Bengen worked closely with me in preparing an earlier version of this article. I thank Dr. Gary Winkel, editor of *Enivironment and Behavior*, for useful suggestions and advice.

The Urban Bystander

2

Catherine Genovese, coming home from a night job in the early hours of an April morning, was stabbed repeatedly and over an extended period of time. Thirty-eight residents of a respectable New York City neighborhood admit to having witnessed at least a part of the attack, but not one of them went to her aid or even so much as called the police until after she was dead.

We are all certain that we would have done better. Our indignation toward the residents of Kew Gardens swells to a sense of outrage. The crime, or more precisely, the lack of civic response to it, was so vile that Senator Russell of Georgia read the *New York Times* account of it into the *Congressional Record*. The fact that it *was* Senator Russell is an indication of the complex social reactions touched off by this neighborhood tragedy.

It is noteworthy, first, that anger is directed, not toward the crime, nor the criminal, but toward those who failed to halt the criminal's actions. It is a curious shift, reminiscent of recent trends in moralizing about the Nazi era. Writers once focused on the sins of the Nazis; it is now more fashionable to discuss the complicity of their victims. The event is significant, also, for the way it is being exploited. Senator Russell is but one case in point. In his home state, several brutal murders of Negroes have taken place before large crowds of unprotesting white onlookers, but the Senator has never felt called upon to insert reports of *these* brutalities into the *Record*. The crime against Miss Genovese no longer exists in and of itself. It is rapidly being assimilated to the uses and ideologies of the day.

For example, the Kew Gardens incident has become the occasion for a general attack on the city. It is portrayed as callous, cruel, indifferent to the needs of the people, and wholly inferior to the small town in the quality of its personal relationships. The abrasiveness of urban life cannot be argued; it is not true, however, that personal relationships are necessarily inferior in the city. They are merely organized on a different principle. Urban friendships and associations are not primarily formed on the basis of physical proximity. A person with numerous close friends in different parts of the city may not know the occupant of an adjacent apartment. Some hold this to be an advantage of the city; men and women can conduct lives unmonitored by the constant scrutiny of neighbors. This does not mean that a city dweller has fewer friends than does a villager, or knows fewer persons who will come to his aid; however,

---

This paper was written in collaboration with Paul Hollander and was first published under the title, "The Murder They Heard," *The Nation*, Vol. 198, No. 25 (1964) pp. 602–604. Reprinted by permission of *The Nation*.

it does mean that his allies are not constantly at hand. Miss Genovese required immediate aid from those physically present; her predicament was desperate and not typical of the occasions when we look for the support of friends. There is no evidence that the city had deprived Miss Genovese of human associations, but the friends who might have rushed to her side were miles from the scene of her tragedy.

A truly extraordinary aspect of the case is the general readiness to forget the man who committed a very foul crime. This is typical of social reactions in present-day America. It begins to seem that everyone, having absorbed a smattering of sociology, looks at once beyond the concrete case in an eager quest for high-sounding generalizations that imply an enlightened social vista. What gets lost in many of these discussions—and what needs at least a partial restoration—is the notion that people may occasionally be responsible for what they do, even if their acts are criminal. In our righteous denunciation of the thirty-eight witnesses we should not forget that they did not commit the murder; they merely failed to prevent it. It is no more than clear thinking to bear in mind the moral difference.

A related and equally confusing error is to infer ethical values from the actual behavior of people in concrete situations. For example, in the case of Miss Genovese we must ask: did the witnesses remain passive because they thought it was the right thing to do, or did they refrain from action *despite* what they thought or felt they should do? We cannot take it for granted that people always do what they consider right. It would be more fruitful to inquire why, in general and in this particular case, there is so marked a discrepancy between values and behavior. What makes people choose a course of action that probably shames them in retrospect? How do they become reduced to resignation, acquiescence and helplessness?

Those who vilify the residents of Kew Gardens measure them against the standard of their own ability to formulate high-minded moral prescriptions. But that is hardly a fair standard. It is entirely likely that many of the witnesses, at the level of stated opinion, feel quite as strongly as any of us about the moral requirement of aiding a helpless victim. They too, in general terms, know what *ought* to be done, and can state their values when the occasion arises. This has little, if anything, to do with actual behavior under the press of circumstances.

Furthermore, we must distinguish between the facts of the murder as finally known and reported in the press, and the events of the evening as they were experienced by the Kew Gardens residents. We can now say that if the police had been called after the first attack, the woman's life might have been saved, and we tend to judge the inaction of the Kew Gardens residents in the light of this lost possibility. That is natural, perhaps, but it is unrealistic. If those men and women had had as clear a grasp of the situation as we have now, the chances are that many of them would have acted to save Miss Genovese's life. What they had, instead, were fragments of an ambiguous, confusing and doubtless frightening episode—one, moreover, that seemed totally incongruous in a respectable neighborhood. The very lack of correspondence between the violence of the crime and the character of the neighborhood must have created a sense of unreality which inhibited rational action. A lesser crime, one more in character with the locale—say, after-hours rowdiness from a group of college students—might have led more readily to a call for the police.

The incongruity, the sheer improbability of the event predisposed many to reject the most extreme interpretation: that a young woman was in fact being murdered outside the window. How much more probable, not to say more consoling, was the interpretation that a drunken party was sounding off, that two lovers were quarreling, or that youths were playing a nasty prank. Bruno Bettleheim, in *The Informed Heart*, describes how resistant many German Jews were to the signs around them of impending disaster. Given any possibility for fitting events into an acceptable order of things, men are quick to seize it. It takes courage to perceive clearly and without distortion. We cannot justly condemn all the Kew Gardens residents in the light of a horrible outcome which only the most perspicacious could have foreseen.

Why didn't the group of onlookers band together, run out into the street and subdue the assailant? Aside from the fact that such organization takes time, and that the onlookers were not in communication (who in such a community knows his neighbor's phone number?), there is another factor that would render such action almost impossible. Despite our current fears about the contagion of violence in the mass media, the fact remains that the middle-class person is totally unequipped to deal with its actual occurrence. More especially, he is unable to use personal violence, either singly or collectively, even when it is required for productive and socially valued ends.

More generally, modern societies are so organized as to discourage even the most beneficial, spontaneous group action. This applies with particular sharpness to the law-abiding, respectable segments of the population—such as the people of Kew Gardens—who have most thoroughly accepted the admonition: "do not take the law into your own hands." In a highly specialized society such people take it for granted that certain functions and activities—from garbage collection to fire protection; from meat certification to the control of criminals —are taken care of by specially trained people. The puzzle in the case under consideration is the reluctance to supply to the police even the barest information which it was essential they have if they were to fulfill their acknowledged functions.

Many facts of the case have not been made public, such as the quality of the relationship between Miss Genovese and the community, the extent to which she was recognized that night, and the number of persons who knew her. It is known that her cries for help were not directed to a specific person: they were general. But only individuals can act, and as the cries were not specifically directed, no particular person felt a special responsibility. The crime and the failure of community response seem absurd to us. At the time, it may well have seemed equally absurd to the Kew Gardens residents that not one of the neighbors would have called the police. A collective paralysis may have developed from the belief of each of the witnesses that someone else must surely have taken that obvious step.

If we ask why they did not call the police, we should also ask what were the alternatives. To be sure, phoning from within an apartment was the most prudent course of action, one involving the minimum of both physical inconvenience and personal involvement with a violent criminal. And yet, one has to assume that in the minds of many there lurked the alternative of going down to the street and defending the helpless woman. This, indeed, might have been felt as the ideal response. By comparison, a mere phone call from the safety of home may have seemed a cowardly compromise with what should be done. As often happens, the ideal solution was difficult, probably dangerous; but, as also happens, the practical, safe alternative may have seemed distasteful in the light of the ideal. Awareness of an ideal response often paralyzes a move toward the less than ideal alternative. Rather than accept the belittling second-best, the person so beset prefers to blot out the whole issue. Therefore, he pretends that there is nothing to get upset about. Probably it was only a drunken brawl.

The symbolic significance of "the street" for the middle-class mentality may have some relevance to the case. Although it cannot explain in full the failure to grab the telephone and call the police, it may account in part for the inertia and indifference. For the middle-class resident of a big city the street and what happens on the street are often symbolic of all that is vulgar and perilous in life. The street is the antithesis of privacy, security and the support one derives from contemplating and living amidst prized personal possessions. The street represents the world of pushing and shoving crowds, potentially hostile strangers, sweat, dust and noise. Those who spend much time on the street have nothing better to do and nowhere better to go: the poor, the foot-loose, the drifters, juvenile delinquents. Therefore, the middle-class person seeks almost automatically to disengage himself from the life of the street; he is on it only from necessity, rarely for pleasure. Such considerations help explain the genesis of attitudes that prevented the witnesses from making the crucial phone call. The tragic drama was taking place on the street, hence hardly relevant to their lives; in fact, in some ways radically opposed to their outlook and concerns.

In an effort to make the strongest possible case against the Kew Gardens citizens, the press has ignored actual dangers of involvement, even at the level of calling the police. They have treated the "fears" of the residents as foolish rationalizations, utterly without basis. In doing so they have conveniently forgotten instances in which such involvement did not turn out well for the hero. One spectacular case in the early fifties, amply publicized by the press, concerned the misfortune of Arnold Schuster. While riding in the subway this young Brooklyn man spotted Willie Sutton, an escaped criminal. He reported this information to the police, and it led to Sutton's arrest. Schuster was proclaimed a hero, but before a month was up Schuster was dead—murdered in reprisal for his part in Sutton's recapture. Schuster had done nothing more than phone the police.

The fact is that there *are* risks even in minimal forms of involvement, and it is dishonest to ignore them. One becomes involved with the police, with the general agents of publicity that swarm to such events, and possibly with the criminal. If the criminal is not caught immediately, there is the chance that he will learn who called the police (which apartment did they enter first, whose pictures are in the papers, etc.) and may fear that the caller can identify him. The caller, then, is of special concern to the criminal. If a trial is held, the person who telephoned is likely to be a witness. Even if he is jailed, the criminal may have underworld friends who will act to avenge him. One is a responsible citizen and a worthy human being, not because of the absence of risk but because one acts in the face of it.

In seeking explanations for their inaction, we have not intended to defend, certainly not to excuse, Kew Gardens' passive witnesses. We have sought, rather, to put ourselves in their place, to try to understand their response. The causes we have suggested are in no way sufficient reason for inaction. Perhaps we should have started with a more fundamental question: Why should anyone have gone to the aid of the victim? Why should anyone have taken the trouble to call the police? The answer must be that it is a matter of common decency to help those who are in distress. It is a humane and compassionate requirement in the relations between people. Yet how generally is it observed? In New York City it is not at all unusual to see a man, sick with alcohol, lying in a doorway; he does not command the least attention or interest from those who pass by. The trouble here, as in Kew Gardens, is that the individual does not perceive that his interests are identified with others or with the community at large. And is such a perception possible? What evidence is there in the American community that collective interests have priority over personal advantage?

There are, of course, practical limitations to the Samaritan impulse in a major city. If a citizen attended to every needy person, if he were sensitive to and acted on every altruistic impulse that was evoked in the city, he could scarcely keep his own affairs in order. A calculated and strategic indifference is an unavoidable part of life in our cities, and it must be faced without sentimentality or rage. At most, each of us can resolve to extend the range of his responsibilities in some perceptible degree, to rise a little more adequately to moral obligations. City life is harsh; still, we owe it to ourselves and our fellows to resolve that it be no more harsh than is inevitable.

3

The Idea of Neighborhood

To understand the problem a sociologist has in handling the concept of neighborhood, the reader must retrieve the cognitive maps of childhood. If you grew up in a large city, you knew best those living on your own block. Awareness of the city radiated outward, with the density of information diminishing rapidly with the distance from home. Beyond a few blocks on either side, street names grew vague and faces unfamiliar. The area of comfortable familiarity constituted the experience of neighborhood. (For those raised in Brooklyn or the Bronx, psychological boundaries were set at 5 ± 2 streets from one's home stoop.)

Yet we know that cities do not consist of an indefinitely large number of neighborhoods each centering on one of millions of inhabitants only a slight spatial remove from his fellows. Rather there is a small number of social labels applied to definable geographic areas. Because population characteristics of a city are continuously variable, with no clear demarcation between one side of the street and the other, society imposes categorical labels on specific geographic realms. Neighborhood categories are not simply found in nature, but are consensually imposed definitions. This is the first sense in which communities are socially constructed according to Suttles's analysis.

A neighborhood label, once affixed, has real consequences, Suttles points out. For outsiders it reduces decision-making to more manageable terms. Instead of dealing with the variegated reality of numerous city streets, the resident can form a set of attitudes about a limited number of social categories and act accordingly. Thus a mother will instruct her child to stay out of Harlem, or judge that a boy who lives in Riverdale is probably acceptable for her daughter. Newcomers may be attracted or repelled by areas defined with a high or a low prestige label. For those who live within it, the neighborhood defines areas relatively free of intruders, identifies where potential friends are to be found or where they are to be cultivated, minimizes the prospects of status insult, and simplifies innumerable daily decisions dealing with spatial activities. Thus the mental map of neighborhoods is not superfluous cognitive baggage, but performs important psychological and social functions.

But what sets the boundaries on neighborhoods: ethnic homogeneity, physical barriers, economic characteristics? All of these play a part, but in the final

This paper was a review of *The Social Construction of Communities,* by Gerald D. Suttles, Chicago: University of Chicago Press, 1972. It was first published in *Science* **178** (November 1, 1972), pp. 494–495. Copyright © 1972 by the American Association for the Advancement of Science.

analysis it is a creative social construction. Most often the neighborhood boundary is an arbitrary street or intersection, rather than a physical barrier. Thus, in New York City, Harlem "begins" on the north side of 96th Street. The demographic approach, which equates neighborhoods with particular concentrations of ethnic or racial types, is less interesting for Suttles than the question "How are varying proportions of racial, ethnic, and income groups selectively highlighted in the reputation of local communities?"

If the neighborhood exists first as a creative social construction, it nonetheless possesses a number of important properties. First, it becomes a component of an individual's identity, "a stable judgmental reference against which people are assessed...." (That is why when you ask a person what city he comes from he will tell you without blush, but when you ask about his neighborhood the question may be considered too personal for casual conversation; for the neighborhood is a status-differentiating component.) A neighborhood may derive its reputation from several sources: first, from the master identity of the area of which it is a part (Yorkville is part of the fashionable East Side); second, through comparison and contrast with adjacent communities; and third, from historic claims, a game, Suttles points out, in which all communities can win, since the new community offers the image of an area unshackled by tradition, and the older community takes pride in its association with the past. The best time to capture the "meaning" of a neighborhood, it occurs to this reviewer, is on moving day, when two sets of pertinent associations are revealed: those generated by people moving in, and those disclosed by people moving out.

Readers will also recognize that neighborhoods deemed "desirable" need not always have the best physical features. Consider the upper East Side in New York City. Unless an apartment overlooks Central Park, it is an area devoid of breathing space, consisting of stone towers built on acres of unrelieved pavement. Park Avenue is a fuming canyon of hydrocarbons. It is a wonder not only that people will pay exorbitant Park Avenue rents and maintenance charges but that they are willing to live there at all. Note that Harlem, which in popular imagery possesses only rat-infested slums, actually contains a considerable amount of attractive housing. But none of this figures in the public image of these two areas. The images are social constructions linked to but not wholly identifiable with the facts.

We define urban communities, therefore, because the concept simplifies the complicated and inchoate qualities of the city, dividing it into differentiable segments and thereby rendering it cognitively manageable.

What then of the idea of a community as first and foremost a group of people bound together by common sentiments, a primordial solidarity? In Suttles's eyes, the view is poorly realized in fact and represents an overromanticized view of social life. Communities do lead to social control, they do "segregate people to avoid danger, insult, and status claims"; but whatever sentiments are engendered by neighborhoods are strictly tied to functional realities and can in no sense be treated as gratuitous expressive solidarity. Moreover, the notion of a closely interdependent, self-contained community, having its prototype in the rural village, was never an appropriate model for urban living. Of greater pertinence to an anlaysis of urban life are the *multiple* levels of community organization in which the resident participates.

The smallest of these units is the "face block." For children it is the prescribed social world carved out by parents. It is here that face-to-face relations are most likely, and the resulting institutional form is the block association. Next, in Suttles's typology, is the "defended neighborhood," which is the smallest segment of the city recognized by both residents and outsiders as having some corporate identity, and possessing many of the facilities needed to carry out the daily routine of life. The defended neighborhood frequently lacks official recognition, and its boundaries, because they have no legal status, are often precarious. Street gangs arise which protect it from unwanted incursions by outsiders.

The urban resident also participates in the "community of limited liability," a larger realm possessing an institutionally secure name and boundaries. The concept, originally developed by Morris Janowitz, emphasizes the "intentional, voluntary, and especially the partial and differential involvement of residents in their local communities." Frequently an external agent, such as a community newspaper, is the most important guardian of a community's sense of boundaries, purposes, and integrity. A single individual may be defined as living in several such communities. The multiple claims on the person may limit and even paralyze active involvement in any of them.

Even larger segments of the city, such as an entire East Side area, may also take shape in response to environmental pressures, creating an "expanded community of limited liability." Thus an individual may find himself picketing to keep a highway not just out of his neighborhood, but out of the entire South Side.

Thus what Suttles teaches us is that the concept of neighborhood is not adequate to handle the multiple levels of urban organization in which the individual participates. Varied levels of community organization are created as responses to the larger social environment. Neighborhoods cannot be seen as a society in microcosm. They never were, and never can be. The urban community is a form of social differentiation within a total society.

Does Suttles's analysis have a bearing on the contemporary issue of "community control"? It suggests, first, that the fully self-contained community within the city is a fiction. The urban community can be a differentiated but never a fully autonomous unit within the larger urban context. Second, Suttles points out that the idea of a centralized government is not incompatible with a well-served local community. "One of the sources of community weakness in most American cities is that many mayors are responsible to local communities but have little direct recourse to the federal levels at which major power and resources are located." In Sweden, in contrast, the mayors of certain local communities are appointed by the central government but this strengthens rather than weakens the resources available to the community.

It is a central theme of Suttles's analysis that "total societies are not made up from a series of communities, but communities are areas which come into being through their recognition by the wider society." Suttles overstates the case. Sometimes cities do develop through the coalescing of smaller communities, which continue to maintain their identity. London is a good example. To some extent it depends on the phase of a city's development under discussion. In later stages of development, when a city's origins are no longer relevant to its functioning, the social-constructive approach may well constitute the dominant mode of defining neighborhoods. More important, is the point really worth a great deal of theoretical fuss?

The book has other faults: It is repetitious and disjointed, with a number of essays only tangentially related to the main theme. Yet these flaws are unimportant alongside the book's considerable achievements. First, it helps break away from the limiting view of Park, Burgess, and others that "a city consists of a mosaic of little worlds which touch but do not interpenetrate." The urban community is a form of social differentiation within a total society. Second, Suttles teaches us that the concept of neighborhood is not adequate to handle the multiple levels of urban organization in which the individual participates. Participation ranges from the face block to larger segments of the city. Third, Suttles shows that there is no necessary discontinuity between how we experience neighborhoods, communities, cities, and so on and the sociological concepts needed to describe them. Neighborhoods are not primarily segments of real estate but collective representations existing in the minds of inhabitants, and attaining reality through social consensus. This is a stimulating viewpoint of great heuristic value. Fourth, he demonstrates that the phenomenon of mental maps, developed by Kevin Lynch and others, is not a disembodied esthetic or cognitive phenomenon but is part of the ongoing life of individuals, with practical meaning and significance. Fifth, Suttles translates the concept of territoriality, so foolishly caricatured in the work of Ardrey, Morris, and others, into its proper human context. He recognizes the importance of territoriality in human life, without equating it with its animal expression. Finally, his book is a work of considerable originality and insight; the author is a keen observer, bringing the same order of sensitivity to urban analysis that Erving Goffman has applied to the study of small-scale social interaction. And in both cases, we emerge with a sense of clarified perception.

4

The Familiar Stranger: An Aspect of Urban Anonymity

Nothing is more characteristic of urban life than the fact that we often gain extreme familiarity with the faces of a number of persons, yet never interact with them. At my railroad station, for example, I have stood at a commuter station for several years, often in the company of people whom I have never gotten to know. The faces and the people are treated as part of the environment, equivalent to the scenery, rather than persons with whom one talks, exchanges greetings.

Harry From, one of my students, wrote that the familiar stranger is the end product of a process, which like friendship, takes time. Moreover, it is a covert process and often leads to a frozen relationship. To become a familiar stranger a person (1) has to be observed, (2) repeatedly for a certain time period, and (3) without any interaction.

There is a powerful rule at work among familiar strangers; the further away from the scene of their routine encounter, the more likely they will interact with each other. Thus if they encounter each other in a faraway country, they are most likely to acknowledge each other, engage in conversation, and even experience a warm surge of familiarity and friendship. Why is it that people who have not in several years spoken to each other, while standing in each other's presence, are in a distant setting moved to address each other as persons?

Barriers build up between familiar strangers which become difficult to surmount, so that when the familiar stranger needs to make a request, he prefers to make it to a total stranger rather than a familiar though hitherto unacknowledged face.

Extraordinary incidents, such as a flood, help move people out of their impersonal relations. The incident itself is temporary, and thus involves not an extended commitment, but only one that lasts as long as the temporary disruption of routine.

A few years ago several students at The City University of New York attempted to study the phenomenon of the familiar stranger. They got up early in the morning, and went out to the commuter stations that feed into New York City. They photographed large clusters of commuters, many standing back to back at the station, or staring straight ahead. Each figure in the photograph was numbered, the photographs were duplicated, and the students returned the next week distributing the photographs to the commuters, with a cover letter explaining our purposes, and a questionnaire dealing with the phenomenon of the

This paper was first published in the *Division 8 Newsletter,* Division of Personality and Social Psychology, Washington: American Psychological Association, July 1972.

(a)

(b)

Fig. 4.1 *Typical photographs distributed to commuters, used in the study of the familiar stranger.*

familiar stranger. We found that 89.5 percent of those questioned reported at least one familiar stranger. The average commuter claimed 4.0 individuals at the station whom he recognized but never spoke to, compared to a mean of 1.5 individuals with whom he conversed. Some familiar strangers turn out to be "socio-metric stars" in that they are recognized by a large proportion of commuters at their station, even if never spoken to.

Many passengers told us they often think about their fellow commuters, trying to figure out what kind of lives they lead, what their jobs are like, etc. They have a fantasy relationship to familiar strangers that may never eventuate in action. But it is a real relationship, in which both parties have agreed to mutually ignore each other, without any implication of hostility. Indeed, sometimes only the right circumstance is needed to change the relationship. Consider this: A woman collapsed on the streets of Brooklyn, not far from her apartment house. She had been a familiar stranger to another resident of the street for years. The resident immediately took responsibility for the unconscious woman, not only calling an ambulance, but riding with her to the hospital to make certain she was treated properly, and to assure that her possessions were not stolen by ambulance attendants. She said later that she had felt a special responsibility for the woman, because, they had seen each other for years, even if they had never spoken. The familiar stranger status is not the absence of a relationship, but a special form of relationship, that has properties and consequences of its own.

Why do familiar strangers exist? It is a response to overload: in order to handle all the possible inputs from the environment we filter out inputs so that we allow only diluted forms of interaction. In the case of the familiar stranger, we permit a person to impinge on us perceptually, but close off any further interaction. In part this is because perceptual processing of a person takes considerably less time than social processing. We can see a person at a glance, but it takes more time to sustain social involvement. If the temporal relations were reversed, that is, if perception took a longer amount of time than social communication, a quite different phenomenon would result: We would typically talk with people whom we did not have time to visually perceive.

A Psychological Map of New York City[1]   5

A city consists of streets, squares and buildings that exist in objective, geographic space. But there is also a psychological representation of the city that each inhabitant carries around in his head. When a man comes to a strange city, at first he does not know his way around. He sticks close to a few known reference points, such as his hotel or the main shopping street, and quickly feels disoriented if he strays from these few familiar paths. With increasing experience, he begins to build up a picture in his mind of how the streets connect with one another, the relationship among paths, and specific turns he must take to move from one point to another. He acquires a representation of the city which we may call a psychological map. A psychological map is the city as mirrored in the mind of an individual. The acquisition of an adequate representation of the city may be a slow process, filled with confusion, and inevitably only partial in its achievement. Very few individuals, if any, have a total grasp of all of the streets and intersections of a major metropolis; but each of us holds at least the fragment of such a map.

In this paper, we shall describe a psychological map of New York City constructed by our research team. But before going further, I would like to raise some general questions about psychological maps and review some of the work that has been carried out in this field. We start with the notion that the person has a psychological representation of some features of the environment. The first question, then, in constructing a mental map, concerns the units of the environment that are to be mapped. In previous research, the scale of maps has varied from those of small campuses to the maps people have in their head of the entire world (Saarinen, 1971; Hooper, 1970; Stea, 1969; Gould, 1967). There is an important difference, of course, in acquiring a mental map of one's campus and that of the world. The campus map is mediated by direct experience, moving about the university buildings and piecing scenes together into some cognitive structure. The image of the world is learned not from direct exposure, but through formal schemata of it as represented in maps and atlases.

Once we have decided what units of geography are to be mapped, we need to decide which psychological features are of greatest interest. The most basic question is whether a given geographical entity exists at all in a person's cognitive repertory. If asked to draw a map of Central America, does he include Costa Rica and El Salvador? If asked about New York City neighborhoods, is

This paper was written in collaboration with Judith Greenwald, Suzanne Kessler, Wendy McKenna, and Judith Waters. It was first published in *American Scientist,* Vol. 60, No. 2 (March–April 1972), pp. 194–200. Reprinted by permission, *American Scientist,* Journal of Sigma Chi, The Scientific Research Society of North America.

the subject aware of the existence of Chelsea and Morningside Heights? And beyond the identification of an element lies the question of whether he knows the geographic position of one entity in relation to another. (He may be able to name Chelsea, but not know its position in relation to other neighborhoods.) In addition to these purely cognitive features, the individual may possess a set of attitudes or feelings toward different parts of the region or city. In principle, it is possible to map an entire city, block by block, in terms of *any* definable psychological dimension (i.e., perceived level of safety-danger). Gould (1967) has mapped the geography of England in terms of the residential desirability of its varying regions.

The major methodological problem in all this is how to externalize the mental map, that is, how to get it out of the individual's subjective experience and onto paper for public scrutiny. One simple method is to ask a person to draw a map of the area in question, say a city, showing all of the streets he knows, and indicating all of the neighborhoods and landmarks he can think of. A decade ago, Kevin Lynch (1960), at MIT, asked a group of Bostonians to do this. While certain landmarks, such as Paul Revere's house and the Boston Common, as well as paths linking them, turned out to be widely known, large areas of the city were not represented in typical mental representations. Certain neighborhoods hardly existed at all in the minds of Bostonians. This again highlights the difference between the cartographer's map and the psychological map. Donald Hooper (1970) informally applied this cognitive mapping technique to New York City with similar results. The psychological representation of New York was found to be localized in downtown landmarks, with much of the city having no cognitive representation at all.

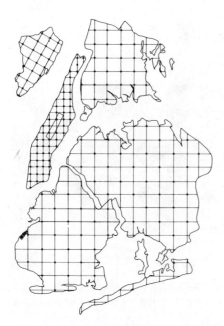

Fig. 5.1. *The stylized map of the five boroughs, on p. 61 shows the percentages of correct placements in neighborhoods of 152 viewing points in the city. The map to the left shows the grid that formed the basis of selection of the viewing points. Photographs taken at some of the grid intersections are shown on the following pages.*

Once the map of a single individual has been externalized, the next problem is that of aggregating the individual maps so as to be able to draw some general conclusion. The problem is that unique configurations are always difficult to aggregate in any meaningful fashion. One is reminded of the work of a nineteenth-century criminologist who attempted to find the average criminal type by superimposing the photographed faces of many criminals onto a single photographic plate, using the resulting portrait as an ideal or average type. Unfortunately, the resulting face was virtually nondescript and resembled no one, criminal or otherwise.

However, the problem of aggregation can be reduced by imposing appropriate constraints. The greater the number of constraints imposed on the subject in externalizing his map, the more readily the production of several individuals can be combined. The psychological map devised by our team is heavily constrained. Subjects are asked to make a simple unidimensional judgment (i.e., whether they can or cannot recognize several scenes of New York). The results of all subjects are then combined without difficulty. This procedure generates a second general type of psychological map, one which takes for granted an objective geographic map, and attempts to plot psychological characteristics onto it. It parallels the approach of a meteorologist mapping weather. In a weather map variables such as temperature, barometric pressure, and wind direction are made at various points and are plotted onto a preexisting map of the region. Similarly, our psychological map attempts to plot a psychological variable onto the geography of New York City.

Fig. 5.2 *Queens (Q–7), Woodside houses between Broadway and 31st Avenue. The percentages of subjects who correctly identified this view are: borough, 22 percent; neighborhood, 3 percent; street, 0.9 percent.*

Psychologists have not been the only persons interested in psychological maps. Geographers such as David Stea (1969), Peter Gould (1967), and Thomas Saarinen (1971) have tried not merely to describe cognitive representations but also to develop concepts for analyzing such maps. Stea asks: "What are the elements out of which people mentally organize large geographic spaces?" and concludes that people think in terms of *points* (New York, Chicago, Canada, etc.). Further, he concludes that these points may be arranged in some *hierarchy* (some are larger, more important, desirable, etc.); that the areas are *bounded* with clear or fuzzy lines of demarcation; that people think in terms of *paths* connecting different points and whether *barriers* block any pair of points. Stea says that "it matters not a whit that we cannot directly observe a mental map.... If a subject behaves as if such a map existed, it is sufficient justification for the model."

In typical studies employing these concepts, subjects are asked to make distance, direction, or size estimates of geographic points. Average results are then compared to the objective reality, the point of interest being the type of deviation from reality contained in the mental images. Thus Griffin (1948) argues that the relative areas ascribed to various regions reflect the importance individuals assigned to them. We have all seen the map of the "New Yorker's idea of the United States," in which the city occupies a vast area of the country, and the Midwest is shrunk to a fraction of its actual size.

A final question concerns the manner in which individuals use mental maps in everyday life to locate themselves in the environment or navigate from one point to another. The question of orientation was raised as early as 1913 by Trowbridge, and continues as a lively issue. Stea suggests that two very different mental approaches may be used in moving from one point to another. In one case, the person proceeds on the basis of a set of specific operations, so that the map consists less of an overall image than a sequence of directional instructions tied to specific cues. The person starts off in an initial direction until he comes to cue_1, such as a building or landmark, at which point he turns right or left until he gets to cue_2, and so forth, until his destination is reached. In a second strategy, the individual proceeds not in terms of a sequence of operations but through a generalized image of the city. Through successive approximations, he zeroes in on the target, constantly referring his position to his knowledge of the city's structure. This second strategy allows for the use of alternative routes, whereas the former method does not. Moreover, Stea points out that in the specific sequence method, "if you miss a cue [choice point], you're lost."

The capacity to form such a representation of the overall structure of the city depends not only on the individual but on the city as well, and the degree to which it is imagible. A highly imagible city does not mean that every point is equally identifiable. Rather, there are clearly identifiable focal points throughout the city which are interconnected and thus form a coherent picture. Lynch, in his seminal work, *The Image of the City* (1960), argues that high imagibility is a crucial condition for a livable and enjoyable social setting. Moreover, imagibility is crucial in orienting an individual in a city, in communicating a sense of place to him that immediately informs him of location, direction, etc. The total absence of such orienting features is an unnerving experience. It is interesting that the anxiety inherent in such disorientation is most acutely expressed in

Fig. 5.3 *Manhattan (M–26), the entrance to Central Park at West 72nd Street (the Dakota). The percentages of subjects who correctly identified this view are: borough, 90 percent; neighborhood, 59 percent; street, 39 percent.*

nightmares in which an individual wanders aimlessly in vaguely familiar but elusively unidentifiable streets.

The imagibility of different parts of the city is interesting for another reason. It allows us to define the psychological boundaries of a city, which need not, of course, coincide with its political boundaries. The methods used by Lynch and others are natural starting points in the assessment of a city's imagibility. But the next step, we felt, should be in the direction of precision by constructing a map that goes beyond landmark specification to the measurement of the exact degree of cognitive significance of any one point in the city relative to any other point. The remainder of this paper describes the method we employed in obtaining a cognitive map of New York City. The key paradigm underlying the psychological map presented here takes the form: If an individual is placed at random at a point in the city, how likely is he to know where he is?

In order for a person to know his location three requirements must be met: First, the scene he confronts needs to be differentiable in some respect from other scenes in the city. If all buildings look exactly the same, a person cannot know where he is. Second, he must match the unique input against some memory of it. The memory may have been acquired through direct exposure, or indirectly through the study of photographs, maps, or hearsay. Third, even if an individual can recognize a scene, he cannot necessarily place it in relation to other parts of the city. ("This street is terribly familiar, but I don't have the slightest idea where we are.") Placing the scene in the larger framework is a final requirement if we are to say that the subject knows where he is.

Our main goal, then, was to make a precise assessment of just which parts of New York City are easiest to recognize and which are most difficult. Our problem was to devise methods that would uncover, in an objective and reliable fashion, the mental representations of New York City held by its residents.

SAMPLING AND PROCEDURE

Only by applying an objective method of scene sampling can assertions drawn from a limited number of cases be applied to the phenomenon as a whole. To illustrate this point, consider the case of a casual investigator who wants to know whether Manhattan or Brooklyn is more recognizable.

He shows a group of people a picture of the Empire State Building to represent Manhattan and his uncle's garage to represent Brooklyn. He would find, no doubt, that more people could recognize the Empire State Building in Manhattan than his uncle's garage in Brooklyn. But that would hardly be an objective basis for asserting that Manhattan was more recognizable than Brooklyn. In one case, he deliberately chose a well-known landmark, and in the other, an insignificant structure. A Brooklyn lover could as easily bias his photographs in the opposite way, photographing the Brooklyn Academy of Music and an insignificant hot dog stand in Manhattan. The only way to control this kind of bias is to introduce an objective method of geographic sampling that could be readily applied not only in New York but in any city in the world (should comparative studies be attempted).

There are many objective ways to choose a set of viewing points. We decided to take advantage of the fact that the entire world is mapped on a coordinate system, lines of latitude and longitude, and that they form regular intersections, so that any point on earth can be specified in terms of these coordinates. While the lines of latitude and longitude appear very far apart on the usual maps, it is possible to obtain maps that carry the system down to a very fine coordinate system. We selected a grid system based on the 1000-meter Universal Transverse Mercator grid ticks shown in U. S. Geological Survey maps of New York City. Wherever a 1000-meter line of latitude intersected a 1000-meter line of longitude, we took a viewing point for our study.

For economy, we systematically thinned out the viewing points in the Bronx, Brooklyn, Queens, and Staten Island, and the final pattern of viewing points is shown in Fig. 5.1. We ended up with 25 viewing points in the Bronx, 22 in Brooklyn, 31 in Queens, 20 in Staten Island, and 54 in Manhattan. Since we wanted to use a large number of subjects, we could not take the subjects to each location, and instead we showed them color slides and asked them to identify the location pictured. A professional photographer was instructed to take a picture that would give the most information to the viewer (e.g., a building rather than an empty lot).

Since familiarity with different parts of the city probably depends on place of residence, we needed a representative sample of all New Yorkers. Thus the most important variable on which our 200 subjects differed was place of residence: they were geographically representative of the population distribution by borough, based on the 1960 census. Subjects were recruited with an advertisement in *New York Magazine,* whose readers, we assumed, would be interested in the city and thus motivated to participate. The total sample represented a particular segment of the New York population. Though some were in their teens and some in their sixties, the majority of the subjects were young adults in their twenties, with a mean age of 28.9. The sex distribution paralleled the city's, with a slight majority of women. According to the Hollingshead scale of social position (1957), the median subject held a job at the minor professional level and had completed college. The median subject had lived in his neighborhood five to ten years and in New York City over 20 years.

Subjects were assembled in groups in a large lecture room with a screen in front. Upon arrival, each was given an answer booklet and a neighborhood map and told to become familiar with the map, which was divided into 54 neighborhoods. They were informed that the main purpose of the study was to discover how well people can recognize various parts of the city. The color slides were then projected onto the screen, and the subjects were asked to imagine that they were viewing these scenes from the window of a bus that was touring the city. The subjects were then asked to indicate in the answer booklet which of the five boroughs they believed the scene was located in. They were also called upon to identify the scene in terms of more exacting criteria—in what neighborhood the scene was to be found and, beyond that, on which precise street. The entire procedure took about ninety minutes.

RELATIVE RECOGNIZABILITY

Based on the proportion of subjects who were able to place each of the 152 scenes in (a) its correct borough, (b) its correct neighborhood, and (c) its exact street location, we may now ask a series of questions concerning the relative recognizability of each of the five boroughs. (It is possible that the figures are somewhat inflated by the fact that if a person took a guess he would be correct 20 percent of the time in any case.)

What proportion of the scenes from each borough were correctly attributed to that borough? By summing the percentage of correct responses for all points in the borough and dividing this figure by the number of points, we arrive at the overall characterization of the borough in terms of an arithmetic mean:

Bronx	25.96%
Brooklyn	35.79
Manhattan	64.12
Queens	39.64
Staten Island	26.00

Clearly, Manhattan emerges as the most recognizable of the five boroughs, with about twice as many correct placements as the others.

There is another way to look at the data. Of the 26 viewing points that were placed in the correct borough by at least 75 percent of the participants, 23 viewing points fall in Manhattan. This certainly corresponds to our generally held notion that Manhattan is better known than other parts of the city.

Fig. 5.4 *This stylized map of New York City shows the correct placement of scenes at 152 viewing points in the city, placed according to neighborhood.*

Fig. 5.5 *Manhattan (M–13), 125th Street between 7th and 8th Avenues. The percentages of subjects who correctly identified this view are: borough, 86 percent; neighborhood, 78 percent; street, 49 percent.*

However, our data tell us more than this, for we may now adopt a more stringent criterion of recognition and ask: What proportion of the scenes in each borough were placed in their correct *neighborhood*? Another way of formulating this is to ask to what degree a street scene communicates to the person the neighborhood he is in. Examining the information on neighborhood placement, we find very substantial differences according to borough:

Bronx	5.85%
Brooklyn	11.42
Manhattan	31.98
Queens	10.76
Staten Island	5.40

A randomly selected scene in Manhattan is five times more likely to be placed in its correct neighborhood than a randomly selected scene in the Bronx; Manhattan scenes do almost three times as well as scenes in Brooklyn and Queens. The superior information value of Manhattan becomes even more pronounced when a more exacting criterion of recognition is applied. When we ask subjects to identify each scene in terms of *street location*, we find the following distribution of accurate guesses:

Bronx	2.56%
Brooklyn	2.83
Manhattan	15.52
Queens	2.21
Staten Island	0.6

Fig. 5.6 *Manhattan (M–8), 147th Street between Riverside Drive and Broadway. The percentages of subjects who correctly identified this view are: borough, 50 percent; neighborhood, 18 percent; street, 9 percent.*

The reader must again be reminded that these scenes were not selected because of the likelihood they would be recognized, but were mechanically sampled completely independent of their scenic value.

This overall picture holds true no matter which borough the person comes from. A resident of Queens is four times more likely to identify a street location in Manhattan than in his own borough (3.76 percent for his home borough of Queens vs. 15 percent for Manhattan). Areas of Queens have often been accused of being nondescript, and taxi drivers are reputed to fear entering Queens lest they never find their way out. And with good reason, when even the people who live in Queens are lost in their home borough compared with the sense of place they experience in Manhattan! Thus it is correct to say that New York City is not merely culturally but also imagistically rooted in Manhattan.

Aside from Manhattan, residents recognize their own borough better than they recognize any other, and they are better at recognizing their own borough than people from any of the others. But these results are overshadowed by the pre-eminence of Manhattan in the psychological map of all New Yorkers, irrespective of where they live (see Table 5.1).

We have been interested not only in the correct guesses made by subjects but also in the kinds of errors they made. When a subject misclassified a scene from the Bronx, where did he tend to place it? Table 5.2 presents a matrix which indicates not only the percentage of subjects who accurately guessed the correct borough but also the percentage of subjects who erred, broken down according to the boroughs which are mistakenly guessed. It appears that, while Manhattan is rarely confused with any other borough, the Bronx, Brooklyn, and Staten

Table 5.1 Percent of correct borough, neighborhood, and street placement by borough of residence.

Borough of residence	Bronx			Brooklyn			Manhattan			Queens			Staten Island		
	B	N	S*	B	N	S	B	N	S	B	N	S	B	N	S
Bronx	40.94	14.40	6.58	21.99	5.78	0.69	69.93	34.77	18.24	33.66	7.72	1.51	18.88	4.44	0.28
Brooklyn	18.63	2.27	1.32	49.19	19.89	5.37	67.41	26.18	11.57	37.15	8.70	1.46	28.87	5.32	0.32
Manhattan	25.58	5.55	2.19	28.97	7.95	2.46	65.09	38.03	21.04	34.71	8.81	2.48	27.95	5.00	0.91
Queens	25.67	5.18	2.52	34.50	8.50	1.17	66.43	31.71	15.00	54.54	15.15	3.76	20.00	2.40	0.20
Staten Island	12.04	0.92	0.0	36.46	9.62	3.85	59.38	24.11	8.93	18.18	3.79	1.52	61.25	30.00	3.75

* B = borough; N = neighborhood; S = street.

Island are often thought to be Queens. It is as though subjects said to themselves: "Well, I don't really know where that was taken, but it looks as if it might be Queens." One could refer to the phenomenon as a Queens response bias. While the largest percentage of subjects either guessed the correct borough or answered "Don't know" (in the case of the Bronx and Staten Island), the second largest percentage of subjects guessed Queens.

Table 5.2 Matrix of classifications showing correct percentages as well as misclassifications, by borough.

When the borough was:	Percent of subjects who identified scenes as:					Combined errors	Don't know
	Bx	B	M	Q	S.I.		
Bronx	**25.96**	14.89	6.92	17.33	3.48	42.62	31.51
Brooklyn	10.33	**35.79**	8.08	18.17	2.94	39.12	25.00
Manhattan	7.81	8.17	**64.12**	3.44	0.49	19.88	15.89
Queens	8.82	14.76	2.94	**39.64**	4.94	31.46	28.52
Staten Island	11.45	10.15	1.50	21.70	**26.00**	44.80	29.05

Finally, we may ask whether the residents of any one borough are better at recognizing the city as a whole than the residents of any other borough. As shown in Table 5.3, the differences among residents of the five boroughs are not very large on any of the categories. In other words, there is no evidence that residents of any particular borough are more accurate at recognizing the city as a whole than residents of any other borough.

What general principles account for the major findings of the study? First, an area can only be recognized if people are exposed to it. As we might expect, Manhattan's high index of recognizability is due, in important measure, to the fact that, as the cultural and entertainment core, it attracts persons from all over the city. Even a highly distinctive architectural display will not be widely

Table 5.3 Average percent correct (over all boroughs) according to where subject lives.

Borough of residence	Borough	Neighborhood	Street
Bronx	37.08	13.42	5.46
Brooklyn	40.25	12.47	4.01
Manhattan	36.46	13.07	5.82
Queens	40.23	12.59	4.53
Staten Island	37.46	13.69	3.61
All subjects combined	38.30	13.08	4.64

Fig. 5.7 *Brooklyn (B–3), Adelphi Street between Fulton Street and Atlantic Avenue. The percentages of subjects who correctly identified this view are: borough, 48 percent; neighborhood, 27 percent; street, 2 percent.*

recognized if it is too far off the beaten path; centrality in relation to major population flow is crucial.

The second major factor seems to be the overall architectural or social distinctiveness of the area. Columbus Circle and Rockefeller Center impress themselves because of their unique configuration of spaces and buildings. Chinatown and Little Italy communicate themselves through cultural and racial features of their respective neighborhoods. The degree to which a scene in the city will be recognized can be summarized by the formula

$$R = f(C \times D),$$

in which R is recognition, C stands for centrality to population flow, and D represents social or architectural distinctiveness.

We have seen that New York City, as a psychological space, is very uneven. It is not at all clear that such world cities as London, Paris, Tokyo, and Moscow have comparably uneven psychological textures. It would be extremely interesting to construct a similar psychological map of other major cities of the world to determine how successfully each city, in all its parts, communicates to the resident a specific sense of place which locates him in the city, assuages the panic of disorientation, and allows him to build up an articulated image of the city as a whole. Contours could be drawn around the psychological core of the city to show whether it is compressed or coextensive with the city around it. My guess is that Paris holds together better than New York because it has focal points that are more successfully distributed throughout the city. In addition, if only out of a sense of scientific duty, we ought to take the psychological map to the drearier cities of the world. It would probably turn out that their index of recognizability is about on a par with that of Queens or the Bronx. The deeper misfortune of their inhabitants is that they cannot take a subway into a vibrant and highly imagible core.

There is a moral here for the outlying boroughs. The construction of identifiable monuments in their neighborhoods, the addition of distinctive decorative touches to their houses, and emphasis on local color would help them emerge from the gray, nondescript character they now possess into more vivid and exciting locales.

NOTE

1. This research would not have been possible without the public-spirited assistance of *New York Magazine* and its executive editor, Sheldon Zalaznick. Over a thousand volunteers were recruited through its advertising pages. Thanks are also due to Pacy Markman for his talent in recruiting subjects and to Lynne Goodstein for assistance in graphics.

REFERENCES

EMERSON, W., 1969, "A review of geographic and psychologic research into the structure of environmental images," University of Minnesota, unpublished.

GOULD, P, 1967. "Structuring information on spacio-temporal preferences," *J. Regional Science*, Vol. 7, No. 2 (supplement).

GRIFFIN, D., 1948, "Topographical orientation," *Foundations of Psychology*, New York: J. Wiley.

HOOPER, D., reported in S. Milgram, 1970, "The experience of living in cities," *Science*, Vol. 167.

LYNCH, K., 1960, *The Image of the City*. Cambridge, Mass.: MIT and Harvard University Press.

MILGRAM, S., 1970, "The experience of living in cities," *Science*, Vol. 167.

SAARINEN, T., 1971, "The use of projective techniques in geographic research," mimeo.

STEA, D., 1969, "Environment perception and cognition: Toward a model for mental maps," Student Publication of the North Carolina State University School of Design, Vol. 18.

STEA, D., 1969, "The measurement of mental maps: An experimental model for studying conceptual spaces," Studies in Geography #17: Behavioral Problems in Geography: A Symposium, Northwestern University.

TROWBRIDGE, C. C., 1913, "On fundamental methods of orientation and imaginary maps," *Science*, Vol. 38.

Psychological Maps of Paris[1]   6

In this report we shall explore the way in which Parisians mentally represent their city. It is not an examination of Paris as a geographic reality, but rather of the way that reality is mirrored in the minds of its inhabitants. And the first principle is that reality and image are imperfectly linked. The Seine may course a great arc in Paris, almost forming a half circle, but Parisians imagine it a much gentler curve, and some think the river a straight line as it flows through the city.

Paris, the city of stone, is the template from which the mental map draws its structure, but it is not the same as the map. The person harboring a mental model of Paris may die, but the city endures. The city may vanish through flood or nuclear holocaust, but the maps encoded in millions of human brains are not thereby destroyed.

The main problem in investigating a mental entity is to learn how to render it observable. The person's mental image of Paris is not like his driver's license, something he can pull out for inspection. Rather, we shall have to tease the information from the subject, using whatever means psychology can offer to inspect the contents of the mind (Downs and Stea, 1973).

It is not quite as easy as simply asking the person. First, many of the concepts people have about cities are nonverbal, spatial ideas. They are not easily translated into words, particularly on the part of subjects of limited education. Moreover, Parisians are all exposed to stereotypes about their city, readily available clichés, which do not so much tap their personal ideas of the city, as their immersion in a world of prepackaged platitudes. We want to get at something more personal and more closely tied to direct experience.

HANDDRAWN MAPS

To begin, our 218 subjects, drawn from each of the 20 arrondissements (i.e., administrative sectors) of Paris in proportion to their numbers, were asked to draw a map of Paris in which they were to mention all of the elements of the city that came to mind; they could illustrate their maps with monuments, squares, neighborhoods, streets, or whatever elements spontaneously occurred to them. They were told further that their sketch should not resemble a tourist map

This paper was written in collaboration with Mme. Denise Jodelet. The research was supported by a fellowship to the senior author from the John Simon Guggenheim Memorial Foundation, and by a grant from the Délégation Générale à la Recherche Scientifique, an agency of the French Government. It was first published in *Environmental Psychology: People and Their Physical Settings* (second edition), H. M. Proshansky, W. H. Ittelson, and L. G. Rivlin (eds.), New York: Holt, Rinehart and Winston, 1976. Reprinted by permission of the author.

of Paris, but ought to express their personal view. Let us now consider the maps of some of the subjects:

Map 108 (Fig. 6.1). The subject is a 25-year-old commercial agent, with university degrees in physical chemistry. His first entries on the map were Boulevard St. Germain and St. Michel, then the Faculté des Sciences at Jussieu, suggesting that his student experience remains dominant. The modern structures of the Zamanski Tower at the Faculté des Sciences and the 50-story Maine-Montparnasse office tower are prominently shown. Youthful subjects, more often than their elders, include these contemporary elements as if the mental maps of the old were internalized a long time ago and cannot admit these recent additions. Rising in the northwest, the massive office complex, La Défense, is given an almost projective significance, as it hovers menacingly alongside the city. The map expresses the central dilemma of contemporary Paris: how can it preserve its distinctive character, formed in earlier centuries, while coming to grips with modernity?

Map 070 (Fig. 6.2). Map 070 is drawn by a 50-year-old woman who, at the time of the interview, lived in the 12th arrondissement; however, for 15 years she

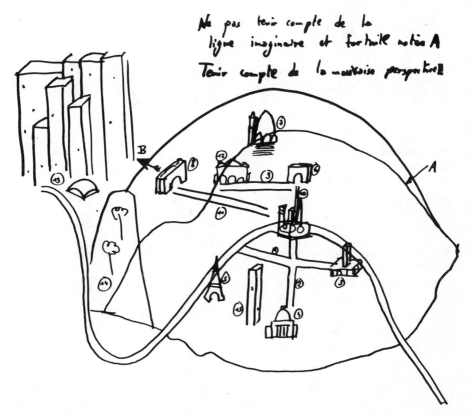

Fig. 6.1 *Map 108.*

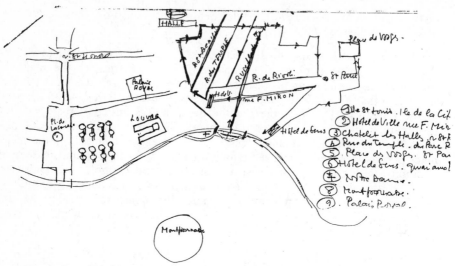

Fig. 6.2 *Map 070.*

had resided in the 4th, which she maps with scrupulous detail, even to the point of indicating the one-way street directions for automobiles. She centers her map not on Paris as a whole, but on a segment of it that has special meaning to her. Yet she is able to link her personal experience to highly public landmarks such as the Louvre and the Palais Royale. Perhaps it is characteristic of Paris that one can readily fuse private and public aspects of life through the network of streets and landmarks.

Map 215 (Fig. 6.3). This subject is a 33-year-old butcher who lives in the 11th arrondissement. At first the map looks confusing, but we begin to discern the elements of a set of life circumstances when we examine it closely. He does not forget to include his home arrondissement, which is something of a hidden one to most subjects. Nor does he neglect La Villette, where the major stockyards and slaughterhouses of Paris are to be found. One can imagine his visits to the great exposition hall at the Porte de Versailles, to see displays of meat cutting equipment, motorcycles, and perhaps automobiles. Faubourg St. Antoine, of revolutionary significance, is placed on the Left Bank, where it would seem to belong politically.

We are most confused, perhaps, by the inverted curvature he has given to the Seine; the disposition of elements along the river seem all out of line with reality. Yet if Etoile, Maison de la Radio, and the Porte de St. Cloud deviate from their true spatial coordinates, they do preserve a meaningful topological sequence.

Map 037 (Fig. 6.4). A mental map is not limited to reality, but may incorporate visions of how a city ought to be. This subject, an architect, organizes the city around the Place de la Concorde. He envisages a major avenue stretching south from the Place, over the Seine, piercing the Chambre

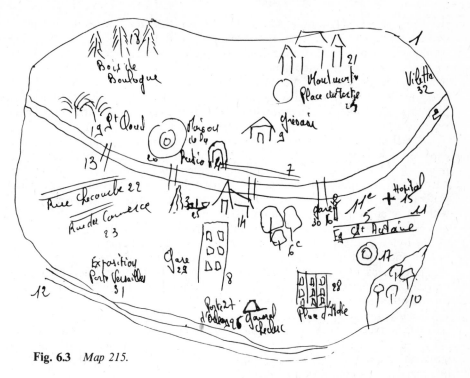

Fig. 6.3 *Map 215.*

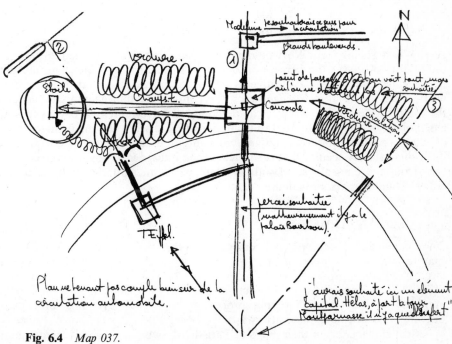

Fig. 6.4 *Map 037.*

des Députés, and continuing south into the heart of the Left Bank, terminating in an impressive structure (as yet unrealized). From that point, a broad avenue would sweep northwest to reveal the Eiffel Tower, and another northeast leading to the colonnade of Madeleine (displaced from its present location). Such mental maps are fanciful. Yet Paris as it exists was born first as a set of ideas, and the Paris to come is also germinating in the minds of architects and city planners. The subject's concern with problems of automobile traffic represents a realistic attention to the city's most severe environmental problem.

It is clear the subjects did not merely derive their maps from personal, direct experience with the city. They learned them, in part, from other maps. Street maps of Paris, prepared by technically skilled cartographers, are an inherent part of contemporary Parisian culture. Probably not a single subject could have generated a map of the city accurately showing its form and basic structure without reference in his own mind to maps he has already seen. But through processes of selectivity, emphasis, and distortion, the maps become projections of life styles, and express emotional cathexes of the participants.

Second, neither the city, nor the mental maps of the city, are simple agglomerations of elements; they are structures. It is the essence of structure that displacement of one element is not an isolated event, but has consequences for the other elements with which it is linked.

Finally, a map that a person draws of his city is not his mental map, but is only a clue to it. He may not be able to draw very well; he may have images in his mind which he cannot put on paper. He may make errors in his initial strokes that complicate his later completion of the map. But still, the sketch is an opening into his conception of the city.

PARIS AS A COLLECTIVE REPRESENTATION

A city is a social fact. We would all agree to that. But we need to add an important corollary: the perception of a city is also a social fact, and as such needs to be studied in its collective as well as its individual aspect. It is not only what *exists* but what is *highlighted* by the community that acquires salience in the mind of the person. A city is as much a collective representation as it is an assemblage of streets, squares, and buildings. We discern the major ingredients of that representation by studying not only the mental map in a specific individual, but by seeing what is shared among individuals. Toward this end, we turn from the clinical use of individual maps to an actuarial analysis of the entire group of maps provided by the subjects.

EMERGING ELEMENTS

The sequence that spontaneously emerges as subjects sketch their maps of Paris may tell us what is uppermost in their minds when they think of the city. What is most salient is probably what comes out first. With this point in mind, from the outset we had asked our subjects to number each element as they drew it, emphasizing that the numbering process is to accompany their process of drawing, and not be applied afterward.

Most subjects begin their maps of Paris by drawing a rough ellipse designating the city limits. Unlike many cities in the United States, such as Los Angeles, which do not possess a strong form and whose boundaries bleed off into surrounding areas, Paris possesses a clear boundary and its form impresses itself on the inhabitants. The boundary is sharply etched by the *périphérique,* a highway wrapped around the city, separating the city from the densely populated suburbs, and providing a contemporary moat-in-motion to replace the historic walls.

Within the city there are almost a thousand different elements included in the maps of our subjects, but only one feature is the first entry of a large number of participants, the Seine. After the city limits are sketched, it is the element that far and away is drawn first. It is not only a basic geographic fact of the city, but its most salient psychological fact as well, and much of the subjects' subsequent mapmaking is organized around it.

But there is a serious distortion in the way the Seine is represented. In reality the path of the Seine resembles a wave that enters Paris at the Quai Bercy, rises sharply northward, tapers slightly as it flows into separate streams around the islands, initiates its flat northernmost segment at the Place de la Concorde, then turns sharply in a great 60° bend at the Place d'Alma to flow out of the southwestern tip of the city. But in their drawings, 91.6 percent of the subjects understated the river's degree of curvature. Several subjects pulled it through the city as a straight line, and the typical subject represented the Seine as a gentle arc of slight but uniform curvature.

Because the course of the river is made to resemble an arc of gentle convexity, some subjects find it necessary to force the river through the Bois de Boulogne, and there is no space for the Auteuil and Passy districts. Accordingly, these districts are eliminated or displaced to the Left Bank.

Figure 6.5 compares the actual course of the Seine to the average curvature imparted by the subjects.

Why does this systematic distortion occur? Quite clearly it reflects the subjects' experience. Although the Alma bend of the Seine is apparent in high aerial views of the city, it is not experienced as a sharp curve in the ordinary walk or drive through the city. The curve is extended over a sufficient distance so that the pronounced turn of the river is obscured. Such long, slow curves have, in almost all studies of orientation in cities, proved to be the most confusing, and difficult to reconstruct (Lynch, 1960).

We return now to the general question of the sequence with which the elements are set down. After the Seine, Notre Dame and Île de la Cité are set down most often as the first entries. The three elements of the Seine, Île de la Cité, and Notre Dame are at the very heart of the idea of Paris. Lutèce was born on the Île de la Cité; Notre Dame was constructed there 800 years ago. The sequence with which subjects enter their elements in the handdrawn maps recapitulates this history.

Unlike a city such as New York, whose psychological core has shifted continuously northward (and now focuses on the area between 34th and 86th Streets), the psychological center of Paris has remained true to its origins, building outward from the Seine, never shifting its center away from its historic root. The remarkable stability of the "heart of Paris" confers a dimension of permanence to the city's psychological structure.

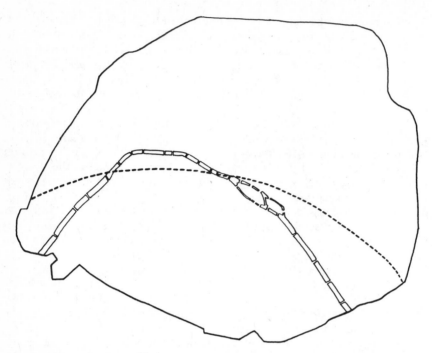

Fig. 6.5 *Perceived curvature of the Seine. The dotted line represents the median curvature imparted to the Seine in the subject's hand-drawn maps. It is superimposed on the actual course of the river.*

THE MAJOR ELEMENTS

Altogether our subjects entered 4,132 elements in their maps, an average of 19 for each subject. If the city did not impress on its inhabitants a sense of its structure, its highlights and nodes, we would find little agreement among the subjects. But, in fact, time and again we find the same locations, showing up in the handdrawn maps. Indeed, about half of all the 4,132 elements are accounted for by only 26 locations.

We need to translate the frequency of information into cartographic form. Perhaps we can take a cue from Rand McNally. When the population of a city is large, Rand McNally translates this information into **BOLD TYPOGRAPHY**, and the population of a small city is expressed by smaller print. In Fig. 6.6 we have shown the names of the locales, streets, and monuments in a size proportional to the number of people who cited them; that is, in proportion to their salience to the Parisians.

Parisians like to say that there is a tourist Paris, but the real Paris is something quite apart. But if we examine the maps produced by the subjects, we see that time and again tourist Paris—the famous monuments and landmarks—reappears as the basic structuring devices in their own productions of the city. Paris is integral, and it is not possible to efface l'Etoile, the Louvre, and others from any intelligent representation of the city.

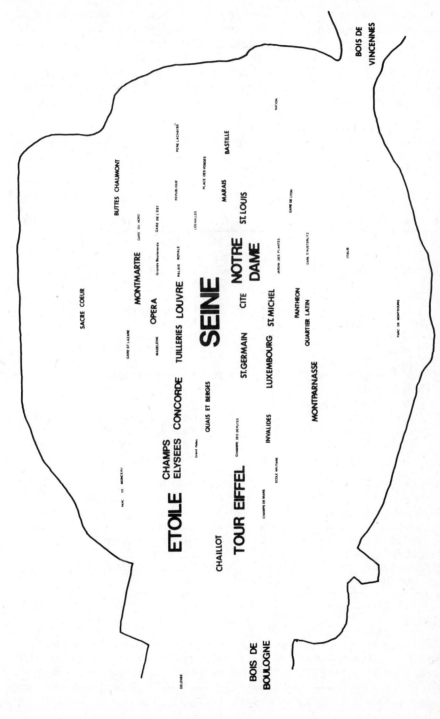

Fig. 6.6 *The 50 most frequently cited elements. The name of each locale is shown in a size proportional to the number of subjects who included it in their handdrawn maps of Paris.*

In scoffing at tourist Paris, Parisians imply they have access to a much deeper treasure, and choose to dissociate themselves from the city's public aspect. But, of course, the very greatness of Paris and its attraction to millions reside in its very availability as a city.

In Table 6.1 we have listed by rank, and irrespective of when the items appeared in the subject's map, the fifty elements of the Paris cityscape listed most frequently by the subjects.

Table 6.1   The fifty elements most frequently included in the hand-drawn maps of Paris.

Rank	Name of element	Percent of maps in which this element appears	Rank	Name of element	Percent of maps in which this element appears
1.	Seine	84.3	26.	Bastille	22.1
2.	Limites de Paris	81.5	27.	Quartier Latin	20.7
3.	Etoile, Arc de Triomphe	61.9	28.	Panthéon	20.7
			29.	Place des Vosges	18.4
4.	Notre Dame	55.5	30.	Gare de Lyon	18.4
5.	Tour Eiffel	54.6	31.	Champ de Mars	17.9
6.	Bois de Boulogne	49.1	32.	Madeleine	17.9
7.	Louvre	45.4	33.	Parc Monceau	17.0
8.	Concorde	45.4	34.	Parc de Montsouris	16.6
9.	Champs Elysées	40.4	35.	Gare St. Lazare	16.6
10.	Jardin du Luxembourg	38.5	36.	Jardin des Plantes	16.1
11.	Bois de Vincennes	38.1	37.	Gare de l'Est	15.6
12.	Gare et Tour Montp.	35.3	38.	Palais Royale	15.2
13.	Île de la Cité	33.9	39.	Gare du Nord	14.7
14.	Tuileries	33.5	40.	Place de la République	14.3
15.	Butte Montmartre	32.1	41.	Gare d'Austerlitz	13.8
16.	Chaillot, Trocadero	32.1	42.	Père Lachaise	12.9
17.	Île de St. Louis	31.7	43.	Porte, Place d'Italie	12.4
18.	St. Germain	31.2	44.	Place de la Nation	12.0
19.	Opéra	30.7	45.	Chambre des Députés	11.5
20.	Boulevard St. Michel	30.1	46.	École Militaire	11.5
21.	Invalides	29.8	47.	Les Halles	10.1
22.	Marais	26.2	48.	Grand, Petit Palais	9.7
23.	Buttes Chaumont	24.4	49.	La Défense	9.7
24.	Sacre Coeur	23.4	50.	Grands Boulevards	9.2
25.	Quais, Berges	22.5			

LINKS

No city consists of a set of isolated elements floating in an urban vacuum, but some cities possess a dense set of pathways tying its varied monuments and squares together. A city is either barren or fertile, depending on the degree to which its varied elements are woven into an interconnected web. The sum becomes greater than the parts by virtue of their relationship to each other. To uncover the associational structures of Paris, we posed the following problem to our subjects:

> We shall name an element in the Paris scene, then we would like you to wander with the mind's eye to the next specific element in your own mental imagery, which we would then like you to write down. For example, if we say "Tour Eiffel" you might summon up the scene in your mental imagery, probe around mentally, and say "Palais de Chaillot" or "Pont d'Iéna," or you might think of the Champ de Mars. Whatever comes to mind as forming a natural connection is what interests us.

In this way we hoped to see how the varied elements in the subject's mental structure of Paris were held together. The 20 stimulus locales that we provided the subjects are listed in Table 6.2.

Table 6.2   Mental links to twenty stimulus locales.

Stimulus locales	*A* Number of locales with which stimulus locale is linked by 10 percent of the subjects or more	*B* Percent of subjects who fail to link stimulus locale with any other locale
Arc de Triomphe	6	.5
Notre Dame	6	1.8
Place de la Concorde	6	1.8
L'Opéra	6	2.3
Sacre Coeur	2	2.3
Le Louvre	4	3.7
Tour Eiffel	5	5.1
Gare St. Lazare	1	5.5
Bois de Vincennes	3	6.9
Porte St. Martin	2	11.0
Le Panthéon	6	11.5
Tour St. Jacques	4	12.4
Place de la Nation	2	13.3
École Militaire	3	13.8
Place de la République	2	16.1
Lion de Belfort	3	18.4
Parc des Buttes Chaumont	0	20.2
Place d'Italie	3	22.5
Père Lachaise	0	27.0
Parc de Montsouris	1	34.0

In Column *A* we have indicated the number of links forged between each stimulus location and some other location by at least 10 percent of the subjects. For example, there are six such links for the Arc de Triomphe, five links for the Tour Eiffel, and so on. There is a great difference in the degree to which the different stimulus locales are embedded in a context of mental associations.

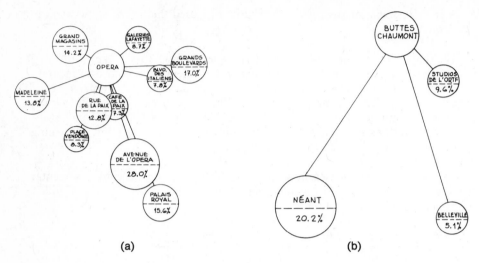

(a)   (b)

Fig. 6.7 *(a) Association to Opéra. Shows all associations to the stimulus locale Opéra made by at least 5 percent of the subjects. (b) Associations to Buttes Chaumont. Shows all associations to the stimulus locale Buttes Chaumont made by at least 5 percent of the subjects.*

Among the most richly embedded sites are Arc de Triomphe, l'Opéra, Notre Dame de Paris, and Panthéon. The most weakly embedded are Buttes Chaumont and Père Lachaise.

The structure of associations for two of the stimulus locales is shown in the "molecules" in Fig. 6.7.

By linking up the separate molecules at points of overlap, one may map the entire network of associations for the city, the reticulate structure of its images.

A related measure of the "embeddedness" is the proportion of subjects who are unable to give any association whatsoever to a stimulus location. As Column *B* of Table 6.2 shows, this varies greatly from one location to the next. Fewer than one percent of the subjects were unable to provide an association to the Arc de Triomphe, while 34 percent were unable to provide any association for the Parc de Montsouris. The former is a well-embedded element, while the latter is poorly articulated with the main structure of the city.

Although we asked our subjects to concentrate on geographic, visual elements, they often included purely social or historical features such as "La Guillotine" or "clochards," as if these elements could simply not be excluded from the meaning of a particular locale. We used this information to create an additional map (Fig. 6.8); one in which each locale is surrounded by the verbal associations it stimulated.

RECOGNITION OF PARISIAN SCENES

There are numerous representations of things that a person cannot externalize through drawing or verbal recall. He may be able to see a loved one's face in his mind's eye without being able to draw it. But he is likely to recognize it if shown

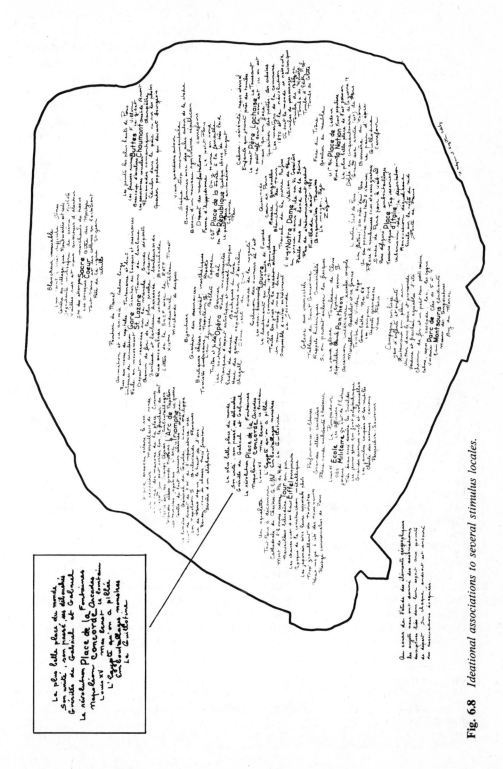

Fig. 6.8 *Ideational associations to several stimulus locales.*

a photograph. And the same is true of cities. A person may have encoded visual aspects of the city that can be most sensitively uncovered through recognition, that is by seeing if the person can match an external stimulus to some memory of it. Accordingly, to supplement the method of "free recall" used in drawing maps of the city, we presented subjects with 40 photographed scenes of Paris, which they were asked to identify. Correct recognition shows that a scene is an active part of the subject's representation of the city, even if he did not spontaneously include it in his map.

We scored recognition by noting the percentage of subjects who correctly identified the scene, and as Table 6.3 shows, this ranged from 100 percent for Etoile to under 5 percent for Rue de Cambrai and Place d'Israël. We may touch briefly on four aspects of the recognition data: *icons of the city, confusions, class differences,* and *paradoxical unknowns* (see Fig. 6.9).

Icons of the City

All of the groups shown the photographs, whether professionals or workers, recognized the same four scenes with the greatest degree of accuracy: Etoile, Notre Dame, Place de la Concorde, and the Palais de Chaillot. What distinguishes these scenes is not so much their beauty, as their monumentality,

Table 6.3 Recognition of Parisian scenes.

Scenes Shown to Group I*	Percent of S's who correctly identified scene	Scenes Shown to Group II*	Percent of S's who correctly identified scene
Etoile	100.0	Place Denfert	
Notre Dame	98.5	Rochereau	94.4
Place de la Concorde	97.0	Place Vendôme	90.8
Palais de Chaillot	93.3	Place de la République	81.6
Mosque	82.8	Parc Monceau	80.5
Louvre (Porte la Tremoille)	79.0	Place du Tertre	79.3
Places des Vosges	70.1	Porte de St. Cloud	61.0
Porte St. Martin	67.0	Square du Vert Galant	59.8
UNESCO (Place Fontenoy)	52.0	École des Beaux Arts	58.7
Musée des Arts		Place des Victoires	56.3
Africains	46.4	Arène de Lutèce	55.2
Place Furstenberg	44.8	Fontaine Molière	55.2
Parc de Montsouris	44.8	Eglise d'Alésia	54.0
Eglise Orthodox	44.8	Fontaine des Innocents	49.4
Place Félix Eboué	39.6	Place St. André des Arts	31.0
Avenue d'Italie	36.6	Mémorial du Martyr Juif	23.0
Monument de la		Passage Dellesert	20.7
Déportation	30.6	Avenue Clichy	16.1
Fontaine Cuvier	37.7	Place Rodin	12.6
Avenue des Gobelins	7.5	Pont Bir Hakeim	12.6
Place d'Israël	4.5	Place de Santiago	6.9
Rue de Cambrai	4.5		

*Twenty scenes were shown to each of two groups of subjects, studied at different times.

Icon: *Etoile, 100 percent correct identification.*

Confusion: *Porte St. Martin, 67.0 percent identification. Often misidentified as Porte St. Denis.*

Class differences: *UNESCO at Place Fontenoy, 52 percent correct overall. Professionals, 67 percent; workers, 24 percent.*

Unknown: *Place D'Israël, identified by 4.5 percent of the subjects.*

Fig. 6.9 *Representative photographs used in the recognition test.*

special historic significance, and scenic grandeur. (To this group one could, without doubt, add the Eiffel Tower, and Sacre Coeur (Sondages, 1951)). Each of these scenes has come to be indelibly associated with Paris, not merely within the city, but abroad as well. One might conclude, therefore, that those sites which are universally identifiable among residents serve as internationally circulated symbols of the city. This formula is, however, too simple: Denfert Rochereau, with its imposing Lion de Belfort, though recognized by 94 percent of the subjects, in no way functions as an international symbol. (This raises questions of urban iconography too complex to discuss here. We may also ponder why Paris is so richly endowed with exportable symbols, while such great urban centers as São Paulo and Chicago lack them entirely.)

Confusions

In the mental representation of a city, two quite separate geographic locales may be collapsed into a single imagined site. Thus, many Parisians mentally combined the nonsectarian Monument de la Déportation (located on the Île de la Cité) and the Mémorial du Martyr Juif (located in St. Paul) into a single locale, believing there is only one such monument, rather than the two that actually exist. Porte St. Martin was frequently misidentified as Porte St. Denis, highlighting the psychologically interchangeable character of the two arches.

Class Differences

Class factors shape the maps of the subjects by segregating rich and poor residentially, and also by transmitting a class-linked culture to various segments of the population. Thus, Place Furstenberg is recognized by 59 percent of the professional subjects, but only 17 percent of the workers; UNESCO headquarters by 67 percent versus 24 percent. The icons of the city, however, are recognized equally by all groups, serving as integrative elements in the urban culture.

Paradoxical Unknowns

When a city is deficient in fine squares and architecture, mediocre locales may be widely publicized because they are the best of what is available. But in Paris, a surfeit of riches creates an opposite situation. Competition for a place in the mind is fierce; many worthy locales are excluded. Thus Place Felix Eboué, which displays an impressive and monumental fountain, is recognized by less than half of the Parisians, while 87 percent of the subjects cannot identify Place Rodin. Place d'Israël, which could serve as an architectural showpiece, sinks to virtual obscurity—identified by only 4.47 percent of the subjects. Locational factors play some part. But more critically, the data highlight how the mental maps which Parisians internalize are not only individual products, but are in an important degree social constructions. Any one of these last scenes possesses sufficient aesthetic value to serve as a widely known feature of the Parisian environment. If society chose to publicize Place Rodin, the square could become as famous as (God forbid) the urinating statue of Brussels. Social definition determines, through selectivity and reiteration, which features of the city acquire salience in the mental maps of the inhabitants.

PARIS, KNOWN AND UNKNOWN

The photographic recognition test tells us about the knowledge of specific landmarks, but we wanted a more general picture of the known and unknown parts of the city. Accordingly, we provided each subject with an illustrated map of the city, which we overprinted with the boundaries of the 80 administrative districts (*quartiers*). We asked each subject to study his map and indicate the ten quartiers with which he was most familiar, and those that were least familiar to him. By combining the response for all subjects, we generate a gradient of asserted familiarity across the entire city.

The five most familiar quartiers are contiguous and center on the Quartier Latin and Île de la Cité. The next five choices accrete to this cluster, but also extend to the Champs Elysées and Etoile. When subjects are asked to list the quartier they know least well, we find a striking movement away from the center of Paris to the peripheral arrondissements.

Figure 6.10 shows how these data, translated into respective arrondissements, delineate a ring of unknown areas around the core of Paris. Curiously, in this map the boundary between known and unknown parts of the city retraces

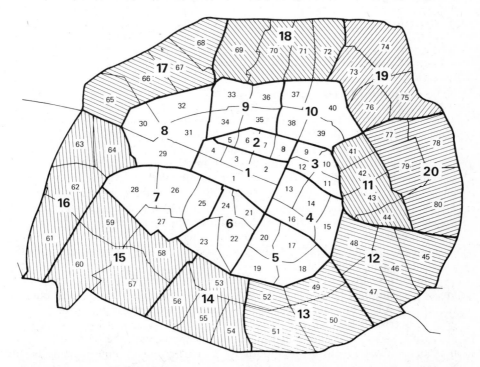

Fig. 6.10 *Least known areas of Paris, by arrondissment. The shaded portion of the map indicates the ten arrondissments that contain areas subjects indicate they know least well.*

part of the route of the last wall of Paris, the Férmiers Généraux. Although the wall was torn down in 1859 its effects endure in the mental maps of contemporary Parisians, with the least familiar parts of the city lying outside the boundary where the wall once stood.

The residential patterns of Paris create a class basis to known and unknown parts of the city. Generally speaking, the wealthier segments of the population live in the western part of the city, and the poorer classes live in the east. It is not surprising, therefore, that the areas least known to the working-class subjects should differ from those of the middle-class professionals, as Table 6.4 shows. While all of the least-known arrondissements are on the periphery of Paris, there is no overlap between the class-linked perceptions. It is only a knowledge of the central arrondissements of Paris that is claimed by both groups.

Table 6.4   Least familiar arrondissements by social class.

		Middle class		*Working class*
Rank	*Arrond.*	*Percent of S's indicating a quartier in this arrondissement to be among the least familiar*	*Arrond.*	*Percent of S's indicating a auartier in this arrondissement to be among the least familiar*
1	20	69.3	15	61.0
2	19	68.2	13	58.5
3	12	62.5	17	53.7
4	18	61.4	16	51.2

SOCIAL PERCEPTIONS

While ethnic turfs have a salient place in the representation of New York, with exception of the North African districts, and the Jewish quarter around St. Paul, they do not figure greatly in the mental maps of Paris. The city does not have the multiple ethnic concentrations found in New York, and areas are not selectively highlighted and affixed with an ethnic label, a process Suttles (1972) has shown to be important in the definition of ethnic neighborhoods. In pre-World War II Paris, areas of the city were rich in residents from particular provinces, and subjects continue to identify the quartiers around Gare de Montparnasse as *Paris des Bretons*. On the other hand, the Chinese community that once flourished behind the Gare de Lyon receives no representation   the maps of contemporary Parisians.

Subjects locate the very poor in the northeastern districts; while the wealthy are overwhelmingly situated in the 16th arrondissement, at the western edge of the city (Table 6.5). This is a sharply differentiated perception, with no geographic overlap between the two groups. The criminally dangerous areas of Paris are identified with the 18th and 19th arrondissements, with the greatest threat to personal safety ascribed to the Goutte d'Or quartier, which houses many North African immigrants.

The responses to several purely personal questions appear to derive from

Table 6.5 Qualities ascribed to different areas of Paris.

Qualities	The arrondissements in which the quality on the left is most frequently located, ranked 1–4, and the percentage of all subjects locating the quality within this arrondissement.* (N = 218)			
	1	2	3	4
Paris of the rich	16	17	8	7
	87.6%	20.6%	18.3%	17.0%
Paris of the poor	18	19	20	13
	38.5%	31.7%	29.8%	11.0%
Dangerous Paris	18	9	10	19
	38.5%	31.7%	29.8%	11.0%
Areas you like best	6	4	1	5
	70.6%	65.1%	57.8%	51.4%
Areas in which you would refuse to live under any circumstances	18	19	10	8
	37.2%	27.1%	18.3%	17.0%
Areas you know best	6	1	5	8
	73.9%	61.5%	58.3%	57.8%
Areas you know least well	20	13	19	18
	60.1%	58.7%	57.3%	55.0%
Snobbish Paris	16	6	8	17
	49.1%	15.1%	14.7%	9.6%
"Paris des Bretons"	15	4	6	—
	50.0%	34.9%	23.4%	—
Where you would move if you became wealthy	6	4	7	16
	33.9%	31.2%	24.8%	21.6%
Friendlier, more relaxed atmosphere	6	5	4	7
	30.3%	22.5%	18.3%	14.7%
Greatest loss of pleasant qualities because of urban renewal	15	1	13	6
	43.1%	14.2%	13.8%	10.1%

*Subjects were instructed to give all responses in terms of quartiers and not arrondissements. (There are four quartiers in each arrondissement.) But we have integrated the results and presented them in terms of arrondissements for ease of comprehension, particularly for those familiar with the city.

this rough socioeconomic map. When subjects are asked if there is a quartier they would refuse to live in under any circumstances, they cite the quartiers around Goutte d'Or (quartiers 71, 72, 73, 74).

The deepest affection for the city is reserved for its central historic areas, with the best-liked quartiers falling out in the 6th, followed by 4th, 1st, and 5th arrondissements. Along related lines, subjects were asked to engage in a pleasant financial fantasy: *Suppose you came into a great deal of money, and could afford to live anywhere in Paris. Where would you move to?* The arrondissements exerting the greatest residential attraction are, in order of popularity, 6th, 4th, 7th, and 16th. The single most desired location is the Île de St. Louis. Popular with all groups, and particularly so with younger Parisians, 36.2 percent of those under 30 speculated that if they had a financial windfall they would move there, to the island in the middle of Paris, but removed from the bustle.

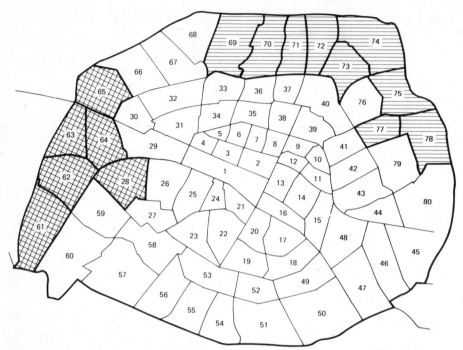

Fig. 6.11 *Perception of rich and poor areas. Shows all quartiers which at least 10 percent of the subjects indicated as among the right (grating) or poor (stripes) areas of Paris.*

The subjects' attachment to "le vieux Paris" is expressed in a somewhat different form when they responded to the following hypothetical problem: *Suppose you were about to go into exile, and had a chance to take only one last walk through the city. What would be your itinerary?* Each subject was given an unmarked street map and was asked to trace a final itinerary of not more than three kilometers. Many idiosyncratic routes appeared as subjects traced paths through childhood neighborhoods, sites of romantic encounters, and so on. But when we focus on the commonly selected paths (any street segment transversed by at least five of the subjects) a definite pattern is revealed (Fig. 6.13). The densest network of walks are along the quais of the Seine, on the Île de la Cité and the Quartier Latin. (Smaller numbers of subjects chose to stroll through Place des Vosges, Palais Royale, and Montmartre.) And a considerable group chose to walk along the Champ Elysées. Paris contains more than 3500 streets within its limits (Hillairet, 1964), but the concentration of choices on only a score of these reveals the few which have a shared emotional significance.

INTUITIONS AND SECRETS

Before drawing the report to a close, we wish to make a few additional observations about Paris and the processes of its mental representation. A person may know many things about a city while not being aware that he possesses such knowledge; and such implicit knowledge may be widely shared.

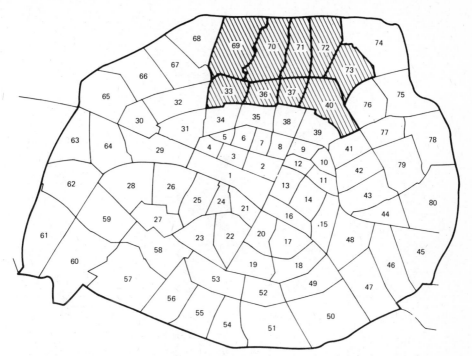

Fig. 6.12 *Paris dangereux. Indicates the quartiers perceived as being the most dangerous, from the standpoint of criminal activity.*

Consider the following hypothetical situation we presented to the subjects:

> Suppose you were to meet someone in Paris, a person whom you had never met before, and you knew the exact date and time of the meeting, but not the place. Assume the person you were to meet operated under the similar handicap of not knowing where you would wait for him. Where in Paris would you wait so as to maximize the chances of encountering the person?

Subjects were encouraged to use their intuition in answering the question, but this did not prevent many of them from denouncing the question as illogical, stupid, and unanswerable. But those who responded ($N = 188$) demonstrated that a set of appropriate—even intelligent—responses was possible. (An answer to this question may be considered "appropriate" if it is selected by a large number of other respondents, and thus represents a shared intuition of where others are likely to wait.) Two principles governed the choice of locales (a) some subjects selected a location that was unequivocally representative of the city, (b) other subjects chose locales that by custom and practice had become institutionalized waiting places (much as the clock at Grand Central Station in New York serves this function).

Six locations accounted for more than 50 percent of all answers, as Table 6.6 shows. The largest number of Parisians indicated they would wait by the Eiffel Tower, the preeminent symbol of Paris in modern times. (What would the

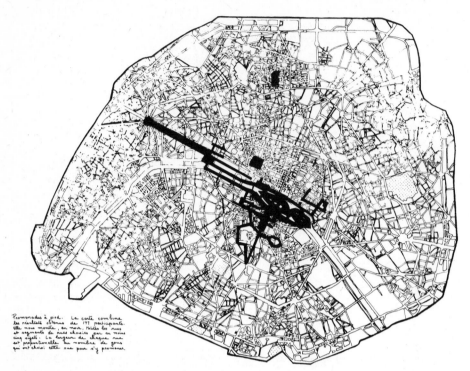

Fig. 6.13 *Last walks before going into exile. The black paths indicate all street segments chosen by at least five subjects. The width of each segment is proportional to the number of subjects who traverse segment during their last walk.*

dominant response have been prior to its construction in 1889? We have no psychological maps to tell us.) The second most popular choice was the Monument des Morts at the Gare St. Lazare. The consensus generated by this question shows that the inhabitants share an implicit, intuitive knowledge of the city that can be crystalized given the proper stimulus.

A second observation is that even poorly known areas of a city may exercise a fascination for the inhabitant: thus, three-fourths of the subjects answered affirmatively when asked if there was any part of Paris they did not know well but were attracted to. (The most popular choice was *le Marais,* a once unfashionable area that has recently experienced a renaissance.) And subjects generated the names of 155 different locales when asked if they had come across any places of particular beauty or interest that were unknown to the general public. Among their responses were: quaint provincial streets off the Parc de Montsouris; Villa Montmorency, a rustic residential enclave of several acres into which the noise of the surrounding streets scarcely penetrates; the courtyards off the Rue de Sèvres, which represent the inner folds of the convoluted brain of Paris, providing a great deal more surface area than a mere skimming of the surface would suggest; Canal St. Martin; Place des Peupliers; Cour du Rohan, and numerous others. Many of the so-called "places of beauty" were actually

Table 6.6 Meeting places chosen to maximize encounter.

Location	Percent of subjects selecting this location (N = 188)
Tour Eiffel	16.5
Monument des Morts	
(Gare St. Lazare)	8.0
Etoile	7.4
Opéra	7.4
Blvd. St. Germain	6.9
Notre Dame	6.9
Blvd., Pl. St. Michel	6.9

cited by a large number of subjects, yet more important is the subject's attitude that the city yields some secrets to him alone, and that Paris is intricate, variegated, and inexhaustible in its offerings.

But it is false to end this report as a panegyric. For many Parisians assert that the city is declining in quality, succumbing to vehicular pollution, noise, and the flight of artisans from the city; they assert that urban renewal is destroying a good deal of the beauty of Paris, and they locate its worst effects in the 15th, 1st, and 13th arrondissements, where modern apartment buildings and office towers have replaced the greater charm, but also the greater decrepitude, of the older structures.

The problem for modern Paris, then, is to learn something about the transmutation of charm into its contemporary forms, and to learn it quickly, before the old is brutally replaced by the new, and only the street patterns remain.

SUMMARY

In this paper we described a number of psychological maps of Paris generated by its inhabitants, detailed representations of the city expressed in cartographic form, rather than as simple opinions, attitudes, and words. The peculiar value of such mental maps is that they tease out the person's view of a city in a way that permits a ready comparison with the reality. They allow a treatment of the city's spatial character in a way that words frequently avoid. And they show how urban space is encoded, distorted, and selectively represented, while yet retaining its usefulness to the person. For the image of the city is not just extra mental baggage; it is the necessary accompaniment to living in a complex and highly variegated environment.

Such maps are multi-dimensional. They contain cognitive and also emotional and intuitive components, and a variety of procedures is needed to bring them to light. The maps are not only individual products; they are shaped by social factors, and therefore acquire the status of collective representations—that is, symbolic configurations of belief and knowledge promoted and disseminated by the culture.

Appendix   Distribution of subjects by sex and arrondissement.

Arrondissement	Percent of subjects in study (N = 218)			Percent distribution according to 1968 census
	Men	Women	Total	
1	1.6	2.2	1.8	1.3
2	0.8	2.2	1.4	1.4
3	3.2	1.1	2.3	2.2
4	4.8	1.1	3.2	2.2
5	4.0	4.3	4.1	3.2
6	2.4	1.1	1.8	2.7
7	4.8	2.2	3.7	3.4
8	2.4	3.3	2.8	2.7
9	2.4	5.4	3.7	3.4
10	4.8	4.3	4.6	4.5
11	6.3	4.3	5.5	7.0
12	8.7	4.3	6.9	6.1
13	4.0	4.3	4.1	5.8
14	7.1	6.5	6.9	6.2
15	8.7	12.0	10.1	9.1
16	8.7	5.4	7.3	8.4
17	7.1	8.7	7.8	8.3
18	7.1	14.1	10.1	9.4
19	6.3	5.4	6.0	5.5
20	4.8	7.6	6.0	7.2

NOTE

1. Grateful acknowledgment is made to Professor Serge Moscovici for his generous aid, and to Anne André, Ben Zion Chanowitz, Alexandra Milgram, and Judith Waters for research assistance. The services of the Institut Français d'Opinion Publique were employed in interviewing the working-class segment of our sample and in computer analyzing the data from all subjects. The assistance of Paris MENSA is gratefully acknowledged.

REFERENCES

DOWNS, R. M., AND STEA, D., *Image and Environment: Cognitive Mapping and Spatial Behavior.* Chicago: Aldine, 1973.

GOULD, P., AND WHITE, R., *Mental Maps.* Baltimore: Penguin Books, 1974.

HILLAIRET, J., *Dictionnaire Historique des Rues de Paris.* Paris: Les Editions de Minuits, 1964.

LYNCH, K., *The Image of the City.* Cambridge, Mass.: The MIT Press, 1960.

Sondages: Revue Française de l'Opinion Publique, 1951, No. 2., pp. 1–41. "Paris, une enquête psychosociale." Anonymous.

SUTTLES, G., *The Social Construction of Communities.* Chicago: University of Chicago Press, 1972.

THE INDIVIDUAL
AND AUTHORITY

Part 2

Introduction

An experimental paradigm is a plan for exploration. It does not guarantee what will be found, nor what the ultimate cost of the undertaking will be, but it creates a point of entry into an uncharted domain. Since World War II, three important human conflicts have been explored through the experimental paradigms of social psychology. Each exposes the individual to a dilemma, and allows the individual to resolve it in a way consistent with or in opposition to moral values. The first is the dilemma of truth versus conformity examined in Asch's experiment on group pressure. The second is the conflict between altruism and self-interest systematically examined in the work of Latané and Darley. And the third is the conflict between authority and conscience dealt with in my experiment on obedience.

Each paradigm poses a problem for the individual: Should I tell the truth or go along with the group? Should I involve myself in other peoples' troubles or remain aloof? Should I hurt an innocent person or disobey authority? These problems were not invented by social psychologists. They are inevitable dilemmas of the human condition. Every person must confront them simply by being a member of society.

The experiments share an important technical feature. The dependent measure in each case is a morally significant act. Thus the experiments acquire a *prima facie* interest, because they show what variables increase or decrease the performance of acts which are not only concrete and measurable, but speak to significant human values. Yet in the final analysis, the contribution of social psychology is an intellectual rather than a moral contribution. It shows that the course of action in each situation cannot be explained by a simple moral judgment, but resides in an analysis of the situational components of each dilemma.

The origins of the obedience study as a laboratory paradigm are described in detail later in this chapter (p. 94). But the laboratory paradigm merely gave scientific expression to a more general concern about authority, a concern forced upon members of my generation, in particular upon Jews such as myself, by the atrocities of World War II. Susan Sontag, the social critic, described her reaction upon first seeing photographs of the death camps:

> ...One's first encounter with the photographic inventory of ultimate horror is a kind of revelation, perhaps the only revelation people are granted now, a negative epiphany. For me, it was photographs of Bergen–Belsen and Dachau which I came across by chance in a bookstore in Santa Monica in July, 1945. Nothing I have seen—in photographs or in real life—ever cut me as sharply, deeply, instantaneously. Ever since then, it has seemed plausible to me to think of my life as being divided into two parts: before I saw those photographs (I was twelve) and after.

92

My life was changed by them, though not until several years later did I understand what they were about.

The impact of the holocaust on my own psyche energized my interest in obedience and shaped the particular form in which it was examined.

"Some Conditions of Obedience and Disobedience to Authority" presents a survey of the obedience experiments, and prior to publication of my book[1] was the most comprehensive description of the research. The article first appeared in *Human Relations* in 1965, then was reprinted in *The American Journal of Psychiatry*, followed by a critique of Martin Orne and Charles Holland. They applied a "demand characteristic" analysis to the obedience studies. Shortly afterward, I was invited to give a colloquium at the University of Pennsylvania. I suggested that this be in the form of a debate between myself and Professor Orne. Dr. Orne graciously consented, and we were perhaps both astonished to see an auditorium filled with several hundred spectators eager for gladiatorial combat. It was a good debate, conducted on a high level, and ultimately productive of deeper understanding. "Interpreting Obedience: Error and Evidence," which appeared in 1972, summarizes my views on this matter.

A stinging and unexpected challenge to the obedience experiment appeared in the form of an ethical criticism by Dr. Diana Baumrind. "Ethical Issues in the Study of Obedience" constitutes my reply to Dr. Baumrind; it spells out my views on the ethical aspects of the investigation. There is one point, however, that should have received greater emphasis. The central moral justification for allowing my experiment is that it was judged acceptable by those who took part in it. Criticism of the experiment that does not take account of the tolerant reaction of the participants has always seemed to me hollow. This applies particularly to criticism centering on the use of technical illusion (or "deception," as the critics prefer to say) that fails to relate this detail to the central fact that subjects find the device acceptable. The participant, rather than the external critic, must be the ultimate source of judgment in these matters.

Acts of obedience and disobedience may be examined in the laboratory, but their most crucial expression occurs in the real world. The experiments were begun in 1960. Five years later the nation was deeply involved in an unpopular war in southeast Asia, and thousands of young men fled to Canada to avoid the draft, while others declared themselves war resisters and went to prison. During the Vietnam War, psychiatrist Willard Gaylin interviewed a number of these resisters, and I was asked to review his book, *War Resisters in Prison*, for *The Nation* (p. 147).

Social psychology is a cumulative discipline. Investigators with greater or lesser creativity build on the contributions of those who precede them. In a recent interview,[2] Dr. Richard Evans asked about the experimental antecedents of the obedience studies, then moved on to a discussion of the ethical and social implications of these investigations. The following is a portion of that interview, the conversational syntax and tone of which I have made no attempt to formalize.

Evans: ... One of your experiments has received wide attention. It was a kind of outgrowth of the group pressure study, testing just exactly what people will do under pressure from an experimenter, a scientist in a kind of laboratory setting. How did you happen to begin thinking in terms of this type of experiment? Maybe you would describe it briefly for us.

Milgram: Very often, when there's an idea, there are several points of origin to it. It doesn't necessarily develop in linear fashion from what one has been working on previously. I was working for Asch in Princeton, New Jersey, in 1959–1960. I was thinking about his group pressure experiment. One of the criticisms that had been made of his experiments is that they lack a surface significance, because, after all, an experiment with people making judgments of lines has a manifestly trivial content. So the question I asked myself is: How can this be made a more humanly significant experiment?

It seemed to me that if, instead of having a group exerting pressure on the judgments about lines, the group could somehow induce something more significant from the person, then that might be a step in giving a greater face significance to the behavior induced by the group. Could a group, I asked myself, induce a person to act with severity against another person?...I envisioned a situation very much like Asch's experiment in which there would be a number of confederates and one naive subject, and instead of confronting the lines on a card, each one of them would have a shock generator. In other words, I transformed Asch's experiment into one in which the group would administer increasingly higher levels of shock to a person, and the question would be to what degree an individual would follow along with the group. That's not yet the obedience experiment, but it's a mental step in that direction.

Then I wondered how one would actually set it up. What would constitute the experimental control in this situation? In Asch's experiment, there is a control—the proportion of correct judgments the person makes in the absence of group pressure. So I said to myself, "Well, I guess I would have to study a person in this situation in the absence of any group pressure. But then, how would one get the person to increase the shocks? I mean, what would be the force that would get him to increase the shocks?" And then the thought occurred, "Well, I guess the experimenter would have to tell him to give higher and higher shocks. Just how far will a person go when an experimenter instructs him to give increasingly severe shocks?" Immediately I knew that that was the problem I would investigate. It was a very excited moment for me, because I realized that although it was a very simple question, it was one that would admit itself to measurement, precise investigation. One could immediately see the variables to be studied, with the dependent measure being how far a person would go in administering shocks.

Evans: Well, let's be a little bit more specific. We could talk about authority in the form of the experimenter, or we could talk about group pressure, acquiescence to the group. There's a very interesting distinction here.

Milgram: There are both features in common and features that are different. What we have in common is, in both instances, the abdication of individual judgment in the face of some external social pressure. But there are also factors that are quite different. I would like to call what happens to Asch's subjects "conformity," and I would like to

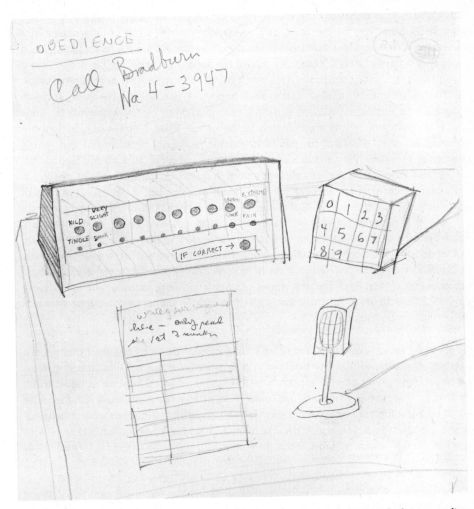

Fig. I.3 *Early sketch of the simulated shock generator used in the obedience studies. (Princeton, Spring 1960).*

call what happens in my experiment "obedience." In conformity, as illustrated by Asch's experiment, there is no explicit requirement on the part of the group members that a person go along with them. Indeed, the presence of an explicit requirement might even eliminate the person's yielding. The individual members of Asch's group give their judgments; there's a felt pressure to comply with them, but there's no explicit demand to do so. In the obedience situation, the experimenter explicitly prescribes certain behavior. That's one difference.

A second very important difference is that in conformity, as illustrated in Asch's experiment, you're dealing basically with a process of which the end product is the homogenization of behavior. The pressure is not that you be better than me, or worse than me, but that you be the same as me. Obedience arises out of differentiation of social structure. You don't start from the assumption that we are the same; one person starts with a higher status. You don't repeat his action; you execute his order. And it doesn't lead to homogenization of behavior, but rather to some kind of division of labor.

There's another distinction that's quite important psychologically. After subjects have been in Asch's experiment and they are questioned by the experimenter, they almost invariably deny that they gave in to the group. Even if errors in judgment are pointed out, they will tend to ascribe them to their own deficiencies. But in the obedience experiment, the result is the opposite. The subjects disclaim any responsibility for their action. So I think there are factors in common, certainly. We're dealing in both cases with what I would call the abdication of individual initiative in the face of some external social pressure. But there are also these distinguishing aspects to it.

And in a broader philosophic way they're quite different also....Conformity is a natural source of social control in democracy, because it leads to this homogenization. But obedience in its extreme forms is the natural expression of fascistic systems, because it starts with the assumption of differences in the rights of people. It's no accident that in Nazi Germany, the virtues of obedience were extolled, and at the same time an inherent part of the philosophy was the idea of inferior and superior groups; I mean, the two go together.

Evans: As an example, let me just take a current piece of research that we are involved in dealing with a very fascinating phenomenon in our culture—smoking. Now we have some pretty good evidence, and this is one of the things we're going to be looking at, that perhaps smoking begins as a reaction to peer pressure. On the other hand, we have the very interesting fact that authority stresses that this type of behavior is going to lead to cardiovascular disease, cancer, etc., etc. Here you have at once peer and authority pressure. In terms of this distinction you made, how could you resolve this type of situation?

Milgram: I'll try. First, the word "authority" is used in many different ways. When we talk about a medical authority, we're talking about someone with expertise. That's not quite the same as the kind of authority I was studying, which is someone perceived to have the right to control one's behavior. When a teenager hears an authority on television saying he shouldn't smoke, he doesn't accept the fact that that person has the right to control behavior. Secondly, you still have these conflicts between peer pressure and authority pressure. In one of the experiments I carried out, it was shown that when peers in my experimental situation rebelled against the experimenter, they tremendously undercut his power. I think the same thing is operating here; you have pressures from an authority, but you have pressures from peers which sometimes neutralize this. It's only when you have, as you have in my experiment, an authority who in the basic experiment operates in a free field without countervailing pressures other than the victim's protests that you get the purest response to authority. In real life, of course, you're confronted with a great many countervailing pressures that cancel each other out.

Evans: One of the things, of course, that you're acutely aware of is that partly because of Congressional pressure, partly because of some—what would we say—some second looks at our consciences in the behavioral sciences, we are beginning to get increasingly concerned now about the whole matter of what rights we have with respect to our subjects. When you were doing that earlier obedience to authority study, it's very clear that you were operating completely within the ethical framework of psychologists in those days. You debriefed the subjects, and there was really no harm done to the victims, and so on. However, in the present utilization of subjects, we are very hung up on the phrase, "informed consent," and this raises a very tough problem for the investigator. For example, do you think you could have done that experiment if you followed the present ethical standards of "informed consent"? Let's say that you were about to engage in an experiment where the subjects were going to be exposed to a certain amount of stress. One type of stress might be the fact that you're going to be ordering somebody to get shocked.

Milgram: Well first of all, before you do the experiment, you don't know there will be stress.

Evans: All right, that's a good point.

Milgram: The subject must make a decision, but we don't know if it's going to be accompanied by stress. Many of the most interesting things we find out in experimentation you don't learn until you carry it out. So to talk about "informed consent" presumes that you know the fundamental consequences of your experiment, and that just isn't the case for my investigations. That's one aspect of the problem; it's not the entire problem, however. There is the fact that misinformation is used in these experiments, that illusions are used. For example, in my obedience experiment, the victim does not actually *get* the shocks; although the subject is *told* he is getting the shocks. Furthermore, it's an experiment on obedience, in which the subject is the focus of the experiment rather than the other person, but a cover story attempts to deflect attention from that. Now could the experiment be run if we told people beforehand that this was going to be the case ? Not in its particulars. It is possible that one could develop a system whereby people are told generally that they're asked to be in a psychology experiment, and that in psychology experiments illusions are sometimes used. Sometimes stress arises. Perhaps a subject pool of such persons who are not necessarily used immediately could be created. They would then be invited to an experiment, having been given the general instruction that these things may but don't necessarily happen in psychological experimentation. That would be one way of handling the problem....

Evans: Of course one of the points made about informed consent is that after all we're dealing, often, with a purely phenomenological situation. How can you give informed consent in advance as a human subject in an experiment when the total mass of feelings and experiences and sensitivities, even pain, cannot really be verbalized?

Milgram: Well, I think to some extent that's true, added to the fact that one is very often ignorant of what will happen before an experiment. Reactions to such situations can be diverse. Ninety percent of the subjects can react in a perfectly calm way; others can become agitated. But then we must know whether psychology is excluding stress and agitation from its domain of study. Do we really want to say that any of these aversive emotions are to be excluded from psychological inquiry? I think that's a question that's yet to be resolved, but my personal vote is "no." At the same time I don't want to be put in the position of saying that I'm *for any kind* of experimentation.

Evans: Were you surprised by the reaction to your obedience experiment?

Milgram: I must say that I was totally astonished by the criticism that my experiment engendered. I thought what I was doing was posing a very legitimate question. How far would people proceed if they were asked to give increasingly severe shocks to another person? I thought that the decision rested with the subject. Perhaps that was too naive an assumption from which to start an investigation.

It is true that technical illusions were used in the experiment. I would not call them deceptions, because that already implies some base motivation. After all, the major illusion used was that the person did not receive shocks. One might have imitated the investigators who have done studies in traumatic avoidance conditioning where human beings are, in fact, shocked to near-tetanizing levels. I chose not to. I thought that the illusion was used for a benign purpose.

I'm convinced that much of the criticism, whether people know it or not, stems from the results of the experiment. If everyone had broken off at slight shock or moderate shock, this would be a very reassuring finding and who would protest? Indeed, I would say that there's a tendency these days to make inferences about the experimenter's motives on the basis of the results of his investigations, and I think that's a very pernicious tendency. Personally, and even professionally, I would have been very pleased if people had broken off at mild shock.

Evans: Were you surprised that they went so far?

Milgram: I was, but if they had not been so obedient, it would not have prevented my research program. I would simply have studied the variables leading to an increase or diminution in the amount of obedience. And in fact, one could say that the results that I got threw a wrench into the program in that many variables were washed out because too many people obeyed. One didn't have that distribution of responses—that bell-shaped distribution—that would have been most convenient for studying the effects of specific variables.

Evans: There have been statements made by people about both the work of Zimbardo and yourself which I think it's only fair to hear you react to. Some people have suggested, some journalists particularly, that both you and Dr. Zimbardo got involved in experiments that were exciting, interesting, unique, and that because of the uproar about the ethics, you have begun to rationalize, by trying to extrapolate from your findings something relating to a bigger picture. For example, in the case of Zimbardo, he has now become a strong advocate for prison reform, arguing that this little experiment will teach mankind how horrible prisons are. In your case, you have, more or less, extrapolated the whole question of the dangers of authoritarian rule in American culture. In your book, *Obedience to Authority*, you go into this. Now, Dr. Zimbardo is not here to speak for himself, but what about your reaction to this?

Milgram: The very first article that I wrote on obedience ["Behavioral Study of Obedience"], before anyone had really reacted to the experiments, discussed the societal problem. So it's not true that trying to find the larger application of the issue is motivated by ethical criticism. Beyond that, what disturbs me somewhat is the absence of any assumption of good will and good faith. I believe that a certain amount of good will is necessary on the part of society for the conduct of any enterprise. Criticisms of that sort seem to me to start from some assumption of bad faith on the part of the investigators, which I don't believe, in my case or the Zimbardo case, has anything to do with the truth.

Evans: Were there any criticisms of this particular effort that have troubled you that perhaps we haven't mentioned?

Milgram: Well, I think the question of the limits of experimentation is a real one. I believe that there are many experiments that should not be carried out. I don't oppose criticism, because I think there's a societal function served by it. The investigator wants to study things. Society, in the form of certain critics, will establish limits. I think the net outcome will be a kind of equilibrium between scientific values and other values, but I don't believe that most investigators, certainly myself, are limited to scientific values. There are thousands of experiments that could be very useful from the standpoint of increasing knowledge that one would never carry out, because in one's own estimation, they would violate moral principles. It doesn't mean that one doesn't think of them. For example, an experiment in which neonates are deposited onto a deserted island, and one watches their development over three generations, assuming they survive, would be stupendously informative, but grossly immoral.

Evans: Well now, moving to another area of your work that is extremely intriguing, we have the research dealing with the experience of living in cities. While in your earlier experiment you were studying obedience to authority and the resulting cruelty, at the same time, beginning to become noticeable, were cases like the famous Kitty Genovese case, where we had another kind of, shall we say, horrendous reaction to a fellow man. But in this case, rather than the administering of shock under experimental conditions, the apathy was what was cruel. The work of Darley and Latané (1970), and a great deal of subsequent work, has gone very carefully into trying to understand something about the nature of this so-called bystander apathy, also asking: Is there any real altruism in man? The findings of this line of research suggest that there's some cause for optimism. It seems to me that in your analysis of living in the cities (Milgram, 1970), in a very broad and fascinating way, you extend some of these interpretations, and so it might be kind of interesting to hear what led you in this particular direction.

Milgram: May I, before doing that, try to draw some connections between the bystander work and the work on authority?

Evans: Oh yes, certainly.

Milgram: To some extent, a lot of bystander work shows that when society becomes complicated, there are specialized organizations set up, such as the police, which have authority in particular domains, and then people abdicate responsibility to them. After all, in the Genovese case, people thought it was not their responsibility; it was the responsibility of those in authority—that is, the police—to do something about this matter. The particular tragedy in the Genovese case was that no one even notified the police. There's another thing that comes out in some of the other Latané and Darley studies—I'm thinking particularly of the smoke experiment. They've shown that a group of people is less likely to respond to an emergency than a single individual. That really shows how ineffectively people function in the absence of authority. When there's no group structure, when there's no predesignated leadership, it can lead to enormous inefficiency. You see, none of these issues is really one-sided. Under certain circumstances, authority is very useful. It wouldn't exist in human society, I assure you, if it did not serve important adaptive functions.

NOTES

1. S. Milgram, *Obedience to Authority: An Experimental View* (New York: Harper & Row,1974).
2. R. Evans (ed.), *The Making of Psychology: Discussions with Creative Contributors* (New York: Alfred Knopf, 1976).

REFERENCES

Asch, S., 1958. "Effects of group pressure upon modification and distortion of judgments." In *Readings in Social Psychology*, 3rd ed., eds. E. E. Maccoby, T. M. Newcomb, and E. L. Hartley. New York: Holt.

Korte, C., and Milgram, S., 1970. "Acquaintance networks between racial groups: application of the small world method." *J. Pers. Soc. Psychol.* 15: (2) 101–8.

Latané B., and Darley, J., 1970. *The Unresponsive Bystander: Why Doesn't He Help?* New York: Appleton.

Lynch, K., 1960. *The Image of the City*. Cambridge, Mass.: M.I.T. Press and Harvard University Press.

Milgram, S., 1963. "Behavioral study of obedience." *J. Abnorm. Soc. Psychol.* 67: 371–78.

———, 1965. "Some conditions to obedience and disobedience to authority." *Hum. Rel.* 18: (1) 57–76.

———, 1967. "The small world problem." *Psychol. Today* 1: (1) 60–67.

———, 1970a. "The experience of living in cities." *Science* 167: 146–168.

————, 1970*b*. "The experience of living in cities: a psychological analysis." In *Psychology and the Problems of Society,* eds. F. F. Korten, S. W. Cook, and J. I. Lacey. Washington, D. C.: American Psychological Association.

————, 1972. "Interpreting obedience." In *The Social Psychology of Psychological Research,* ed. A. Miller. New York: Free Press.

————, 1974*a*. *Obedience to Authority.* New York: Harper & Row.

————, 1974*b*. "The city and the self." Time-Life Films: Time-Life Building, Rockefeller Center, New York, N. Y. 10020.

Travers, J., and Milgram, S., 1969. "An experimental study of the small world problem." *Sociometry* 32: (4) 425–43.

Zimbardo, P., *et al.,* 1973. "The mind is a formidable jailer: a Pirandellian prison." *The New York Times,* p. 38, April 8, 1973.

Some Conditions of Obedience and Disobedience to Authority[1]

7

The situation in which one agent commands another to hurt a third turns up time and again as a significant theme in human relations. It is powerfully expressed in the story of Abraham, who is commanded by God to kill his son. It is no accident that Kierkegaard, seeking to orient his thought to the central themes of human experience, chose Abraham's conflict as the springboard to his philosophy.

War too moves forward on the triad of an authority which commands a person to destroy the enemy, and perhaps all organized hostility may be viewed as a theme and variation on the three elements of authority, executant, and victim.[2] We describe an experimental program, recently concluded at Yale University, in which a particular expression of this conflict is studied by experimental means.

In its most general form the problem may be defined thus: if X tells Y to hurt Z, under what conditions will Y carry out the command of X and under what conditions will he refuse. In the more limited form possible in laboratory research, the question becomes: If an experimenter tells a subject to hurt another person, under what conditions will the subject go along with this instruction, and under what conditions will he refuse to obey. The laboratory problem is not so much a dilution of the general statement as one concrete expression of the many particular forms this question may assume.

One aim of the research was to study behavior in a strong situation of deep consequence to the participants, for the psychological forces operative in powerful and lifelike forms of the conflict may not be brought into play under diluted conditions.

This approach meant, first, that we had a special obligation to protect the welfare and dignity of the persons who took part in the study; subjects were, of necessity, placed in a difficult predicament, and steps had to be taken to ensure their wellbeing before they were discharged from the laboratory. Toward this end, a careful, post-experimental treatment was devised and has been carried through for subjects in all conditions.[3]

TERMINOLOGY

If Y follows the command of X we shall say that he has obeyed X; if he fails to carry out the command of X, we shall say that he has disobeyed X. The terms to

This paper was first published in *Human Relations,* Vol. 18, No. 1 (1965), pp. 57–75. The research was supported by grants from the National Science Foundation and from a small grant from the Higgins Fund of Yale University. Reprinted by permission of the author.

obey and to *disobey*, as used here, refer to the subject's overt action only, and carry no implication for the motive or experiential states accompanying the action.[4]

To be sure, the everyday use of the word *obedience* is not entirely free from complexities. It refers to action within widely varying situations, and connotes diverse motives within those situations: a child's obedience differs from a soldier's obedience, or the love, honor, and *obey* of the marriage vow. However, a consistent behavioral relationship is indicated in most uses of the term: in the act of obeying, a person does what another person tells him to do. *Y* obeys *X* if he carries out the prescription for action which *X* has addressed to him; the term suggests, moreover, that some form of dominance-subordination, or hierarchical element, is part of the situation in which the transaction between *X* and *Y* occurs.

A subject who complies with the entire series of experimental commands will be termed an *obedient* subject; one who at any point in the command series defies the experimenter will be called a *disobedient* or *defiant* subject. As used in this report the terms refer only to the subject's performance in the experiment, and do not necessarily imply a general personality disposition to submit to or reject authority.

SUBJECT POPULATION

The subjects used in all experimental conditions were male adults, residing in the greater New Haven and Bridgeport areas, aged 20 to 50 years, and engaged in a wide variety of occupations. Each experimental condition described in this report employed 40 fresh subjects and was carefully balanced for age and occupational types. The occupational composition for each experiment was: workers, skilled and unskilled: 40 percent; white collar, sales, business: 40 percent; professionals: 20 percent. The occupations were intersected with three age categories (subjects in 20's, 30's, and 40's, assigned to each condition in the proportions of 20, 40, and 40 percent, respectively).

THE GENERAL LABORATORY PROCEDURE[5]

The focus of the study concerns the amount of electric shock a subject is willing to administer to another person when ordered by an experimenter to give the "victim" increasingly more severe punishment. The act of administering shock is set in the context of a learning experiment, ostensibly designed to study the effect of punishment on memory. Aside from the experimenter, one naïve subject and one accomplice perform in each session. On arrival each subject is paid $4.50. After a general talk by the experimenter, telling how little scientists know about the effect of punishment on memory, subjects are informed that one member of the pair will serve as teacher and one as learner. A rigged drawing is held so that the naïve subject is always the teacher, and the accomplice becomes the learner. The learner is taken to an adjacent room and strapped into an "electric chair."

The naïve subject is told that it is his task to teach the learner a list of paired associates, to test him on the list, and to administer punishment whenever the learner errs in the test. Punishment takes the form of electric shock, delivered to the learner by means of a shock generator controlled by the naïve subject. The teacher is instructed to increase the intensity of electric shock one step on the generator on each error. The learner, according to plan, provides many wrong answers, so that before long the naïve subject must give him the strongest shock on the generator. Increases in shock level are met by increasingly insistent demands from the learner that the experiment be stopped because of the growing discomfort to him. However, in clear terms the experimenter orders the teacher to continue with the procedure in disregard of the learner's protests. *Thus, the naïve subject must resolve a conflict between two mutually incompatible demands from the social field. He may continue to follow the orders of the experimenter and shock the learner with increasing severity, or he may refuse to follow the orders of the experimenter and heed the learner's pleas. The experimenter's authority operates not in a free field, but against ever-mounting countervailing pressure from the person being punished.*

A few technical points need to be considered before the findings of the study are described. For the purpose of delivering shock, a simulated shock generator is used, with 30 clearly marked voltage levels that range from 15 to 450 volts. (Each level is activated by one of 30 individual lever switches set in a horizontal line.) The naïve subject is given a sample shock of 45 volts to convince him of the authenticity of the instrument. The generator bears verbal designations that range from "Slight Shock" to "Danger: Severe Shock."

The responses of the victim are standardized on tape, and each protest is coordinated to a particular voltage level on the shock generator. Starting with 75 volts the learner begins to grunt and moan. At 150 volts he demands to be let out of the experiment. At 180 volts he cries out that he can no longer stand the pain. At 300 volts he refuses to provide any more answers to the memory test, insisting that he is no longer a participant in the experiment and must be freed. In response to this last tactic, the experimenter instructs the naïve subject to treat the absence of an answer as equivalent to a wrong answer, and to follow the usual shock procedure. The experimenter reinforces his demand with the statement: "You have no other choice, you must go on!" (This imperative is used whenever the naïve subject tries to break off the experiment.) If the subject refuses to give the next higher level of shock, the experiment is considered at an end. A quantitative value is assigned to the subject's performance based on the maximum-intensity shock he administered before breaking off. Thus any subject's score may range from zero (for a subject unwilling to administer the first shock level) to 30 (for a subject who proceeds to the highest voltage level on the board). For any particular subject and for any particular experimental condition, the degree to which participants have followed the experimenter's orders may be specified with a numerical value, corresponding to the metric on the shock generator.

This laboratory situation gives us a framework in which to study the subject's reactions to the principal conflict of the experiment. Again, this conflict is between the experimenter's demands that he continue to administer the electric shock, and the learner's demands, which become increasingly more insistent, that the experiment be stopped. The crux of the study is to vary systematically the factors believed to alter the degree of obedience to the experimental commands, to learn under what conditions submission to authority is most probable and under what conditions defiance is brought to the fore.

PILOT STUDIES

Pilot studies for the present research were completed in the winter of 1960; they differed from the regular experiments in a few details: for one, the victim was placed behind a silvered glass, with the light balance on the glass such that the victim could be dimly perceived by the subject (Milgram, 1961).

Though essentially qualitative in treatment, these studies pointed to several significant features of the experimental situation. At first no vocal feedback was used from the victim. It was thought that the verbal and voltage designations on the control panel would create sufficient pressure to curtail the subject's obedience. However, this was not the case. In the absence of protests from the learner, virtually all subjects, once commanded, went blithely to the end of the board, seemingly indifferent to the verbal designations ("Extreme Shock" and "Danger: Severe Shock"). This deprived us of an adequate basis for scaling obedient tendencies. A force had to be introduced that would strengthen the subject's resistance to the experimenter's commands, and reveal individual differences in terms of a distribution of break-off points.

This force took the form of protests from the victim. Initially, mild protests were used, but proved inadequate. Subsequently, more vehement protests were inserted into the experimental procedure. To our consternation, even the strongest protests from the victim did not prevent all subjects from administering the harshest punishment ordered by the experimenter; but the protests did lower the mean maximum shock somewhat and created some spread in the subject's performance; therefore, the victim's cries were standardized on tape and incorporated into the regular experimental procedure.

The situation did more than highlight the technical difficulties of finding a workable experimental procedure: It indicated that subjects would obey authority to a greater extent than we had supposed. It also pointed to the importance of feedback from the victim in controlling the subject's behavior.

One further aspect of the pilot study was that subjects frequently averted their eyes from the person they were shocking, often turning their heads in an awkward and conspicuous manner. One subject explained: "I didn't want to see the consequences of what I had done." Observers wrote:

> ...subjects showed a reluctance to look at the victim, whom they could see through the glass in front of them. When this fact was brought to their attention they indicated that it caused them discomfort to see the victim in agony. We note, however, that although the subject refuses to look at the victim, he continues to administer shocks.

This suggested that the salience of the victim may have, in some degree, regulated the subject's performance. If, in obeying the experimenter, the subject found it necessary to avoid scrutiny of the victim, would the converse be true? If the victim were rendered increasingly more salient to the subject, would obedience diminish? The first set of regular experiments was designed to answer this question.

IMMEDIACY OF THE VICTIM

This series consisted of four experimental conditions. In each condition the victim was brought "psychologically" closer to the subject giving him shocks.

In the first condition (Remote Feedback) the victim was placed in another room and could not be heard or seen by the subject, except that, at 300 volts, he pounded on the wall in protest. After 315 volts he no longer answered or was heard from.

The second condition (Voice Feedback) was identical to the first except that voice protests were introduced. As in the first condition the victim was placed in an adjacent room, but his complaints could be heard clearly through a door left slightly ajar and through the walls of the laboratory.[6]

The third experimental condition (Proximity) was similar to the second, except that the victim was now placed in the same room as the subject, and $1\frac{1}{2}$ feet from him. Thus he was visible as well as audible, and voice cues were provided.

The fourth, and final, condition of this series (Touch-Proximity) was identical to the third, with this exception: The victim received a shock only when his hand rested on a shockplate. At the 150-volt level the victim again demanded to be let free and, in this condition, refused to place his hand on the shockplate. The experimenter ordered the naïve subject to force the victim's hand onto the plate. Thus obedience in this condition required that the subject have physical contact with the victim in order to give him punishment beyond the 150-volt level.

Forty adult subjects were studied in each condition. The data revealed that obedience was significantly reduced as the victim was rendered more immediate to the subject. The mean maximum shock for the conditions is shown in Fig. 7.1.

Expressed in terms of the proportion of obedient to defiant subjects, the findings are that 34 percent of the subjects defied the experimenter in the Remote condition, 37.5 percent in Voice Feedback, 60 percent in Proximity, and 70 percent in Touch-Proximity.

How are we to account for this effect? A first conjecture might be that as the victim was brought closer the subject became more aware of the intensity of his suffering and regulated his behavior accordingly. This makes sense, but our evidence does not support the interpretation. There are no consistent differences in the attributed level of pain across the four conditions (i.e. the amount of pain experienced by the victim as estimated by the subject and expressed on a 14-point scale). But it is easy to speculate about alternative mechanisms:

Empathic cues. In the Remote and to a lesser extent the Voice Feedback conditions, the victim's suffering possesses an abstract, remote quality for the subject. He is aware, but only in a conceptual sense, that his actions cause pain to another person; the fact is apprehended, but not felt. The phenomenon is common enough. The bombardier can reasonably suppose that his weapons will inflict suffering and death, yet this knowledge is

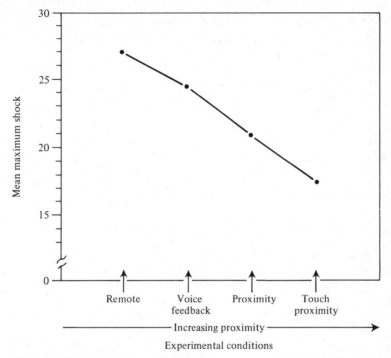

Fig. 7.1   *Mean maxima in proximity series.*

divested of affect and does not move him to a felt, emotional response to the suffering resulting from his actions. Similar observations have been made in wartime. It is possible that the visual cues associated with the victim's suffering trigger empathic responses in the subject and provide him with a more complete grasp of the victim's experience. Or it is possible that the empathic responses are themselves unpleasant, possessing drive properties which cause the subject to terminate the arousal situation. Diminishing obedience, then, would be explained by the enrichment of empathic cues in the successive experimental conditions.

Denial and narrowing of the cognitive field. The Remote condition allows a narrowing of the cognitive field so that the victim is put out of mind. The subject no longer considers the act of depressing a lever relevant to moral judgement, for it is no longer associated with the victim's suffering. When the victim is close it is more difficult to exclude him phenomenologically. He necessarily intrudes on the subject's awareness since he is continuously visible. In the Remote condition his existence and reactions are made known only after the shock has been administered. The auditory feedback is sporadic and discontinuous. In the Proximity conditions his inclusion in the immediate visual field renders him a continuously salient element for the subject. The mechanism of denial can no longer be brought into play. One subject in the Remote condition said: "It's funny how you really begin to forget that there's a guy out there, even though you can hear him. For a long time I just concentrated on pressing the switches and reading the words."

Reciprocal fields. If in the Proximity condition the subject is in an improved position to observe the victim, the reverse is also true. The actions of the subject now come under proximal scrutiny by the victim. Possibly, it is easier to harm a person when he is unable to observe our actions than when he can see what we are doing. His surveillance of the action directed against him may give rise to shame, or guilt, which may then serve to curtail the action. Many expressions of language refer to the discomfort or inhibitions that arise in face-to-face confrontation. It is often said that it is easier to criticize a man "behind his back" than to "attack him to his face." If we are in the process of lying to a person it is reputedly difficult to "stare him in the eye". We "turn away from others in shame" or in "embarrassment" and this action serves to reduce our discomfort. The manifest function of allowing the victim of a firing squad to be blindfolded is to make the occasion less stressful for him, but it may also serve a latent function of reducing the stress of the executioner. In short, in the Proximity conditions, the subject may sense that he has become more salient in the victim's field of awareness. Possibly he becomes more self-conscious, embarrassed, and inhibited in his punishment of the victim.

Phenomenal unity of act. In the Remote condition it is more difficult for the subject to gain a sense of *relatedness* between his own actions and the consequences of these actions for the victim. There is a physical and spatial separation of the act and its consequences. The subject depresses a lever in one room, and protests and cries are heard from another. The two events are in correlation, yet they lack a compelling phenomenological unity. The structure of a meaningful act—*I am hurting a man*—breaks down because of the spatial arrangements, in a manner somewhat analogous to the disappearance of phi phenomena when the blinking lights are spaced too far apart. The unity is more fully achieved in the Proximity condition as the victim is brought closer to the action that causes him pain. It is rendered complete in Touch-Proximity.

Incipient group formation. Placing the victim in another room not only takes him further from the subject, but the subject and the experimenter are drawn relatively closer. There is incipient group formation between the experimenter and the subject, from which the victim is excluded. The wall between the victim and the others deprives him of an intimacy which the experimenter and subject feel. In the Remote condition, the victim is truly an outsider, who stands alone, physically and psychologically.

When the victim is placed close to the subject, it becomes easier to form an alliance with him against the experimenter. Subjects no longer have to face the experimenter alone. They have an ally who is close at hand and eager to collaborate in a revolt against the experimenter. Thus, the changing set of spatial relations leads to a potentially shifting set of alliances over the several experimental conditions.

Acquired behavior dispositions. It is commonly observed that laboratory mice will rarely fight with their litter mates. Scott (1958) explains this in terms of passive inhibition. He writes: "By doing nothing under...circumstances [the animal] learns to do nothing, and this may be spoken of as passive inhibition... this principle has great importance in teaching an individual to be peaceful, for it means that he can learn not to fight simply by not fighting." Similarly, we may learn not to harm others simply by not harming them in everyday life. Yet this learning occurs in a context of proximal relations with others, and may not be generalized to that situation in which the person is physically removed from us. Or possibly, in the past, aggressive actions against others who were physically close resulted in retaliatory punishment which extinguished the original form of response. In contrast, aggression against others at a distance may have only sporadically led to retaliation. Thus the organism learns that it is safer to be aggressive toward others at a distance, and precarious to be so when the parties are within arm's reach. Through a pattern of rewards and punishments, he acquires a disposition to avoid aggression at close quarters, a disposition which does not extend to harming others at a distance. And this may account for experimental findings in the remote and proximal experiments.

Proximity as a variable in psychological research has received far less attention than it deserves. If men were sessile it would be easy to understand this neglect. But we move about; our spatial relations shift from one situation to the next, and the fact that we are near or remote may have a powerful effect on the psychological processes that mediate our behavior toward others. In the present situation, as the victim is brought closer to the subject ordered to give him shocks, increasing numbers of subjects break off the experiment, refusing to obey. The concrete, visible, and proximal presence of the victim acts in an important way to counteract the experimenter's power to generate disobedience.[7]

CLOSENESS OF AUTHORITY

If the spatial relationship of the subject and victim is relevant to the degree of obedience, would not the relationship of subject to experimenter also play a part?

There are reasons to feel that, on arrival, the subject is oriented primarily to the experimenter rather than to the victim. He has come to the laboratory to fit into the structure that the experimenter—not the victim—would provide. He has come less to understand his behavior than to *reveal* that behavior to a competent scientist, and he is willing to display himself as the scientist's purposes require. Most subjects seem quite concerned about the appearance they are making before the experimenter, and one could argue that this preoccupation in a relatively new and strange setting makes the subject somewhat insensitive to the triadic nature of the social situation. In other words, the subject is so concerned about the show he is putting on for the experimenter that influences from other parts of the social field do not receive as much weight as they ordinarily would. This overdetermined orientation to the experimenter would account for the relative insensitivity of the subject to the victim, and would also lead us to believe that alterations in the relationship between subject and experimenter would have important consequences for obedience.

In a series of experiments we varied the physical closeness and degree of surveillance of the experimenter. In one condition the experimenter sat just a few feet away from the subject. In a second condition, after giving initial instructions, the experimenter left the laboratory and gave his orders by telephone. In still a third condition the experimenter was never seen, providing instructions by means of a tape recording activated when the subjects entered the laboratory.

Obedience dropped sharply as the experimenter was physically removed from the laboratory. The number of obedient subjects in the first condition (Experimenter Present) was almost three times as great as in the second, where the experimenter gave his orders by telephone. Twenty-six subjects were fully obedient in the first condition, and only nine in the second (Chi square obedient vs. defiant in the two conditions, df = 14.7; $p < 0.001$). Subjects seemed able to take a far stronger stand against the experimenter when they did not have to encounter him face to face, and the experimenter's power over the subject was severely curtailed.[8]

Moreover, when the experimenter was absent, subjects displayed an interesting form of behavior that had not occurred under his surveillance. Though continuing with the experiment, several subjects administered lower shocks than were required and never informed the experimenter of their deviation from the correct procedure. (Unknown to the subjects, shock levels were automatically recorded by an Esterline-Angus event recorder wired directly into the shock generator; the instrument provided us with an objective record of the subjects' performance.) Indeed, in telephone conversations some subjects specifically assured the experimenter that they were raising the shock level according to instruction, whereas in fact they were repeatedly using the lowest shock on the board. This form of behavior is particularly interesting: although these subjects acted in a way that clearly undermined the avowed purposes of the experiment, they found it easier to handle the conflict in this manner than to precipitate an open break with authority.

Other conditions were completed in which the experimenter was absent during the first segment of the experiment, but reappeared at the point that the subject definitely refused to give higher shocks when commanded by telephone. Although he had exhausted his power via telephone, the experimenter could frequently force further obedience when he reappeared in the laboratory.

Experiments in this series show that the *physical presence* of an authority is an important force contributing to the subject's obedience or defiance. Taken together with the first experimental series on the proximity of the victim, it would appear that something akin to fields of force, diminishing in effectiveness with increasing psychological distance from their source, have a controlling effect on the subject's performance. As the victim is brought closer, the subject finds it harder to administer shocks to him. When the victim's position is held constant relative to the subject, and the authority is made more remote, the subject finds it easier to break off the experiment. This effect is substantial in both cases, but manipulation of the experimenter's position yielded the more powerful results. Obedience to destructive commands is highly dependent on the proximal relations between authority and subject.

(a) Shock generator used in the experiments. Fifteen of the 30 switches have already been depressed.

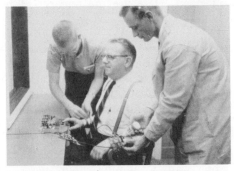

(b) The learner is strapped into a chair and electrodes are attached to his wrist. Electrode paste is applied by the experimenter. The learner provides answers by depressing switches that light up numbers on an answer box.

(c) The subject receives a sample shock from the generator.

(d) The subject breaks off the experiment. On the right, an event recorder wired into the generator automatically records the switches used by the subject. (From the film Obedience, distributed by the New York University Film Library.)

Fig. 7.2 *Photographs of the obedience experiments.*

TENSIONS

The description of final scores does not fully convey the character of the subjects' performance, and it would be useful to interrupt our reporting of quantitative relationships to remark on the subjects' general reaction to the situation.

One might suppose that a subject would simply break off or continue as his conscience and temperament dictated. Yet this is very far from what happened. There were powerful reactions of tension and emotional strain in a substantial proportion of the participants. Persons were observed to sweat, tremble, stutter, bite their lips, and groan as they found themselves increasingly implicated in the experimental conflict. Some sense of the subjects' mood can be found in a transcript of their remarks at break-off point. Here are the remarks of two defiant subjects:

> Is he banging?...Is he hurt out there? Well, I don't want to be responsible for anything that happens to him. No, I can't go on with it. I don't know whether he's all right or not. I mean he may have a heart condition or something; I wouldn't feel right doing it. He's banging for help. He's evidently in trouble or he wouldn't bang...I don't see any sense to this—to knocking him out or something. I just can't see it.
> [*Subject refuses to administer shocks*]   [*Subject 0108*]

> The man is banging. He wants to get out...I'm sorry. If the man wants to get out I'd just as soon stop...I don't want to administer any more [extremely excited]...I will gladly refund the check, but I will not harm this man...I'm sorry, I will not give him any more if he obviously wants to get out. There is no money in the world that will make me hurt another individual.   [*Subject 010X*]

And here is a transcript from an obedient subject. He began the experiment calmly, but became increasingly tense as the experiment proceeded. After administering the 150-volt shock, he began to address the experimenter in agitated tones:

> *150 volts delivered.* You want me to keep going?
> *165 volts delivered.* That guy is hollering in there. There's a lot of them here. He's liable to have heart condition. You want me to go?
> *180 volts delivered.* He can't stand it! I'm not going to kill that man in there! You hear him hollering? He's hollering. He can't stand it. What if something happens to him?...I'm not going to get that man sick in there. He's hollering in there. You know what I mean? I mean I refuse to take responsibility. He's getting hurt in there. He's in there hollering. Too many left here. Geez, if he gets them wrong. There's too many of them left. I mean who is going to take responsibility if anything happens to that gentleman?
> [*The experimenter accepts responsibility.*] All right.
> *195 volts delivered.* You see he's hollering. Hear that. Gee, I don't know.
> [*The experimenter says: 'The experiment requires that you go on.'*]—I know it does, sir, but I mean—hugh—he don't know what he's in for. He's up to 195 volts.

210 volts delivered.

225 volts delivered.

240 volts delivered. Aw, no. You mean I've got to keep going up with the scale? No sir. I'm not going to kill that man! I'm not going to give him 450 volts!

[*The experimenter says: 'The experiment requires that you go on.'*]—I know it does, but that man is hollering there, sir...

Despite his numerous, agitated objections, which were constant accompaniments to his actions, the subject unfailingly obeyed the experimenter, proceeding to the highest shock level on the generator. He displayed a curious dissociation between word and action. Although at the verbal level he had resolved not to go on, his actions were fully in accord with the experimenter's commands. This subject did not want to shock the victim, and he found it an extremely disagreeable task, but he was unable to invent a response that would free him from *E*'s authority. Many subjects cannot find the specific verbal formula that would enable them to reject the role assigned to them by the experimenter. Perhaps our culture does not provide adequate models for disobedience.

One puzzling sign of tension was the regular occurrence of nervous laughing fits. In the first four conditions 71 of the 160 subjects showed definite signs of nervous laughter and smiling. The laughter seemed entirely out of place, even bizarre. Full-blown, uncontrollable seizures were observed for 15 of these subjects. On one occasion we observed a seizure so violently convulsive that it was necessary to call a halt to the experiment. In the post-experimental interviews subjects took pains to point out that they were not sadistic types and that the laughter did not mean they enjoyed shocking the victim.

In the interview following the experiment subjects were asked to indicate on a 14-point scale just how nervous or tense they felt at the point of maximum tension (Fig. 7.3). The scale ranged from "not at all tense and nervous" to "extremely tense and nervous." Self-reports of this sort are of limited precision and at best provide only a rough indication of the subject's emotional response. Still, taking the reports for what they are worth, it can be seen that the distribution of responses spans the entire range of the scale, with the majority of subjects concentrated at the center and upper extreme. A further breakdown showed that obedient subjects reported themselves as having been slightly more tense and nervous than the defiant subjects at the point of maximum tension.

How is the occurrence of tension to be interpreted? First, it points to the presence of conflict. If a tendency to comply with authority were the only psychological force operating in the situation, all subjects would have continued to the end and there would have been no tension. Tension, it is assumed, results from the simultaneous presence of two or more incompatible response tendencies (Miller, 1944). If sympathetic concern for the victim were the exclusive force, all subjects would have calmly defied the experimenter. Instead, there were both obedient and defiant outcomes, frequently accompanied by extreme tension. A conflict develops between the deeply ingrained disposition not to harm others and the equally compelling tendency to obey others who are in authority. The subject is quickly drawn into a dilemma of a deeply dynamic character, and the presence of high tension points to the considerable strength of each of the antagonistic vectors.

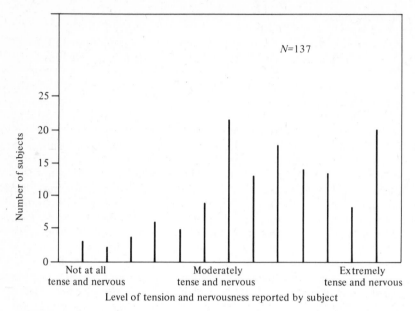

Fig. 7.3 *Level of tension and nervousness: the self-reports on "tension and nervousness" for 137 subjects in the Proximity experiments. Subjects were given a scale with 14 values ranging from "not at all tense and nervous" to "extremely tense and nervous." They were instructed: "Thinking back to that point in the experiment when you felt the most tense and nervous, indicate just how you felt by placing an X at the appropriate point on the scale." The results are shown in terms of midpoint values.*

Moreover, tension defines the strength of the aversive state from which the subject is unable to escape through disobedience. When a person is uncomfortable, tense, or stressed, he tries to take some action that will allow him to terminate this unpleasant state. Thus tension may serve as a drive that leads to escape behavior. But in the present situation, even where tension is extreme, many subjects are unable to perform the response that will bring about relief. Therefore there must be a competing drive, tendency, or inhibition that precludes activation of the disobedient response. The strength of this inhibiting factor must be of greater magnitude than the stress experienced, or else the terminating act would occur. Every evidence of extreme tension is at the same time an indication of the strength of the forces that keep the subject in the situation.

Finally, tension may be taken as evidence of the reality of the situations for the subjects. Normal subjects do not tremble and sweat unless they are implicated in a deep and genuinely felt predicament.

BACKGROUND AUTHORITY

In psychophysics, animal learning, and other branches of psychology, the fact that measures are obtained at one institution rather than another is irrelevant to the interpretation of the findings, so long as the technical facilities for measurement are adequate and the operations are carried out with competence.

But it cannot be assumed that this holds true for the present study. The effectiveness of the experimenter's commands may depend in an important way on the larger institutional context in which they are issued. The experiments described thus far were conducted at Yale University, an organization which most subjects regarded with respect and sometimes awe. In post-experimental interviews several participants remarked that the locale and sponsorship of the study gave them confidence in the integrity, competence, and benign purposes of the personnel; many indicated that they would not have shocked the learner if the experiments had been done elsewhere.

This issue of background authority seemed to us important for an interpretation of the results that had been obtained thus far; moreover it is highly relevant to any comprehensive theory of human obedience. Consider, for example, how closely our compliance with the imperatives of others is tied to particular institutions and locales in our day-to-day activities. On request, we expose our throats to a man with a razor blade in the barber shop, but would not do so in a shoe store; in the latter setting we willingly follow the clerk's request to stand in our stockinged feet, but resist the command in a bank. In the laboratory of a great university, subjects may comply with a set of commands that would be resisted if given elsewhere. *One must always question the relationship of obedience to a person's sense of the context in which he is operating.*

To explore the problem we moved our apparatus to an office building in industrial Bridgeport and replicated experimental conditions, without any visible tie to the university.

Bridgeport subjects were invited to the experiment through a mail circular similar to the one used in the Yale study, with appropriate changes in letterhead, etc. As in the earlier study, subjects were paid $4.50 for coming to the laboratory. The same age and occupational distributions used at Yale and the identical personnel were employed.

The purpose in relocating in Bridgeport was to assure a complete dissociation from Yale, and in this regard we were fully successful. On the surface, the study appeared to be conducted by Research Associates of Bridgeport, an organization of unknown character (the title had been concoted exclusively for use in this study).

The experiments were conducted in a three-room office suite in a somewhat run-down commercial building located in the downtown shopping area. The laboratory was sparsely furnished, though clean, and marginally respectable in appearance. When subjects inquired about professional affiliations, they were informed only that we were a private firm conducting research for industry.

Some subjects displayed skepticism concerning the motives of the Bridgeport experimenter. One gentleman gave us a written account of the thoughts he experienced at the control board:

> ...Should I quit this damn test? Maybe he passed out? What dopes we were not to check up on this deal. How do we know that these guys are legit? No furniture, bare walls, no telephone. We could of called the Police up or the Better Business Bureau. I learned a lesson tonight. How do I know that Mr. Williams [the experimenter] is telling the truth...I wish I knew how many volts a person could take before lapsing into unconsciousness...
>
> [*Subject 2414*]

Another subject stated:

> I questioned on my arrival my own judgment [about coming]. I had doubts
> as to the legitimacy of the operation and the consequences of participation.
> I felt it was a heartless way to conduct memory or learning processes on
> human beings and certainly dangerous without the presence of a medical
> doctor.   [*Subject 2440V*]

There was no noticeable reduction in tension for the Bridgeport subjects.
And the subjects' estimation of the amount of pain felt by the victim was
slightly, though not significantly, higher than in the Yale study.

A failure to obtain complete obedience in Bridgeport would indicate that the
extreme compliance found in New Haven subjects was tied closely to the
background authority of Yale University; if a large proportion of the subjects
remained fully obedient, very different conclusions would be called for.

As it turned out, the level of obedience in Bridgeport, although somewhat
reduced, was not significantly lower than that obtained at Yale. A large
proportion of the Bridgeport subjects were fully obedient to the experimenter's
commands (48 percent of the Bridgeport subjects delivered the maximum shock
versus 65 percent in the corresponding condition at Yale).

How are these findings to be interpreted? It is possible that if commands of
a potentially harmful or destructive sort are to be perceived as legitimate they
must occur within some sort of institutional structure. But it is clear from the
study that it need not be a particularly reputable or distinguished institution.
The Bridgeport experiments were conducted by an unimpressive firm lacking
any credentials; the laboratory was set up in a respectable office building with
title listed in the building directory. Beyond that, there was no evidence of
benevolence or competence. It is possible that the *category* of institution, judged
according to its professed function, rather than its qualitative position within
that category, wins our compliance. Persons deposit money in elegant, but also
in seedy-looking banks, without giving much thought to the differences in
security they offer. Similarly, our subjects may consider one laboratory to be as
competent as another, so long as it is a scientific laboratory.

It would be valuable to study the subjects' performance in other contexts
which go even further than the Bridgeport study in denying institutional support
to the experimenter. It is possible that, beyond a certain point, obedience
disappears completely. But that point had not been reached in the Bridgeport
office: almost half the subjects obeyed the experimenter fully.

FURTHER EXPERIMENTS

We may mention briefly some additional experiments undertaken in the Yale
series. A considerable amount of obedience and defiance in everyday life occurs
in connection with groups. And we had reason to feel in light of the many group
studies already done in psychology that group forces would have a profound
effect on reactions to authority. A series of experiments was run to examine
these effects. In all cases only one naïve subject was studied per hour, but he

performed in the midst of actors who, unknown to him, were employed by the experimenter. In one experiment (Groups for Disobedience) two actors broke off in the middle of the experiment. When this happened 90 percent of the subjects followed suit and defied the experimenter. In another condition the actors followed the orders obediently; this strengthened the experimenter's power only slightly. In still a third experiment the job of pushing the switch to shock the learner was given to one of the actors, while the naïve subject performed a subsidiary act. We wanted to see how the teacher would respond if he were involved in the situation but did not actually give the shocks. In this situation only three subjects out of forty broke off. In a final group experiment the subjects themselves determined the shock level they were going to use. Two actors suggested higher and higher shock levels; some subjects insisted, despite group pressure, that the shock level be kept low; others followed along with the group.

Further experiments were completed using women as subjects, as well as a set dealing with the effects of dual, unsanctioned, and conflicting authority. A final experiment concerned the persoanl relationship between victim and subject. These will have to be described elsewhere, lest the present report be extended to monographic length.

It goes without saying that future research can proceed in many different directions. What kinds of response from the victim are most effective in causing disobedience in the subject? Perhaps passive resistance is more effective than vehement protest. What conditions of entry into an authority system lead to greater or lesser obedience? What is the effect of anonymity and masking on the subject's behavior? What conditions lead to the subject's perception of responsibility for his own actions? Each of these could be a major research topic in itself, and can readily be incorporated into the general experimental procedure described here.

LEVELS OF OBEDIENCE AND DEFIANCE

One general finding that merits attention is the high level of obedience manifested in the experimental situation. Subjects often expressed deep disapproval of shocking a man in the face of his objections, and others denounced it as senseless and stupid. Yet many subjects complied even while they protested. The proportion of obedient subjects greatly exceeded the expectations of the experimenter and his colleagues. At the outset, we had conjectured that subjects would not, in general, go above the level of "Strong Shock." In practice, many subjects were willing to administer the most extreme shocks available when commanded by the experimenter. For some subjects the experiment provided an occasion for aggressive release. And for others it demonstrated the extent to which obedient dispositions are deeply ingrained and engaged, irrespective of their consequences for others. Yet this is not the whole story. Somehow, the subject becomes implicated in a situation from which he cannot disengage himself.

The departure of the experimental results from intelligent expectation, to some extent, has been formalized. The procedure was to describe the experimental situation in concrete detail to a group of competent persons, and to ask them to predict the performance of 100 hypothetical subjects. For purposes of indicating the distribution of break-off points, judges were provided with a diagram of the shock generator and recorded their predictions before being informed of the actual results. Judges typically underestimated the amount of obedience demonstrated by subjects.

In Fig. 7.3, we compare the predictions of forty psychiatrists at a leading medical school with the actual performance of subjects in the experiment. The psychiatrists predicted that most subjects would not go beyond the tenth shock level (150 volts; at this point the victim makes his first explicit demand to be freed). They further predicted that by the twentieth shock level (300 volts; the victim refuses to answer) 3.73 percent of the subjects would still be obedient; and that only a little over one-tenth of one percent of the subjects would administer the highest shock on the board. But, as the graph indicates, the obtained behavior was very different. Sixty-two percent of the subjects obeyed the experimenter's commands fully. Between expectation and occurrence there is a whopping discrepancy.

Why did the psychiatrists underestimate the level of obedience? Possibly, because their predictions were based on an inadequate conception of the determinants of human action, a conception that focuses on motives *in vacuo*. This orientation may be entirely adequate for the repair of bruised impulses as revealed on the psychiatrist's couch, but as soon as our interest turns to action in larger settings, attention must be paid to the situations in which motives are expressed. A situation exerts an important press on the individual. It exercises constraints and may provide push. In certain circumstances it is not so much the kind of person a man is, as the kind of situation in which he is placed, that determines his actions.

Many people, not knowing much about the experiment, claim that subjects who go to the end of the board are sadistic. Nothing could be more foolish than an overall characterization of these persons. It is like saying that a person thrown into a swift-flowing stream is necessarily a fast swimmer, or that he has great stamina because he moves so rapidly relative to the bank. The context of action must always be considered. The individual, upon entering the laboratory, becomes integrated into a situation that carries its own momentum. The subject's problem then is how to become disengaged from a situation which is moving in an altogether ugly direction.

The fact that disengagement is so difficult testifies to the potency of the forces that keep the subject at the control board. Are these forces to be conceptualized as individual motives and expressed in the language of personality dynamics, or are they to be seen as the effects of social structure and pressures arising from the situational field?

A full understanding of the subject's action will, I feel, require that both perspectives be adopted. The person brings to the laboratory enduring dispositions toward authroity and aggression, and at the same time he becomes enmeshed in a social structure that is no less an objective fact of the case. From the standpoint of personality theory one may ask: What mechanisms of personality enable a person to transfer responsibility to authority? What are the motives underlying obedient and disobedient performance? Does orientation to authority lead to a short-circuiting of the shame-guilt system? What cognitive

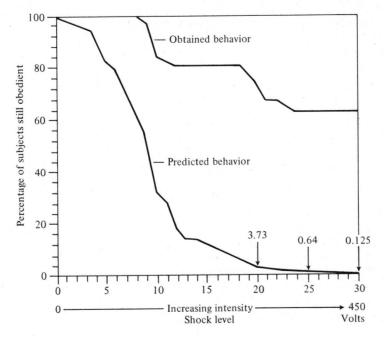

Fig. 7.4 *Predicted and obtained behavior in voice feedback.*

and emotional defenses are brought into play in the case of obedient and defiant subjects?

The present experiments are not, however, directed toward an exploration of the motives engaged when the subject obeys the experimenter's commands. Instead, they examine the situational variables responsible for the elicitation of obedience. Elsewhere, we have attempted to spell out some of the structural properties of the experimental situation that account for high obedience, and this analysis need not be repeated here (Milgram, 1963). The experimental variations themselves represent our attempt to probe that structure, by systematically changing it and noting the consequences for behavior. It is clear that some situations produce greater compliance with the experimenter's commands than others. However, this does not necessarily imply an increase or decrease in the strength of any single definable motive. Situations producing the greatest obedience could do so by triggering the most powerful, yet perhaps the most idiosyncratic, of motives in each subject confronted by the setting. Or they may simply recruit a greater number and variety of motives in their service. But whatever the motives involved—and it is far from certain that they can ever be known—action may be studied as a direct function of the situation in which it occurs. This has been the approach of the present study, where we sought to plot behavioral regularities against manipulated properties of the social field. Ultimately, social psychology would like to have a compelling *theory of situations* which will, first, present a language in terms of which situations can be defined; proceed to a typology of situations; and then point to the manner in which definable properties of situations are transformed into psychological forces in the individual.[9]

POSTSCRIPT

Almost a thousand adults were individually studied in the obedience research, and there were many specific conclusions regarding the variables that control obedience and disobedience to authority. Some of these have been discussed briefly in the preceding sections, and more detailed reports will be released subsequently.

There are now some other generalizations I should like to make, which do not derive in any strictly logical fashion from the experiments as carried out, but which, I feel, ought to be made. They are formulations of an intuitive sort that have been forced on me by observation of many subjects responding to the pressures of authority. The assertions represent a painful alteration in my own thinking; and since they were acquired only under the repeated impact of direct observation, I have no illusion that they will be generally accepted by persons who have not had the same experience.

With numbing regularity good people were seen to knuckle under the demands of authority and perform actions that were callous and severe. Men who are in everyday life responsible and decent were seduced by the trappings of authority, by the control of their perceptions, and by the uncritical acceptance of the experimenter's definition of the situation, into performing harsh acts.

What is the limit of such obedience? At many points we attempted to establish a boundary. Cries from the victim were inserted; not good enough. The victim claimed heart trouble; subjects still shocked him on command. The victim pleaded that he be let free, and his answers no longer registered on the signal box; subjects continued to shock him. At the outset we had not conceived that such drastic procedures would be needed to generate disobedience, and each step was added only as the ineffectiveness of the earlier techniques became clear. The final effort to establish a limit was the Touch-Proximity condition. But the very first subject in this condition subdued the victim on command, and proceeded to the highest shock level. A quarter of the subjects in this condition performed similarly.

The results, as seen and felt in the laboratory, are to this author disturbing. They raise the possibility that human nature or, more specifically, the kind of character produced in American democratic society cannot be counted on to insulate its citizens from brutality and inhumane treatment at the direction of malevolent authority. A substantial proportion of people do what they are told to do, irrespective of the content of the act and without limitations of conscience, so long as they perceive that the command comes from a legitimate authority. If in this study an anonymous experimenter could successfully command adults to subdue a fifty-year-old man and force on him painful electric shocks against his protests, one can only wonder what government, with its vastly greater authority and prestige, can command of its subjects. There is, of course, the extremely important question of whether malevolent political institutions could or would arise in American society. The present research contributes nothing to this issue.

In an article titled "The Dangers of Obedience," Harold J. Laski wrote:

> ...civilization means, above all, an unwillingness to inflict unnecessary pain. Within the ambit of that definition, those of us who heedlessly accept the commands of authority cannot yet claim to be civilized men.
>
> ...Our business, if we desire to live a life, not utterly devoid of meaning and significance, is to accept nothing which contradicts our basic experience merely because it comes to us from tradition or convention or authority. It may well be that we shall be wrong; but our self-expression is thwarted at the root unless the certainties we are asked to accept coincide with the certainties we experience. That is why the condition of freedom in any state is always a widespread and consistent skepticism of the canons upon which power insists.

NOTES

1. This research was supported by two grants from the National Science Foundation: NSF G–17916 and NSF G–24152. Exploratory studies carried out in 1960 were financed by a grant from the Higgins Funds of Yale University. I am grateful to John T. Williams, James, J. McDonough, and Emil Elges for the important part they played in the project. Thanks are due also to Alan Elms, James Miller, Taketo Murata, and Stephen Stier for their aid as graduate assistants. My wife, Sasha, performed many valuable services. Finally, I owe a profound debt to the many persons in New Haven and Bridgeport who served as subjects.

2. Consider, for example, J. P. Scott's analysis of war in his monograph on aggression:

   ...while the actions of key individuals in a war may be explained in terms of direct stimulation to aggression, vast numbers of other people are involved simply by being part of an organized society.
   ...For example, at the beginning of World War I an Austrian archduke was assassinated in Sarajevo. A few days later soldiers from all over Europe were marching toward each other, not because they were stimulated by the archduke's misfortune, but because they had been trained to obey orders. (Slightly rearranged from Scott (1958), *Agression*, p. 103.)

3. It consisted of an extended discussion with the experimenter and, of equal importance, a friendly reconciliation with the victim. It is made clear that the victim did *not* receive painful electric shocks. After the completion of the experimental series, subjects were sent a detailed report of the results and full purposes of the experimental program. A formal assessment of this procedure points to its overall effectiveness. Of the subjects, 83.7 percent indicated that they were glad to have taken part in the study; 15.1 percent reported neutral feelings; and 1.3 percent stated that they were sorry to have participated. A large number of subjects spontaneously requested that they be used in further experimentation. Four-fifths of the subjects felt that more experiments of this sort should be carried out, and 74 percent indicated that they had learned something of personal importance as a result of being in the study. Furthermore, a university psychiatrist, experienced in outpatient treatment, interviewed a sample of experimental subjects with the aim of uncovering possible injurious effects resulting from participation. No such effects were in evidence. Indeed, subjects

typically felt that their participation was instructive and enriching. A more detailed discussion of this question can be found in Milgram (1964).

4. *To obey* and *to disobey* are not the only terms one could use in describing the critical action of *Y*. One could say that *Y* is cooperating with *X*, or displays conformity with regard to *X*'s commands. However, *cooperation* suggests that *X* agrees with *Y*'s ends, and understands the relationship between his own behavior and the attainment of those ends. (But the experimental procedure, and, in particular, the experimenter's command that the subject shock the victim even in the absence of a response from the victim, preclude such understanding.) Moreover, cooperation implies status parity for the co-acting agents, and neglects the asymmetrical, dominance-subordination element prominent in the laboratory relationship between experimenter and subject. *Conformity* has been used in other important contexts in social psychology, and most frequently refers to imitating the judgments or actions of others when no explicit requirement for imitation has been made. Furthermore, in the present study there are two sources of social pressure; pressure from the experimenter issuing the commands, and pressure from the victim to stop the punishment. It is the pitting of a common man (the victim) against an authority (the experimenter) that is the distinctive feature of the conflict. At a point in the experiment the victim demands that he be let free. The experimenter insists that the subject continue to administer shocks. Which act of the subject can be interpreted as conformity? The subject may conform to the wishes of his peer or to the wishes of the experimenter, and conformity in one direction means the absence of conformity in the other. Thus the word has no useful reference in this setting, for the dual and conflicting social pressures cancel out its meaning.

In the final analysis, the linguistic symbol representing the subject's action must take its meaning from the concrete context in which that action occurs; and there is probably no word in everyday language that covers the experimental situation exactly, without omissions or irrelevant connotations. It is partly for convenience, therefore, that the terms *obey* and *disobey* are used to describe the subject's actions. At the same time, our use of the words is highly congruent with dictionary meaning.

5. A more detailed account of the laboratory procedure can be found in Milgram (1963). A similar and independently evolved experimental procedure, employing a shock generator, victim, and learning task, was reported by Buss (1961). Buss used the technique for studying aggression, not obedience, and did not make use of the fundamental measure employed in the present study: break-off points.

6. It is difficult to convey on the printed page the full tenor of the victim's responses, for we have no adequate notation for vocal intensity, timing, and general qualities of delivery. Yet these features are crucial to producing the effect of an increasingly severe reaction to mounting voltage levels. (They can be communicated fully only by sending interested parties the recorded tapes.) In general terms, however, the victim indicates no discomfort until the 75-volt shock is administered, at which time there is a light grunt in response to the punishment. Similar reactions follow the 90- and 105-volt shocks, and at 120 volts the victim shouts to the experimenter that the shocks are becoming painful. Painful groans are heard on administration of the 135-volt shock, and at 150 volts the victim cries out, 'Experimenter, get me out of here! I won't be in the experiment any more! I refuse to go on!' Cries of this type continue with generally rising intensity, so that at 180 volts the victim cries out, 'I can't stand the pain', and by 270 volts his response to the shock is definitely an agonized scream. Throughout, he insists that he be let out of the experiment. At 300 volts the victim shouts in desperation that he will no longer provide answers to the memory test; and at 315 volts, after a violent scream, he reaffirms with vehemence that he is no longer a participant. From this point on, he provides no answers, but

shrieks in agony whenever a shock is administered; this continues through 450 volts. Of course, many subjects will have broken off before this point.

A revised and stronger set of protests was used in all experiments outside the Proximity series. Naturally, new baseline measures were established for all comparisons using the new set of protests.

There is overwhelming evidence that the great majority of subjects, both obedient and defiant, accepted the victims' reactions as genuine. The evidence takes the form of: (a) tension created in the subjects (see discussion of tension); (b) scores on "estimated-pain" scales filled out by subjects immediately after the experiment; (c) subjects' accounts of their feelings in post-experimental interviews; and (d) quantifiable responses to questionnaires distributed to subjects several months after their participation in the experiments. This matter will be treated fully in a forthcoming monograph.

(The procedure in all experimental conditions was to have the naïve subject announce the voltage level before administering each shock, so that—independently of the victim's responses—he was continually reminded of delivering punishment of ever-increasing severity.)

7. Admittedly, the terms *proximity, immediacy, closeness,* and *salience-of-the-victim* are used in a loose sense, and the experiments themselves represent a very coarse treatment of the variable. Further experiments are needed to refine the notion and tease out such diverse factors as spatial distance, visibility, audibility, barrier interposition, etc.

The Proximity and Touch-Proximity experiments were the only conditions where we were unable to use taped feedback from the victim. Instead, the victim was trained to respond in these conditions as he had in Experiment 2 (which employed taped feedback). Some improvement is possible here, for it should be technically feasible to do a proximity series using taped feedback.

8. The third condition also led to significantly lower obedience than this first situation, in which the experimenter was present, but it contains technical difficulties that require extensive discussion.

9. My thanks to Professor Howard Leventhal of Yale for strengthening the writing in this paragraph.

REFERENCES

BUSS, ARNOLD H., 1961. *The Psychology of Aggression.* New York and London: John Wiley.

KIERKEGAARD, S., 1843. *Fear and Trembling.* English edition, Princeton: Princeton University Press, 1941.

LASKI, HAROLD J., 1929 "The dangers of obedience." *Harper's Monthly Magazine* **159**, June, 1–10.

MILGRAM, S., 1961. "Dynamics of obedience: experiments in social psychology." Mimeographed report, *National Science Foundation*, January 25.

———, 1963. "Behavioral study of obedience." *J. Abnorm. Soc. Psychol.* **67**, 371–378.

———, 1964. "Issues in the study of obedience: a reply to Baumrind." *Amer. Psychol.* **19**, 848–852.

MILLER, N. E., 1944. "Experimental studies of conflict." In J. McV. Hunt (ed.), *Personality and the Behavior Disorders.* New York: Ronald Press.

SCOTT, J. P., 1958. *Aggression.* Chicago: University of Chicago Press.

Interpreting Obedience: Error and Evidence[1]

8

Thus far we have been singularly unsuccessful in finding an experimental task which would be discontinued, or indeed refused by subjects in an experimental situation...(M. Orne, 1962)

In the October 1968 issue of the *International Journal of Psychiatry,* Orne and Holland sought to reinterpret the findings of my experimental studies of obedience and disobedience to authority. In this paper, I shall discuss their comments and, beyond this, address myself to some of the related questions that have formed part of Orne's thinking, and which have found their way into his critique.[2]

To begin, I note that Orne does not question the behavioral outcomes obtained in the obedience experiments, but focuses on the psychological meaning behind them. This point of agreement on behavior is important. First, it gives us a common empirical starting point for our discussion. Second, it places a burden on the critic. Let us leave open for the moment whether the subject's state of mind is characterized by the suspiciousness and disbelief that Orne postulates, assuming only that the subject complies outwardly with the experimenter. The critic must still ask *why* subjects respond with a show of outward compliance. The forces in a situation that constrain a person to adhere to required external forms cannot be dismissed as inconsequential. Nor in my view is such compliance most profitably seen as a methodological wrinkle but rather as a social fact of interest in its own right. An orientation in terms of demand characteristics, then, is questionable on two counts: (1) it treats compliance merely as if it were an impediment to research, thereby deflecting attention from the substantive issues underlying such compliance; and (2) it is presented as an explanation while it functions mainly as a depreciatory label.

There is a further implication in the locus of Orne's criticism. It is certainly legitimate to accept the behavioral facts and carry out arguments in regard to the psychological attitudes that lie behind them. However, a warning is in order: namely, this shift in no way diminishes the need for evidence in support of argumentation. I am afraid Orne has assumed that once he has moved the argument off the level of behavioral evidence, he is free to proceed on the basis of speculation and anecdote. In this he is quite wrong. Systematic evidence is of decisive importance and must be brought to bear on the argument.

This paper was first published in *The Social Psychology of Psychological Research*, Arthur G. Miller (ed.), New York: The Free Press, 1972, pp. 139–154. Reprinted by permission of the author.

II

What characterizes Orne's piece is gross overstatement of a point that has an element of validity, is corrected for with relative ease by control procedures, and ought to be seen in its proper place. Orne's first major argument is that subjects do not accept the experimental situation at face value. To make matters perfectly clear, let us state explicitly what subjects may fail to believe: (1) they may not believe the experiment is about memory and learning; (2) they may not believe the learner is getting painful shocks; (3) they may not believe the learner is the focus of experiment. Only the second of these points is critical, for as long as the subject believes he is transmitting painful shocks to the learner on command of the experimenter, the essential manipulatory intent of the experiment is achieved. The fact is that most subjects do believe that the shocks are painful, some subjects are unsure about it, and a few subjects do not believe it. This has been assessed at points during the experiment, immediately after the experiment, and in questionnaire and interview studies a year after the experiment. Orne asserts that no evidence has been presented on this question. This is false. The first published report states:

> With few exceptions subjects were convinced of the reality of the experimental situation, that they were administering shocks to another person, and the most potent shocks were extremely painful. In the post-experimental interview subjects were asked: "How painful to the learner were the last few shocks that you administered to him?" Subjects were instructed to indicate their answers on a printed 14-point scale, ranging from "Not at all painful" to "Extremely painful." The modal response was 14 (Extremely painful) with the mean at 13.42 [1963, p.375].

Moreover, the occurrence of tension provided striking evidence of the subject's genuine involvement in the experimental conflict, and this has been observed and reported throughout in the form of representative transcripts (1963), scale data (1965b), and filmed accounts (1965a). In the course of a recent debate with Orne (1969), a member of the audience pointed out that he would be willing to consider Orne's interpretation a possibility if, indeed, subjects gave evidence of a wry, tongue-in-check attitude, but that Orne's view was untenable in view of the formidable tension and strain observed. Orne's suggestion that the subjects only *feigned* sweating, trembling, and stuttering to please the experimenter is pathetically detached from reality, equivalent to the statement that hemophiliacs bleed to keep their physicians busy. To be sure, I could certainly improve my image with D. Baumrind (1964) and others who have criticized the experiment because of the tension it induced, constructing a defense on Orne's interpretation, but this would be utterly false, for the conflict *was* present, intensely experienced, and cannot be wished or theorized away.

In all experimental conditions the level of pain was interpreted as very high, bordering on the upper extreme. In condition (02), Voice Feedback (when the victim is audible but not visible), the mean on the 14-point scale for obedient subjects is 11.36 and falls within the "extremely painful" zone of the scale. More than half the obedient subjects use the extreme upper point on the scale, and at least one subject indicated by a + sign that "extremely painful" was not a

Table 8.1 Subjects' estimate of pain felt by victim.

Condition	Obedient S's $\bar{x}$	n	Defiant S's $\bar{x}$	n	$\bar{x}$
Remote victim	13.50	(20)	13.27	(11)	13.42
Voice feedback	11.36	(25)	11.80	(15)	11.53
Proximity	12.69	(16)	11.79	(24)	12.15
Touch proximity	12.25	(28)	11.17	(12)	11.93
Coronary tape(a)	11.40	(26)	12.25	(14)	11.70
Coronary tape (b)	11.98	(20)	12.05	(20)	12.02
Bridgeport replication	11.79	(19)	11.81	(18)	11.80
Women as subjects	12.88	(26)	12.07	(14)	12.60
Experimenter departs	11.67	(31)	12.39	(9)	11.83

strong enough designation. Of the 40 subjects in this condition, two indicated on the scale (with scores of 1 and 3) that they did not think the victim received painful shocks, and both subjects were obedient. These subjects, it would appear, were not successfully exposed to the manipulatory intent of the experimenter. But even this is not so simple, since denial of an unpleasant action can serve a defensive function, and some subjects come to view their performance in a favorable light only by reconstructing what their state of mind was when they were administering shocks. The question is: Did they hold their disbelief as a firm hypothesis or as a fleeting notion among many other notions?

The broad quantitative picture of subjects' testimony on belief can be examined, among other ways, by scrutinizing responses to a follow-up questionnaire distributed about a year after subjects participated in the study. Item 4 of the questionnaire is reprinted below, along with the distribution of responses to it.

There are several ways to describe the results. Emphasizing the positive side, one could say that only 4 percent of the subjects were certain the learner was *not*

Table 8.2 Response to question on belief in follow-up questionnaire.

During the experiment			All subjects
1. I fully believed the learner was getting painful shocks.	62.5% (230)	47.9% (139)	56.1% (369)
2. Although I had some doubts, I believed the learner was *probably* getting the shocks.	22.6% (83)	25.9% (75)	24.0% (158)
3. I just wasn't sure whether the learner was getting the shocks or not.	6.0% (22)	6.2% (18)	6.1% (40)
4. Although I had some doubts, I thought the learner was probably not getting the shocks.	7.6% (28)	16.2% (47)	11.4% (75)
5. I was certain the learner was not getting the shocks.	(5)	(11)	(16)

getting any shocks, while 96 percent, in some degree or other, felt the learner was receiving the shocks. Or one could put the most negative interpretation possible on the results by asserting that only half of the subjects fully accepted the experimental deception. But the fairest treatment of the data is to say that three-quarters of the subjects (the first two categories), by their own testimony, acted under the belief that they were administering painful shocks. It would have been an easy out at this point to have denied that the hoax had been accepted. But only a fifth of the group indicated having had serious doubts.

David Rosenhan of Swarthmore College carried out a replication of the obedience experiment in order to obtain a base measure for further studies of his own. He took elaborate interviewing steps. Among other things, he established the interviewer as a person independent of the experiment, who demands a detailed account of the subject's experience and probes the issue of belief even to the point of asking, "You really mean you didn't catch on to the experiment?" On the basis of highly stringent criteria of full acceptance, Rosenhan reports that (according to the determination of independent judges), 68.9 percent of the subjects thoroughly accepted the authenticity of the experiment. Examining the performance of these subjects, he reports that 85 percent were fully obedient. (Rosenhan, it must be pointed out, employed a subject population that was younger than that used in the original experiments, and this, I believe, accounts for the higher level of obedience.[3])

When my experimental findings are subjected to a comparable type of analysis, they are not altered in any substantial manner. For example, in condition (02), Voice Feedback, of those subjects who indicated acceptance of the deception (categories 1 and 2), 58 percent were obedient; of those who indicated category 1, 60 percent were obedient. Over all experimental conditions this manner of controlling the data slightly reduced the proportion of obedient-to-defiant subjects. The changes leave the relations among conditions intact and are inconsequential for interpreting the meaning or import of the findings.

In sum, the majority of subjects accept the experimental situation as genuine; a few do not. Within each experimental condition it was my estimate that two to four subjects did not think they were administering painful shocks to the victim, but I adopted a general rule that no subject be removed from the data, because selective removal of subjects on somewhat inprecise criteria is the quickest way to inadvertently shape hypotheses. Even now I am not willing to dismiss those subjects, because it is not clear that their rejection of the technical illusion was a cause of their obedience or a consequence of it. Does it not occur to Orne that cognitive processes may serve to rationalize behavior that the subject has felt compelled to carry out? It is simple indeed for a subject to explain his behavior by stating he did not believe the victim received shocks, and some subjects come to this position as a post facto explanation of their actions. The explanation has no cost to them and goes a long way toward preserving their positive self-conception. It has the additional benefit of demonstrating how astute and clever they were to penetrate a carefully laid cover story.

More important, however, is to be able to see the role of denial in the total process of obedience and disobedience, for denial is not a *deus ex machina* that descends on the laboratory and sweeps away all else. It is rather one specific cognitive adjustment of several that occur in the experiment, and needs to be properly placed in terms of its functioning in the performance of some subjects.

III

Leaving the evidential basis of this discussion, let us now consider the arguments Orne offers to support his idea that subjects see through the experimental illusions. Orne says, first, that the subjects of psycholological experiments tend to "view their task as a problem-solving situation which requires them to determine the 'real' situation and respond appropriately." I do not share the belief that people by and large are suspicious, distrustful and given to outguessing scientific authorities; nor do I think that among postal clerks, high-school teachers, salesmen, engineers, and laborers—our typical subjects—a great deal is known about psychological experiments. It is true, as Orne says, that within university circles a certain "scuttlebutt" develops about such endeavors, but it is very much a matter of local campus culture and, as Orne must surely know, not relevant to this study, which relied on a general not a campus population (1963,1965b). Some of our subjects were highly intelligent, others of very limited intellectual ability. Very few of them approached the experiment with implicit distrust of the experimenter. Rather than trying to outwit him, subjects occasionally wanted to engage him in personal problems and probably held the idea of a psychiatric interview in their image of psychology. What kind of world does Orne postulate? It is a world populated with mutually suspicious persons, each with concealed motives and working at cross purposes. I do not believe this corresponds to reality, not even the reality of a psychological experiment. I am struck by the fact that Orne not only approaches the question of experimentation from an acutely suspicious point of view, but assumes experimental subjects possess a similar outlook. He supposes that they, too, are searching for concealed motives and hidden meanings, while, in fact, this is true for only a small fraction of subjects of characteristically paranoid outlook.

Orne contends that there are incongruities in the experimental process that give away the deception. He says that a subject would find it implausible that he be required to administer shocks to an individual to test a presumed relation between punishment and learning when the experimenter could as easily give the shocks himself. Yet Orne could determine, by reading that portion of the instructions reprinted in the initial report of the experiment (1963), that a role was assigned to the subject and a reason for his administering the shocks was given. Each subject was told:

> We don't know how much punishment is best for learning, and we don't know how much difference it makes as to who is giving the punishment, whether an adult learns best from a younger or an older person than himself, or many things of that sort. So in this study we are bringing together a number of adults of different occupations and ages. And we're asking some of them to be teachers and some of them to be learners. We want to find out just what effect different people have on each other as teachers and learners, and also what effect punishment will have on learning in this situation.

Another source of doubt, according to Orne, is "The incongruity between the relatively trivial experiment and the imperturbability of the E on the one hand...and the extremity of the victim's suffering...." One could argue with equal conviction that people usually do not assess the relative importance of scientific studies and that the cool, competent stance of the experimenter is the typical posture of authority in modern times, so that casting him in this role contributes to the plausibility of the situation. But the argument can only be resolved by assessment of the subject's acceptance of the situation.[4]

A major problem with the demand characteristic approach is that it is always *post facto*. Orne is quite incapable of knowing what the results of a scientific experiment will be. He only knows how to argue after the results are in. Moreover, he forgets that from the standpoint of a "demand characteristic" analysis, virtually all of the cues in the obedience experiment communicate the necessity to break off the experiment, yet many subjects are unable to do so.

Finally, at times Orne describes the experiment backwards, implying that the subject is told right off to administer dangerous shocks to a screaming person. Far from it, there is an important developmental aspect to the experiment which comes to constrain and control the subject's behavior. The early stages of the experiment are quite proper, even uneventful; it is only gradually as the shock levels intensify that conflict arises. The earlier parts of the experiment, in which any reasonable person would participate, only gradually ease the subject into a conflict; when conflict arises the subject has already routinized his behavior, committed himself to the procedure and, in consequence, is locked into the situation. The shifting, step by step, and piecemeal escalation of shocks plays an important part in exacting obedience, and, moreover, sets the experiment apart from other studies, such as the nitric acid study, which lack this temporal component.

IV

Since Orne makes frequent reference to the experiments he has carried out, some comments ought to be made about them. Many of them are not experiments at all, but only incidents involving one or two individuals. Orne rarely carries his incidents out in sufficient numbers to view the full range of responses to them. Yet they represent, relatively speaking, strong points in Orne's style of inquiry, for often he dispenses with evidence altogether and turns with an air of authority to anecdotes. The anecdotal method does not have much standing in science and has never, to my knowledge, settled anything. Nonetheless, we may critically examine some of Orne's stories, if only to expose the flawed logic with which they are applied to present issues.

Orne tells us that about eighty years ago a hypnotized woman was induced to perform many seemingly antisocial acts, such as stabbing a victim, but could not be induced to undress before an assemblage of males. Orne concludes that the woman did not believe she was inflicting stab wounds. First, this is a gratuitous assumption. Neither Orne nor I have the slightest idea of what went through this woman's mind, and there is no evidence now to help us decide.

But there is a more significant point. Orne asserts that an act such as undressing possesses an irreducible meaning that "transcends the context"

[Orne, 1968, p.228] and therefore cannot be elicited by a hypnotist. One imagines the hypnotist standing Svengali-like over the poor girl, intoning, "You are in my power: Undress! Undress!" All very fine, but it is hard to see what this has to do with the exercise of authority through ordinary channels of social structure, which is the subject matter of the experiments on obedience.

A military officer does not need to rely on animal magnetism or Svengali-like poses to exact compliance from his subordinates. The parties are embedded in a socially defined hierarchical structure and this fact dominates their behavior. Social structure is not a mysterious thing. From the standpoint of the participating subject it is the conviction that another person, by virtue of his status, has the right to prescribe behavior for him.

Let us return to undressing the girl, but now shift from the irrelevant issue of hypnotism to the pertinent question of social structure. It is well known that under a proper set of role relationships, e.g., when visiting a gynecologist, a woman not only undresses but allows her body to be thoroughly inspected. So we are left to conclude that not even hypnotism can bring about what is readily and routinely accomplished by legitimized societal roles. And that is precisely what we have investigated: our subjects are not hypnotized, but they are defined into social roles that place them in a position of subordination vis-à-vis the experimenter.

Let us note a further point. The woman taking part in her medical checkup does not deny that she is undressing before a male stranger but she defines the meaning of the act in a manner that permits it. In the experiment the subject does not deny he is shocking the victim, but he defines the meaning of his act in terms of the constructive purposes outlined by the experimenter. This is not an alternative to complying with authority, but is the typical cognitive concomitant of such compliance.[5]

Orne asserts that direct inferences about obedience in real life cannot be drawn from an experimental context. His documentation consists of a speculative anecdote that is offered as a parallel to the obedience experiment, but which on analysis proves to be misleading and without pertinence.

Orne states:

Anyone who believes direct inference about obedience in real life can be drawn from an experimental context should ask his secretary to type a letter and, after making certain there are no errors, ask her to tear it up and retype it. With rare exceptions, two or three such trials should be sufficient to ensure that the E will require a new secretary.

It is hard to see that this anecdote has anything to do with my obedience experiment or real life. In the experiment, the act of shocking the victim is coordinated to a set of rational purposes concerning advancement of knowledge about the effects of punishment on learning. Nor does the anecdote have much to do with obedience in other settings. Not even in the army are individuals ordered to perform a destructive act for its own sake. The burning of a village containing innocent civilians is carried out with the explanation that it is to impress the populace, or to frighten the inhabitants into cooperating, or to enforce a system of military justice. Were the secretary in Orne's anecdote provided a set of rational purposes for the destructive act, Orne's story would end differently.

The criminal-act experiments on which Orne rests much of his argument also bear little resemblance to the obedience experiment or to life outside the laboratory. In these experiments, the subject is simply told to stab or throw nitric acid at a human target. Orne contends that the subject knows that no one really will be harmed and therefore obeys. It is the same in the obedience experiment, Orne says. But it is not the same. An important feature of the nitric acid experiment is that a meaningless act is arbitrarily demanded of the subject. In the obedience experiments, the act of shocking the victim is tightly embedded in a set of socially constructive purposes, namely, the furtherance of knowledge in regard to memory and learning processes. Obedience occurs not as an end in itself but as an instrumental element in a situation that the subject construes as significant and meaningful. Further, in contrast to the nitric acid study, in the obedience experiment the experimenter explicitly denies the possibility of harm. He states, "Although the shocks can be extremely painful, they cause no permanent tissue damage." (The subject also watches, after the electrode is attached to the victim's wrist, the application of a paste "to avoid blisters and burns.") The indications of harm come from other sources, and the subject must weigh information from his own senses against his trust in and dependence on the experimenter. Most of Orne's analysis ignores this critical aspect of the experiment and is simply not relevant to it.[6]

In summary, the several points on which the obedience experiment differs from the models provided by Orne are: First, we are not dealing with the *personal power* of the experimenter as in the case of hypnosis but, quite explicitly, with the consequence of social structure for action. A clearly defined hierarchical relationship exists between subject and authority. Second, the purposes which authority defines are not senseless and stupid (as in the nitric acid study) but are readily accepted by the subject as worthwhile. Third, the experiment has an important temporal aspect to it. It begins with the mutual consent of all parties and only gradually leads into conflict.

V

The issue of ecological validity comes down to two very different though equally important points that are not kept clearly distinct in Orne's thinking. The first question is: Within the context of a psychological experiment, will a subject accept that he is administering painful shocks to another person against his will? The question must be resolved by resorting to evidence and not simply rhetoric. The second question, which is analytically quite separate, is: Does the behavior established in the laboratory have any generality beyond the circumstances in which it was observed, or is the experimental situation so special that nothing that was observed can contribute to a general view of the functions of obedience in wider social life?

Orne observes that behavior is legitimized in the subject-experimenter relationship. He sees this only as getting in the way of establishing general truths, while in actuality, it is precisely an understanding of behavior *within* legitimized social relationships that the investigation seeks to attain. What Orne can construe only as an impediment is in fact a strategic research opportunity.

Orne wishes to show the uniqueness of the psychological experiment as a context for eliciting behavior, but his manner of supporting the view is specious. Thus he informs us that "it was essential for the subject to be in an actual subject-experimenter relationship in order to have him carry out these actions; despite repeated attempts not one of our colleagues could be induced to attempt any one of these acts." This merely says that the presence of legitimized, hierarchical role relations is needed for exacting compliance. And this is correct. But the further implication that only the subject-experimenter relationship possesses this quality is not merely gratuitous, but blind to the reality of social life, which is replete with hierarchical structures, and which in significant measure is composed of them. Orne's colleagues did not comply for the same reason that, during a parade, when the marshal shouts "left face" the military band turns left but the onlooking pedestrians do not. One group consists of subordinates in a hierarchical structure and the other does not. We can in a despairing moment conclude that this establishes the uniqueness of a parade as a social situation, or we can see through to the deeper principle that only persons defined into a hierarchical structure will respond to it. It is precisely those situations in which a person is defined into a hierarchical structure that constitutes the subject matter of the obedience experiment.

Perhaps the main source of confusion in Orne's thinking is his failure to keep clearly in mind the distinction between social occasions that are hierarchically organized and those that are not. To move from a discussion of one into the other, without taking account of the critical change, can only lead to muddled thought.

The occasion we term a psychological experiment shares its essential structural properties with other situations composed of subordinate-superordinate roles. In all such circumstances the person responds not so much to the content of what is required but on the basis of his relationship to the person who requires it. Indeed, I am tempted to assert this principle in more drastic form: where legitimate authority is the source of action, *relationship overwhelms content.* That is what is meant by the importance of social structure and that is what is demonstrated in the present experiment.

VI

The obedience experiment makes use of a technical illusion, namely that the learner was receiving shocks, when in fact he was an actor. Orne asserts that, according to his analysis, cues in the experiment would not allow the subject to accept this illusion. In fact, observation and data show that Orne's conjecture is wrong, that most subjects do accept the illusion.

There are, to be sure, many alternative methods for accruing evidence, and if the use of a technical illusion is the stumbling block to confidence in the results, then the investigator who wishes to study obedience can do two things. First, he can study the performance of only those subjects who fully accept the illusion. We have already discussed how the data of Milgram and Rosenhan, controlled in this manner, continue to yield levels of obedience comparable to those reported in the original articles. A second approach is to study situations in which no illusion is required because the naïve subject himself serves as the victim. Even when subjects cannot possibly deny the genuineness of what they are doing, because it is happening to them, they comply in extraordinary degree. Thus Turner and Solomon (1962) and Shor (1962) have reported that subjects willingly accept near traumatizing shocks when serving in their experiments. Kudirka (1965) presents an experiment of unusual interest in which subjects were instructed to perform a highly noxious, although not dangerous, task, namely, eating bitter crackers (they were soaked in strong quinine solution). The crackers were extremely distasteful and give rise to facial distortions, grunts, groans, and in some subjects feelings of nausea. Since in this experiment the subject is himself the victim, none of Orne's criticism relating to deception is applicable. The question is whether compliance with the experimenter will occur in any significant degree. The first finding was that the requirement of obedience was so powerful that the experiment could not be done with the experimenter present: virtually all subjects obeyed. Kudirka, therefore, consciously weakened the experimenter's authority by removing him from the laboratory. Even under these circumstances 14 of the 19 subjects continued to the end of the experiment, each one ingesting, frequently with considerable disgust, 36 quinine soaked crackers.

Orne himself (1962b) has used the example of subjects carrying out extremely boring, stupid, and meaningless tasks (such as performing endless serial additions, then tearing up answer sheets) to show the power of the experimenter to induce action in his subjects. He says that although these actions may appear stupid, subjects perform them because they occur within a psychological experiment. When Orne moves on to the obedience experiment, however, he shifts his argument. The power of the experimenter, which Orne so carefully demonstrated, suddenly evaporates. Whereas his subjects genuinely did carry out actions prescribed by the experimenter, Orne would have us believe that my subjects did not. This is, at best, twisted logic, and Orne really cannot have it both ways. On the one hand he asserts an extreme degree of control over the subject, and on the other hand he denies this control exists in the present experiment. It is far more logical to see the obedience experiment as climaxing a consistent line of research demonstrating the power of authority, a line that can be traced to Frank (1944), through Orne (1962b), and into the present research.

His argument is further weakened by his failure to come to grips with the Bridgeport variation of the experiment in which the university setting was eliminated. For years Orne has pointed to the benignity of the university and hospital setting and the manner in which these specific contexts invalidate experimental studies of antisocial behavior. Insofar as Orne's general position is concerned, the implication of the Bridgeport experiment would seem to be that the university context may be less important than thought in the elicitation of antisocial behavior and that whatever elementary social structure is required for its elicitation can function independently of established, benevolent organizations.

At the conclusion of his critical evaluation, Orne calls for "experiments that are not recognized as such by the subjects" to elucidate the true nature of man. I call his attention, then, to a study in which a group of nurses, on duty in hospital wards, were the unknowing subjects (Hofling, *et al.*, 1966). The nurses were given over the telephone an irregular order to administer medication. The voice of the caller, purporting to be a known physician, was unfamiliar to the nurse; the medicine was not on the ward stocklist and thus unauthorized; the dose requested was double the maximum dose shown on the pill box; and the procedure of ordering medication by telephone was in violation of hospital policy. Yet of the 22 nurses tested in this fashion, 21 gave the medication as ordered. In reply to a questionnaire, a majority of a control group of nurses said that they would not have given the medication. The parallel results found in Hofling's results in a naturalistic setting and those found in my laboratory study are striking and lend support to the ecological validity of my laboratory findings.

Ecological validity refers to mapping the range of conditions under which a phenomenon will appear. If Orne is saying there are more experiments to be done, and the present experiments do not give all the answers, I entirely agree with him. But the ultimate effect of Orne's work seems to be the denial of scientific knowledge.

Orne does a disservice of his high methodological ideas when he pursues his doctrines so zealously that, in order to make them fit, he misstates the manner in which the obedience study was conducted (p.143), or continues to insist on his presuppositions in the face of contrary evidence (p.139). For we must then ask whether this theory is a useful scientific analysis or shades into an autistic construction in which the themes of conspiracy, distrust, contaminants, and concealed motives play a commanding part. Without question, one may legitimately ask whether the subjects believed the victim received painful shocks, but the answer resides in evidence, not the infallibility of Orne's presuppositions.

Orne's arguments, built largely on anecdotes, are slippery and shift to meet the needs of a limited intellectual orientation. Their aim seems to be to deny the reality of a phenomenon, whether it be hypnosis (1959,1965), sensory deprivation (1964), general experimentation (1962b), or obedience (1968). Orne's doctrine begins with a population of subjects who are actively suspicious and distrustful, except when trust is the ingredient that will render the experiment invalid; then they are trustful (Orne,1968,p.291). Demand characteristics come next: The experimenter is not really studying what he wants to study, for the subject has thwarted the possibility of objective inquiry by giving him only what he wants to hear. Evidence for this view is nonexistent, and indeed, Sigall, Aronson, and Van Hoose (1970) have recently reported a study showing it does not hold up.

In any case, Orne realizes that the argument of the "cooperating subject" cannot invalidate the obedience experiment, since the experimenter makes quite explicit to the subject what he "wants," and the degree to which the subject gives him what he "wants" constitutes the actual experimental measure. Accordingly, Orne again shifts his argument, arguing that outward behavior is not what it seems to be, and there are hidden meanings beneath the surface. One might note that Orne's interest in the hidden meaning is pursued in disregard of the manifest meaning of the behavior and, indeed, is employed to discount what is most apparent.

Orne does not hesitate to use the obedience experiment to discredit hypnotic phenomena (1965); having done this he next turns to discredit the obedience experiment, introducing irrelevant arguments and misstatements of fact along the way. He next asserts the unqualified uniqueness of psychological experiments, so that nothing found within them has relevance to anything else. The overall pattern of this work does not point to the possibilities for studying phenomena, but only to the possibility for discrediting them. Orne does not see a possible link between the compliance found in his studies and the compliance observed in the obedience experiments, for his aim in reporting his findings of compliance is to show how impossible the experimental situation was for determining scientific truth. Finally, there is no substance in things, only methodological wrinkles. This seems to me the history of the school of social psychology which Orne has assiduously cultivated. I do not believe that, in its present one-sided form, it constitutes a contribution to our understanding of human behavior. While specific details of this viewpoint are sometimes plausible, the rigid presuppositions animating such ideology invariably deform the total picture until it no longer corresponds with reality.

Certain methodological correctives derived from this point of view can, I believe, be of value. Increased experimental sophistication in the form of careful interviewing and avoidance of obvious pitfalls (e.g., employing psychology majors as subjects) can enhance the quality of experimentation. But these steps are only helpful when detached from the tunnel vision of conspiratorial thought and applied with a sense of balance to the problem at hand.

VII

Despite the rhetorical vigor of the Orne and Holland piece, it contains a good deal of error and much that is irrelevant. Let us summarize its major deficiencies:

1. Orne's case rests on the supposition that subjects do not believe they are administering painful shocks to the learner. He builds this case not by looking at evidence, but by anecdote and by weaving a speculative analysis not based on fact. In doing so he disregards information obtained by direct observations, interviewing, quantitative scales, and questionnaire studies, all of which indicate that most subjects accept the experiment at face value.

2. If we are uneasy about the degree to which the authenticity of the experiment was experienced by a fraction of the subjects, we may take the step of considering only those subjects for whom we are certain the manipulatory intent was most fully achieved. For the critical question is not whether some subjects disbelieved, but whether, among these who did fully believe, performance was such that the major conclusions are altered. The data of several investigators show that the phenomenon of obedience holds up for subjects who fully accepted the experiment at face value.

3. Orne mechanically applies a critique of the experiments based on his criticism of hypnotic phenomena. This is the wrong model. Obedience to authority explicitly treats of the consequences of social structure for behavior. The experimental situation is constructed of hierarchically defined role relations. All of Orne's illustrations showing the power of social structure do not, as he believes, invalidate the findings, but only serve to show how general is the phenomenon.

4. If deception is the key issue, then all that the investigator interested in obedience needs to do is to study behavior in which the subject himself is the victim, in which case Orne's criticism of plausibility cannot apply. Studies of this sort have been reported. All the evidence, including that obtained by Orne, points to the extreme compliance of subjects in obeying the experimenter and carrying out acts that are stupid, tedious, noxious, and painful. Orne himself writes he could not find any task which subjects would refuse to do. That was an insight he ought to have taken seriously and pursued to its logical conclusion.

5. Orne asserts that the university context invalidates studies of antisocial behavior, but fails to come to grips with a replication of the experiment run with no visible university affiliation.

6. The trouble with "demand characteristics" is that those who rely on the concept are incapable of predicting the results of an experiment and only know how to apply the label after the facts are in. Then, any number of "demand characteristic" analyses can be formulated. Indeed, the strongest case can be made for the view that all of the cues in the study tell the subject of the necessity to break off. Yet many of them are unable to break with authority.

7. The basic logical contradication in Orne's argument is that at one moment he argues for the extreme compliance of subjects to experimental commands, and at the next he argues against the reality of such compliance. A set of shifting arguments is employed in the service of nihilistic outlook. With far greater logic, one can set the obedience experiment in a context of research that shows, with increasing clarity and force, the profound consequences of submission to authority, a line of research to which Orne's early work (1962b) has contributed in an important way.

NOTES

1. The author wishes to thank Barbara Kline, Mary Englander, and Lynne Steinberg for assistance in preparing this paper.

2. For brevity of reference I shall employ Orne's name exclusively in dealing with the above paper. This is not in any way meant to diminish the contribution of Dr. Holland to the paper, but rather is used to be concise and to focus my criticism on a well-known body of methodological philosophy which has appeared under Orne's name.

3. Holland's thesis (1969), though it contains many serious flaws of procedure which are fatal to the successful replication of the experiment, nonetheless offers supporting data on this issue. By Holland's own calculation, only a quarter of the subjects were successfully subjected to the manipulatory intent of the experiment. He would be perfectly correct, then, in looking at these subjects and determing the proportion of obedient subjects. It turns out that 70 percent of his "good" subjects are obedient, a figure that slightly exceeds my own figures, but is nonetheless of the same order of magnitude. Unfortunately, Holland carried out the study in 1967, and employed as his subjects students in an introductory psychology class. The author should have steered as far clear from psychology undergraduates as possible, for they would constitute the worst possible subjects for an experiment in which prior knowledge of the experiment is a fatal contaminant.

4. Recently, Ring, Wallston, and Corey (1970) carried out an obedience experiment in which the experimenter's behavior was made more animated and responsive, and this does not lead to any decrement in obedience. Instead of electric shock, the authors substituted excruciatingly painful noise fed to the subject's ear. Ninety-one percent of the subjects were maximally obedient.

5. Orne may properly pose the question: Can one devise an *experiment* in which women will undress? Of course it is possible to devise such an experiment. Naturally, the act of undressing would have to be coordinated to a set of rational purposes that the subject could accept. Indeed, an experiment has already been carried out by Masters and Johnson (1966) at Washington University in which, in the course of studies of sexual response, women—some prostitutes but others ordinary girls—not only undressed before the investigators but masturbated and engaged in coitus as well. Can we expect Orne to write an article arguing that the women did not really think they were engaging in coitus because of the imperturbable quality of the investigators?

6. Incidentally, Orne believes that if unhypnotized subjects throw nitric acid at individuals it is because they believe they will not really harm the other individual. My guess is that there is more to it than this, that in some degree they do not feel accountable for what they are doing.

REFERENCES

BAUMRIND, D., "Some thoughts on ethics of research: After reading Milgram's 'Behavioral study of obedience.'" *American Psychologist,* 1964, **19**: 421–423.

FRANK, J. D., "Experimental studies of personal pressure and resistance." *Journal of General Psychology,* 1944, **30**: 23–64.

HOFLING, C. K., BROTZMAN, E., DALRYMPLE, S., GRAVES, N., AND PIERCE, C. M., "An experimental study in nurse-physician relationships." *The Journal of Nervous and Mental Disease,* 1966, **143** (2): 171–180.

HOLLAND, C. H., "Sources of variance in the experimental investigation of behavioral obedience." Unpublished doctoral dissertation, University of Connecticut, 1967.

KUDIRKA, N. K., "Defiance of authority under peer influence." Unpublished doctoral dissertation, Yale University, 1965.

MASTERS, W. H., AND JOHNSON, V. E., *Human Sexual Response,* Boston: Little, Brown and Co., 1966.

MILGRAM, S., "Behavioral study of obedience." *Journal of Abnormal and Social Psychology,* 1963, **67**: 371–378.

———, *Obedience* (a filmed experiment). Distributed by the New York University Film Library, Copyright 1965 (a).

———, "Some conditions of obedience and disobedience to authority." *Human Relations,* 1965, **18**: 57–75 (b).

ORNE, M. T., "The nature of hypnosis: Artifact and essence." *Journal of Abnormal and Social Psychology,* 1959, **58**: 277–299.

———, "Antisocial behavior and hypnosis: Problems of control and validation in empirical studies." In G. H. Estabrooks (ed.), *Hypnosis: Current problems.* New York: Harper and Row, 1962 (a).

———, "On the social psychology of the psychological experiment: With particular reference to demand characteristics and their implications." *American Psychologist,* 1962, **17** 11): 776–783 (b).

ORNE, M. T., AND EVANS, F. J., "Social control in the psychological experiment: Antisocial behavior and hypnosis." *Journal of Personality and Social Psychology,* 1965, **1**, 189–200.

ORNE, M. T., AND HOLLAND, C. C., "On the ecological validity of laboratory deceptions." *International Journal of Psychiatry,* 1968, **6** (4): 282–293.

ORNE, M. T., AND MILGRAM, S., "Obedience or demand characteristics." A debate held at the University of Pennsylvania on February 19, 1969.

ORNE, M. T., AND SCHEIBE, K. E., "The contribution of nondeprivation factors in the production of sensory deprivation effects." *Journal of Abnormal and Social Psychology,* 1964, **68** (1): 3–12.

ORNE, M. T., SHEEHAN, P. W., AND EVANS, F. J., "Occurrence of post-hypnotic behavior outside the experimental setting." *Journal of Personality and Social Psychology,* 1968, **9** (2, Pt. 1): 189–196.

RING, K., WALLSTON, K. AND COREY, M., "Mode of debriefing as a factor affecting subjective reaction to a Milgram-type obedience experiment—an ethical inquiry." *Representative Research in Social Psychology,* 1970, **1** (1): 67–88.

ROSENHAN, D., "Some origins of concern for others." In P. Mussen, J. Langer, and M. Covington (eds.), *Trends and Issues in Developmental Psychology.* New York: Holt, Rinehart & Winston, 1969.

————, "Obedience and rebellion: Observations on the Milgram three-party paradigm." In preparation.

SHOR, R. E., "Physiological effects of painful stimulation during hypnotic analgesia under conditions designed to minimize anxiety." *International Journal of Clinical and Experimental Hypnosis,* 1962, **10**: 183–202.

SIGALL, H., ARONSON, E., AND VAN HOOSE, T., "The cooperative subject: Myth or reality?" *Journal of Experimental Social Psychology,* 1970, **6**:1–10.

TURNER, L. H., AND SOLOMON, R. L., "Human traumatic avoidance learning: Theory and experiments on the operant-respondent distinction and failures to learn." *Psychological Monographs,* 1962, **76** (40, whole no. 559).

9

Ethical Issues
in the Study of Obedience

Obedience serves numerous productive functions in society. It may be ennobling and educative and entail acts of charity and kindness. Yet the problem of destructive obedience, because it is the most disturbing expression of obedience in our time, and because it is the most perplexing, merits intensive study.

In its most general terms, the problem of destructive obedience may be defined thus: If X tells Y to hurt Z, under what conditions will Y carry out the command of X, and under what conditions will he refuse? In the concrete setting of a laboratory, the question may assume this form: If an experimenter tells a subject to act against another person, under what conditons will the subject go along with the instruction, and under what conditions will he refuse to obey?

A simple procedure was devised for studying obedience (Milgram, 1963). A person comes to the laboratory and, in the context of a learning experiment, he is told to give increasingly severe electric shocks to another person. (The other person is an actor, who does not really receive any shocks.) The experimenter tells the subject to continue stepping up the shock level, even to the point of reaching the level marked "Danger: Severe Shock." The purpose of the experiment is to see how far the naïve subject will proceed before he refuses to comply with the experimenter's instructions. Behavior prior to this rupture is considered "obedience" in that the subject does what the experimenter tells him to do. The point of rupture is the act of disobedience. Once the basic procedure is established, it becomes possible to vary conditions of the experiment, to learn under what circumstances obedience to authority is most probable, and under what conditions defiance is brought to the fore (Milgram, 1965).

The results of the experiment (Milgram, 1963) showed, first, that it is more difficult for many people to defy the experimenter's authority than was generally supposed. A substantial number of subjects go through to the end of the shock board. The second finding is that the situation often places a person in considerable conflict. In the course of the experiment, subjects fidget, sweat, and sometimes break out into nervous fits of laughter. On the one hand, subjects want to aid the experimenter; and on the other hand, they do not want to shock the learner. The conflict is expressed in nervous reactions.

In a recent issue of *American Psychologist*, Diana Baumrind (1964) raised a number of questions concerning the obedience report. Baumrind expressed concern for the welfare of subjects who served in the experiment, and wondered whether adequate measures were taken to protect the participants. She also questioned the adequacy of the experimental design.

Patently, "Behavioral Study of Obedience" did not contain all the information needed for an assessment of the experiment. But it is clearly indicated in the referencences and footnotes (pp. 373,378) that this was only one of a series of reports on the experimental program, and Baumrind's article was deficient in information that could have been easily obtained. I thank the editor for allotting space in this journal to review this information, to amplify it, and to discuss some of the issues touched on by Baumrind.

At the outset, Baumrind confuses the unanticipated outcome of an experiment with its basic procedure. She writes, for example, as if the production of stress in our subjects was an intended and deliberate effect of the experimental manipulation. There are many laboratory procedures specifically designed to create stress (Lazarus, 1964), but the obedience paradigm was not one of them. The extreme tension induced in some subjects was unexpected. Before conducting the experiment, the procedures were discussed with many colleagues, and none anticipated the reactions that subsequently took place. Foreknowledge of results can never be the invariable accompaniment of an experimental probe. Understanding grows because we examine situations in which the end is unknown. An investigator unwilling to accept this degree of risk must give up the idea of scientific inquiry.

Moreover, there was every reason to expect, prior to actual experimentation, that subjects would refuse to follow the experimenter's instructions beyond the point where the victim protested; many colleagues and psychiatrists were questioned on this point, and they virtually all felt this would be the case. Indeed, to initiate an experiment in which the critical measure hangs on disobedience, one must start with a belief in certain spontaneous resources in men that enable them to overcome pressure from authority.

It is true that after a reasonable number of subjects had been exposed to the procedures, it became evident that some would go the end of the shock board, and some would experience stress. That point, it seems to me, is the first legitimate juncture at which one could even start to wonder whether or not to abandon the study. But momentary excitement is not the same as harm. As the experiment progressed there was no indication of injurious effects in the subjects; and as the subjects themselves strongly endorsed the experiment, the judgment I made was to continue the investigation.

Is not Baumrind's criticism based as much on the unanticipated findings as on the method? The findings were that some subjects performed in what appeared to be a shockingly immoral way. If, instead, every one of the subjects had broken off at "slight shock," or at the first sign of the learner's discomfort, the results would have been pleasant and reassuring, and who would protest?

PROCEDURES AND BENEFITS

A most important aspect of the procedure occurred at the end of the experimental session. A careful post-experimental treatment was administered to all subjects. The exact content of the dehoax varied from condition to condition and with increasing experience on our part. At the very least all subjects were told that the victim had not received dangerous electric shocks. Each subject had a friendly reconciliation with the unharmed victim, and an extended discussion with the experimenter. The experiment was explained to the defiant subjects in a way that supported their decision to disobey the experimenter. Obedient subjects were assured of the fact that their behavior was entirely normal and that their feelings of conflict or tension were shared by other participants. Subjects were told that they would receive a comprehensive report at the conclusion of the experimental series. In some instances, additional detailed and lengthy discussions of the experiments were also carried out with individual subjects.

When the experimental series was complete, subjects received a written report which presented details of the experimental procedure and results. Again their own part in the experiments was treated in a dignified way and their behavior in the experiment respected. All subjects received a follow-up questionnaire regarding their participation in the research, which again allowed expression of thoughts and feelings about their behavior.

The replies to the questionnaire confirmed my impression that participants felt positively toward the experiment. In its quantitative aspect (see Table 9.1), 84 percent of the subjects stated they were glad to have been in the experiment; 15 percent indicated neutral feelings, and 1.3 percent indicated negative feelings. To be sure, such findings are to be interpreted cautiously, but they cannot be disregarded.

Table 9.1 Excerpt from questionnaire used in a follow-up study of the obedience research.*

Now that I have read the report, and all things considered...	Defiant	Obedient	All
1. I am very glad to have been in the experiment	40.0%	47.8%	43.5%
2. I am glad to have been in the experiment	43.8%	35.7%	40.2%
3. I am neither sorry nor glad to have been in the experiment	15.3%	14.8%	15.1%
4. I am sorry to have been in the experiment	0.8%	0.7%	0.8%
5. I am very sorry to have been in the experiment	0.0%	1.0%	0.5%

*Ninety-two percent of the subjects returned the questionnaire. The characteristics of the nonrespondents were checked against the respondents. They differed from the respondents only with regard to age; younger people were overrepresented in the nonresponding group.

Further, four-fifths of the subjects felt that more experiments of this sort should be carried out and 74 percent indicated that they had learned something of personal importance as a result of being in the study. The results of the interviews, questionnaire responses, and actual transcripts of the debriefing procedures will be presented more fully in a forthcoming monograph.

The debriefing and assessment procedures were carried out as a matter of course and were not stimulated by any observation of special risk in the experimental procedure. In my judgment, at no point were subjects exposed to danger and at no point did they run the risk of injurious effects resulting from participation. If it had been otherwise, the experiment would have been terminated at once.

Baumrind states that, after the subject has performed in the experiment, he cannot justify his behavior and must bear the full brunt of his actions. By and large it does not work this way. The same mechanisms that allow the subject to perform the act, to obey rather than to defy the experimenter, transcend the moment of performance and continue to justify his behavior for him. The same viewpoint the subject takes while performing the actions is the viewpoint from which he later sees his behavior, that is, the perspective of "carrying out the task assigned by the person in authority."

Because the idea of shocking the victim is repugnant, there is a tendency among those who hear of the design to say "people will not do it." When the results are made known, this attitude is expressed as "if they do it they will not be able to live with themselves afterward." These two forms of denying the experimental findings are equally inappropriate misreadings of the facts of human social behavior. Many subjects do, indeed, obey to the end, and there is no indication of injurious effects.

The absence of injury is a minimal condition of experimentation; there can be, however, an important positive side to participation. Baumrind suggests that subjects derived no benefit from being in the obedience study, but this is false. By their statements and actions, subjects indicated that they had learned a good deal, and many felt gratified to have taken part in scientific research they considered to be of significance. A year after his participation one subject wrote:

> This experiment has strengthened my belief that man should avoid harm
> to his fellow man even at the risk of violating authority.

Another stated:

> To me, the experiment pointed up...the extent to which each individual
> should have or discover firm ground on which to base his decisions,
> no matter how trivial they appear to be. I think people should think more
> deeply about themselves and their relation to their world and to other
> people. If this experiment serves to jar people out of complacency, it will
> have served its end.

These statements are illustrative of a broad array of appreciative and insightful comments by those who participated.

The five-page report sent to each subject on the completion of the experimental series was specifically designed to enhance the value of his experience. It layed out the broad conception of the experimental program as well as the logic of its design. It described the results of a dozen of the experiments, discussed the causes of tension, and attempted to indicate the possible significance of the experiment. Subjects responded enthusiastically; many indicated a desire to be in further experimental research. This report was sent to all subjects several years ago. The care with which it was prepared does not support Baumrind's assertion that the experimenter was indifferent to the value subjects derived from their participation.

Baumrind's fear is that participants will be alienated from psychological experiments because of the intensity of experience associated with laboratory procedures. My own observation is that subjects more commonly respond with distaste to the "empty" laboratory hour, in which cardboard procedures are employed, and the only possible feeling upon emerging from the laboratory is that one has wasted time in a patently trivial and useless exercise.

The subjects in the obedience experiment, on the whole, felt quite differently about their participation. They viewed the experience as an opportunity to learn something of importance about themselves, and more generally, about the conditions of human action.

A year after the experimental program was completed, I initiated an additional follow-up study. In this connection an impartial medical examiner, experienced in outpatient treatment, interviewed 40 experimental subjects. The examining psychiatrist focused on those subjects he felt would be most likely to have suffered consequences from participation. His aim was to identify possible injurious effects resulting from the experiment. He concluded that, although extreme stress had been experienced by several subjects,

> ...none was found by this interviewer to show signs of having been harmed by his experience.... Each subject seemed to handle his task [in the experiment] in a manner consistent with well established patterns of behavior. No evidence was found of any traumatic reactions.

Such evidence ought to be weighed before judging the experiment.

OTHER ISSUES

Baumrind's discussion is not limited to the treatment of subjects, but diffuses to a generalized rejection of the work.

Baumrind feels that obedience cannot be meaningfully studied in a laboratory setting: The reason she offers is that "The dependent, obedient attitude assumed by most subjects in the experimental setting is appropriate to that situation [p. 421]." Here, Baumrind has cited the very best reason for examining obedience in this setting, namely that it possesses "ecological validity." Here is one social context in which compliance occurs regularly. Military and job situations are also particularly meaningful settings for the study of obedience precisely because obedience is natural and appropriate to these contexts. I reject Baumrind's argument that the observed obedience does not count because it occurred where it is appropriate. That is precisely why it *does* count. A soldier's obedience is no less meaningful because it occurs in a pertinent military context. A subject's obedience is no less problematical because it occurs within a social institution called the psychological experiment.

Baumrind writes: "The game is defined by the experimenter and he makes the rules [p. 421]." It is true that for disobedience to occur the framework of the experiment must be shattered. That, indeed, is the point of the design. That is why obedience and disobedience are genuine issues for the subject. *He must really assert himself as a person against a legitimate authority.*

Further, Baumrind wants us to believe that outside the laboratory we could not find a comparably high expression of obedience. Yet, the fact that ordinary citizens are recruited to military service and, on command, perform far harsher acts against people is beyond dispute. Few of them know or are concerned with the complex policy issues underlying martial action; fewer still become conscientious objectors. Good soldiers do as they are told, and on both sides of the battle line. However, a debate on whether a higher level of obedience is represented by (a) killing man in the service of one's country, or (b) merely shocking them in the service of Yale science, is largely unprofitable. The real question is: What are the forces underlying obedient action?

Another question raised by Baumrind concerns the degree of parallel between obedience in the laboratory and in Nazi Germany. Obviously, there are enormous differences: Consider the disparity in time scale. The laboratory experiment takes an hour; the Naxi calamity unfolded in the space of a decade. There is a great deal that needs to be said on this issue, and only a few points can be touched on here.

1. In arguing this matter, Baumrind mistakes the background metaphor for the precise subject matter of investigation. The German event was cited to point up a serious problem in this human situation: the potentially destructive effect of obedience. But the best way to tackle the problem of obedience, from a scientific standpoint, is in no way restricted by "what happened exactly" in Germany. What happened exactly can *never* be duplicated in the laboratory or anywhere else. The real task is to learn more about the general problem of destructive obedience using a workable approach. Hopefully, such inquiry will stimulate insights and yield general propositions that can be applied to a wide variety of situations.

2. One may ask in a general way: How does a man behave when he is told by a legitimate authority to act against a third individual? In trying to find an answer to this question, the laboratory situation is one useful starting point—and for the very reason stated by Baumrind—namely, the experimenter does constitute a genuine authority for the subject. The fact that trust and dependence on the experimenter are maintained, despite the extraordinary harshness he displays toward the victim, is itself a remarkable phenomenon.

3. In the laboratory, through a set of rather simple manipulations, ordinary persons no longer perceived themselves as a responsible part of the causal chain leading to action against a person. The means through which responsibility is cast off, and individuals become thoughtless agents of action, is of general import. Other processes were revealed that indicate that the experiments will help us to understand why men obey. That understanding will come, of course, by examining the full account of experimental work and not alone the brief report in which the procedure and demonstrational results were exposed.

At root, Baumrind senses that it is not proper to test obedience in this situation, because she construes it as one in which there is no reasonable alternative to obedience. In adopting this view, she has lost sight of this fact: A substantial proportion of subjects do disobey. By their example, disobedience is shown to be a genuine possibility, one that is in no sense ruled out by the general structure of the experimental situation.

Baumrind is uncomfortable with the high level of obedience obtained in the first experiment. In the condition she focused on, 65 percent of the subjects obeyed to the end. However, her sentiment does not take into account that within the general framework of the psychological experiment obedience varied enormously from one condition to the next. In some variations, 90 percent of the subjects *dis*obeyed. It seems to be *not* only the fact of an experiment, but the particular structure of elements within the experimental situation that accounts for rates of obedience and disobedience. And these elements were varied systematically in the program of research.

A concern with human dignity is based on a respect for a man's potential to act morally. Baumrind feels that the experimenter *made* the subject shock the victim. This conception is alien to my view. The experimenter tells the subject to do something. But between the command the outcome there is a paramount force, the acting person who may obey or disobey. I started with the belief that every person who came to the laboratory was free to accept or to reject the dictates of authority. This view sustains a conception of human dignity insofar as it sees in each man a capacity for *choosing* his own behavior. And as it turned out, many subjects did, indeed, choose to reject the experimenter's commands, providing a powerful affirmation of human ideals.

Baumrind also criticizes the experiment on the grounds that "it could easily effect an alteration in the subject's...ability to trust adult authorities in the future [p. 422]." But I do not think she can have it both ways. On the one hand, she argues the experimental situation is so special that it has no generality; on the other hand, she states it has such generalizing potential that it will cause subjects to distrust all authority. But the experimenter is not just any authority. He is an authority who tells the subject to act harshly and inhumanely against another man. I would consider it of the highest value if participation in the experiment could, indeed, inculcate a skepticism of this kind of authority. Here, perhaps, a difference in philosophy emerges most clearly. Baumrind sees the subject as a passive creature, completely controlled by the experimenter. I started from a different viewpoint. A person who comes to the laboratory is an active, choosing adult, capable of accepting or rejecting the prescriptions for action addressed to him. Baumrind sees the effect of the experiment as undermining the subject's trust of authority. I see it as a potentially valuable experience insofar as it makes people aware of the problem of indiscriminate submission to authority.

CONCLUSION

My feeling is that viewed in the total context of values served by the experiment, approximately the right course was followed. In review, the facts are these: (a) At the outset, there was the problem of studying obedience by means of a simple experimental procedure. The results could not be foreseen before the experiment was carried out. (b) Although the experiment generated momentary stress in some subjects this stress dissipated quickly and was not injurious. (c) Dehoax and follow-up procedures were carried out to insure the subject's well-being. (d) These procedures were assessed through questionnaire and psychiatric studies and were found to be effective. (e) Additional steps were taken to enhance the value of the laboratory experience for participants, for example, submitting to each subject a careful report on the experimental program. (f) The subjects themselves strongly endorse the experiment, and indicate satisfaction at having participated.

If there is a moral to be learned from the obedience study, it is that every man must be responsible for his own actions. This author accepts full responsibility for the design and execution of the study. Some people may feel it should not have been done. I disagree and accept the burden of their judgment.

Baumrind's judgment, someone has said, not only represents a personal conviction, but also reflects a cleavage in American psychology between those whose primary concern is with *helping* people and those who are interested in *learning* about people. I see little value in perpetuating divisive forces in psychology when there is so much to learn from every side. A schism may exist, but it does not correspond to the true ideals of the discipline. The psychologist intent on healing knows that his power to help rests on knowledge; he is aware that a scientific grasp of all aspects of life is essential for his work, and is in itself a worthy human aspiration. At the same time, the laboratory psychologist senses his work will lead to human betterment, not only because enlightenment is more dignified than ignorance, but because new knowledge is pregnant with humane possibilities.

REFERENCES

BAUMRIND, D., "Some thoughts on ethics of research: After reading Milgram's 'Behavioral study of obedience.'" *Amer. Psychologist,* 1964, **19**, 421–423.

LAZARUS, R., "A laboratory approach to the dynamics of psychological stress." *Amer. Psychologist,* 1964, **19**, 400–411.

MILGRAM, S., "Behavioral study of obedience." *J. Abnorm. Soc. Psychol.,* 1963, **67**, 371–378.

———, "Some conditions of obedience and disobedience to authority." *Hum. Relat.,* 1965, **18**, 57–76.

10

Disobedience in the Sixties

Americans who are unwilling to kill for their country are thrown into jail. And our generation learns, as every generation has, that society rewards and punishes its members not in the degree to which each fulfills the dictates of individual conscience but in the degree to which the actions are perceived by authority to serve the needs of the larger social system. It has always been so. Jesus was a good man by any standard of individual morality but a threat to the structure of Roman authority. Every epoch produces its share of highly moral individuals whose very purity pushes them into conflict with the state. The task of democracy is to strive to reconcile the disparity between individual conscience and societal needs.

Resisting induction into the military is a crime only in the purely technical sense that federal statutes provide penalties for it. But the resisters are the very opposite of criminals. First, they act out of moral ideals, not in opposition to them. Second, while the criminal's actions are geared to personal profit, the resister willingly suffers loss to uphold a moral ideal. Third, while the criminal seeks to evade the law, the resister offers himself to it. Nor is the resister a revolutionary: for he accepts the legitimacy of authority without being willing to serve it in specifically immoral ways. Finally, he is not truly alienated: one who has no deep involvement with his country can depart from it without the pains of incarceration.

Willard Gaylin, a psychiatrist, sets out to examine the motives and thoughts of a group of men in prison for war resistance. He moves to a consideration of the flaws of the prison system, and ineluctably is forced to extend his concern to the idea of incarceration itself as a civilized human practice. "The more I thought of it, the more monstrous it seemed that anyone should have the power to deprive another human being of five years of life—merely as punishment." He is right, of course, and putting men in cages will surely come to be seen as one of the barbarisms of our age. It becomes doubly shameful when the men in jail have acted on principles of conscience.

The actual chances of landing in jail vary enormously from one person to the next, depending largely on whether the resister has the wit, cash and proper legal counsel to circumvent the law. With proper religious credentials he is more likely to be granted C.O. status. Inequity in the application of the draft laws is one of the recurrent themes in this subtle and moving account of Gaylin's research.

This paper was a book review of *In the Service of Their Country: War Resisters in Prison*, by Willard Gaylin, New York: Viking, 1970. The review was first published in *The Nation*, Vol. 211, No. 1 (July 6, 1970). Reprinted by permission of *The Nation*.

All of the men studied are war resisters in a special sense. When a man decides that he will not enter the armed forces, several options are open to him. He can go underground (a strategy best suited to ghetto blacks, for whom there are poor administrative records). He can flee the country, or he can attempt to circumvent induction by whispering concocted sexual secrets to the psychiatrist at the induction center. Some dedicated resisters enter the army with the aim of subverting it from within, and they, no doubt, constitute the most dangerous element from the standpoint of the military.

Gaylin's interviewees chose a different course. They refused induction and offered themselves for imprisonment. Even after imprisonment the options were not fully closed, for each man had to decide whether to continue his resistance by refusing to cooperate with prison authorities in any degree, or to serve as a model prisoner. Typically, war resisters chose the latter course, a position that is consistent with their moral stance.

Life in prison is rotten, and it becomes increasingly clear that it is not merely the time taken from normal living that counts as punishment but immersion in a kind of social hell, consisting of tedium, senseless authoritarian routine, and the need to protect oneself from depredations of fellow inmates. Gaylin became a well-liked visitor to the resisters who looked forward to a break from the routine of prison life and a sympathetic ear. The research method thus exemplifies the constructive possibilities of scientific inquiry. The very process of inquiry brought a ray of light to the men. Gaylin's own sensitivity and professional tact ensured that the men did not perceive themselves as guinea pigs. This was further assured by Gaylin's temperate use of psychiatric doctrines. In seeking to find unconscious motives, the author does not discredit conscious ones. He views psychoanalytic concepts as complementary to everyday levels of explanation, and in no way supplants them. He refuses to start with the assumption that going to jail itself constitutes a neurotic symptom.

Gaylin used as his main tool of investigation the psychoanalytic interview, adhering to Freud's doctrine that "it is only when you stop asking questions that the truth emerges." Only occasionally does he turn the subject matter in a direction of interest to him. Mostly he wants to examine the ideas and feelings that the resisters summon up.

The procedure shows the strengths and limitations of the psychiatric interview. Each life is presented vividly and makes sense in its own terms; it is difficult to find generalizations applicable to all the cases. Gaylin is sparse on interpretation, preferring that the client paint his own portrait. The most promising scientific fact deals with birth order: almost all of the war resisters are first sons, suggesting that some special relationship to authority, implicit in the role of the son-who-will-replace-the-father, is at the motivational root of the resister's act.

Gaylin's sympathies lie with the resisters, not so much, I suspect, because they resisted war in general but because they resisted involvement in a particularly odious war. The reader's sympathies will be correspondingly colored by the general antipathy to the Vietnamese adventure. It is not at all clear that the moral advantage the resisters acquire at this particular moment in American history would automatically apply to resistance to all wars at all times.

Although in some respects going to prison has the quality of an act of martyrdom, it differs in that life does not end with the act; it is only interrupted. We have yet to understand how the resister comes retrospectively to fit the experience into the broader pattern of his life. In this connection, it would be helpful to speak to those who had resisted in other wars, and who have now gained a perspective on their actions. Resistance in World War II could serve as a particularly interesting point of comparison, since refusal to serve in the armed forces was not at the time viewed sympathetically by any sizable fraction of the population.

We admire the resisters for their moral stance, but this is not to be confused with an effective political act. The resisters did not win converts in prison; their individual decisions have no effect on the efficiency of the war machine: the man who refuses to go into the army is simply replaced by the next in line. So, we confront a morally inspired, but politically ineffective act of the lone individual against the system. The burden of effective resistance is thus shifted to those willing to sacrifice individual purity for the attainment of practical political goals: evasion of prison, organized collective action, and a willingness to be personally tainted are the price of maximally effective resistance, and are exemplified in the actions of men of stature such as Willy Brandt, who fled Germany to fight Nazism in the Norwegian underground. Some Germans have never forgiven Brandt, but the nation did elect him Premier. It remains to be seen whether Americans will allow similar political opportunities to those who have taken up the battle in Canada.

Since there will always be individuals who refuse induction on moral grounds, the nation must work to eradicate deficiencies in the law. Until the recent Supreme Court decision, belief in a Supreme Being was a *sine qua non* of C.O. status. Philosophic convictions that function as a religion may now be sufficient grounds for granting exemption from military service. But the person must be opposed to all wars. This does not yet reflect the process whereby moral judgments are formed. A person may, on moral grounds, be willing to fight in one war, yet find participation in another war morally repugnant. The law must come to recognize this reality, and permit selective conscientious objection. The technical difficulty is to devise procedures for separating those objections that are rooted in morality and those that are simply self-serving. Finally, the country needs to provide war resisters not the brutal and meaningless experience of prison but constructive forms of alternative national service. The impact of Gaylin's book will help move us in this direction.

THE INDIVIDUAL AND THE GROUP

Part 3

Introduction

How is a group possible? Each participant in the group is a complex individual with purposes and motives of his own, and yet the group is able to function effectively, even with harmony. This must be due to the fact that each individual member adjusts his behavior with reference to the other participants; social psychologists attempt to understand the nature and extent of that adjustment. The effects of groups—small groups as well as the larger aggregation of individuals we term a crowd—are explored in the following pages.

Having made these general observations, it still becomes necessary to find a clear way to study group effects. For me, the decisive paradigm was contained in the group pressure experiments of Solomon E. Asch.

In Asch's experiments, a group of four to six subjects was shown a line of a certain length and had to say which of three lines matched it. All but one of the subjects in the group had been secretly instructed beforehand to select one of the wrong lines on each trial. The naïve subject was so placed that he heard the answers of most of the group before he had to announce his own decision. Asch found that under this form of social pressure, a large fraction of subjects went along with the group rather than accept the unmistakable evidence of their own eyes.

I had the good fortune to work for and with Professor Asch at both Harvard and Princeton. Asch was inspiring, particularly when he was not teaching formally but was simply exposing his cerebral processes in the course of conversation. He is a man of quiet intellectual brilliance.

Most of the papers in this section are variations on the theme of Asch's experiment. I mean "variations" in the musical sense of the term, the way Brahms wrote variations on Haydn. As in music, sometimes the theme of the master is clear and little adorned. Sometimes the original motif is all but obscured, as the variations take off in new directions and become virtually independent of their origins. Probably the master doesn't always like the way his themes are shifted in key and emphasis. *Tant pis*. For me, Asch's experiment rotates as a kind of permanent intellectual jewel. Focus analytic light on it, and it diffracts energy into new and interesting patterns.

Indeed, in my graduate teaching, I have often designed variations of his experiment to carry out as a class exercise, or simply as thought-experiments. The following ten such variations are among my favorites.

1. *Pro-social conformity.* In Asch's experiment, the group is shown to limit, constrain, and distort the individual's response. One variant examined the pro-social effects of group pressure. Subjects were free to decide on an amount to contribute to a series of charities. Confederates upped the amount for each of eight charities, and, under the influence of the group, subjects donated ever-increasing amounts to the charities.

152

"Liberating Effects of Group Pressure" (p. 188) continues this tradition of constructive conformity.

2. *Sequential influence.* In Asch's experiments, the naïve subject faces the unanimous opinion of a simultaneously assembled group. In this variant, subjects are exposed to the unanimous opinion of several individuals, but each confederate confronts the subject individually, on different days, during the course of a week. The influence summates and approximates that of a simultaneously assembled group.

3. *Influencing the alienated.* How would a group influence a person who was negatively oriented toward it? Students were asked to design experimental techniques for influencing the alienated. Some students believed the group can induce the behavior it wants by publicly calling for the opposite, on the assumption that the hostile person will perform contrary to what he thinks the group wants. Others emphasize that it is better to work on reducing the alienation.

4. *Action conformity.* Asch's subjects yield in regard to a verbal judgment. But can the group induce the person to perform *actions* he would not otherwise engage in? What is the range of significant behavior that the group can shape? (See "Group Pressure and Action Against a Person," p. 178.)

5. *Enduring effects of yielding.* In Asch's experiment, the consequence of the subject's yielding does not transcend the laboratory hour. It is a fully self-contained experience. Is this the basis of the group's power? Would a person as readily conform to the group in regard to acts that endure beyond the laboratory hour? For example, would subjects expose their foreheads to a permanent green dye if all of the confederates appeared to do so? Would a naïve subject be willing to sign a marriage certificate if the group sheepishly did so? This is a critical and as yet untested variant.

6. *The group's response to pressure.* Asch's experiment examines how an individual responds to pressures exerted by a group. But how do *groups* respond when they are under the unanimous pressure of a larger field of groups? Asch's partnership variation touches on but does not fully develop this issue.

7. *The conformity of inaction.* Asch's subjects are influenced by a majority that takes a positive action (making a definite judgment). But can a group induce passivity by the example of its own inaction? This shades into typical bystander experiments.

8. *Forewarned subjects.* In this variant, we expressly informed subjects that from time to time members of the group would deliberately give incorrect answers. This changed the basic psychological character of the experience, but surprisingly, some subjects still went along with the group as a kind of reflexive imitation.

9. *Repetition of stimulus.* Subjects in an auditory variation of the Asch experiment (subjects heard two tones and were asked to indicate which was the longer; the group gave the incorrect answer) were free to request a repetition of the stimulus before giving their judgments. Subjects were therefore free to clarify their perception, but few subjects requested a repetition of the tones. This is particularly true of those who yield to the group in their judgment of tonal lengths. Their conformity is so deep, it does not permit them to reduce uncertainty, even when they have an opportunity to do so.

10. *Black box conformity.* In the Asch study, the subject and the group have equal access to the stimulus material. My student, Rita Dytell, carried out a "black box" variation, in which the group had access to the stimulus material but not the subject. This corresponds to the fact that we must often decide whether to accept judgments made by others on events which they have observed but which we have not.

Each variation, substantially inspired by the Asch paradigm, sheds light on a new aspect of social influence and speaks to the immense fecundity of the original experiment.

There is a progression in the several experimental papers reprinted in this section. In "Nationality and Conformity," the effect of group pressure on individual judgments is studied and is shown to vary—a little—from one national setting to the next. The purpose was to use the Asch experiment as a measuring instrument to study the level of conformity in two national cultures. As a result of this experience, I became less interested in national cultures and more interested in the effects of group pressure. Surely it is not limited to changing a person's verbal pronouncement.

The issue of verbal conformity is, of course, extremely important. The entire climate of a community comes to be determined by the freedom which individuals feel to express themselves. The capacity of groups to stultify original expression or dissenting ideas is an important fact of social life. But conformity extends beyond the merely verbal. The very deeds of the person may come to be shaped by the group, and this notion is brought within an experimental framework in "Group Pressure and Action Against a Person." (p. 178)

I have explained elsewhere (p. 94) how the obedience experiments are related to Asch's experiments twice removed—first by substitution of a consequential act for a verbal judgment, and then by focusing on the authority rather than the group. In "Liberating Effects of Group Pressure," we come full circle. The group breaks the yoke of authority, and by its example restores the person's integrity against authoritarian excess.

In real life, the constructive uses of group pressure go considerably beyond this experimental demonstration. Individuals frequently seek out groups whose pressures and standards will help them develop and maintain desired ends. We may welcome the pressures to conform to a group whose values are enlighted and which strengthens our own ideals.

The themes of individual submission to group pressure, the conflict of conscience and authority, and the constructive role that groups have on the individual seem to me central to an individual's experience with the social world. The basic fact of human experience is that we are born into a social matrix, yet each of us strives to be an individual. The social matrix is indispensable to our lives, equips us with language and the habits of civilized men and women, endows us with goals, values, and the needed company of one another. Yet once the values are given to us, they become our very own and the individual must strive to maintain individual conscience, judgment, and critical intellect against the pressures of the crowd, and the assertive strength of doctrinaire authority.

Fig. I.4 *Norwegian subject in group pressure study. (Illustration by Roy Superior.)*

What is most distinctive about people is what they have gotten from others: language, habits of rational thought, humane values. Yet to maintain what is best, an individual often needs to stand alone against the crowd and against authority. A person internalizes these values and must then defend them even against the society that gave them. Though enormous pressures may bear down on a person to abandon critical intelligence, dispense with conscience, and surrender humanity, that person will often prove hardy and resilient, transcend the pressure of the moment, and reaffirm the power and integrity of one's own spirit. Well, as our experiments show, it does not always happen this way. But it remains a worthy ideal.

In addition to the experimental articles, a few excerpts are reprinted from my dissertation, *Conformity in Norway and France*, completed in 1960. The excerpt on ethics (p. 174) is perhaps ironic in that the experiments on obedience were to become a few years later a focus of ethical controversy. Irrespective of the ethical status of the obedience experiment, the specific implication of some critics that I was indifferent to ethical matters is hardly borne out by this early empirical research into experimental ethics.

The excerpt on Norwegian life (p. 171) is included as an example of commentary on larger issues affecting the experiment. Of special importance are the Norwegians' strong sense of group identification and the high degree of social responsibility, issues which could not be fully dealt with in the laboratory.

The section ends with an excerpt from my chapter, "Crowds," written for the *Handbook of Social Psychology*. The difference between crowds and groups is, of course, one of degree. A crowd is a very large group of people which is relatively unorganized and with at least a minimum of interaction. To study crowd phenomena first hand, I immersed myself in episodes of crowd activity, a task that was not difficult, given the ubiquitous social protests of the 1960's. The snapshots on pages 157 and 158, taken at a civil rights rally, illustrate aspects of crowd structure and process which I later described in the *Handbook* chapter (pp. 206–231).

An interest in crowds is healthy for social psychology. It directs the scientist's vision beyond the one-way observation room to meeting halls and the outdoor urban setting where protests are held, rallies take place, and the spontaneous interactions of people occur. All this can only have a tonic effect on a discipline periodically enfeebled by academic preoccupations not tied to the real social world.

REFERENCES

Asch, S. E., 1956. "Studies of independence and conformity: I. A minority of one against a unanimous majority." *Psychological Monographs*, **70** (9, Whole No. 416).

Dytell, R., 1970. "An analysis of how people use groups as a source of information on which to base judgments." Unpublished doctoral dissertation, The City University of New York.

(a) Crowd focus

(b) Differential participation

(c) Crowd boundaries

(d) Communication within the crowd

Fig. 1.5 *Upon receiving the assignment to write a chapter on crowds, the author immersed himself in crowd activities for first-hand observation. Many of the observations were subsequently incorporated into the chapter. Above, the author's photographs of the Boston Civil Rights rally of March 14, 1965.*

(e) Internal substructures

(f) Polarization

(g) Social control

(h) Distillation effect

Fig. I.5 *(continued)*

11   Nationality and Conformity

People who travel abroad seem to enjoy sending back reports on what people are like in various countries they visit. A variety of national stereotypes is part and parcel of popular knowledge. Italians are said to be "volatile," Germans "hard-working," the Dutch "clean," the Swiss "neat," the English "reserved," and so on. The habit of making generalizations about national groups is not a modern invention. Byzantine war manuals contain careful notes on the deportment of foreign populations, and Americans still recognize themselves in the brilliant national portrait drawn by Alexis de Tocqueville more than 100 years ago.

And yet the skeptical student must always come back to the question: "How do I know that what is said about a foreign group is true?" Prejudice and personal bias may color such accounts, and in the absence of objective evidence it is not easy to distinguish between fact and fiction. Thus the problem faced by the modern investigator who wishes to go beyond literary description is how to make an objective analysis of behavioral differences among national groups. By this he means simply an analysis that is not based on subjective judgments and that can be verified by any competent investigator who follows the same methods.

It is easy to show objectively that people in different countries often speak different languages, eat different foods and observe different social customs. But can one go further and show national differences in "character" or "personality"? When we turn to the more subtle dimensions of behavior, there is very little evidence to make a case for national differences. It is not that such differences are to be denied out of hand; it is just that we lack sufficient reliable information to make a clear judgment.

Before reporting the results of my own study let me refer briefly to some earlier efforts to achieve objectivity in studying this elusive problem. One approach has been to examine the literature and other cultural products of a nation in the hope of identifying underlying psychological characteristics. For example, Donald V. McGranahan of Harvard University studied successful stage plays performed in Germany and the U.S. and concluded that German stage characters were more devoted to principles and ideological notions, whereas the Americans were more concerned with the attainment of purely personal satisfactions. The obvious limitation of such a study is that the behavior and attitudes under examination are the synthetic ones of the stage and may bear little or no resemblance to those of real life.

This paper was first published in *Scientific American*, Vol. 205, No. 6 (December 1961), pp. 45–51. Reprinted by permission. Copyright © 1961 by Scientific American, Inc. All rights reserved. Illustrations are by Bernarda Bryson.

Another indirect approach has relied on the tools of clinical psychology. This method was pioneered by anthropologists in the study of small, primitive societies and has only recently been applied to modern urban nations. These studies rely heavily on such tests as the Rorschach ink-blot test and the thematic apperception test (TAT). In the latter the subject is shown a drawing of a situation that can be variously interpreted and is asked to make up a story about it. The major difficulty here is that the tests themselves have not been adequately validated and are basically impressionistic.

Finally, sample surveys of the type developed by Elmo Roper and George Gallup in this country have been applied to the problem. Geoffrey Gorer, an English social scientist, based his study *Exploring English Character* on a questionnaire distributed to 11,000 of his compatriots. The questions dealt with varied aspects of English life, such as courtship patterns, experiences in school and practices in the home. Unfortunately there are many reasons why an individual's answer may not correspond to the facts. He may deliberately distort his answers to produce a good impression, or he may have genuine misconceptions of his own behavior, attributable either to faulty memory or to the blindness people often exhibit toward their own actions and motivations.

These methods should not be dismissed as unimportant in the study of national characteristics. Yet in principle if one wants to know whether the people of one nation behave differently from those of another, it would seem only reasonable to examine the relevant behavior directly, and to do so under conditions of controlled observations in order to reduce the effects of personal bias and to make measurement more precise.

An important step in this direction was reported in 1954 by an international team of psychologists who worked together as the Organization for Comparative Social Research. This team studied reactions to threat and rejection among school children in seven European nations, using hypotheses advanced by Stanley Schachter of Columbia University. The inquiry was not specifically designed to study national characteristics but chiefly to see if certain concepts regarding threat and rejection would hold up when tested in different countries. In the course of the study certain differences between countries did turn up, but the investigators felt they were not necessarily genuine. Conceivably they were due to defects in the experiment or to inadequacies in the theory behind it. Although its focus was on theory validation, this study is a landmark in cross-national research. Unfortunately the Organization for Comparative Social Research halted its research program when the study was completed.

My own investigation was begun in 1957. My objective was to see if experimental techniques could be applied to the study of national characteristics, and in particular to see if one could measure conformity in two European countries: Norway and France. Conformity was chosen for several reasons. First, a national culture can be said to exist only if men adhere, or conform, to common standards of behavior; this is the psychological mechanism underlying all cultural behavior. Second, conformity has become a burning issue in much of current social criticism; critics have argued that people have become too sensitive to the opinions of others, and that this represents an unhealthy development in modern society. Finally, good experimental methods have been developed for measuring conformity.

Fig. 11.1 *The conformity experiment required that the subject discriminate between the lengths of two tones heard through headphones, and measured the extent to which he went along with wrong answers given—it seemed to him—by five other subjects listening to the same tones. Actually no other subjects were present; the illusion was created by tape recordings. The top drawing by Bernarda Bryson shows what the subject saw as he entered the experimental room. The middle drawing shows what the subject, seated in the far left-hand booth, imagined the situation to be while he was taking the test. The drawing at the bottom shows the actual situation.*

The chief tool of investigation was a modified form of the group-pressure experiment used by Solomon E. Asch and other social psychologists. In Asch's original experiment a group of half a dozen subjects was shown a line of a certain length and asked to say which of three other lines matched it. All but one of the subjects had been secretly instructed beforehand to select one of the "wrong" lines on each trial or in a certain percentage of the trials. The naïve subject was so placed that he heard the answers of most of the group before he had to announce his own decision. Asch found that under this form of social pressure a large fraction of subjects went along with the group rather than accept the unmistakable evidence of their own eyes.

Our experiment is conducted with acoustic tones rather than with lines drawn on cards. Five of the subjects are confederates of the experimenter and conspire to put social pressure on the sixth subject. The subjects listen to two tones and are asked to say which is the longer. The five confederates answer first and their decisions are heard by the subject, who answers last. The confederates have been instructed to announce wrong answers on 16 of the 30 trials that constitute one experiment.

We elected to use tones rather than lines because they are better suited to an experimental method using "synthetic groups." Two psychologists working at Yale University, Robert Blake and Jack W. Brehm, had discovered that group-pressure experiments can be conducted without requiring the actual presence of confederates. It is sufficient if the subject thinks they are present and hears their voices through headphones. With tape recordings it is easy to create synthetic groups. Tapes do not have to be paid by the hour and they are always available.

When the test subject entered our laboratory, he saw several coats on hangers and immediately got the impression that others were present. He was taken to one of six closed booths, where he was provided with headphones and a microphone. As he listened to the instructions through the headphones he overheard the voices of the other "subjects" and assumed that all the booths were occupied. During the actual experiment he would hear five taped answers before he was asked to give his own.

Except when we made a technical slip the subject never caught on to the trick. Most subjects became deeply involved in the situation, and strong tensions were generated when they realized they must stand alone against five unanimous opponents. This situation created a genuine and deeply felt conflict that had to be resolved either through independence or conformity.

Once we had refined our techniques at Harvard University we were ready to experiment abroad with Norwegian and French subjects. In which of the two national environments would people go along with the group more and in which would there be greater independence?

Most of the students used in the Norwegian study were students attending the University of Oslo. Because this is the only full-fledged university in Norway, a good geographic representation was obtained. Our test sample included students from beyond the Artic Circle, from the fiord country of western Norway and from Trondheim, the former Viking capital.

When the study moved to Paris, French students were selected who matched the Norwegians in age, level of education, fields of study, sex, marital status, and —so far as possible—social class. Once again a good geographic distribution was

Fig. 11.2 *Norwegian subjects were from the University of Oslo, which has students from the entire country. The dots on the map show the home town or county of the 100 students involved.*

obtained, because students from all parts of France came to study in Paris. A few of the French subjects came from French North African cities. Those used in the experiment were culturally as French as people living on the mainland; they were of French parentage and had been educated in French lycées.

In Norway the entire experiment was conducted by a native Norwegian and all the recorded voices were those of natives. In France the experiments were conducted by native Frenchmen. Much effort was made to match the tone and quality of the Norwegian and French groups. We made many recordings until people who were sensitive to the nuances of both languages were satisfied that equivalent group atmospheres had been achieved.

Twenty Norwegian subjects and the same number of French subjects were studied in the first set of experiments. The Norwegian subjects conformed to the

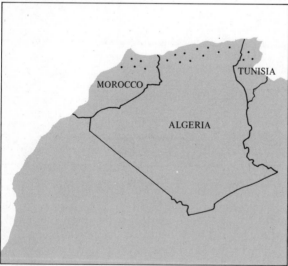

Fig. 11.3 *French subjects were students in Paris chosen to match the Norwegians as closely as possible. The dots show the home department (or area of North Africa) of 95 students.*

group on 62 percent of the critical trials (that is, trials in which the group deliberately voted wrong); the French subjects conformed to the group on 50 percent of the critical trials.

After each subject had taken part in the experiment he was told its true character and was asked to give his reactions. Almost all participants in both countries had accepted the experiment at face value and admitted feeling the strong pressure of the group. A Norwegian student from a farm in Nordland, above the Arctic Circle, said: "I think the experiment had a very ingenious arrangement. I had no idea about the setup until it was explained to me. Of course, it was a little embarrassing to be exposed in such a way." A self-critical student from Oslo remarked: "It was a real trick and I was stupid to have fallen into the trap.... It must be fun to study psychology." Similar reactions were obtained in France, where students were impressed with the idea of psychological experimentation. (In neither country is psychological research as widespread

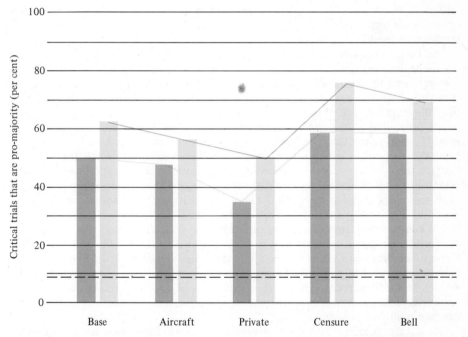

Fig. 11.4 *Level of conformity was higher for Norwegians (light tint) than French subjects (darker tint) in all five test situations, but fluctuated similarly for both. The broken black line indicates the error level of control groups of both nationalities in the absence of pressure. The first set of bars gives results for the basic experiment. In the next situation, significance was increased by an announcement that the test results would affect aircraft safety. This "aircraft" factor was maintained in subsequent tests, in one of which the subjects recorded their answers privately instead of announcing them. In the "censure" situation, critical comments (on tape) stepped up pressure on the subjects. In a final experiment, censure continued and the subjects were allowed to request repetition of the test tones by sounding a bell; fewer Norwegians and Frenchmen proved "bold" enough to do so.*

or as intensive as it is in the U. S., so that subjects are relatively unsophisticated about psychological deceptions.)

It would have been superficial, of course, to conduct just one experiment in Norway, another in France and then draw conclusions. In a second experiment we undertook to change the subject's attitude toward the importance of the experiment itself to see if this might alter the original findings. In this new series of trials (and in all subsequent ones) the subjects were told that the results of the experiments would be applied to the design of aircraft safety signals. In this way their performance was linked to a life-and-death issue. As one might have predicted, the subjects this time showed somewhat greater independence of the group, but once again the level of conformity was higher in Norway (56 percent) than it was in France (48 percent).

One possibility that had to be considered at the outset was that Norwegians and Frenchmen differ in their capacity for discriminating tonal lengths and that this led to the greater number of errors made by Norwegians in the group situation. We were able to show, however, by giving each subject a tone-discrimination test, that there was no difference in the level of discrimination of students in the two countries.

In both of the first two conformity experiments the subjects were required to do more than decide an issue in the face of unanimous opposition: they were also required to announce that decision openly for all to hear (or so the subject thought). Thus the act had the character of a public statement. We all recognize that the most obvious forms of conformity are the public ones. For example, when prevailing standards of dress or conduct are breached, the reaction is usually immediate and critical. So we decided we had better see if the Norwegians conformed more only under public conditions, when they had to declare their answers aloud. Accordingly, we undertook an experiment in both countries in which the subject was allowed to record his answers on paper rather than announce them to the group. The experiments were performed with a new group of 20 Norwegian and 20 French students.

When the requirement of a public response was eliminated, the amount of conformity dropped considerably in both countries. But for the third time the French subjects were more independent than the Norwegians. In Paris students went along with the group on 34 percent of the critical trials. In Oslo the figure was close to 50 percent. Therefore elimination of the requirement of a public response reduced conformity 14 percentage points in France but only 6 percentage points in Norway.

It is very puzzling that the Norwegians so often voted with the group, even when given a secret ballot. One possible interpretation is that the average Norwegian, for whatever reason, believes that his private action will ultimately become known to others. Interviews conducted among the Norwegians offer some indirect evidence for this conjecture. In spite of the assurances that the responses would be privately analyzed, one subject said he feared that because he had disagreed too often the experimenter would assemble the group and discuss the disagreements with them.

Another Norwegian subject, who had agreed with the group 12 out of 16 times, offered this explanation: "In the world now, you have to be not too much in opposition. In high school I was more independent than now. It's the modern way of life that you have to agree a little more. If you go around opposing, you might be looked upon as bad. Maybe this had an influence." He was then asked, "Even though you were answering in private?" and he replied, "Yes. I tried to put myself in a public situation, even though I was sitting in the booth in private."

A fourth experiment was designed to test the sensitivity of Norwegian and French subjects to a further aspect of group opinion. What would happen if subjects were exposed to overt and audible criticism from the conspiratorial group? It seemed reasonable to expect a higher degree of conformity under these conditions. On the other hand, active criticism might conceivably lead to a greater show of independence. Moreover, the Norwegians might react one way and the French another. Some of my associates speculated that audible criticism would merely serve to annoy the French subjects and make them stubborn and more resistant to the influence of the group.

To test these notions we recorded a number of appropriate reactions that we could switch on whenever the subject gave a response that contradicted the majority. The first sanction, in both Norway and France, was merely a slight snicker by a member of the majority. The other sanctions were more severe. In Norway they were based on the sentence "Skal du stikke deg ut?" which may be translated: "Are you trying to show off?" Roughly equivalent sentences were used with the French group. In Paris, when the subject opposed the group, he might hear through his headphones: "Voulez-vous faire remarquer?" ("Trying to be conspicuous?")

In both Norway and France this overt social criticism significantly increased conformity. In France subjects now went along with the majority on 59 percent of the critical trials. In Norway the percentage rose to 75 percent. But the reactions of subjects in the two countries was even more striking. In Norway subjects accepted the criticism impassively. In France, however, more than half the subjects made some retaliatory response of their own when the group criticized them. Two French students, one from the Vosges mountain district and the other from the Department of Eure-et-Loire, became so enraged they directed a stream of abusive language at their taunters.

Even after we explained in the interview session that the entire experimental procedure had been recorded on tape, many of the subjects did not believe us. They could not understand how we could interject comments with such verisimilitude, particularly since we could not predict how they would respond at any given moment. This was achieved by making use of two tape recorders. One played the standard tape containing tones and the group judgments, with "dead" time for the subject; the other contained only the set of "criticisms" from members of the group. The two instruments could be controlled independently, allowing us to inject a remark whenever the subject's responses made it appropriate. The remarks followed the subject's·independent responses immediately, creating a highly spontaneous effect.

Another series of experiments was designed to aid in the interpretation of the earlier findings. For example, many Norwegian subjects rationalized their behavior by stating in the interview that they went along with the others because they doubted their own judgment, and that if they had been given a chance to dispel this doubt they would have been more independent. An experiment was

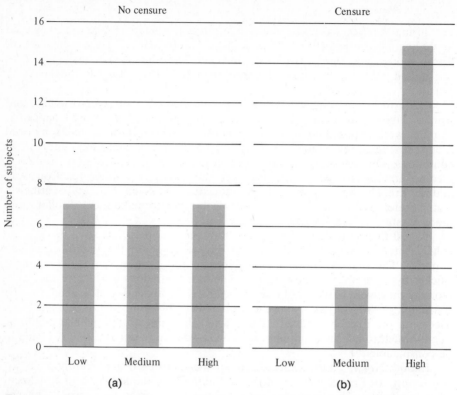

Fig. 11.5 *Effect of censure was to increase conformity. The charts show the degree of conformity among 20 Norwegians in the absence of censure (a) and when censure was introduced in the form of criticism (b) The "low"-conformity category includes those who gave 6 or fewer promajority responses out of 16; "medium" is 7 to 11, and "high" is 12 or more.*

therefore carried out to test this notion. The subject was given a chance to reexamine the stimulus materials before giving his final judgment. He did this by sounding a bell in his booth whenever he wished to hear a pair of tones again. As before, the subject was openly censured by the group if he failed to conform, but he was not censured merely for asking to hear the tones repeated. It turned out that even the relatively simple act of requesting a repetition must be construed as an act of considerable independence. Only five of the Norwegians asked for a repetition of a tone on any trial, whereas 14 of the French subjects were "bold" enough to do so. And again the French showed more independence over-all, voting with the group on 58 percent of the critical trials, compared with 69 percent for the Norwegians.

The study next moved out of the university and into the factory. When we tested 40 Norwegian industrial workers, we found that their level of conformity was about the same as that of the Norwegian students. There was, however, one important difference. Students were often tense and agitated during the experiment. The industrial workers took it all with good humor and frequently were amused when the true nature of the experiment was explained. We have not yet managed to study a comparable group of industrial workers in France.

No matter how the data are examined they point to greater independence among the French than among the Norwegians. Twelve percent of the Norwegian students conformed to the group on every one of the 16 critical trials, while only 1 percent of the French conformed on every occasion. Forty-one percent of the French students but only 25 percent of the Norwegians displayed strong independence. And in every one of the five experiments performed in both countries the French showed themselves to be the more resistant to group pressure.

These findings are by no means conclusive. Rather they must be regarded as the beginning of an inquiry that one would like to see extended. But incomplete as the findings are, they are likely to be far more reliable than armchair speculation on national character.

It is useful, nevertheless, to see if the experimental results are compatible with a nation's culture as one can observe it in daily life. If there were a conflict between the experimental findings and one's general impressions, further experiments and analysis would be called for until the conflict had been resolved. Conceivably the discrepancy might be due to viewing the culture through a screen of stereotypes and prejudices rather than seeing it with a clear eye. In any case, in our study experiment and observation seem to be in reasonable agreement. For whatever the evidence may be worth, I will offer my own impressions of the two countries under examination.

I found Norwegian society highly cohesive. Norwegians have a deep feeling of group identification, and they are strongly attuned to the needs and interests of those around them. Their sense of social responsibility finds expression in formidable institutions for the care and protection of Norwegian citizens. The heavy taxation required to support broad programs of social welfare is borne willingly. It would not be surprising to find that social cohesiveness of this sort goes hand in hand with a high degree of conformity.

Compared with the Norwegians, the French show far less consensus in both social and political life. The Norwegians have made do with a single constitution, drafted in 1814, while the French have not been able to achieve political stability within the framework of four republics. Though I hardly propose this as a general rule of social psychology, it seems true that the extreme diversity of opinion found in French national life asserts itself also on a more intimate scale. There is a tradition of dissent and critical argument that seeps down to the local *bistro*. The high value placed on critical judgment often seems to go beyond reasonable bounds; this in itself could account for the comparatively low degree of conformity we found in the French experiments. Furthermore, as Stanley Schachter has shown, the chronic existence of a wide range of opinion helps to free the individual from social pressure. Much the same point is made in recent studies of U.S. voting behavior. They reveal that the more a person is exposed to diverse viewpoints, the more likely he is to break away from the voting pattern of his native group. All these factors would help to explain the relatively independent judgments shown by French students.

The experiments demonstrate, in any case, that social conformity is not exclusively a U.S. phenomenon, as some critics would have us believe. Some amount of conformity would seem necessary to the functioning of any social system. The problem is to strike the right balance between individual initiative and social authority.

One may ask whether or not national borders really provide legitimate boundaries for the study of behavioral differences. My feeling is that boundaries are useful only to the extent to which they coincide with cultural, environmental or biological divisions. In many cases boundaries are themselves a historical recognition of common cultural practice. Furthermore, once boundaries are established they tend to set limits of their own on social communication.

For all this, a comparison of national cultures should not obscure the enormous variations in behavior within a single nation. Both the Norwegians and the French displayed a full range of behavior from complete independence to complete conformity. Probably there is no significant national comparison in which the extent of overlap does not approach or match the extent of differences. This should not prevent us, however, from trying to establish norms and statistically valid generalizations on behavior in different nations.

We are now planning further research in national characteristics. In a recent seminar at Yale University students were given the task of trying to identify behavioral characteristics that might help to illuminate the Nazi epoch in German history. The principal suggestions were that Germans might be found to be more aggressive than Americans, to submit more readily to authority and to display greater discipline. Whether these assumptions will hold up under experimental inquiry is an open question.

NOTE

1. The research in Norway was carried out at the Institute for Social Research, Oslo, and at the Psychological Institute of the University of Oslo. Special thanks are due to Erik Rinde and Asa Grude Skaard, of these respective institutions, for their generous cooperation. In France, Dr. Robert Pagès, of the University of Paris, was most helpful in securing facilities for the conduct of the research. My research assistants were Guttorm Langaard and Michel Maugis.

REFERENCES

ASCH, S. E., "Effects of group pressure upon the modification and distortion of judgement." In H. Guetzkow (ed.), *Groups, Leadership and Men.* Pittsburgh: The Carnegie Press, 1951.

BLAKE, R. R., and BREHM, J. W., "The use of tape recording to simulate a group atmosphere." *J. Abnorm. and Soc. Psychol.,* 1954, **49**, 311–313.

CASTBERG, F., *The Norwegian way of Life.* London: W. Heinemann, 1954.

GORER, G., *Exploring English Character.* New York: Criterion Books, 1955.

INKELES, A., and LEVINSON, D. J., "National character: the study of modal personality and sociocultural systems." In G. Lindzey (ed.), *Handbook of Social Psychology* (Vol. II). Cambridge, Mass.: Addison-Wesley, 1954, pp. 977–1020.

McGRANAHAN, D. V., and WAYNE, I., "German and American traits reflected in popular drama." *Human Relations,* 1948, I, 429–455.

RODNICK, D., *The Norwegians: a study in national culture.* Washington: Public Affairs Press, 1955.

SCHACHTER, S., NUTTIN, J., DE MONCHAUX, C., MAUCORPS, P. H., OSMER, D., DUIJKER, H., ROMMETVEIT, R., and ISRAEL, J., "Cross-cultural experiments on threat and rejection." *Human Relations,* 1954, **7**, 403–439.

12 Conformity and Norwegian Life

Norwegian society is highly cohesive. Norwegians have a deep feeling of group identification, and they are strongly attuned to the wants and interests of those around them. The possibilities for action are constantly referred to the manner in which this action will impinge on others, and behavior is regulated accordingly.

Norwegians are a very considerate people, and they possess a high degree of social responsibility. This social closeness, sense of cohesiveness, and concern for others is revealed in many aspects of Norwegian life: On the one hand, it is given expression in formidable social institutions for the care and protection of people. Highly developed schemes of social welfare have evolved in modern Norway. There is a pervasive concern for the well-being of others and a willingness to support systems of public welfare through heavy taxation.

On the other hand, this cohesiveness, social closeness, finds expression in an extreme democratic conformism. There is a strong feeling that one must not try to show oneself as better than the next man. Displays of personal brilliance are discouraged. Even at the level of primary education, school children are discouraged from raising their hands too often. Norwegians play down qualitative differences among men; it is part of their egalitarian ethos.

In Norway not even the King can put on airs. He symbolizes the unity of the Norwegian people, but he wears a business suit, shops in the local market, and sends his children to the public schools. Almost anyone can arrange an interview with him. He is not thought to possess special personal qualities absent from the average Norwegian.

A Norwegian who attempts to place himself in the foreground by his actions, who tries to set himself apart from others, is violating tenets of good behavior. This norm is particularly well entrenched in Norwegian social life, and was reflected in the behavior of Norwegians in the experiment.

There are important regional differences in Norway, but within any particular region there is very general accord with regard to basic issues. Norwegians argue and debate a good deal, but they phrase their arguments within a framework of fundamental values that is rarely violated. To cite a mundane example: Norwegians may argue whether a sewage disposal plant should be placed in this end of town, or that end of town, but *none* will argue for the value of dirt. Many Frenchmen, also, believe ardently in the value of sanitation, but

Excerpted from my doctoral dissertation, *Conformity in Norway and France: An Experimental Study of National Characteristics*, Cambridge, Mass.: Harvard University, 1960, pp. 197–203. Reprinted by permission of the President and Fellows of Harvard University. The late Gordon W. Allport was my thesis advisor and the research was supported by a fellowship from the Social Science Research Council.

that did not prevent one Parisian student from telling me: "Sewage disposal plant! Who wants to get rid of refuse? Dirt is God's gift to humanity, the creative matrix out of which all art and imagination arise. Show me a clean city, and you are showing me a sterile culture." Most Frenchmen would say such a thing only as a joke, but this particular student happened to be serious. No Norwegian—even in jest—would argue beyond questions of location, financing, and design of the sewage disposal plant. In Norway, arguments occur within a clearly defined structure of consensus.

In the political sphere Norwegians do have party alignments, but again, there is such general agreement on the way the state should be organized that matters in the Storting proceed with admirable smoothness, and there is good will among members of different political groups.

It is no wonder, then, that the experiment created a particularly intense conflict for the Norwegian subjects: it required that accord be destroyed with regard to a very fundamental issue.

Oslo, although it is the capital, has a small town, provincial aspect to it that contrast sharply with such sophisticated cities as Paris and Copenhagen. There is in Oslo a greater continuity with rural traditions; most of the present inhabitants are not more than two generations removed from the farm. In numbers, it is a city of only 400,000, and even for this size, seems small. In any particular circle, such as students or lawyers, there will be face to face contact among a substantial proportion of all members. Thus to some extent Oslo culture is governed by its small town qualities. In this connection it is well to mention the *Janteloven* (a well know literary reference among educated Norwegians). The "Jante Laws" refer to the ten "commandments" imposed on the individual by provincial society.[1] Three of the commandments are:

Du skal ikke innbille dig at du er bedre enn *oss*.
(*Thou shalt not believe thyself better than us.*)

Du skal ikke tro at du vet mere enn *oss*.
(*Thou shalt not believe thou knowest more than us.*)

Du skal ikke tro du er klopere enn *oss*.
(*Thou shalt not think thou art wiser than us.*)

It was almost as if many experimental subjects in Norway were striving to observe these "commandments." The small scale of Norwegian society is probably an important determinant of the high level of conformity found there.

The pressures for conformity being great, the requirements for good behavior being so pervasive, do Norwegians have any socially acceptable mechanisms for achieving relief from these pressures? I think they do in at least two forms, drunkenness, and escape from the field through sport and travel. The quantity of alcohol consumed in Norway is less astonishing than the way it is used. Norwegians imbibe large amounts of alcohol in a short time, so that they become drunk. Indeed, intoxication appears to be the goal. At a party among educated young people, the first fifteen minutes is typically sedate, almost stiff. Guests sit around, talk quietly, and drink *aquavit*. Within an hour everyone is drunk, but seriously so. Parties get loud, rowdy, and often wild. It is astonishing to see Oslo late on Saturday night. One will always find intoxicated persons reeling in the streets, often singing. Alcohol is an important device for achieving respite from the requirements of strict conformity to good behavior, which is the typical behavior of Norwegians.

A second mechanism of release from group pressure is to escape from the field; this is done in a socially approved way in the form of long, solitary hikes and, in the winter, through ski journeys. Norwegians often say that they wish, sometimes, to be alone in the mountains. A student from Western Norway remarked that he often felt the need to escape into the valleys, and that he found solace there. One finds a good many expressions of this sentiment among Norwegians.

Travel to foreign countries is a second device for escaping from the field, and Norwegians go abroad in large numbers. To be sure, there is a widespread and genuine interest in foreign lands and peoples, but travel also brings relaxation from the strong social pressures of home. Many Norwegians become less inhibited in a foreign milieu, but they are rarely able to maintain this stance upon returning to Norway.

Norwegian society, then, is small in scale and cohesive; there is strong group feeling and attention to the welfare and opinions of others. There is a widespread internalization of common values, a high degree of social responsibility, a tendency to play down individual differences (and, in particular, characteristics that make one person outstanding relative to another). There is a high degree of democratic conformism.

It must not be thought, however, that conformity to group norms is either a painful or, in some sense, a degrading experience. It depends on the content of the norms. The Norwegian way of life has at its core, values that are humanitarian, egalitarian, and progressive. Adherence to such standards can be elevating.

NOTE

1. I am grateful to Mr. Ulf Torgersen for introducing me to the "Jante Laws" (as well as to many other aspects of Norwegian society). The *Janteloven* stem from a satirical novel by the Danish author, Aksel Sandemose, which was published in Norwegian under the title, "En Flyktning Kryser Sitt Spor" (A Runaway Crosses His Path). Oslo: Tiden Norsk Forlag, 1933.

Ethics in the Conformity Experiment: An Empirical Study 13

A s part of the study of group pressure in Norway, I investigated the subjects' reactions to the ethics of the experiment. In the laboratory, many subjects revealed aspects of their personalities that might be considered unflattering; conformist subjects felt ashamed or even humiliated when, in the interview, they were confronted with the true nature of the experiment. Furthermore, the subject was invited to the laboratory under false pretenses, and was misinformed by the experimenter while he was there. Subjects were deceived into believing (1) that others were present, (2) that the others were answering honestly, and (3) that the experimental findings would have an important humanitarian application. Although subjects were informed of the true character of the experiment immediately after they had performed in it, the ethical issue remains. With a view toward gauging the subjects' reactions to this issue, a questionnaire was distributed to the Norwegian student subjects.

One hundred and twenty questionnaires were distributed approximately two months after the subjects' participation in the experiment. Ninety-six of these were completed and returned. We assume that a few of the twenty-four that were not returned never reached the addressees, because of incorrect addressing, etc. However, this is not the only factor. In Table 13.1 we compare performance in the experiment with the number of unreturned questionnaires.

Table 13.1 Percentage of persons returning questionnaire as a function of performance in the experiment.

Degree of conformity	Number of questionnaires returned	Number of questionnaires not returned	Percentage of questionnaires returned
Low	29	0	100
Medium	25	6	80.6
High	42	18	70.0

We see that 100 percent of the low conformity subjects, 81 percent of the medium conformity subjects, and only 70 percent of those who had yielded twelve or more times returned the questionnaires.

Excerpted from my doctoral dissertation, *Conformity in Norway and France: An Experimental Study of National Characteristics*, Cambridge, Mass.: Harvard University, 1960, pp. 170–176. Reprinted by permission of the President and Fellows of Harvard University.

Thus, in considering the questionnaires, we should keep in mind that there is a systematic bias in favor of the responses of high independence subjects.

In one question we asked the subject how he had felt immediately after performing in the experiment. The open-ended form allowed for maximum freedom of response and, while a variety of moods are expressed, no subject seems to have been shaken too badly. One subject used the word "brutal" but referred only to his experience in the course of the experiment and not to its enduring effects. Most subjects said they were annoyed with themselves for not having penetrated the true character of the experiment.

In another question, we asked whether, from the present perspective, the subject thought the experiment ethical or unethical. In order to stack the cards against the experimenter, we included two negative, one positive, and one neutral response categories. The results are reproduced in Table 13.2.

Table 13.2 Do you feel now that the experiment was ethical or unethical

Very unethical	0
Unethical	8
Ethical	14
Neither ethical nor unethical	69
	91
(No answer)	5
	$N = 96$

Eight persons reported that the experiment was unethical, but some offered qualifying remarks:

> The experiment is unethical because one gets into it on false premises, but I suppose such an experiment can only be set up in such a way.

> One should perhaps tolerate this much for the benefit of science. All the same, it is not quite right to fool people in this way.

It is clear from the free comments to this question that when subjects judge the experiment to be "ethical" they refer to positive, edifying effects resulting from the experience. Thus one subject in this category wrote:

> I felt as if it was a lesson for me. It's healthy as a prevention against mass mentality.

Others indicated that, despite the discomfort, they had learned much from it.

By far the largest number of subjects declared that the experiment was neither ethical nor unethical. Many indicated that they did not understand how one could use these terms in connection with a scientific experiment. Some responded with the general principle: "Every scientific experiment is beyond ethics." Others pointed out that the ethicality of the experiment would depend on the uses to which its findings were put.

Some students mentioned specific features of the experimental procedure that in their minds kept it above board. One subject wrote:

> When the experiment is kept strongly confidential, and the subjects have volunteered, the experiment in my opinion cannot be either ethical or unethical.

The following themes recur frequently in the students' responses: that subjects had volunteered for the experiment; that the results were kept confidential; and that the purpose of the experiment was explained to them. For most subjects these features counted in favor of the experiment, and compensated for the initial deceptions.

A law student from Oslo expressed the most common reaction when he wrote:

> I must say that the word "ethical"—either with or without the "un"—was never in my thoughts in connection with this experiment. I mean that the test in itself is neither ethical nor unethical, neither moral nor immoral. It might on the other hand serve a moral purpose, namely greater intellectual honesty. If the experiment contributes to this aim, it serves a purpose of immense value.

A less direct approach to the problem was to ask the students how they felt in general about having participated in the experiment. Table 13.3 shows the distribution of answers in terms of the five response categories provided.

Table 13.3   How do you feel now about having been in the experiment?

I'm very glad to have been in the experiment	22
I'm glad to have been in the experiment	48
I am neither sorry nor glad to have been in the experiment	22
I'm sorry to have been in the experiment	1
I'm very sorry to have been in the experiment	0
	93
(No answer)	3
	$N = 96$

It appears that most subjects were glad to have participated, despite the trickery involved. The reasons for this seem to be: First, they understood that any deception used was not primarily for personal gain, but for the advancement of knowledge. They appreciated that they were informed of the true character of the experiment as soon as possible. They understood that whatever their performance may have been, we placed them in a position of trust by revealing the true purpose and methods of the experiment, and they knew that the success of the experimental project depended on their willingness to support this trust. If for twenty minutes we abused their dignity, we reaffirmed it by extending to them our confidence. Third—and this was an unexpected advantage of using tape-recorded stooges—most subjects exhibited relief when they learned that other persons were not really present. The high conformers, especially, were glad that their performances were essentially private, and would be kept confidential.

Again, we remind the reader that twenty-four subjects did not respond to the questionnaire, and they were concentrated among the high conformers. Perhaps, had they responded, we would have had a good many more damaging criticisms on hand. Furthermore, the results are based solely on the sample of Norwegian students. My guess is that responses from the French students would have been more critical. On the basis of the results we have, however, I think it is fair to say that most subjects accept the necessity of deception in this experiment, and do not condemn it morally. That is not to say they should have the last word on the matter. No action is divested of its unethical properties by the expedient of a public-opinion poll; neither is the outcome of such an inquiry irrelevant to the issue.

Group Pressure and Action Against a Person[1]

14

A great many variations of a paradigm provided by Asch (1951) show that there is an intelligible relationship between several features of the social environment and the degree to which a person will rely on others for his public judgments. Because it possesses merits of simplicity, clarity, and reconstructs in the laboratory powerful and socially relevant psychological processes, this paradigm has gained widespread acceptance as a basic technique of research on influence processes.

One feature that has been kept constant through the variations on Asch's work is that verbal judgment has been retained as the end product and basic index of conformity. More generally, a *signal* offered by the subject as representing his judgment has been the focus of study. Most often the signal has taken the form of a verbal pronouncement (Asch, 1956; Milgram, 1961), though mechanical devices which the subject uses to signal his judgment have also been employed (Crutchfield, 1955; Tuddenham & MacBride, 1959).

A distinction can be made between *signal conformity* and *action conformity* in that the immediate consequence of the former is purely informational; the subject states his opinion or reports on his perception of some feature of the environment. Action conformity, on the other hand, produces an immediate effect or alteration in the milieu that goes beyond a contribution of information. It refers to the elicitation of a *deed* by group forces, the induction of an act that is more than communicative in its effect. The act may be directed toward the well being of another person (e.g., a man is induced by group pressure to share bread with a beggar) or it may be oriented toward nonsocial parts of the environment (a delinquent is induced by gang pressure to throw a rock at a shop window).

There is little reason to assume a priori that observations made with regard to verbal conformity are automatically applicable to action. A person may pay lip service to the norms of a group and then be quite unwilling to carry out the kinds of behavior the group norms imply. Furthermore, an individual may accept and even promulgate a group standard at the verbal level, and yet find himself *unable* to translate the belief into deeds. Here we refer not to the distinction between overt compliance and private acceptance, but of the relationship between a genuinely accepted belief and its transformation into behavior.

This paper was first published in the *Journal of Abnormal and Social Psychology*, Vol. 69, No. 2 (August 1964), pp. 137–143. Copyright © 1964 by the American Psychological Association. Reprinted by permission.

The main point of the present experiment is to see if a person will perform acts under group pressure that he would not have performed in the absence of social inducement. There are many particular forms of action that can be inserted into a general group-pressure experimental design. One could study sorting IBM cards, or making paper cutouts, or eating crackers. Convenience makes them attractive, and in several valuable experiments investigators have used these tasks to good advantage (Frank, 1944; French, Morrison, & Levinger, 1960; Raven & French, 1958). But eventually social psychology must come to grips with significant behavior contents, contents that are of interest in their own right and are not simply trivial substitutes for psychologically meaningful forms of behavior. Guided by this consideration, a relatively potent form of action was selected for shaping by group pressure. We asked: Can a group induce a person to deliver punishment of increasing severity to a protesting individual? Whereas Asch and others have shown in what manner group pressure can cause a person to pronounce judgments that contradict his thinking, the present study examines whether group pressure causes a person to engage in acts at variance with his uninfluenced behavior.

METHOD

The details of subject recruitment, subject composition, experimenter's introductory patter, apparatus, and learning task have been described elsewhere (Milgram, 1963) and need only be sketched here.

Subjects consisted of 80 male adults, ranging in age from 20 to 50 years, and distributed in equal numbers, ages, and occupational statuses in the experimental and control conditions.

Procedure for Experimental Condition

General. The basic experimental situation is one in which a team of three persons (including two confederates) tests a fourth person on a paired-associate learning task. Whenever the fourth party makes a mistake the team punishes him with an electric shock. The two confederates suggest increasingly higher shock levels; the experimenter observes in what degree the third member of the team (a naive subject) goes along with or resists the confederates' pressure to increase the voltage levels.

Details. Four adults arrive at a campus laboratory to participate in a study of memory and learning. On arrival each subject is paid $4.50. The experimenter explains that a variety of roles must be performed in the experiment, and that to make role assignments fairly, subjects are to draw printed slips from a hat, each slip designating a particular experimental role. Actually, three of the adults are confederates, and only one naive subject is tested each hour. The drawing is rigged so that the naive subject is always assigned the position, Teacher 3, and Confederate *B* is always the Learner. The role assignments, which the subjects read from the drawn slips, are as [shown on the next page].

The experimenter explains that the purpose of the experiment is to study the effects of punishment on memory in a context of "collective teaching." Confederate *B* is taken to an adjoining room and in full view of the others is

Role title	Participant	Task
Teacher 1	Confederate *C*	First, you will read word pairs to the learner. Then you will read a stimulus word along with four possible answers.
Teacher 2	Confederate *A*	When the learner gives his answer, your task is to indicate whether he is correct or incorrect. When he has erred you will provide him with the correct answer.
Teacher 3	Naive subject	Whenever the learner gives an incorrect answer, you will administer punishment by activating a shock generator.
Learner	Confederate *B*	Your task will be to learn a list of word pairs read to you by Teacher 1.

strapped into an electric-chair apparatus. The experimenter explains the nature of the learning task to the Learner and, passing over a remark made by the Learner concerning a mild heart condition, takes the three teachers to the main experimental room.

They are seated before an imposing shock generator whose essential feature is a horizontal line of 30 lever switches, labeled 15–450 volts, in 15-volt increments. Verbal designations are spread along the line of switches reading: Slight Shock, Moderate Shock, Strong Shock, Very Strong Shock, Intense Shock, Extreme Intensity Shock, and Danger: Severe Shock.

The experimenter restates that the Learner is to be tested on a paired-associate learning task (see Milgram, 1963, for details). Teachers are told that the Learner must be shocked each time he errs in the learning task. The experimenter explains how the level of shock is to be determined:

> Now the amount of punishment given on any trial is decided by the teachers themselves. Each of you will suggest a shock level. And the shock actually administered will be the lowest level suggested by any of the three teachers. In order to keep the experiment running smoothly, give suggested levels in this order: Teacher 1, submit your bid first; Teacher 2, submit your bid second; and Teacher 3, submit your bid third. Remember you can stick to one level or raise or lower your level as you desire, but on any trial, the punishment administered will be the lowest level suggested by any teacher on that trial.

Thus the naive subject finds himself in a position in which, on any trial, he can effectively control the maximum shock administered to the Learner, e.g., the ground rules of the experiment would permit him to hold the shock level down to 15 volts throughout the laboratory session. On the other hand he may go along with or move in the direction of the group choice. It is the naive subject who actually administers the shock by depressing the appropriate lever on the generator (i.e., he always emerges from the rigged drawing as Teacher 3).

The three teachers each have their roles spelled out for them again, and there remains only the task of giving each a sample shock from the generator before the experiment gets under way.

Behavior of teachers 1 and 2 (confederates). According to a prearranged schedule the two confederates at the shock generator call for a one-step increase in the shock level each time the Learner errs. On the first error they both call for Shock Level 1 (15 volts); on the twentieth error they both call for Shock Level 20 (300 volts), and so forth. Their constant unanimity is rendered credible by having Teacher 1 play a somewhat domineering, and Teacher 2 a somewhat submissive type. The confederates, played by adult actors, appear indifferent to the complaints of the Learner.

Behavior of the learner. According to a prearranged schedule the Learner responds to the learning task by providing answers in the proportion of three wrong answers to each correct one. There are a total of 40 trials, 30 of them being critical (occasions when the Learner answers incorrectly).

The Learner's responses are not limited to providing answers. As the shocks administered to him become stronger, he grunts, protests, and demands to be let out of the experiment. Each complaint of the Learner is in fact prerecorded on magnetic tape, and is coordinated to a specific shock level. The protests and expressions of discomfort follow spontaneously the administration of an electric shock.

The Learner indicates no discomfort until the 75-volt shock is administered, at which time there is a slight grunt in response to the punishment. Similar reactions follow the 90- and 105-volt shocks, and at 120 volts the Learner shouts to the experimenter that the shocks are becoming painful. Painful groans are heard on the administration of the 135-volt shock, and at 150 volts the Learner cries out that he wants to be released from the experiment, complaining of a heart disturbance. Cries of this type continue with generally rising intensity, so that at 180 volts, the Learner cries out "I can't stand the pain," and by 285 volts his response to the shock is clearly an agonized scream. At 300 volts the victim shouts in desperation that he will no longer provide answers to the memory test, and so forth through 450 volts. In other words, increases in shock level are met by increasingly severe reactions from the person being punished.

It is to be remembered that this is merely a *potential* series of responses. If a shock no higher than the 75-volt level is administered, only a grunt is heard. As a point of procedure, protests were not repeated at the same shock level, e.g., after the first grunt was used in response to Shock Level 75, no further complaints were introduced until and if a higher shock level were used.

Experimental measures. The principal experimental measure, therefore, is the level of shock administered by the subject on each of the 30 critical trials. The shock levels were automatically recorded by an Esterline-Angus event recorder wired directly into the shock generator, providing us with a permanent record of each subject's performance.

Postexperimental session. An interview and debriefing session were held immediately after each subject's performance. A variety of background measures was obtained, as well as qualitative reactions to the experimental situation.

Control Condition

The purpose of the control condition is to determine the level of shock the naive subject administers to the Learner in the absence of group influence. One naive subject and one confederate (the Learner) perform in each session. The procedure is identical to that in the experimental condition, except that the tasks of Confederates *A* and *C* are collapsed into one role handled by the naive subject. References to collective teaching are omitted.

The naive subject is instructed to administer a shock each time the Learner errs, and the naive subject is told that as teacher he is free to select any shock level on any of the trials. In all other respects the control and experimental procedures are identical.

RESULTS

Figure 14.1 shows the mean shock levels for each critical trial in the experimental and control conditions. It also shows a diagonal representing the stooge-group's suggested shock level on each critical trial. The degree to which the experimental function moves away from the control level and toward the stooge-group diagonal represents the effects of group influence. Inspection indicates that the confederates substantially influenced the level of shock administered to the Learner. The results will now be considered in detail.

In the experimental condition the standard deviation of shock levels rose regularly from trial to trial, and roughly in proportion to the rising mean shock level. However, in the control condition the standard deviation did not vary systematically with the mean through the 30 trials. Representative mean shock levels and standard deviations for the two conditions are shown in Table 14.1. Hartley's test for homogeneity of variance confirmed that the variances in the two conditions were significantly different. Therefore a reciprocal-of-the-square -root transformation was performed before an analysis of variance was carried out.

As summarized in Table 14.2, the analysis of variance showed that the overall mean shock level in the experimental condition was significantly higher than that in the control condition ($p < 0.001$). This is less interesting, however, than the differing slopes in the two conditions, which show the group effects through the course of the experimental session.[2] The analysis of variance test for trend confirmed that the slopes for the two conditions differed significantly ($p < 0.001$).

Examination of the standard deviations in the experimental condition shows that there are large individual differences in response to group pressure, some

Table 14.1 Representative mean shock levels and standard deviations in the experimental and control conditions.

| Trail | Experimental condition | | Control condition | |
	Mean shock level	SD	Mean shock level	SD
5	4.03	1.19	3.35	2.39
10	6.78	2.63	3.48	3.03
15	9.20	4.28	3.68	3.58
20	11.45	6.32	4.13	4.90
25	13.55	8.40	3.55	3.85
30	14.13	9.59	3.38	1.89

subjects following the group closely, others resisting effectively. Subjects were ranked according to their total deviation from the confederates' shock choices. On the thirtieth critical trial the most conforming quartile had a mean shock level of 27.6, while the mean shock level of the least conforming quartile was 4.8. Background characteristics of the experimental subjects were noted: age, marital status, occupation, military experience, political preference, religious affiliation, birth-order information, and educational history. Less educated subjects (high school degree or less) tended to yield more than those who possess a college degree ($\chi^2 = 2.85$, df $= 1$, $p < 0.10$). Roman Catholic subjects tended to yield more than Protestant subjects ($\chi^2 = 2.96$, df $= 1$, $p < 0.10$). No other background variable measured in the study was associated with amount of yielding, though the number of subjects employed was too small for definite conclusions.

The shock data may also be examined in terms of the *maximum* shock administered by subjects in the experimental and control conditions, i.e., the highest single shock administered by a subject throughout the 30 critical trials. The information is presented in Table 14.3. Only 2 control subjects administered shocks beyond the tenth voltage level (at this point the Learner makes his first truly vehement protest), while 27 experimental subjects went beyond this point. A median test showed that the maximum shocks administered by experimental subjects were higher than those administered by control subjects ($\chi^2 = 39.2$, df $= 1$, $p < 0.001$).

Table 14.2 Analysis of variance of shock levels administered in the experimental and control conditions.

Source	df	SS	MS	F
Total between individuals	79	966,947.1	12,239.8	
Between experimental conditions	1	237,339.4	237,339.4	25.37*
Between individuals	78	729,607.7	9,353.9	
Within individuals	2,320	391,813.5	168.9	
Between trials	29	157,361.7	5,426.3	96.04*
Trials × experimental conditions (Trend)	29	106,575.4	3,675.0	65.04*
Remainder	2,262	127,876.4	56.5	

*$p < 0.001$.

Table 14.3 Maximum shock levels administered in experimental and control conditions.

Verbal designation and voltage indication	Number of subject for whom this was maximum shock	
	Experimental	Control
Slight shock		
15	1	3
30	2	6
45	0	7
60	0	7
Moderate shock		
75	1	5
90	0	4
105	1	1
120	1	1
Strong shock		
135	2	3
150	5	1
165	2	0
180	0	0
Very strong shock		
195	1	0
210	2	0
225	2	0
240	1	0
Intense shock		
255	2	0
270	0	0
285	1	0
300	1	0
Extreme intensity shock		
315	2	0
330	0	0
345	1	0
360	2	0
Danger: severe shock		
375	0	1
390	0	0
405	1	0
420	2	0
XXX		
435	0	0
450	7	1

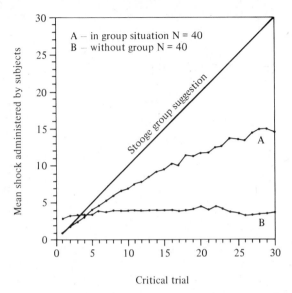

Fig. 14.1 *Mean shock levels in experimental and control conditions over 30 critical trials.*

The main effect, then, is that in the experimental condition subjects were substantially influenced by group pressure. When viewed in terms of the mean shock level over the 30 critical trials, as in Fig. 14.1, the experimental function appears as a vector more or less bisecting the angle formed by the confederates' diagonal and control slopes. Thus one might be tempted to say that the subject's action in the experimental situation had two major sources: it was partly determined by the level the subject would have chosen in the control condition, and partly by the confederates' choice. Neither one nor the other entirely dominates the average behavior of subjects in the experimental condition. There are very great individual differences in regard to the more dominant force.

DISCUSSION

The substantive contribution of the present study lies in the demonstration that group influence can shape behavior in a domain that might have been thought highly resistant to such effects. Subjects are induced by the group to inflict pain on another person at a level that goes well beyond levels chosen in the absence of social pressure. Hurting a man is an action that for most people carries considerable psychological significance; it is closely tied to questions of conscience and ethical judgment. It might have been thought that the protests of the victim and inner prohibitions against hurting others would have operated effectively to curtail the subject's compliance. While the experiment yields wide variation in performance, a substantial number of subjects submitted readily to pressure applied to them by the confederates.

The significance of yielding in Asch's situation is sometimes questioned because the discriminative task is not an issue of self-evident importance for many subjects (Bronowski).[3] The criticism is not easily extended to the present study. Here the subject does not merely feign agreement with a group on a perceptual task of undefined importance; and he is unable to dismiss his action by relegating it to the status of a trivial gesture, for a person's suffering and discomfort are at stake.

The behavior observed here occurred within the framework of a laboratory study presided over by an experimenter. In some degree his authority stands behind the group. In his initial instructions the experimenter clearly legitimized the use of any shock level on the console. Insofar as he does not object to the shocks administered in the course of the experiment, his assent is implied. Thus, even though the effects of group pressure have been clearly established by a comparison of the experimental and control conditions, the effects occurred within the context of authoritative sanction. This point becomes critical in any attempt to assess the relative effectiveness of *conformity* versus *obedience* as means of inducing contravelent behavior (Milgram, 1963). If the experimenter had not approved the use of all shock levels on the generator, and if he had departed from the laboratory at an early stage, thus eliminating any sign of authoritative assent during the course of the experiment, would the group have had as powerful an effect on the naive subject?

There are many points of difference between Asch's investigation and the procedure of the present study that can only be touched upon here.

1. While in Asch's study the *adequate* response is anchored to an external stimulus event, in the present study we are dealing with an internal, unbound standard.

2. A misspoken judgment can, in principle, be withdrawn, but here we are dealing with action that has an immediate and unalterable consequence. Its irreversibility stems not from constraints extrinsic to the action, but from the content of the action itself: once the Learner is shocked, he cannot be un-shocked.

3. In the present experiment, despite the several sources of opinion, there can be but a single shock level on each trial. There is, therefore, a competition for outcome that was not present in the Asch situation.

4. While in the Asch sutdy the focus of pressure is directed toward the subject's judgment, with distortion of public response but an intermediary stage of influence, here the focus of pressure is directed toward performance of action itself. Asch's yielding subject may secretly harbor the true judgment; but when the performance of an action becomes the object of social pressure, there is no comparable recourse to a covert form. The subject who performed the act demanded by the group has yielded exhaustively.

5. In the Asch situation a yielding subject engages in a covert violation of his obligations to the experimenter. He has agreed to report to the experimenter what he sees, and insofar as he goes along with the group, he breaks this agreement. In contrast, in the present experiment the yielding subject acts within the terms of the "subject-experimenter contract." In going along with the two confederates the subject may violate his own inner standards, and the rights of the Learner, but his relationship with the experimenter remains intact at both the manifest and private levels. Subjects in the two experiments are faced with different patterns of social pressure and violate different relationships through social submission.

NOTES

1. This research was supported by Grant NSF G-17916 from the National Science Foundation. My thanks to Taketo Murata of Yale University for computational and statistical assistance.

2. On the first four trials the control group has a higher mean shock than the experimental group; this is an artifact due to the provision that in the experimental condition the shock actually administered and recorded was the lowest suggested by any member of the group; when the subject called for a shock level higher than that suggested by the confederates, it was not reflected in the data. (This situation arose only during the first few critical trials.) By the fifth critical trial the group pressure begins to show its effect in elevating the mean shock level of the naive subjects.

3. J. Bronowski, personal communication, January 10, 1962.

REFERENCES

ASCH, S. E., "Effects of group pressure upon the modification and distortion of judgment." In H. Guetzkow (ed.), *Groups, Leadership, and Men.* Pittsburgh: Carnegie Press, 1951.

———, "Studies of independence and conformity: I. A minority of one against a unanimous majority." *Psychol. Monogr.*, 1956, **70** (9, Whole No. 416).

CRUTCHFIELD, R. S., "Conformity and character." *Amer. Psychologist*, 1955, **10**, 191–198.

FRANK, J. D., "Experimental studies of personal pressure and resistance." *J. Gen. Psychol.*, 1944, **30**, 23–64.

FRENCH, J. R. P., JR., MORRISON, H. W., & LEVINGER, G., "Coercive power and forces affecting conformity." *J. Abnorm. Soc. Psychol.*, 1960, **61**, 93–101.

MILGRAM, S.., "Nationality and conformity." *Scient. American*, 1961, **205**, 45–51.

———, "Behavioral study of obedience." *J. Abnorm. Soc. Psychol.*, 1963, **67**, 371–378.

RAVEN, B. H., & FRENCH, J. R. P., "Legitimate power, coercive power, and observability in social influence." *Sociometry*, 1958, **21**, 83–97.

TUDDENHAM, R. D., & MACBRIDE, P. "The yielding experiment from the subject's point of view." *J. Pers.*, 1959, **27**, 259–271.

Liberating Effects of Group Pressure[1] 15

In laboratory research, the effect of group pressure has most often been studied in its negative aspect; the conspiratorial group is shown to limit, constrain, and distort the individual's responses (Asch, 1951: Blake & Brehm, 1954; Milgram, 1964). Edifying effects of the group, although acknowledged, have rarely been demonstrated with the clarity and force of its destructive potential. Particularly in those areas in which a morally relevant choice is at issue, experimentalists typically examine pressures that diminish the scope of individual action. They have neglected effects that enhance the individual's sense of worth, enlarge the possibilities for action, and help the subject resolve conflicting feelings in a direction congruent with his ideals and values. Although in everyday life occasions arise when conformity to group pressures is constructive, in the laboratory "thinking and investigation have concentrated almost obsessively on conformity in its most sterile forms [Asch, 1959]."[2]

There are technical difficulties to demonstrating the value enhancing potential of group pressure. They concern the nature of the base line from which the group effect is to be measured. The problem is that the experimental subject ordinarily acts in a manner that is socially appropriate. If he has come to the laboratory to participate in a study on the perception of lines, he will generally report what he sees in an honest manner. If one wishes to show the effects of group influence by producing a change in his performance, the only direction open to change is that of creating some deficiency in his performance, which can then be attributed to group influences.

If men tend to act constructively under usual circumstances, the obvious direction of an induced and measurable change is toward inappropriate behavior. It is this technical need rather than the inherently destructive character of group forces that has dictated the lines of a good deal of laboratory research. The experimental problem for any study of *constructive* conformity is to create a situation in which undesirable behavior occurs with regularity and then to see whether group pressure can be applied effectively in the direction of a valued behavior outcome.[3]

EXPERIMENT I: BASE-LINE CONDITION

A technique for the study of destructive obedience (Milgram, 1963) generates the required base line. In this situation a subject is ordered to give increasingly

This paper was first published in the *Journal of Personality and Social Psychology*, Vol. 1, No. 2 (February 1965), pp. 127–134. Copyright © 1965 by the American Psychological Association. Reprinted by permission.

more severe punishment to a person. Despite the apparent discomfort, cries, and vehement protests of the victim, the experimenter instructs the subject to continue stepping up the shock level.

Technique

Two persons arrive at a campus laboratory to take part in a study of memory and learning. (One of them is a confederate of the experimenter.) Each subject is paid $4.50 upon arrival, and is told that payment is not affected in any way by performance. The experimenter provides an introductory talk on memory and learning processes and then informs the subjects that in the experiment one of them will serve as teacher and the other as learner. A rigged drawing is held so that the naive subject is always assigned the role of teacher and the accomplice becomes the learner. The learner is taken to an adjacent room and is strapped into an electric chair.

The naive subject is told that it is his task to teach the learner a list of paired associates, to test him on the list, and to administer punishment whenever the learner errs in the test. Punishment takes the form of electric shock, delivered to the learner by means of a shock generator controlled by the naive subject. The teacher is instructed to increase the intensity of the electric shock one step on the generator on each error. The generator contains 30 voltage levels ranging from 15 to 450 volts, and verbal designations ranging from Slight Shock to Danger: Severe Shock. The learner, according to plan, provides many wrong answers, so that before long the naive subject must give him the strongest shock on the generator. Increases in shock level are met by increasingly insistent demands from the learner that the experiment be stopped because of growing discomfort to him. However, the experimenter instructs the teachers to continue with the procedure in disregard of the learner's protests.[4]

A quantitative value is assigned to the subject's performance based on the maximum intensity shock he administered before breaking off. Thus any subject's score may range from 0 (for a subject unwilling to administer the first shock level) to 30 (for a subject who proceeds to the highest voltage level on the board).

Subjects

The subjects used in the several experimental conditions were male adults residing in the greater New Haven area, aged 20–50 years, and engaged in a wide variety of occupations. Each experimental condition described here employed 40 fresh subjects and was carefully balanced for age and occupational types (see Milgram, 1963, Table 1, for details).

Results and Discussion

In this situation a subject is instructed to perform acts that are in some sense incompatible with his normal standards of behavior. In the face of the vehement protests of an innocent individual, many subjects refuse to carry out the experimenter's orders to continue with the shock procedure. They reject the role

Table 15.1 Distribution of break-off points by condition.

Shock level	Verbal designation and voltage level	Base-line condition (n = 40) (1)	Hypothetical subjects (n = 40) (2)	Disobedient groups (n = 40) (3)	Obedient groups (n = 40) (4)
	Slight shock		3*		
1	15	0	0	0	0
2	30	0	0	0	0
3	45	0	1	0	0
4	60	0	1	0	0
	Moderate shock				
5	75	0	7	0	1
6	90	1	1	0	0
7	105	0	1	1	1
8	120	0	3	0	0
	Strong shock				
9	135	0	2	0	0
10	150	6	9	3←	2
11	165	0	2	4	0
12	180	1	3	1	1
	Very strong shock				
13	195	0	1	4	0
14	210	0	0	12←	0
15	225	0	1	0	0
16	240	0	1	0	0
	Intense shock				
17	255	0	1	0	0
18	270	2	0	4	4
19	285	0	0	0	0
20	300	1	3	2	0
	Extreme intensity shock				
21	315	1	0	3	2
22	330	1	0	0	0
23	345	0	0	0	0
24	360	0	0	1	0
	Danger: severe shock				
25	375	1	0	0	0
26	390	0	0	1	0
27	405	0	0	0	0
28	420	0	0	0	0
	XXX				
29	435	0	0	0	0
30	450	26	0	4	29
	Mean maximum shock	24.55	9.00	16.45	25.70
	Percentage defiant subjects	35.0%	100.0%	90.0%	27.5%

*These three subjects indicated they would refuse to administer even the lowest shock.

assignment of *experimental subject*, assert themselves as persons, and are unwilling to perform actions that violate personal standards of conduct. The distribution of break-off points for this condition is shown in Table 15.1 Column 1. Fourteen of the 40 subjects withdraw from the experiment at some point before the completion of the command series.

The majority of subjects, however, comply fully with the experimenter's commands, despite the acute discomfort they often experience in connection with shocking the victim. Typically these obedient subjects report that they do not wish to hurt the victim, but they feel obligated to follow the orders of the experimenter. On questioning they often state that it would have been "better" not to have shocked the victim at the highest voltage levels. Consider, for example, the remarks of the following obedient subject. He has completed the experiment and is now questioned by an interviewer (who is not the experimenter).

> *I'd like to ask you a few questions. How do you feel?* I feel all right, but I don't like what happened to that fellow in there [the victim]. He's been hollering and we had to keep giving him shocks. I didn't like that one bit. I mean he wanted to get out but he [the experimenter] just kept going, he kept throwing 450 volts. I didn't like that.
>
> *Who was actually pushing the switch?* I was, but he kept insisting. I told him "No," but he said you got to keep going. I told him it's time we stopped when we get up to 195 or 210 volts.
>
> *Why didn't you just stop?* He wouldn't let me. I wanted to stop. I kept insisting to stop, but he said "No."...I figured the voltage we were giving him was quite a bit. I wanted to stop but he [the experimenter] kept insisting not to stop. I mean the fellow in there is hollering "I don't want to do it. I want to get out of here. I want to get out of here!"
>
> *Why didn't you just disregard what the experimenter said?* He says it's got to go on, the experiment.
>
> *Do you feel a little upset?* Well, I mean I feel concerned about the gentleman in there, I do sir...I was getting ready to walk out...I couldn't see the point of going on when the guy is suffering in there. I figured he was having a heart attack or something. That's the reason I wanted to stop....

The subject was then dehoaxed carefully and had a friendly reconciliation with the victim.

There is additional evidence that, in shocking the victim to the end of the command series, subjects are engaging in behavior which they disvalue and see as antithetical to personal and social ideals.

Spontaneous shock levels. In an experimental control reported elsewhere (Milgram, 1964), subjects administer any voltage level they wish in the absence of group or authoritarian pressure. Under this condition the mean maximum shock for 40 subjects is 82.5 volts (level = 5.50); in contrast, under command of the experimenter (in the base-line condition described above) the mean maximum shock is 368.25 volts (level = 24.55). When left on their own, subjects administer far lower shock levels than when under command.

Self-image. When persons who have not performed in the experiment are provided with a description of the experimental situation, and are asked to predict their own performance, almost all subjects see themselves as defying the experimenter at some point in the command series. Moreover, they justify their hypothetical behavior in terms of positive qualities of character, employing such statements as "I'm not the kind of person who is willing to hurt others even for the cause of science."

Column 2 of Table 15.1 shows the anticipated break-off points of 40 adult respondents who were asked to predict their own experimental performance. Hypothetical subjects respond in terms of ideals, values, and positive self-conceptions; these values are frequently overridden by the forces engendered in the concrete laboratory situation.

Moral judgment. Twenty undergraduates were asked to render a moral judgment on the issue of obeying or disobeying the experimenter. After describing the experiment to the respondents in concrete detail, the experimenter asked:

> In terms of the moral and ethical values most important to you, and taking into account the scientific goals served by the research, how *should* you perform in the experimental situation? Should you go through to the end of the experiment or should you break off at some point?

Valued break-off points ranged from 0 to 255 volts with the median at 150 volts. Subjects were also asked to explain at length the values that should guide their behavior in the laboratory situation. A sample statement is given below:

> I would say that one should not even start the shocks, but rather, forcibly withdraw the moment that the outline of the experiment becomes evident. My reasons for saying this are very complex... The first is that the society's morals, which I have absorbed, teach that it is wrong to hurt a man. Morals are usually tied in with religion and this is especially true with Christianity. Having been raised, then, in an old fashioned, staunchly Lutheran family I have internalized the view that hurting a man is wrong, and no amount of intellectual reasoning can shake this belief.

Thus, there is a clear consensus that the only behavior consistent with social values and individual conscience is to defy the experimenter at some point before the completion of the command series. Yet there is a marked discrepancy between this value judgment and the actual performance of subjects in the laboratory. Despite their protests and obvious conflict in shocking the victim, a substantial number of subjects are unable to defy the experimenter's authority, and proceed to administer the highest shock levels commanded by him.

EXPERIMENT II: GROUPS FOR DISOBEDIENCE

We may now examine in what degree group influence can release the subject from authoritarian control, and allow him to act in a direction congruent with his values and personal standards.

The strategy is to replicate Experiment I, but with this difference: the subject is placed in the midst of two peers who defy the experimenter and refuse to punish the victim against his will. In what degree will the pressure created by their action affect the naive subject's behavior?

Technique

Forty fresh subjects were studied in this condition. The procedure is identical to Experiment I with these exceptions: Four persons appear at the laboratory to take part in an experiment on "the effects of collective teaching and punishment on memory and learning." Three subjects are confederates of the experimenter and one is a naive subject. The experimenter explains that three teachers and one learner are to be used in the study, and by means of a rigged drawing, the naive subject is assigned the position of Teacher 3. The roles of Teacher 1, Teacher 2, and learner are filled by the confederates. The learner is strapped into the electric chair and the three teachers are seated before the shock generator. Teacher 1 is told to read the list of word pairs, Teacher 2 informs the subject if he is correct or incorrect in his answers, and Teacher 3 (the naive subject) administers punishment. As in Experiment I, the subjects are instructed to raise the shock level one step each time the learner makes an error. (More detailed descriptions of the group technique can be found in Milgram, 1964.)

Behavior of confederates. The confederates comply with the experimenter through the 150-volt shock. After the 150-volt level is administered Teacher 1 informs the experimenter that he does not wish to participate further, because of the learner's complaints. (It is at the 150-volt shock level that the learner makes his first vehement protest.) The experimenter insists that the subject continue. However, Teacher 1 is not swayed by the experimenter's commands, gets up from his chair in front of the shock generator, and takes a seat in another part of the room. Since the experimenter's efforts to get the subject to return to the generator are futile, the experimenter instructs the remaining two subjects to continue with the experiment. Teacher 3 (the naive subject) is to handle the reading of word pairs, in addition to his regular job of administering electric shock to the learner.

After Shock Level 14 (210 volts) is administered, Teacher 2, expressing concern for the learner, refuses to participate further. The experimenter makes strong efforts to have him continue, but he too leaves his chair in front of the generator and seats himself at an opposite corner of the room, saying "I'm willing to answer any of your questions, but I'm not willing to shock that man against his will; I'll have no part of it."

At this point the naive subject is seated alone in front of the shock generator. He has witnessed the defiant actions of two peers. The experimenter orders the naive subject to continue with the experimental procedure by himself, indicating that it is essential that the experiment be completed.

Results and Discussion

The break-off points of the naive subjects in Experiment II are shown in Table 15.1, Column 3. The arrows at Shock Levels 10 and 14 indicate the points at which each of the confederates defied the experimenter.

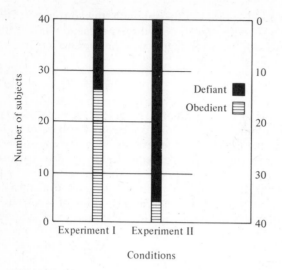

Fig. 15.1 *Proportion of obedient and defiant sub-jects in Experiments I and II.*

Comparing the proportion of obedient to defiant subjects in Experiments I and II, we see that the effect of the confederates' pressure was substantial. In Experiment I, 26 subjects proceeded to the end of the command series; less than one-sixth of this number obeyed fully in the group setting (obedient versus defiant subjects $\chi^2 = 25.81$, df $= 1$, $p < 0.001$). These results are presented graphically in Fig. 15.1. The mean maximum shock in Experiment II (16.45) was also significantly lower than in Experiment II (16.45) was also significantly lower than in Experiment I (24.55, $p < 0.001$).[5]

After Shock Level 14 the second confederate defies the experimenter. Before Level 15 is administered, 25 naive subjects have followed the defiant group, while at the corresponding point in Experiment I only 8 subjects have refused to follow the experimenter's orders. The confederates appear to exert some influence, however, even on those subjects who do not follow them immediately. Between Voltage Levels 17 and 29, 11 subjects in Experiment II break off, while only 6 subjects do so in Experiment I.

In sum, in the group setting 36 of the 40 subjects defy the experimenter while the corresponding number in the absence of group pressure is 14. The effects of peer rebellion are most impressive in undercutting the experimenter's authority. Indeed, of the score of experimental variations completed in the Yale study on obedience none was so effective in undermining the experimenter's authority as the manipulation reported here.[6]

How should we account for the powerful effect of the experimental manipulation? It is probable that in Experiment I many subjects come near to performing the defiant action but cannot quite bring themselves to the point of disobedience. The additional pressure of the group members leads to an increment in the forces oriented toward defiance; the increment is of sufficient strength so that, in combination with pressures for defiance already present, many subjects are carried over the threshold of disobedience.

The strong liberating effect of the peers brings to mind the powerful effect of a partner in Asch's (1951) study. In that experiment negative pressures originated within the group itself so that the conflicting agents (partner versus majority) were internal to the group boundary; in the present study the peers free the subject from an influence that is *external* to the group. Additionally, the partner's support in Asch's study leads to a response that is fundamentally similar in form but different in value from that of the erring majority. In the present study the peers initiate a radically different order of response, one which has no antecedent in the course of the laboratory hour, and which destroys the very framework of the experiment.

Reactions to the confederates. The reactions of naive subjects to the defiant confederates varied considerably and were in part dependent on the exact point where the subject himself defied the experimenter. A subject who quit simultaneously with the first confederate stated, "Well, I was already thinking about quitting when the guy broke off." Most defiant subjects praised the confederates with such statements as, "I thought they were men of good character, yes I do. When the victim said 'Stop,' they stopped [Shock Level 11]."[7] "I think they were very sympathetic people...and they were totally unaware of what was in store for them [Shock Level 14]."

A subject who defied the experimenter at Level 21 qualified his approval: "Well I think they should continue a little further, but I don't blame them for backing out when they did."

A few subjects acknowledged the importance of the confederates in leading to their own defiance: "The thought of stopping didn't enter my mind until it was put there by the other two [Shock Level 14]." "The reason I quit was that I did not wish to seem callous and cruel in the eyes of the other two men who had already refused to go on with the experiment [Shock Level 14]." The majority of subjects, however, denied that the confederates' action was the critical factor in their own defiance.[8]

The fact that obedient subjects failed to follow the defiant group should not suggest that they did not feel the pressure of the confederates' action. One obedient subject stated:

> I felt that I would just look like a real Simon Legree to these guys if I just went on cooly and just kept administering lashes. I thought they reacted normally, and the first thing that came to my mind was to react as they did. But I didn't, because if they reacted normally, and stopped the experiment, and I did the same, I don't know how many months and days you'd have to continue before you got done.

Thus this subject felt the burden of the group judgment, but sensed that in the light of two defections he had a special obligation to help the experimenter complete his work. Another obedient subject, when asked about the nervousness he displayed in the experiment, replied:

> I think it was primarily because of their actions. Momentarily I was ready to go along with them. Then suddenly I felt that they were just being ridiculous. What was I doing following the crowd?...They certainly had a right to stop, but I felt they lost all control of themselves.

And a third obedient subject criticized the confederates more directly, stating:

> I don't think they should have quit. They came here for an experiment, and I think they should have stuck with it.

A closer analysis of the experimental situation points to a number of specific factors that may contribute to the group's effectiveness:

1. The peers instill in the subject the *idea* of defying the experimenter. It may not have occurred to some subjects as a response possibility.

2. The lone subject has no way of knowing whether, in defying the experimenter, he is performing in a bizarre manner or whether this action is a common occurrence in the laboratory. The two examples of disobedience he sees suggest that defiance is a natural reaction to the situation.

3. The reactions of the defiant confederates define the act of shocking the victim as improper. They provide social confirmation to the naive subjects's suspicion that it is wrong to punish a man against his will, even in the context of a psychological experiment.

4. The defiant confederates remain in the laboratory even after withdrawing from the experiment (they have agreed to answer post-experimental questions). Each additional shock administered by the naive subject now carries with it a measure of social disapproval from the two confederates.

5. As long as the two confederates participate in the experimental procedure there is a dispersion of responsibility among the group members for shocking the victim. As the confederates withdraw, responsibility becomes focused onto the naive subject.[9]

6. The naive subject is a witness to two instances of disobedience and observes the *consequences* of defying the experimenter to be minimal.

7. There is identification with the disobedient confederates and the possibility of falling back on them for social support when defying the experimenter.

8. Additionally, the experimenter's power may be diminished by the very fact of failing to keep the two confederates in line, following the general rule that every failure of authority to exact compliance to its commands weakens the perceived power of the authority (Homans, 1961).

Hypothesis of Arbitrary Direction of Group Effects

The results examined thus far show that group influence serves to liberate individuals effectively from submission to destructive commands. There are some who will take this to mean that the direction of group influence is arbitrary, that it can be oriented toward destructive or constructive ends with equal impact, and that group pressure need merely be inserted into a social situation on one side of a standard or the other in order to induce movement in the desired direction.

This view ought to be questioned. Does the fact that a disobedient group alters the behavior of subjects in Experiment II necessarily imply that group pressure can be applied in the other direction with similar effectiveness? A competing view would be that the direction of possible influence of a group is not arbitrary, but is highly dependent on the general structure of the situation in which influence is attempted.

To examine this issue we need to undertake a further experimental variation, one in which the group forces are thrown on the side of the experimenter, rather than directed against him. The idea is simply to have the members of the group reinforce the experimenter's commands by following them unfailingly, thus adding peer pressures to those originating in the experimenter's commands.

EXPERIMENT III: OBEDIENT GROUPS

Forty fresh subjects, matched to the subjects in Experiments I and II for sex, age, and occupational status, were employed in this condition. The procedure was identical to that followed in Experiment II with this exception: at all times the two confederates followed the commands of the experimenter; at no point did they object to carrying out the experimental instructions. Nor did they show sympathy for or comment on the discomfort of the victim. If a subject attempted to break off they allowed the experimenter primary responsibility for keeping him in line, but contributed background support for the experimenter; they indicated their disapproval of the naive subject's attempts to leave the experiment with such remarks as: "You can't quit *now*; this experiment has got to get done." As in Experiment II the naive subject was seated between the two confederates, and in his role of Teacher 3, administered the shocks to the victim.

Results and Discussion

The results, presented in Table 15.1, Column 4, show that the obedient group had very little effect on the overall performance of subjects. In Experiment I, 26 of the 40 subjects complied fully with the experimenter's commands; in the present condition this figure is increased but 3, yielding a total of 29 obedient subjects. This increase falls far short of statistical significance ($\chi^2 = 0.52$, df $= 1$, $p > 0.50$). Nor is the difference in mean maximum shocks statistically reliable. The failure of the manipulation to produce a significant change cannot be attributed to a ceiling artifact since an obedient shift of even 8 of the 14 defiant subjects would yield the 0.05 significance level by chi square.

Why the lack of change when we know that group pressure often exerts powerful effects? One interpretation is that the authoritarian pressure already present in Experiment I has preempted subjects who would have submitted to group pressures. Conceivably, the subjects who are fully obedient in Experiment I are precisely those who would be susceptible to group forces, while those who resisted authoritarian pressure were also immune to the pressure of the obedient confederates. The pressures applied in Experiment III do not show an effect because they overlap with other pressures having the same direction and present in Experiment I; all persons responsive to the initial pressure have already been moved to the obedient criterion in Experiment I. This possibility seems obvious enough in the present study. Yet every other situation in which group pressure is exerted also possesses a field structure (a particular arrangement of stimulus, motive, and social factors) that limits and controls potential influence within that field.[10] Some structures allow group influence to be exerted in one direction but not another. Seen in this light, the hypothesis of the arbitrary direction of group effects is inadequate.

In the present study Experiment I defines the initial field: the insertion of group pressure in a direction opposite to that of the experimenter's commands (Experiment II) produces a powerful shift toward the group. Changing the direction of group movement (Experiment III) does not yield a comparable shift in the subject's performance. The group success in one case and failure in another can be traced directly to the configuration of motive and social forces operative in the starting situation (Experiment I).

Given any social situation, the strength and direction of potential group influence is predetermined by existing conditions. We need to examine the variety of field structures that typify social situations and the manner in which each controls the pattern of potential influence.

NOTES

1. This research was supported by two grants from the National Science Foundation, G–17916 and G–24152. The experiments were conducted while the author was at Yale University. Pilot studies completed in 1960 were financed by a grant from the Higgins Fund of Yale University. My thanks to Rhea Mendoza Diamond for her help in revising the original manuscript.

2. Exceptions become more numerous in moving from the experimental domain to the practice of group therapy and training groups. And surely the *philosophy* of group dynamics stresses the productive possibilities inherent in groups (Cartwright & Zander, 1960).

3. Another solution would be to wait until people who perform in a naturally destructive way come to the laboratory and to use them as subjects. One might deliberately seek out a group of recidivist delinquents who would ordinarily behave in a disvalued manner, and then study group effects on their performance. This would, of course, limit the study to an atypical population.

4. Descriptions of the shock generator, schedule of protests from the learner, and other details of procedure have been described elsewhere and will not be restated here (Milgram, 1963, 1964).

5. Of course the mean maximum shock in the experimental condition is tied to the precise point in the voltage series where the confederates' break-off is staged. In this experiment it is not until Level 14 that both confederates have defied the experimenter.

6. See Milgram, 1965/1974, for additional experiments.

7. Numerals in brackets indicate the break-off point of the subject quoted.

8. Twenty-seven of the defiant subjects stated that they would have broken off without the benefit of the confederates' example; four subjects definitely acknowledged the confederates' rebellion as the critical factor in their own defiance. The remaining defiant subjects were undecided on this issue. In general, then, subjects underestimate the degree to which their defiant actions are dependent on group support.

9. See Wallach, Kogan, and Bem (1962) for a treatment of this concept dealing with risk taking.

10. See, for example, the study of Jones, Wells, and Torrey (1958). Starting with the Asch situation they show that through feedback, the experimenter can foster greater independence in the subject, but not significantly greater yielding to the erring majority. Here, too, an initial field structure limits the direction of influence attempts.

REFERENCES

ASCH, S. E., "Effects of group pressure upon the modification and distortion of judgment." In H. Guetzkow (ed.), *Groups, Leadership, and Men*. Pittsburgh: Carnegie Press, 1951.

————, "A perspective on social psychology." In S. Koch (ed), *Psychology: A Study of a Science*. Vol. 3. *Formulations of the Person and the Social Context*. New York: McGraw-Hill, 1959. Pp. 363–383.

BLAKE, R. R., & BREHM, J. W., "The use of tape recording to simulate a group atmosphere." *Journal of Abnormal and Social Psychology*, 1954, **49**, 311–313.

CARTWRIGHT, D., & ZANDER, A., *Group Dynamics*. Evanston, Ill.: Row, Peterson, 1960.

HOMANS, G. C., *Social Behavior: Its Elementary Forms*. New York: Harcourt, Brace, 1961.

JONES, E. E., WELLS, H. H., & TORREY, R., "Some effects of feedback from the experimenter on conformity behavior." *Journal of Abnormal and Social Psychology*, 1958, **57**, 207–213.

MILGRAM, S., "Behavioral study of obedience." *Journal of Abnormal and Social Psychology*, 1963, **67**, 371–378.

————, "Group pressure and action against a person." *Journal of Abnormal and Social Psychology*, 1964, **69**, 137–143.

————, "Some conditions of obedience and disobedience to authority." *Human Relations*, 1965, **18**, 57–76.

————, *Obedience to Authority: An Experimental View*, New York: Harper & Row, 1974.

WALLACH, M. A., KOGAN, N., & BEM, D. J., "Group influence on individual risk taking." *Journal of Abnormal and Social Psychology*, 1962, **65**, 75–86.

The Drawing Power of Crowds of Different Size[1]

16

In a typical urban setting, when a group of people engage in an action simultaneously, they have the capacity to draw others into the crowd. The actions of the initial group may serve as a stimulus for others to imitate this action. A careful analysis of the details of crowd formation is of obvious interest to a society in which collective action plays an increasingly important part in social life. One theoretical formulation that bears on this problem is that of Coleman and James (1961).

Coleman and James assumed that there is a "natural process" by which free-forming groups acquire and lose members and thus reach specific maximum sizes. They have developed a model that generates a size distribution that closely approximates the actually observed size distribution of many thousands of groups. The central assumption of their model of acquisition and loss are "a constant tendency of a group member to break away, independent of the group, thus producing a loss rate for the group proportional to size; and an acquisition rate for each group proportional to the number of single individuals available to be 'picked up [p. 44].'" Thus the growth of a group is independent of the size of the group and dependent only upon the number of persons who are available to join the group. However, Coleman and James pointed out that "a contagion assumption—that is, an assumption that a person is more likely to join a large group than a small one [p. 44]," might be needed in their model. (Their use of the term "contagion" is not entirely accurate, since this term does not signify in any direct way that a large group is more effective in attracting new persons than a small one. It is preferable, in this connection, to use the phrase "assumption of initial group size.")

This paper reports on the effects which crowds of different sizes had on passersby, following the quantitative approach to the study of crowd behavior outlined by Milgram and Toch (1969).

A few of the basic concepts used in this study need to be clarified. First there is the *stimulus crowd*. This was provided by the investigators and varied in number from 1 to 15. If the crowd is to draw onlookers, then it must be exposed to an *available population*. The population may be finite, and thus exhaustable, or it may be continually replenished as in the present study. The population may

This paper was written in collaboration with Leonard Bickman and Lawrence Berkowitz, and was first published under the title, "Note on the Drawing Power of Crowds of Different Size," in the *Journal of Personality and Social Psychology*, Vol. 13, No. 2 (1969), pp. 79–82. Copyright © 1969 by the American Psychological Association. Reprinted by permission.

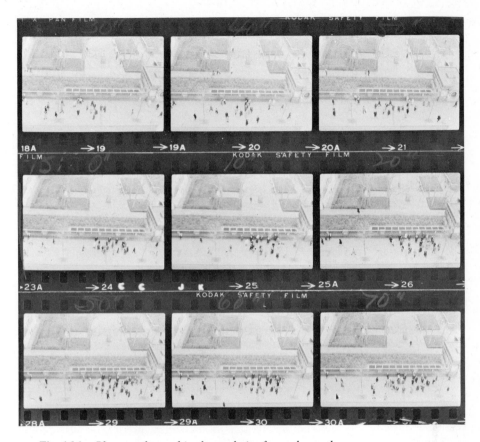

Fig. 16.1 *Photographs used in the analysis of crowd growth.*

also be in various *states of activity*, that is, sitting around (as at a beach) or moving along paths. The available population in the case of the present study consisted of the stream of pedestrians moving along a major city thoroughfare. Finally, the crowd must exhibit some sort of *observable action* that the population can imitate or in some manner respond to. In the present study the stimulus crowd stood on the pavement and looked up at the window of a nearby building. This action, or parts of it, could be adopted by the passersby. The passerby could simply look up at the building where the crowd was staring without breaking stride, or he could make a more complete imitative action by stopping and standing alongside the crowd. Analyses were undertaken for both types of responses.

In sum, the investigators wanted to see in what degree crowds, varying in size from 1 to 15 persons, and all performing the same observable action, would draw persons into their activities.

METHOD

Subjects

The subjects were 1,424 pedestrians on a busy New York City street who passed along a 50-foot length of sidewalk during thirty one-minute trials. The study was conducted on two winter afternoons in 1968.

Procedure

A 50-foot length of sidewalk was designated as the area of observation. At a signal, flashed from the sixth-floor window of an office building across the street from this area of sidewalk, a group of confederates (stimulus crowd) entered the middle of the observation area, stopped, and looked up at the sixth-floor window. This gaze was maintained for 60 seconds. At the end of this period the group was signaled to disperse. After the area was cleared of the gathered crowd the procedure was repeated using a different size stimulus crowd. Five randomly ordered trials were conducted for each of the six different size stimulus crowds. The stimulus crowds were composed of 1, 2, 3, 5, 10, and 15 persons. Motion pictures were taken of the observation area for the 60 seconds during which the stimulus crowd maintained its gaze at the window.

Data Analysis

The motion pictures were analyzed to determine the total number of persons who passed through the observation area and their behavior. Pairs of judges counted the number of persons entering the field; within this group, the number of persons who looked up; and finally the number of persons who stopped.

RESULTS

The first question is whether the number of persons who stop alongside the crowd increases as the size of the stimulus crowd increases. The data are provided in Fig. 16.2 (broken line). While 4 percent of the passersby stopped alongside a single individual looking up, 40 percent of the passersby stopped alongside a stimulus crowd of 15. An analysis of variance was performed on the mean percentage of persons who stopped alongside the crowd (Table 16.1). This analysis indicates that the size of the stimulus crowd significantly affects the proportion of passersby who stand alongside it.

But the influence of the stimulus crowd is not limited to those who stop and stand alongside it. For a larger number of passersby partially adopt the behavior of the crowd by looking up in the direction of the crowd's gaze, while not, however, breaking stride and standing alongside it. Here again the influence of the stimulus crowd increases along with its size. While one person induced 42 percent of the passersby to look up (whether or not they also stopped), the stimulus crowd of 15, all looking in the same direction, caused 86 percent of the passersby to orient themselves in the same direction (Fig. 16.2, solid line). An analysis of variance again confirms the difference in means (Table 16.2).

A trend analysis for unequal intervals was performed on the data (Gaito, 1965). There is a significant linear trend ($F = 101.7$, $p < 0.01$) and a nonsignificant quadratic trend ($F = 0.42$) for the passersby who stopped. However, for the

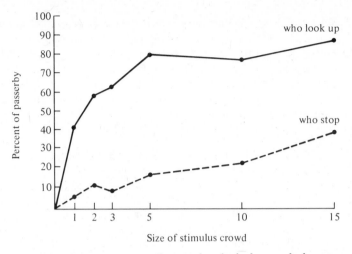

Fig. 16.2 *Mean percentage of passersby who look up and who stop, as a function of the size of the stimulus crowd.*

Table 16.1 Analysis of variance of the proportion of passersby who stop as a function of the size of the stimulus crowd.

Source	SS	df	MS	F
Between	0.423	5	0.085	20.63*
Within	0.099	24	0.004	
Total	0.522	29		

*$p < 0.001$.

passersby who looked up, there are both significant linear ($F = 57.2$, $p < 0.01$) and quadratic ($F = 11.6$, $p < 0.01$) components. This bears on a recent discussion of Gerard, Wilhelmy, and Conolly (1969). In their study, conformity increased in linear fashion as a function of group size, in contrast to Asch (1951), who found a curvilinear relationship. The present study shows that a single set of group-size manipulations can generate both types of functions, depending on the specific dependent variable selected for analysis.

A comparison of those who stop and those who look up shows that while both behaviors increase with the size of the stimulus crowd, the percentage of

Table 16.2 Analysis of variance of the proportion of passersby who look up as a function of the size of the stimulus crowd.

Source	SS	df	MS	F
Between	0.628	5	0.125	16.28*
Within	0.187	24	0.008	
Total	0.815	29		

*$p < 0.001$.

those who only look up is always higher than those who stop, regardless of the size of the stimulus crowd. It appears that the more demanding, in time or effort, the behavior, the less likely it is that the passerby will join it.

Two additional points need to be made. First, it is clear that while the effects of a precipitating group of a given size for the subsequent growth of the crowd were studied, the size of the stimulus crowd increased as soon as persons joined it. Thus, the effect of a stimulus crowd of *constant* size was not studied. In order to do this it would be necessary to withdraw a member of the stimulus crowd as soon as a passerby joined it.

Second, the maximum size which the crowd attains is dependent not only on the initial size of the crowd, but also on the nature of the stimulus to which the passerby is directed. In the present study, passersby were oriented by the gaze of the crowd to a scene that had no special holding power. (Pedestrians looked up to the sixth floor of an office building where some dimly perceived figures were peering back from inside. It was not a scene of compelling interest.) If, instead, an acrobat were performing on the building ledge, the interest of the scene would likely hold crowd members for a longer period of time, and the crowd would grow to a larger maximum size within a one-minute interval (the size of the crowd at any given moment being equal to the initial stimulus crowd plus additions minus withdrawals.) There is some logical basis for joining larger crowds: all other things being equal, the larger the crowd, the more likely its members are attending to a matter of interest.

The results of this study show that the number of persons who will react to, and join in, the observable behavior of a stimulus crowd is related to the size of the stimulus crowd. These findings contradict the acquisition assumption of the Coleman and James model. The acquisition rate is not, as they assume, dependent only upon the number of persons available to join the group. (For the present study, the mean number of such individuals was not significantly different for the different size stimulus crowds.) An assumption of initial group size is indeed necessary.

NOTE

1. This study arose out of a graduate seminar in social psychology conducted by the first author at The City University of New York. Among those who took part in the present study were Stuart Baum, Sheryl Bruder, Fay Crayne, Victor Ernoult, Susan Flinn, Bert Flugman, Henry Glickman, Michael Hoffman, Marcia Kay, Jo Lang, Elaine Lieberman, Nicholas Papouchis, Arthur Shulman, Henry Solomon, Sheila Sperber, and Mark Silverman. The study was supported by The City University of New York and by a small grant from the National Institute of Mental Health, Number 16284-01.

REFERENCES

Asch, S. E. "Effects of group pressure upon the modification and distortion of judgment." In H. Guetzkow (ed.), *Groups, Leadership, and Men.* Pittsburgh: Carnegie Press, 1951.

Coleman, J. S., & James, J., "The equilibrium size distribution of freely-forming groups." *Sociometry*, 1961, **24**, 36–45.

GAITO, J., "Unequal intervals and unequal N in trend analysis." *Psychological Bulletin*, 1965, **63**, 125–127.

GERARD, H. B., WILHELMY, R. A. & CONOLLY, E. S., "Conformity and group size." *Journal of Personality and Social Psychology*, 1968, **8**, 79–82.

MILGRAM, S., & TOCH, H., "Collective behavior: crowds and social movements." In G. Lindzey & E. Aronson (eds.), *The Handbook of Social Psychology*. Vol. 49 (2nd ed.) Reading, Mass.: Addison-Wesley, 1969

Crowds[1] 17

Crowd is a generic term referring to highly diverse conditions of human assemblage: audience, mob, rally, and panic all fall within the definition of crowds. Common to these terms is the idea of human beings in sufficiently close proximity that the fact of aggregation comes to influence behavior. Crowds occur frequently in social life, under some circumstances become the focus of society-wide concern, and during the past century have been subject to scientific analysis on a rudimentary level.

ELEMENTARY FEATURES OF THE CROWD

Any crowd can be seen as a group of points coming into aggregation, growing in size at specifiable rates, evolving new shapes, and possessing certain self-distributing dynamics, coalescing out of larger throngs in a specifiable manner, with boundaries that are sharp or diffuse, permeable or closed to points lying outside the boundary.

While a fully articulated theory linking the variables of macroscopic analysis has not yet been proposed, characterization of the crowd at this level may suggest important regularities. Moreover, this perspective lends itself to empirical inquiry. Spatial aspects of the crowd may be readily recorded with techniques of aerial photography, and time-lapse studies or motion picture films allow the temporal features to be recorded and carefully scrutinized (Millard, 1963). Such methods may make it possible to predict, for example, the eventual size of a crowd on the basis of initial rate of aggregation—a question of considerable theoretical and practical import.

SHAPE AND RUDIMENTARY STRUCTURE

Typical group configurations have often been noted in species of birds, schools of fish, and packs of baboons (Hall, 1966; Lorenz, 1966), but the shape of spontaneous human aggregations has eluded study. Partly, this is because observers generally view crowds from the same plane as the crowd, while the most advantageous perspective for configurational studies is from a position directly overhead. Pending the availability of systematic data, the observer of crowds is limited to a few rough generalizations about basic crowd structures

---

Excerpted from "Collective Behavior: Crowds and Social Movements," which was written in collaboration with Hans Toch and was published in *The Handbook of Social Psychology* (second edition), Vol. IV, G. Lindzey and E. Aronson (eds.), Reading, Mass.: Addison-Wesley, 1969, pp. 507–610. Reprinted by permission of Addison-Wesley.

and their functions. Discussion will begin with one variety of crowd structure, the ring.

The Ring

If individuals are randomly distributed over a flat surface in the starting situation, a point of common interest in the same plane creates a crowd tending toward circularity. The circular arrangement is not accidental but serves an important function. It permits the most efficient arrangement of individuals around a point of common focus (see Fig. 17.1). For experimental purposes, an ideal ring can be created by dragging an object of interest from the ocean and onto a populated beach. A treasure chest will suffice; a circular ring will form around it.

Nature abhors a square crowd. The crowd builds in the form of accretions to the initial circular core.. Even when a ring grows to be many layers thick, the circular shape tends to prevail. Ecological factors, such as the presence of walls or barriers, may prevent the full completion of the ring, but frequently arc segments can be discerned. Whenever we see an assemblage with rectilinear properties, we may infer that it is not a spontaneous grouping, but reflects the imposition of an institutional form on the crowd.

Persons who arrive early tend to be at the center of the ring; those who arrive late tend to be at the fringe. However, there will also be movement of the more ardent or involved members toward the crowd's center, so that fractionation strata, analogous to the strata resulting from the separation of heavy and light particles in a centrifuge, occurs. *Milling* has traditionally been seen as a means of exchanging information (Blumer, 1946), but it also allows people to settle into their proper places in the crowd structure, into more central or peripheral positions. A hypothesis that emerges, therefore, is that those who are most intensely motivated to carry out the crowd's purposes will be disproportionately represented at the crowd's structural core.

The structure of the ring is illustrated in Fig. 17.2. Several features need to be mentioned. The inner area allows a spatial separation of onlookers and speakers. The larger the circumference of the inner boundary, the more individuals can observe the speaker unobstructed by heads and bodies of other members. The inner space also highlights the functional difference between the speaker and onlookers. The dimensions of the inner space are related to a number of variables, such as degree of attraction or repulsion to the speaker, his elevation, the size of the ring, and the pressure from those in the rear. Feshbach and Feshbach (1963) reported on the changes in the dimensions of a ring. They created fear in a group of boys seated in a circle by recounting ghost stories, and noted the effect of the induction.

> Although the diameter of the circle was about eleven feet at the beginning of the story-telling, by the time the last ghost story was completed, it had been spontaneously reduced to approximately three feet.

Boris Sidis (1895) proposed a rudimentary structure in the hostile mob, and described its organization in terms of a "sensory and prehensile nucleus" which

Fig. 17.1 *Crowds in ring form. The scene depicts crowds gathering around entertainers in an open-air Moroccan marketplace. (Loomis Dean for Life, copyright © 1965, Time, Inc.)*

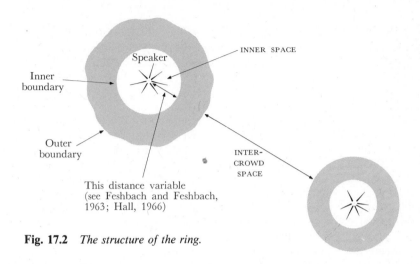

Fig. 17.2 *The structure of the ring.*

is formed in the center of the crowd, but is forced to the front, and a "nucleolinus contained with a nucleolus"—that is, a crowd hero surrounded by his most devoted followers. Sidis' cellular analogy does not help very much, but the underlying idea of a structure within the crowd ought not be be overlooked. Of contemporary writers, Canetti (1962) and Hall (1966) are most attentive to structural features of the crowd.

BOUNDARIES

A boundary defines the limit or extent of the crowd. The two major characteristics of boundaries are (1) permeability and (2) sharpness.

Permeability

Whether a crowd boundary is open or closed to new persons depends on both physical and ideological factors. Descriptively, we must distinguish between penetration of the boundary and accretion to it. Penetration specifies entry from points external to the crowd followed by movement toward the center. Accretion refers to the clustering of persons at the fringes. A densely packed ring surrounding a circus performer may not permit others to get close to the core but allows them to build around the outer fringe. Even accretion, however, may be rejected in the interest of preserving the privacy of an already gathered group. Crowds need not be fully open or closed, but may display selectivity along ideological lines. A proletarian lynch mob in formation is ordinarily open to whites, but violently rejects Negroes (Cantril, 1941).

Permeability works both ways. Once within a crowd, it may be impossible to pass through the outer boundary. Stone-throwing crowds, described in the Old Testament, encircled their victims, creating an impenetrable surround. Celebrities are sometimes unable to extricate themselves from a thick ring of admirers.

Sharpness of Boundary

The definition of crowd boundaries may be clearly demarcated or vague. Measurement is not always easy, particular when the crowd has coalesced out of a larger throng which continues to function in unfocused form around the core. Polarization constitutes the best single measure of the crowd boundary in such cases; as one moves out from the center of the crowd in concentric rings, the proportion of people polarized toward the center may drop off; it is anybody's guess what polarization value defines the exact boundary of the crowd.

Crowd boundaries are also of interest because the junction of two crowds causes a set of distinctive phenomena. The clash of two hostile groups, such as political demonstrators and police, is largely a boundary confrontation. Most of what is especially dramatic occurs at the interface; it is here that blows are cast and clubs are whipped out on the front rank of demonstrators. Frequently, a crowd will disperse after the front phalanxes of both sides have had an initial encounter. But when the boundaries blend into each other, one knows that a form of free interaction is developing and the crisis is deepening. For purposes of measurement, the degree of interpenetration of the two sides can be specified readily in the statistical terms of mixed and unmixed runs. Or one may apply a grid over photographs taken at different phases of a riot, and determine how many squares are mixed, and how many contain unmixed elements, as illustrated in Fig. 17.3.

Solvency is the degree to which one collectivity blends into another when the two of them meet and dissolve their identifications with the original groupings. A parade is usually insolvent, even as it passes through onlookers; but it may be so inundated and interspersed with onlookers that its form disintegrates. Boundary maintenance is an important problem in organized collectivities. As an exception, the anti-nuclear protest march from Aldermaston (Lang, 1960) typically invited onlookers to join the group. Here a fluid boundary between marchers and onlookers was encouraged.

Crowds' boundaries often change by accretion independently of the intentions of those already in the crowd, and a participant's position relative to the boundary can consequently be altered. At the Boston Civil Rights rally of March 14, 1965, the author noted:

> I had been standing on the perimeter of the crowd, but by 2:50 P.M., without doing anything, I found myself no longer on the fringe. A great mass of people had formed behind me, and I was now in a relatively central part of the crowd. Somewhat the same feeling as waiting at the very end of the line at a movie theatre, and then with great surprise noticing how many people had formed behind me. By doing nothing, my position shifted in a changing structure.

The observation is representative of a general property of crowds. There is a separation of intention and consequence. A man becomes immersed in a situation whose properties are continually changing. He decides to stand on the fringe, yet finds himself at the core; he wishes to remain stationary, but the dense flow of bodies carries him forward. The choices made by a plurality of others in interstimulation create altered conditions for him that are independent

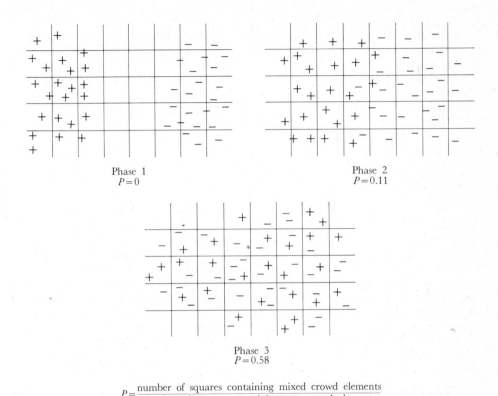

Phase 1
P = 0

Phase 2
P = 0.11

Phase 3
P = 0.58

$$P = \frac{\text{number of squares containing mixed crowd elements}}{\text{number of squares containing any crowd elements}}$$

Fig. 17.3 *The interpenetration of two crowds.*

of his intentions; in turn, his response to the conditions creates constraints and pressures for others.

INTERNAL SUBSTRUCTURES

An assemblage that appears to be undifferentiated may on closer examination possess internal boundaries dividing it into several subgroups. *Lamination* effects are common in crowd formations. For example, outside the Cow Palace in San Francisco during the 1964 nominating convention of the Republican Party, a parade of CORE demonstrators protested the candidacy of Senator Barry Goldwater, but they were surrounded by a pro-Goldwater crowd that attempted to nullify the effect of the CORE demonstration (White, 1965). Laminated crowds composed of antagonistic subgroups constitute ideal predisposing conditions for riots.

In totalitarian countries, the managed mass demonstration has become a common occurrence (Methvin, 1961) and depends for its stability on the creation of invisible but carefully planned internal substructures. Workers parade in the street, seemingly spontaneous, enthusiastic, and unrelated to each other. But each parade participant is embedded in a group of persons who know him, frequently his fellow factory workers. Thus a lack of enthusiasm, or a failure to show the proper amount of spontaneous and uninhibited participation, is discouraged.

Even in the truly spontaneous crowd, friendship ties, family ties, and role relationships constitute substructures and govern the participants to a greater degree than is ordinarily supposed. Most crowds cannot be thought of as an aggregate of isolated points, since a fair proportion of the participants are likely to have specifiable kinship or friendship ties to one or more other participants in the assemblage.

Moreover, a far greater diversity of activity goes on in what appears to be a homogeneously acting crowd than is generally supposed. To cite an example observed by the author: At the height of the Boston Civil Rights rally of March 14, 1965, on first glance the entire audience seemed rapt in attention as a speaker described the brutal treatment he had received at the hands of Mississippi police. More careful scrutiny of the crowd, however, revealed that highly varied activities were in progress. A good proportion of the audience was attending to the speaker. But others were engaged in private conversations. A mother was tying the shoelace of her child. Even business relationships were in evidence: a photographer with a Polaroid camera was circulating in the crowd, photographing participants; he then had no difficulty initiating a seller-client relationship with those whom he had photographed. Recent theories by Turner and Killian (1957) and Lang and Lang (1961) stress differential participation as major features of crowd activity.

POLARIZATION

Polarization provides one index of the "mental unity" of a crowd. Attention, after all, is one aspect of such unity: if the members of a group all face one object, such as a speaker, the group is highly polarized; if they face in many different directions, the degree of polarization is low. A theater audience united by interest in a play will show nearly complete polarization, but if a substantial proportion of the spectators are looking away from the stage, things are not going well for the players.

For most groups, polarization is related to important aspects of structure and function. Polarization is likely to be higher near the center of a crowd than at the fringes. In certain situations, polarization delineates the borders of a crowd. Consider a fairground on a busy day. Many of the observers at any time will be in random motion among exhibits, but a subgroup will be polarized around each attraction. When the borders of the subgroups are not sharp, a quantitative measure of polarization can be used to determine where the splinter groups end and the freely moving mass begins. A crowd, in short, is distinguished from a mere aggregate by some commonality of interest or purpose. As a rough measure of such commonality, polarization is used to specify the borders of crowds and to delineate subgroups within a large assemblage.

Similarly, polarization is related to the breakup of crowds. Diminishing polarization frequently precedes spontaneous breakup of the group, as individuals lose interest and prepare to disengage. Changes in polarization over time reveal much about the workings of a crowd. Sequential records of polarization in a crowd watching political candidates could yield important insights about the effectiveness of speakers. For example, in the 1960 Presidential election, did Kennedy or Nixon characteristically create crowds of higher polarization?

Though writers have discussed polarization (Brown, 1954; Woolbert, 1916), little has been done to explore its empirical applications. As an example of the kind of work that could be undertaken, consider the accompanying photograph of Governor Nelson Rockefeller in the midst of a crowd at Berkeley (Fig. 17.4). An arrow is assigned to each member of the crowd, showing the direction in which his eyes are focused. A radial grid is fitted over the crowd, with Rockefeller in a circle at the center. The resulting diagram (Fig. 17.5) provides a clearer overall picture of polarization than does the photograph itself.

Each individual arrow is extrapolated to test whether it intersects the Rockefeller circle. If an arrow does intersect the circle, the individual is polarized and is assigned a value of 1. If not, he is unpolarized and assigned a value of 0. Polarization for the entire crowd can be represented by the fraction:

$$\frac{\text{sum of polarization values for crowd}}{\text{size of crowd}}.$$

Fig. 17.4 *Governor Nelson Rockefeller in the midst of a crowd at Berkeley. (Courtesy of Wide World Photos.)*

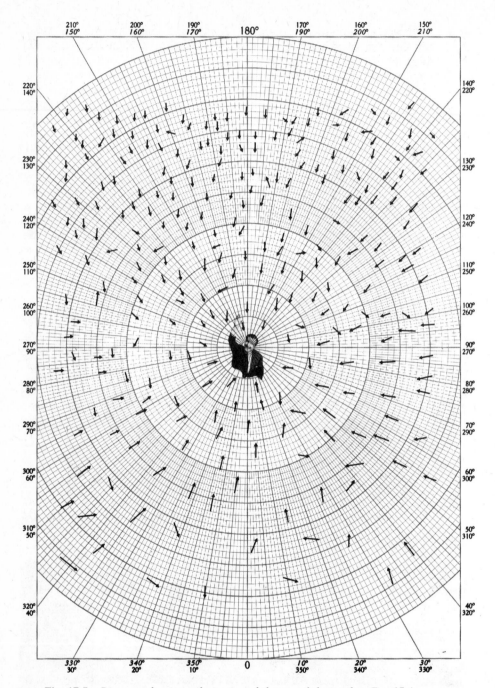

Fig. 17.5 *Diagram showing polarization of the crowd depicted in Fig. 17.4.*

The crowd in the photograph consists of 266 people, of whom 148 are oriented toward Rockefeller. Thus the polarization quotient is 148/266, or about 0.56. The quotient may appear low for this crowd, which on first impression appears to be paying attention to the Governor. Indeed, when persons are asked to indicate the proportion of the crowd looking at Governor Rockefeller, they usually overestimate it. This finding supports Turner's (1964) theory that the sentiments and behavior appropriate to the situation tend to be imputed by observers to all the crowd members.

ECOLOGY: DEPENDENCE ON
PHYSICAL-ENVIRONMENTAL CONDITIONS

There are innumerable points at which the shape of the environment radically affects crowd functioning. The building of wide boulevards in Paris was deliberately planned by Hausman to prevent insurgent crowds from forming barricades across narrow city streets (Pinkney, 1958). Panic depends on a special set of physical conditions, in which there is an aggregate enclosed in a space that has limited exit possibilities such that those who rush for them first can escape, while those who are behind cannot. When an aversive stimulus, such as a fire, occurs in a totally enclosed area where there is no possibility of escape, panic does not develop (Brown, 1965). Also, when the escape routes are not limited but fully open, panic rarely develops (Schultz, 1964).

A typical instance of the dependence of crowd behavior on the exact physical details of the environment is illustrated in the "Brattle Theatre breakdown of norms," observed by the author:

> When patrons arrived at the Brattle Theatre in Cambridge, they purchased tickets and then formed a line along wall A (see Fig. 17.6a). When the line became sufficiently long, it doubled back over wall B.

> Those who had bought their tickets first had priority of entrance according to a well-established understanding among patrons. When the doors to the auditorium were opened the patrons were to proceed in order of arrival and select their seats. However, the corridor in which the doubled over line was formed was an extremely narrow one, so that in order for person X to proceed along the prescribed path, he frequently jostled and bumped into others proceeding in the opposite direction. The internal friction became very great, and eventually the people along wall B would turn around, in violation of the norm. And those at midpoint would become the last to enter. This happened repeatedly. A solution to this problem was found by widening the corridor so as to avoid internal friction (see Fig. 17.6b). This resulted in the orderly and correct sequence of entry into the theatre.

Density

The number of people within a specified space defines the density of the crowd. Jacobs (1967) has computed the density for several crowds assembled to hear speakers in Sproul Plaza on the Berkeley campus. Working with aerial photographs, he tallied the number of persons present, and divided this number into

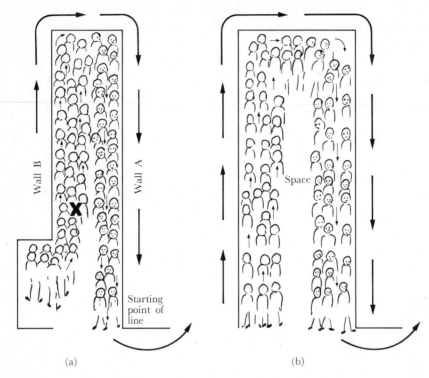

Fig. 17.6 *The Brattle Theatre breakdown of norms.*

the area under observation. The highest density he observed was four square feet per person during a religious gathering (when the absence of a loudspeaker forced listeners to get close to the speaker to hear what he was saying). With loudspeakers present, densities were lower. When Stokeley Carmichael, a militant Negro leader, spoke, Jacobs calculated a crowd density of 5.7 square feet per person; counts of 6.5 and 8.5 square feet per person were observed on other occasions. Jacobs points out that, by applying this formula, official estimates of crowd attendance can often be shown to be grossly exaggerated.

The densest crowds commonly found in day-to-day life are those in the subways of Tokyo. Pushers are employed to pack as many bodies as possible into subway cars. High density, as in the case of the Brattle Theatre, invariably creates problems of internal friction. In Tokyo, slippery coats are sold to subway riders to facilitate their movement through the tightly packed mass (Clark, 1965).

Hall (1966) asserts that there is a psychological sense of crowding that cannot be equated with the simple density of people per unit of space. How a person responds to jostling and shoving will depend on how he feels about being touched by strangers. Further, there exist cultural differences in the tolerance of dense throngs: "The Japanese and Arabs have much higher tolerance for crowding in public spaces and in conveyances than do Americans and Northern Europeans" (Hall, 1966, p. 58).

The work of Calhoun (1962) on Norway rats, Christian (1960) on Sika deer, and Parkes and Bruce (1961) on a variety of animals shows that mammalian populations are controlled by physiological mechanisms that respond to population density, that extreme social disorganization may result from crowding, and that biochemical malfunction and even death occur when animal densities rise above a critical point. The implications for human crowding have not yet been thoroughly investigated.

Rationalizing the Crowd

Many societal devices have been adopted to regulate the relationship of crowds to physical constraints (Cox and Smith, 1961). Some stores handling a large number of customers at once prevent a mob atmosphere by assigning numbers to patrons and serving them according to numerical sequence. The quitting times of employees in large office buildings are staggered to prevent the formation of throngs at the elevator. Cultural norms, such as the dictum "women and children first," prescribe a sequence for leaving a situation of danger. In queuing up for buses, instead of creating a squeeze at the bus door, with its possibility of injury, those waiting assemble themselves in a line, permitting rational entry according to priority. The rationalization of crowd behavior is likely to increase in social life as population densities rise.

The importance of fitting crowd movement to the proper physical environment cannot be exaggerated; designers of theaters and other arenas are now giving serious consideration to the proper flow patterns for efficient evacuation of their structures. Social psychologists, who introduced the idea of crowd phenomena, ought to make a more substantial contribution to this technical problem.

The successful application of computer simulation to fluid dynamics suggests that crowd flow can be simulated, and experiments may be performed without actually herding an army of subjects down laboratory corridors (Harlow and Froom, 1965). Students of crowd phenomena can take advantage of the natural flow of crowds out of stadiums and other areas of high crowd density, and with the aid of photographic and tracer techniques, plot the crowd flow directly.

THE CROWD IN MOTION

The rate at which people walk is ordinarily figured by traffic engineers at four feet per second (Bruce, 1965), with speeds generally decreasing as the density of the crowd rises. The relationship between walking speeds, crowd densities, and time of day is shown in Fig. 17.7.

Acceleration

The term synchronized acceleration refers to a situation in which all crowd members begin to move at the same time. This happens in an army unit when the command "forward march" is given. It may also occur when a common stimulus to start, such as a changing pedestrian light, is perceived by all

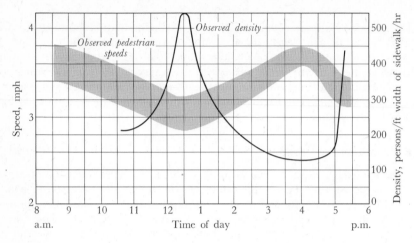

Fig. 17.7 *Relationship between pedestrian walking speeds and density. (From Bruce, 1965.)*

members. But it is relatively rare. Most often the crowd transforms itself from a stationary to moving state by staggered motion. A person waits for the man in front of him to make his move before he starts.

The inefficiency of staggered motion relative to synchronized motion is clear, for in staggered motion the time required to move the crowd is a function of the time it takes the first unit to respond to a stimulus plus the time it takes for the second unit to respond to the $n-1$ unit. Thus:

$$T_d = f(r) \qquad\qquad\qquad \text{for synchronized motion,}$$
$$T_d = f(r_1 + r_{2,1} + r_{3,2} + \cdots + r_{n,n-1}) \qquad \text{for staggered motion}$$

where T stands for the time required for the crowd to move a given distance d, and r is the time required to respond to the stimulus.

If all members of the crowd are moving in the same direction, crushes occur when the nth unit proceeds to move forward before $n-1$ has accelerated sufficiently. More generally, the number of collisions between persons in a crowd is a complex function whose chief variables are the density of the crowd, the rates of acceleration, and the number of directions pursued by the participants.

Man–Vehicle Aggregates

The problem becomes more critical when normal pedestrian rates are augmented by vehicles. A dense aggregate of automobiles driven on a city street, or jammed up at a junction, constitutes a form of contemporary crowd. It is easy to forget, on seeing a traffic snarl, that we are dealing first and foremost with the behavior of human beings, embedded (to be sure) in vehicles, but still responding in terms of crowd psychology. Ritter (1964), a student of urban design, has concerned himself with one aspect of this problem. He notes (p. 34):

> Encased in steel armor almost every driver changes from his pedestrian self into a far more aggressive personality...once tied to the car, people themselves become less sociable, cooperative, rational, considerate, and kind.

Many of the unsavory characteristics Le Bon (1895) attributed to street crowds urban designers now attribute to crowds of drivers. The shock often felt when six or seven people are trampled to death in a theater crush is rarely extended to consideration of highway deaths. If people could walk as rapidly as they drive, the formal identity of the problems would be more generally seen. Crowds of cars have been subjected to theoretical analysis, and some of the ideas developed in this realm are equally relevant to the description of crowds of people.

Distinctive forms of crowd activity have developed in close connection with vehicles in modern times. Motorcycle riots are common (Shellow and Roemer, 1966). The presence of the cycle enhances the participant's feeling that he can speedily leave the scene of the riot, and thus escape legal action—a contemporary extension of the sense of anonymity.

Note. Theorists view traffic as a moving stream with properties of flow, density, and waves (Gazis, 1967). A wave is a tendency of cars in a stream of traffic to bunch together at certain points and then spread out at other points.

Edie and Foote (Edie *et al.*, 1963) demonstrated that waves of congestion could be reduced by separation of cars into groups called platoons. Platoons improve total flow and, since there is less packing together, reduce the number of stops and starts.

Social influence is clearly demonstrable. Herman and Rothery (as reported in Schmeck, 1966) have shown that a fast pacing car will hasten the movement of traffic as surrounding drivers try to maintain the same speed as the lead car. When one car follows another, these investigators have determined, the follower is most concerned with keeping at the same speed as the lead car, but is less concerned with maintaining a uniform distance.

CROWD SIZE

Growth

In a recent television program, the producer staged an automobile accident in the streets of Rome. With the permission of local authorities, two cars were crashed against each other. Though the streets appeared relatively empty, a crowd began to form around the scene of the accident. It grew to a certain extent, perhaps ending up with 100 onlookers arranged in a circle around the cars. The crowd did not grow in unlimited fashion; rather, upon attaining this size, it ceased to grow further. The ultimate size to which an accident crowd will grow is limited by population density in the immediately surrounding area and by other factors, such as the time of day and the diminished visibility which the initial onlookers cause. These features of crowd formation need to be studied further, for though a good deal has been written on the effects produced by crowds once they exist, little has been said about the processes of crowd formation. Canetti (1962) speaks of "crowd crystals" as those initial formations of people which precipitate the growth of larger crowds. Smelser (1963) discusses the general conditions of society that spawn crowd activity.

A field experiment carried out by the first author and his students examined the role of precipitating groups of varying numbers in crowd formation. Precipitating groups made up of 1, 2, 3, 5, 10, and 15 were, in random sequence, placed on a New York City street with heavy pedestrian flow. Members of the group performed a clearly observable action, looking up at the window of a skyscraper, and holding the pose for a period of one minute. Each condition was replicated five times. The investigators photographed the scene with motion picture apparatus, then, by analysis of the film, calculated the proportion of passersby who imitated the action. The results are shown in Fig. 17.8. The proportion of passersby who imitate the "looking up" response increases with precipitating groups of 1 to 5 persons, then levels off with groups of 5, 10, and 15. The attracting power of larger crowds is shown by an additional analysis. Whereas 4.05 percent of the passersby stopped to stand alongside a single person who looked up, 39.98 percent of the passersby stood alongside the precipitating group of 15.

An additional empirical observation on the changing size of crowds is provided by Christopher Millard's study (1963) of the Piazza del Palio. Keeping a minute-by-minute survey of people entering and leaving, he was able to generate a graph showing the number of persons present throughout the day, as

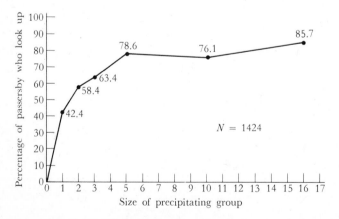

Fig. 17.8 *Percentage of passersby who look up as a function of the size of the percipitating group.*

shown in Fig. 17.9. Using photographic aids and extensive notes, Millard also recorded 1050 incidents that occurred during the period of observation—a type of observational technique that social psychologists could well adapt to the study of crowds, and which in limited form has been attempted by Turner (1964).

The Distillation Effect

Declining crowd size may have important consequences for the composition of the crowd and consequently its disposition for action. At its peak the Boston Civil Rights Rally of March 14, 1965 contained several thousand participants. By 4:05 P.M. (as observed by the author), as a result of departures of those less committed to the rally (partly as a function of boredom and the increasing coldness), only a few hundred of the more ardent and dedicated members were left at the rally. Since stragglers, idle bystanders, and those merely curious had left, the rally now consisted of a dense concentration of dedicated supporters of civil rights. Under circumstances in which extraneous or poorly committed persons are selectively removed from the mass, diminishing crowd size leads to a purer concentration of ardent supporters and a heightened capacity for action. A crowd has a structure viewed against the temporal dimension. To learn who are the most dedicated members of the crowd, one can study the total duration of participation in a crowd and also examine who is the last to leave.

Estimating Crowd Size

The inadequacy of current techniques for estimating crowd size is made clear by an examination of the conflicting reports following crowd episodes. Police

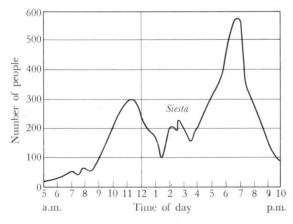

Fig. 17.9 *Changing size of crowds in the Piazza del Palio. (From Millard, 1963, as reproduced in Ritter, 1964.)*

reports are the most common source of estimates, yet Jacobs (1967) has pointed out that police reports "are often double, or triple, and sometimes as much as twenty times the actual number." Estimates of the crowds assembled in St. Peter's Square in Rome, for example, are often as high as one and one-half million. Yet measurements show that the three big areas in front of the basilica which together constitute the square of St. Peter would hold not more than 240,000 persons at two square feet per standee.

Jacobs has presented a formula for estimating crowd sizes that can be carried out by observers on the scene. It consists of adding the length and width of the area occupied by a crowd and multiplying by a density figure, namely, 7 for a loosely composed crowd and 10 for a more compact crowd. He argues that the formula, easily applied, produces an estimate of crowd size accurate to within 20 percent of the size as determined by actual headcount of photographs taken of the crowd. Obviously, Jacob's formula is affected by the shape of the crowd, and could not be applied to an aggregate that is stretched out in a form approaching a line. Multiplying length by width, and dividing the product by a density factor, is more accurate.

A complication is introduced when the crowd does not consist of a stable population, but is composed of continually changing personnel, that is, when there are persons leaving and entering the crowd. Two estimates then become possible: an estimate of the maximum size of the crowd at any one point, and an estimate of the total number of persons who participated in the crowd during the course of its existence. It ought to be possible to sample crowd turnover and to use the sample as the basis of a crowd size estimate. But turnover rates may vary as a function of the location in the structure of the crowd where measurements are made; thus it becomes important to be able to adequately sample representative crowd locations. Methods of estimation must be checked against actual headcounts, a task that is arduous but necessary for establishing the adequacy of any sampling procedure.

The Significance of Numbers

The theoretical significance of numbers for the phenomena of collective behavior is still subject to dispute. Brown (1965), for example, believes that the essence of panic can be captured with only two people, so long as there is operative in the situation a payoff matrix comparable to that in the prisoner's dilemma game.

Yet surely certain crowd phenomena depend for their expression on large numbers. The *surging* of a crowd, for instance, cannot materialize with only a dozen people. At the other extreme, there is clearly a point of superfluity. In the 1963 march on Washington it was estimated that more than 100,000 people were present (Waskow, 1966). Would new phenomena arise after the first 10,000, 30,000, or 50,000? At what size do all the essential features of the large crowd appear? It may be surprisingly small. In Asch's famous laboratory study of group pressure, for example, it was found that groups of three to four confederates produced the maximum group pressure. Increasing the size of the majority even to 15 did not generate any new phenomena or increase the pressure of the group. What is the asymptotic number in crowds?

Argyle (1959) has shown in his examination of revival meetings that the proportion of persons who indicate conversion (by stepping up to the rostrum toward the end of the meeting) increases as the overall size of the audience increases. This could be due to the increased pressure on the potential converts. Or it is possible that the larger audiences have somewhat different compositions than smaller ones, with a higher proportion of people on the threshold of conversion.

Simmel (writing in 1908) more than any other social investigator believed in the importance of *absolute* numbers in determining the quality of social and political events (1964, p. 98):

> ... it is easier for an army of 100,000 to keep a population of ten million under control than it is for a hundred soldiers to hold a city of 100,000 in check, or for one soldier, a village of hundred. The strange thing is that the *absolute* numbers of the total group ... remarkably determine the relations within the group—in spite of the fact that their numerical relations remain the same.

Penrose (1952) has shown that, even in a democracy, a relatively small number of opinionated individuals, by consistently expressing their views by ballot, can come to control disproportionately large populations in which one find a random distribution of opinions.

A related question, as it concerns crowd activity, is this: What proportion of a crowd must pursue a given direction of activity before the behavior spreads and envelops the crowd as a whole? Rashevsky (1951) tried to deal with this question mathematically (see pp. 254–255). Motorcycle riots are traditionally ascribed to one percent who serve as catalysts and precipitate riots. Shellow and Roemer (1966) reported that the "the rowdies have proudly accepted 'one percent' as an honorific epithet, had often emblazoned it on their costume as a badge of commitment."

The very mass of an assemblage can sometimes produce a consequence quite independently of intention. If three people stand on a bridge and simultaneously stomp their feet, nothing happens. If three thousand people perform this action, the bridge may collapse, an effect brought about solely by the increased mass or size of the assemblage. A similar pattern can be ascribed to a good deal of so-called irrational crowd behavior. The sheer number of bodies may cause bottlenecks in narrow corridors, while the pressure exerted by those behind, the accumulated pressure of many bodies pressing on each other, exacerbates the situation. There is thus a separation of consequence from intention owing to the fact of large numbers.

Size and Anonymity

One of the factors presumed to emerge in crowds of sufficiently large size is *anonymity*. Under the cloak of anonymity, according to Le Bon and F. H. Allport, many antisocial impulses are released. The general argument for anonymity is that a crowd member acts in unusual fashion because, by the size and nature of the group, he cannot be singled out and held responsible for his actions. This argument assumes the existence in the individual of a set of antisocial tendencies that are checked only by public opinion or fear of legal or social reprisal.

Turner (1964), in contrast, feels it is the fact that a man *can* be identified by other crowd participants that brings a person into line with their activities. Perhaps, then, one must ask: anonymity with respect to whom? Conceivably, the most effective release of errant impulses occurs when a man can be identified by those crowd participants acting in a deviant manner, but remains anonymous with regard to persons outside the crowd boundary, such as agents of law enforcement.

The police, of course, are most anxious to pierce the protective veil of anonymity that makes reliable identification of rioters so difficult. Technical aids, such as photographic evidence, have proved to be of some use. In the Harlem riot of 1964, police sprayed a fluorescent powder over the participants. The powder was ordinarily invisible, but under proper illumination it could be detected on those who had been in the vicinity of the riot. Such persons could then be prosecuted under existing riot laws.

In his chapter "Anonymity of the Flock," Konrad Lorenz (1966) points out that there is more to anonymity than merely not being recognized. A further protective consequence of being embedded in large numbers is the difficulty a predator will have in apprehending any specific individual (p. 142):

> Just try, yourself, to catch a single specimen from out of a cage full of birds. Even if you do not want a particular individual but intend to empty the whole cage, you will be astonished to find how hard you have to concentrate on a specific bird in order to catch one at all. You will also notice how incredibly difficult it is to concentrate on a certain bird and not allow yourself to be diverted by an apparently easier target. The bird that seems easier to catch is almost never caught, because you have not been following its movements in the immediately preceding seconds and therefore cannot anticipate its next movement.

THE COMPOSITION OF CROWDS

What are the characteristics of the people who make up crowds? When the populace ran through the streets of Paris and stormed the Bastille, who exactly were they? Were they bakers, bums, women, children, criminals, petty bourgeois? For a long time, surprisingly few exact answers could be given to this question. The typical view expressed by Taine and Le Bon was that revolutionary crowds were composed of criminal elements, riffraff, vagrants, or social misfits. Recent historical investigations by such empirically oriented investigators as Soboul (1964), Rudé (1959, 1964), and Tilly (Tilly and Rule, 1964) have brought into question this traditional view. Thus Rudé reports that, although Paris was flooded with unemployed agricultural workers in 1789, they played only a minor role in the tumultuous disturbances that beset the capital that year: "Among 68 persons arrested, and killed in the Reveillon riots in the Faubourg St. Antoine at the end of April, only three were without fixed abode and only three had served previous terms of imprisonment..." (p. 200). Of the

662 persons reported to have been killed in storming the Bastille, all had regular places of residence and had settled occupations. In addition to social class, information on age, literacy, religion, and geographical origin of important historical crowds is now being subjected to the scrutiny of investigators.

In more recent times, also, prison records have served as a useful source of information on those involved in rioting, at least those who were apprehended. In a study of the rioters and looters committed to prison for their participation in the famous Detroit riot of 1943, Akers and Fox (1944) noted the following characteristics of 97 Negroes and eight white men sent to prison. The rioters were disproportionately from states south of the Mason-Dixon line (compared to a nonrioting control group). They were older than nonrioters, less intelligent, and had less education than the control group. They were mostly unskilled workers and many (74 percent) had previously been in conflict with law enforcement agencies.

Wada and Davies (1957) studied a sample of Japanese-Americans who had rioted while in an American internment camp in 1942. Compared to a control group of nonrioters, the rioters differed mainly in their marginality between the two cultures of America and Japan; they also had relative freedom from family ties, and had little economic stake in American society. The authors concluded that rebellion is the work of a minority whose individual circumstances free them to react against the intolerable.

Glenn Lyonns (1965) obtained demographic data on students who participated in the police car demonstration in the 1964 Berkeley uprising. Demonstrators tended to be more politically liberal than the student body as a whole, and tended to reside under conditions of less restrictive housing (apartments rather than dormitories). Again, forms of marginality and 'distance from conventional living appear to characterize the demonstrators.

Changing Composition

What appears to be a continually identifiable crowd frequently experiences change in personnel, as new and different elements move into the crowd and others withdraw. The infusion of a new social element into an ongoing rally or demonstration can serve as the mechanism for changing the activity and direction of the crowd. Craik (1837) reported that criminals frequently infused the crowds of revolutionary France, and gatherings that began with high revolutionary ideals were thus transformed into thieving, destructive mobs. The ruffian element of a community may be drawn into a riotous condition taking advantage of the confusion to turn the direction of the crowd into looting.

The composition of crowds is functionally related to the actions of crowds, and the precise makeup of a crowd may play a very important role in determining the form of collective behavior that arises. Probably, combative riots will not occur with an assemblage containing a high proportion of women and children, because their presence would tend to dampen the movement toward violence. The composition of the crowd may also determine the response to it. Some clergymen displayed themselves prominently in the civil rights demonstrations of the 1960's in the hope that their conspicuous presence as part of the demonstratirs would serve to curtail violent action by antagonistic onlookers. Crowds composed largely of women played an important part in revolutionary France in the eighteenth century, as well as in the Hungarian revolt of 1956. In the latter case it was felt that military forces would be less likely to take action against the women's crowd than against a crowd composed of men.

The composition of any crowd may be ordered in terms of the differential readiness of members to deviate from conventional norms of society. Brown (1954, pp. 846–847) has spelled out the various categories of persons who compose a mob, in terms of their readiness to violate conventional behavior:

1. There may be lawless individuals whose brutal behavior is not completely discontinuous with their private lives.

2. There may be others who readily succumb to the hypnotic powers of father surrogates...not ordinary criminals but simply very susceptible to a certain kind of leadership.

3. With the two impulsive groups above to trigger mob action the *loss of responsibility through anonymity* will bring in the *cautious*. There will be many who are strongly predisposed to criminal action and are only restrained by a fear of punishment.

4. ...there will be those who cannot act until a full-fledged mob is in existence. When large enough numbers can be recruited at the lower thresholds to create an *impression of universality* or to permit the mass to supplant the superego, the *yielders* will become involved.

5. Then there are those *supportive* individuals who cannot be stampeded into action but who do not actively oppose the mob. They draw the line at active participation but are not averse to enjoying the show or even shouting encouragement...

6. Finally there are the *resistant*, whose values are opposed to mob action and who are not unseated by temporary pressures...

Special Compositions

Occasionally, a crowd of people may have a high concentration of some human characteristic especially relevant to the processes of collective behavior. For example, irrationality is often ascribed to crowds (Le Bon, 1895; Martin, 1920). But few observations have been made of crowds of people whom we know to be irrational, that is, mental patients. If, as some say, crowds are paranoiac, we ought to ask: What is a crowd of real paranoiacs like? Do they bear any resemblance to the picture of the "normal" mob described by Le Bon? Would different categories of mental illness lead to crowd reactions of predictably different sorts?

Similarly, the term "childlike" is often used to describe crowds (Strecker, 1940). Why not look at crowds of children? We know *they* are childlike. Do they resemble adult crowds, or is there an important developmental aspects to collective psychology, in the sense that children and adults are governed by different crowd principles?

The importance of language, and the communication of symbolic meaning through slogans, can be studied by the observation of those for whom the factor of language is eliminated. Can crowds of deaf persons get worked up despite the absence of an auditory channel? Can a multilingual crowd, of the sort found at an immigration center, achieve the unity often felt to depend on commonly understood slogans and the harangue of a leader? (Babel crowds, according to Genesis, lead only to confusion and frustration of all concerted action.) It would be easy enough to put a man who does not speak English into an English-speaking crowd and note his reaction. Is he infected with the crowd's excitement anyway? If so, how are we to reinterpret the importance of language in the contagion process?

INFORMATION FLOW IN THE CROWD: RUMOR

Often, there is a process of information seeking and communicating among members of a crowd. Prior to a riot, for example, a great deal of distorted and exaggerated information passes from one participant to another (Lee and Humphrey, 1943; Norton, 1943).

Several theorists have dealt with this communication process as an integral part of crowd theory. Smelser (1963) felt that rumors and related beliefs arise when structural strain is not manageable within the existing framework of action. Thus, rumors are to be expected in panics, crazes, and riots, but may also be part of long-term disturbances such as revolutionary movements and religious secessions. Rumors restructure an ambiguous situation by explaining what has happened, by reporting what is happening, and by predicting what will happen (Smelser, 1963).

The information function of rumors has also been stressed by Turner and Killian (1957) and by Lang and Lang (1961). Rumor allows the individual to refer back to the group for a verified conception of the situation. Once he is able to ascertain that his conception is shared with others, the member of the crowd becomes more willing to act. According to this view, rumors are thought of as collective decision-making processes in which norms emerge to coordinate the action of individual members. A rumor will persist when a collective definition is necessary for action and previous conceptions fail to supply a basis for definition or institutional structures are not adequate to coordinate action.

These theoretical formulations rest heavily on the work of Allport and Postman (1947), in which rumor intensity (both incidence of rumor and rapidity and extensiveness of transmission) was asserted to be an unknown function of the product of interest in the matter being transmitted and ambiguity (that is, incompleteness or unverified character of information). Thus:

$$\text{rumor intensity} = f(\text{interest} \times \text{ambiguity}).$$

Allport and Postman (1947) further agreed that, in the course of being retold, rumors undergo *leveling* (becoming shorter, more concise, more easily grasped) and *sharpening* (becoming selective with a limited number of details perceived and focused on). Just what elements of the rumor are leveled and sharpened depends on the process of assimilation, which is a function of the cognitive and emotional content of the listener's mind.

The Allport-Postman theory and the laboratory experiments on which it is based have been greatly debated. DeFleur (1962) strengthened the theory by showing that evidence for it can be obtained in field as well as laboratory experiments. He gave housewives a pound of coffee and told them a simple slogan, promising another pound if the slogan was remembered three days later. In addition, 30,000 leaflets were dropped, offering a pound of coffee to all who knew the slogan. DeFleur found evidence that the slogan underwent both leveling (shortening) and sharpening (selecting and exaggerating).

However, Peterson and Gist (1951) found no serious distortion during a period of public concern in a community in which there had been a rape and murder of a 15-year-old girl. There were a number of interpretive and speculative propositions put forth concerning the event, but no evidence of leveling or sharpening was found. Peterson and Gist concluded that it was invalid to extrapolate from the laboratory experiments to real-life (and more serious) situations. Their criticism would apply to the DeFleur study as well, since there, just as in laboratory experiments, emotional arousal was relatively slight.

The view of rumor as a series of distortions leads to the conviction that riots could be prevented if the facts were kept straight. The assumption is that rumors are inflammatory, while facts are not. Thus, in a police manual on the control of riots, this advice is given: "The only antidote for poisonous rumor is fact. Get the facts promptly and circulate them as widely as possible" (International Association of Chiefs of Police, 1963, p. 19). Unfortunately, this represents an unduly optimistic view of social conditions and presumes that the objective facts of social life can never be sufficiently bad to precipitate riots. Moreover, exaggeration is not the only type of distortion that occurs in the flow of information. Information can be distorted when objectively true and atrocious facts are concealed or played down in official pronouncements.

Until recently, the flow of information could be described as a process in which an item of information travels outward from a point of origin. It was possible to trace geographically the spread of information through an assemblage. Each point of transmission was physically contiguous. Contemporary technology, however, has destroyed the elegance of the process. In recent mass rallies walkie-talkies have been used to transmit information over areas physically remote from each other. In the Watts riots persons could be seen carrying transistor radios, listening to news reports, then converging on the scene of incidents reported in the news (Cohen and Murphy, 1966). New communication devices are likely to alter further the character of crowd activities—a development foreseen by LeBon (1895), who was the first to note the potential effect of mass media on crowd behavior.

Not only does information move within the crowd, but information about the crowd spreads beyond its immediate activities and may itself precipitate further crowd action. In 1964, one riot seemed to trigger another as Harlem, Rochester, Jersey City, and finally Chicago reeled under the impact of racial outbursts. Rudé has carried out the most careful analysis of such phenomena, tracing the nineteenth-century food riots from southern England to the midlands. He was able to discern a clear pattern of development as one riot touched off another (see Fig. 17.10).

• POOR HARVESTS AND A SUDDEN INCREASE IN THE PRICE OF GRAIN TOUCHED OFF THE RIOTS OF 1766 WHEN SMALL CONSUMERS PANICKED AND POURED INTO THE MARKETS OR RAIDED FLOUR MILLS TO SEEK REDRESS BY COMMON ACTION.
• IN THE COURSE OF 12 WEEKS THE DISTURBANCES SPREAD OVER MUCH OF SOUTHWESTERN ENGLAND AND INTO THE MIDLAND AND EASTERN COUNTIES.
• COUNTY MILITIA, THE MILITARY, THE COURTS AND PRIVATE INITIATIVE WERE ALL NEEDED TO CURB THE RIOTS.
• ALTHOUGH PRICES GENERALLY REMAINED HIGH UNTIL THE SUMMER OF 1768, A TEMPORARY DOWNTREND TOOK PLACE BY OCTOBER 1766, DUE IN PART TO BELATED ACTIONS BY THE GOVERNMENT TO ASSURE MORE PLENTIFUL SUPPLIES.
LOCATION MAP
50 MILES
50 KILOMETERS
Hull
ENGLAND
WALES
MIDLANDS
Chester
Derby
Nottingham
Wolverhampton
Stourbridge
Birmingham
Leicester
Kidderminster
Ludlow
Bewdley
Norwich
Northampton
Bedford
Cambridge
Ipswich
Gloucester
Oxford
Lechlade
Aylesbury
Marlow
Stroud
Tetbury
Malmesbury
Reading
LONDON
Bristol
Bath
SEPT. 20
Newbury
AUG. 7
Trowbridge
Alton
Barnstaple
Salisbury
Southampton
Honiton
Crediton
Exeter
Lyme
Ottery
Sidbury
STARTING POINT OF FOOD RIOTS
LATE JULY, 1766
Redruth
St. Austell
TRM
THE ENGLISH FOOD RIOTS OF 1766

Fig. 17.10 *The spread of crowd activity in the English food riots. (From Rude, 1964.)*

THE CROWD AS A PERCEIVED PHENOMENON

Perception of the crowd, far from being peripheral to the study of crowds, is central to it for a number of reasons. First, the description of crowds, from which theory proceeds, is based on the reports of human observers. Moreover, because of the spontaneous and somewhat unpredictable nature of crowds, it will continue to be based on unaided human observations more than any other source of information. Systematic distortion in reports, of a type reported by Turner (1964, p. 390), may mislead crowd theorists.

Second, the manner in which a participant perceives the crowd around him may greatly alter his own behavior. Ordinarily, the crowd member can be aware of only a small fraction of the crowd's activity at a given time. It is reasonable to guess that he responds primarily to the cues of his immediate neighbors. F. H. Allport (1924) pointed out, however, that though the person responds to the stimuli of those near at hand, he reacts as if they were coming from an

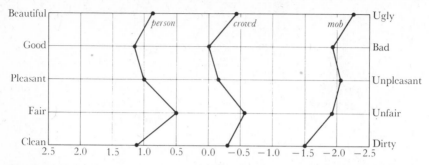

Fig. 17.11 *Attitudes toward the terms* crowd, mob, *and* person. *Students at Harvard University were asked to plot these terms on an attitude scale derived from the semantic differential. With regard to evaluative terms, such as beautiful and ugly, bad and good, clean and dirty,* mob *is given an extremely negative rating, and* crowd *is less favorably plotted than the word* person.

enormously greater number of individuals, and this impression of universality is an important mechanism releasing unconventional behavior. The exact perceptual processes mediating the "impression of universality" need to be examined. Similarly, we have discussed anonymity as a mechanism affecting a person's actions in the crowd. But we know very little about the efficiency with which an individual identifies another person in an aggregate. Neisser's work (1964) on the scanning of elements embedded in larger sets needs to be applied to identification of individuals in an aggregate. Programs of research are needed on the effects of set and prejudice on the perception of crowd activity.

Crowds and Language

The name we attach to a particular mass in action may not be completely free of our political or social purpose. To apply the term *mob* to an assemblage is to condemn it strongly (see Fig. 17.11). The very choice of word may come to exercise an organizing effect on the perception of a collective episode. The Harlem episode of 1963 was termed a "riot" by white radio and television announcers. A Negro in Harlem said he thought it was unfair and definitely "political" to label it this way: "It was a spree, or perhaps a melee." He pointed out that there were comparable activities by white college students on the beach or at Newport, and they were not called riots. We are reminded of Roger Brown's (1954) distinction between the *mass* and the *people*. Similarly, under what conditions group activity is termed a *riot, spree,* or *melee* is a complex problem involving matters of definition, perception, and prejudgment of the group in question.

THEORIES OF THE CROWD

No man is more closely associated with the study of crowds than Gustave Le Bon. Certainly Le Bon was not the first to write on the topic. In 1837, for example, George Craik published his work, "Sketches of Popular Tumults," describing episodes fully as vivid as any Le Bon could draw on half a century later. To what, then, may we attribute Le Bon's special importance? Craik's work, as in the case of other chroniclers of collective behavior (for example, Holinshed, 1577), was not directed principally to the elucidation of general principles. It focused, rather, on particular incidents such as the Naples riot of 1799 or the Birmingham outburst of 1791. Le Bon, too, relied heavily on chronicle and anecdote, but he employed specific incidents to a more ambitious purpose: he sought to define principles common to all crowds. In his attempt to formulate a general theory of crowds—a theory inductively arrived at, however —lies one reason for his special importance.

THE THEORY OF GUSTAVE LE BON

Le Bon's theory was originally presented in two articles in the *Revue Scientifique* (1895), where it shared space with reports on the absorption of light and the analysis of organic compounds. The reports were subsequently combined and offered between hard covers. But the very fact of Le Bon's launching his theory of crowds in a journal devoted to science offers a further clue to his significance. However deficient his own methods, he wished to locate the phenomenon of collective behavior within the province of scientific analysis.

To be sure, Sighele (1901) disputed priority, charging that Le Bon had stolen his ideas, but Sighele's charge is of minor interest, for both authors drew heavily on popular intellectual currents of nineteenth-century Europe. Independent works on crowd behavior appeared almost simultaneously in several countries. The ferment was greatest in France where Le Bon (1895), Tarde (1898), and Sighele (1901) wrote of the mob, and in Italy where Enrico Ferri had devised the title "Collective Psychology" and steered Sighele in the direction of group research (Sighele, p. ii). Even in America, however, Boris Sidis (1895), using terms, language, and ideas remarkably similar to Le Bon's, produced an analysis of mob psychology. It was Le Bon's work, however, that exerted the most effective influence.

What, then, are the components of Le Bon's theory of the crowd? The first and frequently overlooked element is that collective outbursts do not take place in a vacuum, but arise in particular historical epochs, are conditioned by overarching cultural factors, and in turn impress their character on the era in which they occur. There is, thus, a bifurcation in Le Bon's treatment of crowds. On the one hand, he describes far-reaching mass currents characteristic of an entire era, while on the other hand, relatively limited aggregates, such as street crowds, and the psychological mechanisms that operate in them (König, 1958). His first focus initiates an important train of social criticism centering on a general of mass society. The crowd is seen as the hallmark of our age, setting a distinctive tone to the times. The individual is submerged in the mass and a crowd mentality prevails. Ortega y Gasset's *Revolt of the Masses* (1932), Fromm's *Escape from Freedom* (1941), Lederer's *The State of the Masses* (1940), and Arendt's *Origins of Totalitarianism* (1954) each develop this conception in highly individual directions.

Le Bon's second focus, that of the actual street crowd, the manner in which it is formed, the way men are transformed by it, and the mechanisms producing the transformation, comes closer to the concepts of psychology and social psychology. McDougall (1920), Freud (1922), Park and Burgess (1921), Blumer (1946), Turner and Killian (1957), and Lang and Lang (1961), among others, have continued to deal with many of the questions of the street crowd first posed by Le Bon.

Le Bon's fundamental idea is that men undergo a radical transformation in a crowd. Once in the grip of the "law of mental unity of crowds," primitive, irrational elements emerge. Immersed in the crowd, a man loses self-control and may act in a bestial fashion. He can be cruel, savage, irrational, a Jekyl turned Hyde with the crowd itself as elixir. He performs actions that would shock him if carried out when alone. There is a transformation of the first magnitude when a man enter a true psychological crowd.

Such a crowd is dependent not on numbers, but on the "disappearance of conscious personality" and the turning in a fixed direction of the ideas and sentiments of individuals composing such a crowd. There must be a common stimulus before a true psychological crowd is formed. Crowd characteristics appear as emergent properties not predictable from an acquaintance with solitary man. The overarching emergent is nothing less than a *collective mind* (Le Bon, 1903, p. 27):

> Whoever be the individuals that compose it, however like or unlike be their mode of life, their occupations, their character, or their intelligence, the fact that they have been transformed into a crowd puts them in possession of a sort of collective mind which makes them feel, think, and act in a manner quite different from that in which each individual of them would feel, think, and act were he in a state of isolation.

Effects

1. A crowd exercises a dramatic leveling effect on all who are a part of it. No matter how different in aptitude, talent, or temper they may be in an isolated state, in a crowd men become alike. Le Bon explains the *homogeneity* in crowds not merely as the effect of contagion, but by reference to a rudimentary conception of personality. Personality consists of two parts, a superficial conscious layer, where differences between people are located, and an unconscious part which is fundamentally similar from one person to the next. In the crowd, the conscious personality evaporates and with it those superficial differences observable among men.

2. Crowds are intellectually inferior to the individuals who compose it, and manifest all the properties of a retarded mind. A crowd displays rapid shifts of attention, readily accepts fantastic assertions in the absence of evidence, is swayed by images, slogans, and the harangues of a leader.

3. In a crowd, ordinary persons become capable of violent actions that are alien to the solitary individual. The restraints normally governing action are cast off; savage, destructive behavior comes to the fore. "In the life of the isolated individual it would be dangerous for him to gratify these instincts while his absorption in an irresponsible crowd in which in consequence he is assured of impunity gives him entire liberty to follow them" (1903, p. 57). Crowds of decent individuals engage in wanton destruction and indiscriminate murder.

4. Exaggerated emotionalism also comes into play. Participants are intensely excited by fanatical leaders, displaying impulsivity and proneness to extremes of feeling. But, in truth, Le Bon's description of crowd characteristics is less a specification of a given number of properties than a virtually limitless catalog, with a heavy emphasis on all that is stupid, bestial, and primitive in man. (A minor exception occurs in the case of crowds exhorted to heroism.)

Mechanisms

The emergence of crowd properties is brought about by three principal mechanisms:

1. *Anonymity*. Solely from numerical considerations the person in the crowd feels a sense of *invincible power*. The feeling arises when an individual's sense of responsibility disappears, and this in turn is due to a more fundamental fact, the *anonymity of the individual in the crowd*.

2. *Contagion*. Le Bon had been trained as a physician and, impressed with the involuntary manner in which one person contracts a disease from another, perceived a similar mechanism at work in the crowd. He conceived of the state possessed by one person spreading to others like an infectious disease.

3. *Suggestibility*, the third and most important mechanism giving rise to crowd behavior, is a person's uncritical acceptance of the imperatives addressed to him: "...by various processes, an individual may be brought into such condition that having entirely lost his conscious personality he obeys all suggestions of the operator who has deprived him of it and commits acts in utter contradiction with his character and habits" (1903, p. 31). Hypnotism provides the model. Suggestibility, as in the case of contagion, is an open mechanism. Le Bon does not explain why the crowd accepts destructive suggestions rather than constructive ones.

Critique

Le Bon's work has come in for a heavy dose of criticism in recent times (Hofstätter, 1957; Merton, 1960; Turner and Killian, 1957). What are the deficiencies of his approach?

1. A large part of the criticism concerns Le Bon's style. A practicing journalist, Le Bon did not set down his ideas in tidy, ordered fashion. One confronts, rather, a torrential outpouring of insights and observations, repetitious, exaggerated, and unsystematic.

2. Le Bon continually contrasts the irrationality of crowds with a model of the normal, isolated individual. Hofstätter (1957) argues that such a model is inappropriate, for there is an equal amount of stupidity, irrationality, and emotionalism in the lone individual.

3. Le Bon shifts his object of reference with great rapidity, now talking about mobs, sometimes about publics, and on other occasions about juries and parliaments, without adequately distinguishing between types. Furthermore, Le Bon selected the most extreme type of crowd, the hostile mob, and used it as a model for all crowds.

4. Much of Le Bon's exposition reflects the prejudices of his era. He was a racist and accommodated his conception of the crowd to the view that the races of man occupy distinctly different levels on the evolutionary scale. He was a political conservative, fearful of the masses, and scarcely a paragraph of his work is free from an evaluative tone reflecting his patrician stance.

5. Le Bon oscillates in his discussion between the characteristics of the crowd and the characteristics of the individuals who compose it. One might interpret such expressions as "the crowd believes, the crowd imagines, or the crowd feels" as simple short-hand expressions for the way individuals who compose the crowd respond. But in view of Le Bon's strongly asserted notion of "collective mind," it is never clear that this is his intention. The crowd is sometimes viewed as a supraindividual entity, endowed with cognitive processes and a capacity for feeling and believing. Floyd Allport (1924) is typical of those modern positivists who reject the concept of "collective mind," treating it as an obstacle to the scientific analysis of crowds.

6. Le Bon's generalizations are based largely on anecdotal and unsystematic evidence. One senses that, at best, he drew the drapes of his apartment window enough to peek at the rabble below, then closed the velour, ran tremulously to his desk, and dashed off his classic.

Despite these criticisms, his work remains interesting. He presented his theory vividly. More important, a certain prescience on Le Bon's part allowed him to prophesy successfully the role of crowds in our time. His analysis of techniques for influencing crowds, with its stress on repetition, conforms closely to methods subsequently employed by twentieth-century dictators.

Le Bon's work also hit the mark in social psychology. There is scarcely a discussion in his book that is not reflected in the experimental social psychology of this century. His analysis of contagion finds empirical expression in experiments on group pressure and explorations of the process of influence. His dissection of belief systems and the way they are modified is given current expression in the vast quantity of research on attitude change. And it is not merely a highly general discussion that Le Bon provides, but a rich storehouse of imaginative, testable hypotheses. (Consider, as an example chosen at random, his assertion: "At the end of a certain time we have forgotten who is the author of the repeated assertion and we finish by believing it," in essence a statement of the "sleeper effect" confirmed by Hovland, Lumsdaine, and Sheffield, 1949.)

The most important question about Le Bon's theory, however, is this: Are his major assertions true? Does the transformation of a decent, solitary individual actually occur in the manner described by Le Bon? Does he become uncritical, emotional, and capable of acts of enormous destructiveness because he is in a crowd? The sight of a rampaging mob does not necessarily imply that this has occurred. An alternative view would stress the factor of *convergence*, that the mob is formed of those persons who are in fact habitually antisocial and who have been attracted to the mob. So the question remains an open one, but for having posed a question of persistent relevance and impact, Le Bon deserves full credit.

THE PSYCHOANALYTIC VIEW OF COLLECTIVE BEHAVIOR

Freud was so impressed with Le Bon's description of the irrationality of crowds that, when writing his own book on the topic (1922), he devoted a sixth of his manuscript to quotations from the Frenchman's work. He was convinced Le Bon had described a phenomenon of great significance, but he was equally certain Le Bon had not adequately explained it. By extending psychoanalytic theory to the realm of group processes, Freud sought to go beyond Le Bon and uncover the unconscious wellsprings of crowd behavior.

In Freud's scheme, libidinal ties forge the unity among members of the crowd. They cement members together and constitute the essence of "the group mind." The leader plays a crucial role. Libidinal bonds develop between the members of a group and its leader; these are not reciprocated, because the leader cannot love all members with total love. Since the object choice of members is to this extent frustrated, their libidinal relationship with the leader comes to be based on the more primitive process of identification. This involves introjection of the love object, which is then put in place of the ego ideal. In other words, under the leader's influence, the crowd member renounces his own superego and relegates it to the leader. The leader acquires the same relationship to members of the crowd as the hypnotizer to the hypnotized. He thus takes charge of their critical faculties, and they regress to a state of childlike dependence. While the members' relationship to the leader comprises the major force binding the crowd, a second set of relationships comes into play. Each member sees that the other members have in the leader a common ideal. It is by virtue of this common ideal that members also identify with each other ("they are similar to me because they share my leader"). But ties with the leader remain prepotent, and his removal leads to disruption of the group unless a substitute is found. Freud defined "leader" in sufficiently broad terms that it could include symbolic heads of collectivities such as Christ, God, or King. Even an ideal, such as the revolutionary slogan of "Liberté, égalité, fraternité" could qualify, and the crowd could without limitations of conscience exact blood in the name of the revolution.

Violence in the crowd becomes possible, therefore, because the participant is no longer checked by his own superego, but depends on the conscience of the leader. If this is so, then crowds are more or less irrelevant to Freud's explanation of crowd violence; the necessary and sufficient element is the leader. One ought to expect an equally great capacity for violence in a minimal authority situation, in which one person has subjected himself to the authority of a leader, whether or not others are present.

Freud also accepted Le Bon's description of the homogeneity of crowd members. In part, homogeneity is due to the fact that all members come to share a common ego ideal. But there is more to it. Narcissism, the investment of libidinal energy in oneself, works in ordinary circumstances to preserve individual differences and create aversions toward the peculiarities of others (Freud, 1922, p. 43):

[But] individuals in the group behave as though they were uniform, tolerate the peculiarities of other members, equate themselves with them, and have no feeling of aversion toward them. Such a limitation of narcissism can, according to our theoretical views, only be produced by one factor, a libidinal tie with other people. Love for oneself knows only one barrier— love for others.

Thus the principle of the conservation of energy is invoked to explain group homogeneity. In the crowd, the energy required to individualize oneself is withdrawn from the self and is used to cement ties among the members of the crowd and between the members and the leader.

On the whole, it is not easy to subject Freud's theory to empirical tests. Milgram's (1965) studies of obedience to authority lend some experimental support to the view that ordinary persons can relegate superego functions to a leader and act without conscience against another person. But how can one demonstrate that relations among group members derive from ties established with a leader? Since hypnotism serves as the model of the leader-follower relationship, perhaps a group of strangers could be hypnotized; once ties are established between each of the group members and the hypnotizer, bonds should automatically form among the members, and these bonds could be measured by appropriate sociometric devices. Such a procedure, of course, would be heartily disavowed by the orthodox Freudian. Only the standard methods of psychoanalytic inquiry—couch, free association, and all that—could provide appropriate evidence.

One is struck also by the relative *absence* of leadership in recent collective episodes, and indeed, the inability of potential leaders to assume control of a lawless mob. Thus, in the civil rights riots of the 1960's, on several occasions (Waskow, 1966) responsible members of the Negro community tried to becalm tumultuous mobs whose energy seemed to derive not from leaders but from the spontaneous expression of long-standing grievances. Leaders neither initiated the riots nor could they end them.

The importance of Freud's approach lies, in part, in the broad influence it has exerted. A number of works on crowd behavior have been inspired by the psychoanalytic view.

E. D. Martin (1920) was one of the first to apply Freudian principles to an explanation of crowd action, even beating out Freud by a year (the original German version of Freud's book on crowd psychology was published in 1921). Martin accepted the idea of an unconscious mental life, and the accompanying doctrine that real motives are often repressed when they are antisocial: "... a general disguising of the real motive is a characteristic phenomenon of dreams and of mental pathology, and occurs in the crowd by fixing attention of all present upon the abstract and the general" (p. 49).

Each type of crowd (mob, panic, etc.) corresponds to a particular type of repressed impulse that seeks release. The release of antisocial impulses is disguised in the crowd by the use of lofty slogans and ideologies, such as "Liberty, equality, fraternity" or "Bring the boys home." These credos stand in the same relation to the real motives of the crowd as the manifest content of a dream stands in relation to the repressed wish. Moreover, the nature of the repressed material is similar: in both cases it is material that is not acceptable by the standards of conventional morality. According to Martin, "The crowd's spirit will occur most commonly in reference to just those social forms where repression is greatest—in matters political, religious, and moral" (p. 50). Martin fails to explain, however, why the most important domain of psychic repression according to psychoanalytic theory, sexual impulse, does not find more conspicuous release in crowds, give or take an occasional bacchanal.

Martin asserts there is a pathological component to crowds. In the manner of paranoids, crowds sense persecution as well as delusions of grandeur. There is denial. The crowd often projects onto others impulses that are unacceptable to itself. However (p. 106):

> The crowd delusion of persecution, conspiracy, or oppression is...a defense mechanism.... The projection of this hatred on those outside the crowd serves not so much, as in paranoia, to shield the subject from the consciousness of his own hatred, as to provide him with a pretext for exercising it.

Only when members of the crowd are unaware that its lofty preachments are only pretense can it carry out the release of forbidden impulses. Penetration of the disguised material is resisted. Like the wary analysand, the crowd may be extremely intolerant toward those who threaten to reveal its true motives. The crowd cannot tolerate disagreement with its professed purposes, and silences the dissenter with fists.

Redl (1942) attempted to supplement Freud's analysis of the leader's role. His concern was much the same: an examination of the emotional and instinctual events in the members of groups, especially those which happen to center on some focal personality. This focal personality, however, is not quite identical with the "leader" in Freud's sense. Redl's contribution is his terminological refinement, according to which the word "leader" is seen as applying to only one type of role of the person central for group formation and relationships with members, different names being reserved for other forms.

Redl specified ten types of central persons around whom group-formation processes occur. The difference between the various types is based on role differentiation and, specifically, on whether the central person is an object of identification, an object of drives, or an ego support. When the central person is an object of identification, he may be incorporated on the basis of love into the conscience ("Patriarchal Sovereign") or into the ego ideal ("Leader"), or incorporated on the basis of fear through identification with the aggressor ("Tyrant"). The central person may also be an object of love ("Love Object") or aggressive drives ("Aggressive Object"). Finally, as an ego support, the central person may provide means of drive satisfaction ("The Organizer") or means of dissolving conflict situations through assuaging guilt and anxiety.

Janis (1963) applied psychoanalytic formulations to the behavior of groups subjected to extreme anxiety under conditions of external danger (for example, soldiers in battle, surgical patients). He noted a marked upsurge of dependency reactions in such groups and hypothesized that this was the product of a reactivation of separation anxiety. He argued that fear of being abandoned by one's parents persists in latent form in adulthood and is manifested in the need of individuals exposed to danger to be reassured that the significant persons in their lives will not break existing affectionate ties with them. There is a process of psychological replacement that often occurs in such conditions, whereby a company commander may become a symbolic representative of the father, or a fellow soldier a substitute for a brother.

Several writers noted below, though not adhering in close detail to Freud's own theory of group behavior, account for participation in mass events in terms of psychoanalytically oriented concepts.

Some writers emphasize the contribution of the psychological problems of leaders to the shaping of destructive crowds (Gilbert, 1950). Others view the leaders as merely the suppliers of authoritarian doctrines required by the personalities of their followers. An extreme statement of this position is *The Mass Psychology of Fascism*, published in Germany in 1933 by Wilhelm Reich. Reich contended that "a Fuehrer or the advocate of an ideology can succeed only if his ideology or program is concordant with the average structure of the mass individual" (1946, p. 29). Reich traced the attractiveness of Hitler to the patriarchal position of the father in the German family, which "requires sexual inhibition" and eventually causes submission to all authority. Like Reich, Erich Fromm in *Escape from Freedom* (1941) also stressed the role of authoritarian dispositions among the German lower-middle class in creating a receptive milieu for Hitler. Unlike Reich, however, Fromm traced authoritarian character to both economic and psychological factors. Such factors, in combination, may produce a desire for authority which Fromm felt defined the "social character" of a group, and cause it to gravitate to ideologies presented by authoritarian leaders.

Frustration–Aggression Hypothesis

The frustration–aggression hypothesis, an extension of psychoanalytic thinking, was formulated by a group of psychologists at Yale University in the 1930's and applied to the analysis of some forms of collective behavior. The basic postulate introduced by the Yale group asserts "that the occurrence of aggressive behavior always presupposes the existence of frustration and, contrariwise, that the existence of frustration always leads to some form of aggression" (Dollard *et al.*, 1939, p. 1). This premise is elaborated with predictions about the relative amount of aggression to be expected under different circumstances, and about the people against whom aggression would occur. One prediction that relates to *amount* of aggression is that the fury of the destructive reaction will vary with the indignity of the disappointment, or, in the words of the theorists, with the "degree of interference with the frustrated response" (p. 30). An example of this relationship in collective behavior is the following (p. 31):

> The annual per acre value of cotton was computed for fourteen Southern states for the years 1882–1930. The correlation between this index and the number of lynchings in these same fourteen states was −.67; i.e., the number of lynchings (aggression) increased when the amount of interference increased.

The "interference" referred to here is the low price of cotton brought about by market conditions or crop failure. Low cotton prices would affect most acutely the type of "poor white" who composes the rank and file of lynch mobs. This same group has been pinpointed with other indices, such as statistics showing that the most economically deprived Southern counties have been responsible for the largest number of lynchings (Hovland and Sears, 1940, pp. 301–310).

With regard to the *target* of aggression, the theory predicts that victims would be selected in the following order: (1) the "source" of the frustration, (2) other persons, (3) fantasy objects, and (4) the aggressor himself. In collective behavior, an illustration demonstrating the preferred (retaliatory) form of aggression is that of post-World War I race riots in which "the invading and frustrating Negroes were known directly and resented" (Dollard *et al.*, p. 152). The mechanism of reluctantly displaced aggression is illustrated by Nazi anti-Semitism (pp. 154–156). The difficulty with the latter example is that the source of frustration is not easy to specify, since it may include not only the Treaty of Versailles and the impact of inflation and joblessness (Dollard *et al.*, pp. 153–154), but also the hurts sustained by growing German children in pre-World War I authoritarian homes (Adorno *et al.*, 1950; Fromm, 1941). Further, some allowance must be made for the fact that many Nazis may have regarded Jews as the cause of their economic problems to begin with—without having to "displace" from another perceived source of frustration. In other words, whereas the theory sheds important light on a mechanism involved in destructive collective behavior, it is less useful in specifying the nature of the agents involved.

CONTAGION, CONVERGENCE, AND EMERGENT NORM THEORY

Turner (1964), who is chiefly responsible for the statement of emergent norm theory, continually contrasts this approach with theories organized around the ideas of contagion and convergence. Each of these is a mechanism to account for the uniformity of behavior in crowds, the heightened emotion, and the violent antisocial character of the behavior.

Contagion

Contagion is the spread of affect or behavior from one crowd participant to another; one person serves as the stimulus for the imitative actions of another. Bagehot (1869), Le Bon (1895), and Tarde (1903) relied heavily on the mechanism of contagion. McDougall (1920) explained the contagion of feeling by his theory of "the sympathetic induction of emotion," stating that the facial and bodily expression of an emotion in one person instinctively arouses the same emotion in a viewer. He failed to account for those occasions when anger in one party evokes terror in another, or when an expression of lust in the male evokes revulsion in the female. Floyd Allport (1924) extended the notion of contagion by proposing the idea of a *circular reaction*. Quite simply, a person who stimulates another in a crowd sees or hears the intensified response which his behavior has produced in the other; he is in turn restimulated to a higher level of activity by the sight of his neighbor, and so on until ever higher peaks of excitement are achieved. Blumer (1946) elevated the circular reaction to the status of the fundamental mechanism of collective behavior, defining it as "the type of interstimulation wherein the response of one individual reproduces the stimulation that has come from another individual and in being reflected back to this individual reinforces the stimulation. Thus the interstimulation assumes a circular form in which individuals reflect one another's states of feeling and in doing so intensify this feeling." All this is presumed to operate in a roughly mechanical fashion beyond the control of the participants.

Contagion is facilitated by the process of *milling*. In milling, individuals move around one another in more or less aimless fashion, as sheep or cattle do in a herd. They present each other as stimuli, and in turn react to the emotional tones of others. Milling is a process that helps homogenize the crowd and increases the general level of excitement. A spectacular feature of social contagion, according to Blumer, is that "it attracts, and infects individuals, many of whom originally are merely detached and indifferent spectators and bystanders. At first, people may be merely curious about the given behavior, or mildly interested in it. As they catch the spirit of excitement and become more attentive to the behavior, they become more inclined to engage in it" (1946, p. 176).

Is it possible that an initial receptivity to the purposes of the crowd may be a necessary prerequisite of susceptibility? Consider an individual sent into a crowd as an agent of the police to report on crowd vandalism. It seems unlikely that he will be infected with the rising excitement of the crowd. This would suggest that emotional contagion cannot operate in the purely mechanical fashion suggested by Blumer and others. The attitude of the crowd member, how he defines himself relative to the crowd, is of critical importance, and a measure of consent is implied in the crowd participant. The riot police sent to break up a political rally rarely find themselves cheering for the demagogue.

Contagion theorists must face several problems. First, the limits of contagion have not been adequately explained. Sometimes a particular behavior or feeling spreads through a crowd, but often it does not. A failure to specify the conditions of successful contagion is a conspicuous deficiency of this approach. Under what conditions will resistance develop? Perhaps the experimental analyses of McGuire (1962) of the conditions under which a person can develop a resistance to persuasion can be applied to the crowd situation. There is also a failure to specify the spatio-social boundaries within which contagiousness will operate. If contagion accounted for the spread of looting and antisocial behavior in the Los Angeles riot of 1965, why did it not spread in limitless fashion until the entire population of Los Angeles was engaged in these forms of behavior? What are the factors that restricted its spread? (One obvious factor is that a portion of the city was sealed off by armed guards, but even within this quarantine area, sections remained unaffected.)

Finally, contagion, in and of itself, indicates neither the content of the behavior to be diffused nor the variety of shifts that spread through crowds. It leaves open the question of the initial source of the behavior to be diffused and the conditions under which one source will be preferred to another. However, contagion is not so much a theory as it is a specific mechanism which may function in the context of other theoretical mechanisms.

Convergence

If the spread of infectious disease serves as the analog for contagion models, the leukemia ward of a hospital can illustrate convergence. The patients share a common disease, but homogeneity is not due to the fact that they infected one another; rather, they converged on the ward. While contagion theory stresses the transformation of the normal decent individual who is infected by the crowd, convergence theory argues that the crowd consists of a highly unrepresentative grouping of people drawn together *because* they share common qualities. The common qualities preceded formation of the crowd. A hostile mob consists of that small segment of the population unusually prone to aggressive behavior; they have gathered in a crowd as an excuse for expressing qualities which each possesses in isolation. For convergence theories, the composition of the crowd, rather than the interactional mechanisms, becomes the critical focus.

In the mid-1960's a popular singing group known as the Beatles sang before crowds of screaming and swooning teenage girls. The intense emotional expression manifested by the audience may be treated as the effect of contagion, but more likely it represents, at least in part, the convergence of a group already disposed to react in such a manner. When news of a lynch spreads through a Southern town, persons respond to it selectively. Though a great many are subjected to the information of time and place, only a fraction of the town appears. It is likely that these are people most prone to engage in the hostile, punitive act of lynching, with only minimal social support (Cantril, 1941). Thus, convergence, rather than contagion, appears to be the key mechanism. When convergence theory is employed, it is no longer necessary to look for mechanisms within the crowd that bring about homogeneity, since the likeness of members occurs in the very process of crowd formation. Different causes will attract different subsets of the population.

The "outsider," one variant of convergence theory, is frequently invoked in explaining mob violence in an otherwise peaceable town, and indeed, in the case of marauding motorcycle toughs, such as "Hell's Angels," or the English Mods and Rockers riots at English seaside resorts, the accusation seems largely justified (*New York Times*, May 24, 1964).

Shellow and Roemer (1966), reviewing outsider riots centering on sporting events, noted several factors common to them (pp. 12–13):

An influx of outsiders into a small town or circumscribed amusement area, where the number of outsiders was large relative to the number of local inhabitants and police.

The outsiders were distinguished from "locals" by some common feature—
—an intense interest (such as motorcycling), an age group (college youth), race, etc.

The distinction between "locals" and "outsiders" was often made more visible by differences in dress, argot, and other expressive behavior.

A more subtle application of the convergence model attempts to find behind instances of collective outbursts "categories of people within the community who are not fully committed to the dominate mores" (Turner, 1964, p. 387). The prevalence of Negroes in incidents involving wide-scale looting (New York, Los Angeles) may be explained by the fact that many have not accepted white middle-class values, and consider it fair game to acquire goods in moments of social upheaval. But even among the Negro group, only a fraction of the total community participated in the looting, again representing a convergence of those most prone to antisocial behavior.

Convergence is a more elitist theory than contagion, since it implies that all antisocial collective behavior stems from the rabble and that decent, law-abiding citizens are not converted into the lawless.

One merit of convergence theory is that the mechanism can cover a broad range of collective episodes, from the riot and lynch to the deviant social movement. The uniformity of action of a gang of toughs assembled for a brawl, as well as the uniformity of belief among members of the John Birch Society, may both represent the convergence of persons who possessed similar beliefs and action dispositions prior to aggregation.

A difficulty of convergence theory is that of explaining the shifting direction of crowd activity. Assuming that persons possessing a similar behavior disposition are brought together because each wishes his presence in the crowd to serve as an excuse for realizing the disposition in action, how can we account for the continuing homogeneity of the crowd even when its purposes shift? Nor does convergence explain why the like-minded persons come together in the first place, since it implies in its purest form that any one of them would as readily carry out the behavior in isolation. If this is not true, if the dispositions are latent until the like-minded persons converge into a crowd, then we are still left with the problem of explaining what specific mechanisms of the crowd lead to the conversion of the latent impulse into overt action. Perhaps *anonymity* (Le Bon, 1895), or the *feeling of universality* (F. H. Allport, 1924), or the sense of *invincibility* (Le Bon, 1895) acts on those who have assembled. But something must be added to the mere fact of convergence to transform the latent impulse into action.

The issue of contagion versus convergence comes down to this: does a crowd displaying antisocial behavior consist of an ordinary group of persons brought to a state of violence by interstimulation, or is it made up of a special collection of individuals who have converged on the scene, possessed of a set of errant impulses not shared by the population at large? Contagion and convergence are not, of course, mutually exclusive explanations. Both mechanisms could be at work.

Emergent Norm Theory

The explanatory concepts of Le Bon, Freud, Sighele, and McDougall are rooted in the structure of personality and the manner in which the individual is changed by the crowd. Emergent norm theory, as proposed by Turner and Killian (1957) and Turner (1964), employs concepts derived from the study of small groups. Numerous studies in this field show that a group of people allowed to interact freely among themselves will, in time, evolve common standards of behavior (Asch, 1951; Lewin, 1947; Sherif, 1936). Once the standard (or norm) is established, it exercises a constraining effect on group members. There is pressure to adhere to the standard and reluctance to violate it. The emergence of rules of behavior constitutes, from this standpoint, both the chief problem for the study of collective behavior and its most distinctive characteristic.

Emergent norm theory holds that the much heralded *homogeneity* of crowd action, assumed by both contagion and convergence theorists, is false. In fact, most members of a so-called aggressive crowd are not engaged in hostile activity but are simply interested and curious bystanders. The conspicuous actions of relatively few active individuals come to be attributed to the entire crowd. The problem, therefore, is not to explain homogeneity, but rather to explain why the illusion of homogeneity arises. The answer is that a consensus on appropriate conduct is established in the crowd, and crowd members as well as observers refer to this norm, rather than to the actual actions of crowd members, in their characterization of the assemblage. In the establishment of the crowd norm, the action of a few conspicuous and active members comes to be perceived as the dominant course of action. Because it is so perceived, it constrains others to act in a manner consistent with it, inhibits contrary behavior, and justifies converting others to this particular line of action.

Norm theory states, then, that a person acts in a crowd as he does because he perceives it appropriate or required, and not because he is mechanically infected by group emotion or because he has a blind propensity to imitate.

Furthermore, collective behavior is typically characterized by an attempt to define an ambiguous situation and to find cues as to what one is supposed to do. Rumor refers not to the successive transmission of a packaged story with increasing distortion over time (as in the studies of Allport and Postman, 1947), but to a group effort to define what is going on. If there is a search for leadership, it is not Le Bon's "thirst for obedience" nor Freud's identification process, but the desire on the part of members to have others take the responsibility for starting an action that is, initially, of questionable legitimacy.

Emergent norm theory differs in six ways from contagion theory:

1. Norm theory argues that complete uniformity of crowd action is an illusion. Many crowd members simply stand around and by their passivity lend implicit support to the active minority. The proposition that homogeneity is not present in crowds is of great significance. For half a century, social scientists have uttered the catchword "homogeneity" with conviction. Now it is called into question. Moreover, the question can be resolved by resort to the facts. Photographs, films, and videotapes of collective outbursts need to be carefully scrutinized by observers instructed to categorize the behavior in process. This must be done for representative types of crowds, adequately sampled through different phases of their development. It is a mark of our primitive level of knowledge about crowds that not a single tally of this sort exists at the present moment.

2. Under contagion, persons are unwittingly infected with the emotions of others; under a norm, people suppress incongruous moods, but do not necessarily participate in the crowd emotion. They take note of the standard and regulate their behavior appropriately. A buoyant, chattering person, wandering into a funeral service, quickly becomes quiet. It is not automatic infection with the mood of the mourners, but perception of the appropriate norm of behavior, that silences him. In a sense, a "law of mental unity" operates in Turner's theory; it is limited, however, to the unity brought about by the common acceptance of a norm, and does not extend to the indiscriminate contagion of feeling.

3. Contagion works best, Turner asserts, with situations of high emotional arousal, agitation, and excitement. And the general tone of Le Bon, Allport, and Blumer supports this impression. Emergent norm theory, on the other hand, is equally at home with excited as with somber or reverential states. (Despite Turner's assertion, contagion of sad, respectful, or reverential states would not seem beyond the limits of the contagion concept, and Le Bon specifically discusses waves of religiosity spreading over a crowd.)

4. Contagion theory argues that most communication in the crowd consists of messages expressive of the dominant emotion and suggestions for action. Norm theory predicts that most communication will be directed toward (1) attempting to arrive at a conception of what is happening, (2) supplying justification for a course of crowd action, or (3) dispelling conventional norms. A content analysis of crowd communications is required to test the different predictions.

5. Contagion theory fails to account for the limits on crowd excitement and action. Given the infectious spread of emotion and the circular reaction, the crowd should grow ever more extreme in its actions and increasingly agitated over time. A norm, however, can contain a statement of the limits of behavior and define its boundaries. In the Los Angeles riot of 1965, looting and destruction of property were common, but the rioters did not indiscriminately destroy human life. If savage impulses were released, as Le Bon's version of contagion theory would argue, the savagery was remarkably well directed, for whatever sniper fire occurred was directed almost exclusively at the police and related symbols of law enforcement. Destruction was focused, as if regulated by a clearly defined understanding of limits and legitimate targets.

6. Norm theory states that a person must have a social identity if group norms are to be effective over him. Therefore the control of the crowd is greatest among persons who are known to one another. Contagion theory, in the Le Bon tradition, argues the opposite, that anonymity facilitates the spread of crowd emotion and action. Again, a direct empirical confrontation is posed between the two conceptions of collective behavior.

Emergent norm theory contrasts sharply with psychoanalytic interpretations of collective behavior. Martin (1920), as we have seen, recognized that there were many normative sentiments expressed in the crowd; these were not *causes* but merely masking mechanisms, under whose guise repressed impulses could find release. This view explained the seeming paradox that crowds could be both brutal and self-righteous simultaneously. In contrast, emergent norm theory finds primary causal significance in the very material psychoanalysis treats as epiphenomenal. Turner's theory is weighted far more heavily on the rationalistic side.

Emergent norm theory, as it now stands, says little about the content of norms that will arise in collective situations, and specifically, on the violence frequently associated with collective action. Why does one norm emerge rather than another, and what impulses lie behind the emergence of norms that, to all appearances, are destructive not only to a set of outside victims but to the crowd participants as well?

Emergent norm theory does not fully dispense with the idea of contagion. Rather, it displaces the problem of how an emotion comes to be diffused in a crowd, to that of explaining how a group standard comes to be accepted by an aggregate of individuals. One deals, then, with the spread of a cognitive element, but even a cognitive element must start somewhere, and the process of its diffusion is still problematical. While the theory denies homogeneity of feeling and action, it posits a new form of homogeneity: the shared belief in an appropriate standard of conduct by crowd participants.

Because it points to an empirical reexamination of the crowd, and offers a fresh interpretation to crowd episodes which is tied at virtually every point to possible empirical inquiry, Turner's theory deserves the serious attention of social psychologists.

SMELSER'S SOCIOLOGICAL APPROACH

Where other writers content themselves with essayistic approaches to the subject, Smelser (1963) wields a theory that is, above all, systematic. That is, the work in its main outlines is generated from a small number of ideas that are continually reapplied at differing levels of abstraction until a complex theoretical structure is built up. The two main ideas from which the fabric of Smelser's theory is spun out are (1) the notion of *value-added determinants* and (2) the notion of *components of social action*.

According to Smelser (1963), collective behavior occurs when people prepare to act on the basis of a belief that focuses on changing some aspect of society, but it arises only when there is no means of attaining the desired goal through normal institutions of society. It is behavior that occurs, therefore, outside of institutions, and it is behavior that is purposefully oriented toward change.

Smelser's theory strives to be fully sociological in its perspective. In this respect, it departs from the style of psychological analysis initiated by Le Bon, Sighele, and others. It seeks to answer two basic questions: (1) What determines whether an episode of collective behavior of any sort will occur? (2) What determines whether one type of collective behavior rather than another will occur (say, a riot rather than a panic)?

In Smelser's scheme a sequence of six determinants lies behind every episode of collective behavior: (1) structural conduciveness, (2) structural strain, (3) growth and spread of belief, (4) mobilization for action, (5) precipitating factors, and (6) social control. The determinants do not occur in random sequence, but are organized according to the logic of value added.

By "value added," Smelser means that each of the six determinants, beginning with social conduciveness, is necessary for the determinant that follows it and establishes the limits within which the next determinant can operate. Structural strain, for example, must occur within the boundaries established by structural conduciveness, and so on down the line. Temporal sequence is not at issue, since Smelser is concerned with building a formal system that depends on logical relationships only.

The Berkeley Uprising

The determinants and the way they are organized are best understood when brought to bear on the analysis of a concrete case. The Berkeley student protest of 1964 will be used for this purpose. Lipset and Wolin (1965, pp. xi–xii) describe the events:

> As the result of a series of events unprecedented in American university history, the Berkeley campus community lived in a state of unrelieved tension and continuous agitation from September until January. The immediate cause was an announcement by campus officials that a twenty-six-foot strip of land at the entrance to the campus, previously thought by most students and faculty to belong to the City of Berkeley, was the property of the university and subject, therefore, to existing university regulations dealing with political activity. This particular strip happened to be the place where students traditionally conducted political activity involving solicitation of funds and members for off-campus political-action groups, without interference. A student protest movement was rapidly organized, the Free Speech Movement (FSM), and it advanced demands for the drastic reform of university rules and regulations affecting student political activity on campus. A running battle, which lasted almost the entire semester, developed between the administration and the FSM. Before the dispute had run its course, the faculty was drawn in, and the effects of the controversy were registered throughout the entire state. The governor became involved; members of the state legislature began to take sides; thousands of letters and telegrams were sent by alumni, prominent citizens, and interested individuals and groups. Meanwhile the campus was the scene of many unacademic events. There were endless protest meetings, rallies, and silent vigils, with crowds sometimes reaching as many as 7000; there were repeated violations of university rules and civil laws; on two occasions hundreds of police were massed on campus, and the threat of violence seemed immediate and inevitable; three sit-ins occurred, the last culminating in the occupation of the central administration building by 800 students and their forcible removal by an almost equal number of police; and a sympathy strike, launched by teaching assistants, severely interrupted classroom routines. One of the world's largest and most famous centers of learning was brought to the edge of collapse.

Structural conduciveness. This, the first determinant in Smelser's value-added sequence, refers to the very general conditions of social structure that are necessary for a collective episode. Certain fundamental social conditions underlay the Berkeley movement. First, at Berkeley, as at other American universities, administration and student groups have clearly definable identities, and each embodies a somewhat specialized set of interests. Such differentiation is a necessary preliminary to a social movement. Second, unless techniques are available for instituting normative changes, the movement could degenerate into a mere hostile outburst. At Berkeley, students relied on techniques for forcing normative change that were borrowed from the civil rights movement, most specifically the techniques of nonviolent protest and the sit-in. Further, without communication among potential members, no movement could arise. At Berkeley, physical proximity among students facilitated communication; mimeographed handbills and student publications disseminating views of the movement were abundantly in evidence. A final condition of conduciveness concerns the lack of opportunity for other forms of protest. Students could not, for example, readily migrate *en masse* to another college where conditions were more ideal. This could have acted as a valve to siphon off the energy of the movement. The existence of structurally conducive conditions on the Berkeley campus did not ensure a social movement. It merely laid a possible groundwork. No movement would have arisen in the absence of certain conditions of structural strain.

Structural strain. The second determinant of the value-added sequence exists where various aspects of a system are in some way "out of joint" with each other. Strain is a necessary condition of any collective outburst, but it can assume significance as a determinant only within the scope established by the prior conditions of conduciveness. Strain may arise when new knowledge suddenly enables people to do something which had always been desired, but had previously been impossible because requisite skills were lacking. Experience in the civil rights movement and knowledge of its tactics enabled students to strive for a role in policymaking which previously had seemed beyond reach.

Deprivation of a once enjoyed privilege can be an important source of strain. At Berkeley, the Bancroft strip had customarily been used for political activity, but as a result of the administration's decision students were no longer privileged to engage in political recruiting on this property. In addition, this action violated the ideal of free speech. Indeed, the Berkeley protest, which came to be known as the Free Speech Movement, took its name from this focus of strain. But strain, as a set of objective sociological conditions, cannot lead to a collective episode unless people focus on the causes of strain and have beliefs on how to alleviate it. Belief, therefore, is the next determinant in Smelser's scheme.

The growth of a generalized belief. The crux of any analysis of collective behavior is to assess under what set of general beliefs the participants are acting. A generalized belief includes (1) a diagnosis of the forces and agents that cause the strain and (2) a belief about a program which, if instituted, will erase the source of strain. At Berkeley, those who participated in the protest believed that the university administration interfered with their right of free speech, and furthermore, that President Clark Kerr's idea of the multiversity lay behind the unsatisfying impersonality and bureaucratic atmosphere of their institution. Protest of the administration's policy, it was believed, could win for the students the right of full political activity on campus, and force the administration to give up its right of disciplining students for use of campus facilities. The program called for the administration to yield fully on the free speech issue. In a somewhat less clear-cut manner it called for the university to reorganize in a way that would make it more responsive to student needs.

Precipitating factors. Structural conduciveness, strain, and developing beliefs merely set the stage for collective action which, to occur, must be set off by an event. The Berkeley protest was sparked by the announcement that the

Bancroft strip could no longer be used for political recruitment. Subsequent incidents in the Berkeley movement were precipitated by other events. For example, the sit-in at Sproul Hall on December 2 was set off by the administration's announcement that it would discipline four leaders for an earlier incident in the protest. A precipitating factor taken by itself cannot cause a collective episode. In order to do so, it must occur in the context of the other determinants of conduciveness, strain, and generalized belief.

Mobilization of the participants for action. Once the previous determinants have been activated, the only remaining necessary condition is to bring the affected group into action. At Berkeley, a ready and experienced leadership existed in the dissatisfied political groups whose tables had been removed in the Bancroft strip. A potential leadership that was trained in the civil rights movement and committed to its tactics was on hand. Mario Savio, a 21-year-old student who had actively participated in civil rights activities, rose to the fore as a popular student leader. On September 2, for example, he had stood atop a police car and incited a crowd to demonstrate against closing of the Bancroft strip. A report of the Federal Bureau of Investigation asserted that some of the leaders of the Berkeley episode were trained agitators acting in the service of foreign causes.

The operation of social control. This determinant "arches over" all the others, for it consists of the ways in which the agencies of control in the social system discourage or encourage collective behavior. In the Berkeley situation, diverse controlling agencies were at work: the administration, the faculty, and the police. Assemblages of students were permitted on campus, but when the students staged a massive sit-in at Sproul Hall, on orders of the Governor more than 800 demonstrators were forcibly removed and jailed. (This was, incidentally, one of the largest mass arrests in American history.) While the sit-ins were not permitted, a considerable amount of protest activity was tolerated by the administration. Social control is not merely a negative feature. Agencies of control may specifically encourage particular kinds of collective behavior. In some degree the faculty performed this function at Berkeley, in giving general encouragement to a norm-oriented movement (Lipset and Wolin, 1965).

The heart of Smelser's analysis of collective behavior, then, consists in an examination of collective episodes in terms of the six determinants. The same six determinants are to be found in each form of collective behavior, and taken together they fully determine the production of a collective episode. Each of the determinants can appear in a number of forms, and the way different forms combine through the six stages accounts for the type of collective behavior that is produced. One pattern leads to panic, another to craze; other combinations lead to hostile outbursts or social movements. The determinants are not randomly related, but thanks to the logic of value added, nestle into each other like a set of Chinese boxes.

Components of Social Action

The four "components of social action" provide another major organizing construct for Smelser. The components are taken from the writings of Talcott

Parsons (1951) and consist of categories that describe fundamental features of
society:

    1. Values express the most general statement of what is desirable in a
society. Freedom is a value; so is democracy.

    2. Norms are more specific than general values, for they provide rules of
behavior, or guidelines, for the realization of values. For example, if the
value democracy is to operate, rules must be formulated that spell out the
principles of elections.

    3. Mobilization of motivation into organized action specifies who will be
the agents in the pursuit of valued ends, and how the actions of these agents
will be structured into concrete roles. A definition of the electorate, for
example, could fit into this category, as well as a statement of who may run
for office.

    4. Finally, situational facilities, as the lowest component of social action,
refer to the means and obstacles that facilitate or hinder the attainment of
goals. Voting booths would constitute a facility through which elections are
made possible, and the value of democracy is expressed.

Any readjustment of one of the higher components makes for a change in
those components below it, but not necessarily those above it. For example, at
the level of situational facilities, voting boxes may be replaced by high-speed
voting machines without altering the norm that elections be held, or that
democracy be abandoned as a value. But if we proceed in the other direction
and replace the democratic value with an autocratic rule, then the idea of
elections or an electorate, and of voting boxes, becomes superfluous.

What is the relevance of the components of social action to Smelser's theory
of collective behavior?

    1. At every point the components may be applied to the determinants for a
finer analysis of causation. For example, structural strain is defined in terms of
the components of social action. Strain may occur at the level of facilities, at the
level of roles, or at the level of values.

    2. The components help define the several forms of collective behavior. In the
cases of *panic* and *craze*, people prepare to act on the basis of a belief
concerning *facilities*. In a *hostile outburst*, people act on the basis of a belief
focusing on persons felt to be responsible for the evil on hand (*level of
mobilization*). The *norm-oriented social movement*, which seeks to change ways of
doing things, but not the overall values of society, comes next. The American
civil rights movement of the 1960's, which seeks equality for the Negro, a
generally accepted value in American society, is attempting to eliminate segregation, a device that prevents equality. But it does not seek to eradicate basic
democratic values. The most radical form of collective episode is the *value-
oriented social movement*. It aims to induce societal changes of the most fundamental character, that is, at the level of societal values. The French Revolution,
which instituted a new set of values for that nation, constituted such a movement. The Black Muslim movement, in the degree that it seeks to replace the

democratic value of equality with an ideal of Negro superiority, could be defined as a value-oriented movement.

3. Finally, the general nature of collective behavior comes to be defined in terms of the components of action (Smelser, 1963, p. 71):

> ...it is a search for solutions to conditions of strain by moving to a more generalized level of resources. Once the generalization has taken place, attempts are made to reconstitute the high-level component. At this point, however, the critical feature of collective behavior appears. Having redefined the high level component, people do not proceed to respecify, step by step, down the line to reconstitute social action. Rather, they develop a belief which "short circuits" from a very generalized component directly to the focus of strain. The accompanying expectation is that the strain can be relieved by a direct application of a generalized component.

Consider the case of Negroes in a Mississippi town who are denied access to a restaurant. The major components of social action in this situation, from general to specific, are:

1. Values: Equality for Americans.

2. Norms: The mores of a Southern community. Negroes do not eat with whites. Separate but equal.

3. Mobilization (roles): The role of the white restaurateur in preserving the Southern norms. Subordinate role of Negroes.

4. Facilities: Lack of access to white restaurants.

These circumstances engender a situation of strain for the Negro community. The search for a solution does not remain fixed at the level of facilities. Rather it tends upward. The difficulty in using the restaurant is seen as interfering with the value of equality. The nature of the relevant value is reconstituted in this way: While equality may have been taken to mean "separate but equal," the strain created at the restaurant leads to a respecification of what equality entails. "Separate but equal" is read out of the meaning of equality. Having redefined the high-level component of the value equality, the Negro community attempts a direct application of this value at the level of facilities. Negro marchers bearing posters demanding "Equality For All" parade before the restaurant and Negro students sit-in at the lunch counter. Members have attempted a direct application of the high-level component (value) to the specific. In doing so, the intermediate components of social action have been short-circuited. The mores of the Southern community have not been changed, nor have relevant persons (in their role of restaurateurs, patrons, waitresses, etc.) come to accept the application of the reconstituted value to the specific level of facilities. It is this situation that gives collective behavior its clumsy and sometimes destructive character.

There are thus two aspects to collective behavior. First, a specific problem at a low level gives rise to a belief that focuses on a higher-level component. The distinctive character of collective behavior, according to Smelser, is that the group then attempts to apply this higher-level value, once redefined, directly to the specific locus of strain. In this respect, collective behavior is akin to magical thinking in that the intermediate instrumentalities for the achievement of a goal are short-circuited. Le Bon, too, sensed the exercise of magical thinking in the crowd, and Smelser's theory gives it a more rigorous theoretical underpinning.

Critique of Smelser

1. The Berkeley movement, which we have used for illustrative purposes, does not fit neatly into any Smelser's forms of collective behavior. If it was a norm-oriented movement, it possessed few of the enduring features generally associated with such movements. It was temporary, with a relatively transient organizational structure that both arose and evaporated rapidly. Nor could it be termed a hostile outburst, partly because its duration lasted over a period of months, but more critically, because it was a nonviolent episode. Smelser's classification is not fully adequate to an exact characterization of the event.

2. Smelser's theory employs as its central postulate the notion of a generalized belief, implying a unitary outlook at the root of collective action. But it is clear from the Berkeley episode that students with the most diverse and contradictory sets of beliefs were drawn to the protest; it was not a generalized belief, but a series of rather distinct, frequently contradictory, and at times idiosyncratic beliefs that accompanied action (Lipset and Wolin, 1965).

3. Nor is it clear that Smelser's theory meets the single most critical feature of a scientific explanation: that its truth can be denied in the face of contradictory fact. At the outset, it is not possible to coordinate the major concepts of structural conduciveness, strain, etc., to empirical events in an exact and unequivocal manner (Davis, 1964). Social analysts independently assessing the Berkeley episode could not agree on what constituted strain in the Berkeley situation, nor even what constituted the critical precipitating incident (Feuer, 1964; Glazer, 1965; Selznick, 1965). Second, even if it were possible to link each of Smelser's concepts to specific empirical events, it is not clear what propositions are to be refuted. Smelser's scheme is less a theory than a taxonomic structure, a general set of rubrics useful for describing a collective episode but not itself open to disconfirmation.

4. Smelser's value-added theory does not of itself generate hypotheses. The fact that Smelser himself offered insights in such profusion was due to his personal grasp of a wide variety of sociological and historical materials, and to his own ingenuity, rather than to the theory. Turner (1964) tried to apply the value-added theory and concluded it was a useful way of organizing material, but he was not sure that it contributed new knowledge.

5. Finally, we must return to the question: If all collective episodes have the same set of six determinants, why does one type of collective behavior arise rather than another? The levels themselves are merely empty categories. The particular conditions that must obtain at each category determine the type of collective behavior. Where do these particular conditions come from? Are they specified or derived from the major lines of the theory? The particular conditions are *ad hoc*, derived from other theories, or simply brought in intuitively.

Thus the major lines of the theory, the six determinants and the components, are not really theory but metatheory, onto which Smelser must graft a true specification of causes.

Nevertheless, Smelser's theory is a brilliant attempt to incorporate a wide range of determinants into a systematic interpretation of collective behavior, with attention given to both immediate and distal sources of collective action.

MATHEMATICAL THEORIES OF CROWDS

Mathematics is not a form of magic which can create substance out of the vacuum of an ill-conceived theory. However, there are real advantages to the symbolic formalization of models:

1. The mathematical theorist must make perfectly explicit all variables and the relationships among them. No verbal haze can obscure the essential postulate of the model.

2. Similarly, the theorist must specify assumptions which are necessary for the model to function but which are not part of the model itself. In the area of collective behavior, for example, it is frequently necessary to assume that the group under examination is of constant size, or that it is homogeneously mixed. The need for explication of such assumptions may force the theorist to consider crucial but unexamined aspects of the phenomenon he wishes to explain.

3. Once a theory has been translated into mathematical terms, a highly developed set of formal rules can be applied to investigate relationships among the variables. Such investigation can produce subtle and unexpected conclusions. Perhaps the most significant outcome of current mathematical approaches to crowd behavior (such as the existence of a propensity to imitate) can generate striking predictions about aggregates (such as the rapid spread of a behavior through a crowd). Such predictions require no change in the customary behavior patterns of individuals. Rather, they proceed mechanically from the simple fact of large numbers.

Attempts to apply mathematics to crowd behavior were in evidence as early as 1898, when Boris Sidis proposed a theory of mob energy which filtered down from the mob's leader to his followers. Arbitrarily, Sidis decided that the energy awakened in each follower should be half that emanating from the mob leader, and that the energy awakened by mutual excitation among the followers should for each individual be halved again. The resulting expression for total "energy" predicts growth of that quantity as approximately the square of mob size. Plainly, Sidis' quantitative results must be taken with a grain of salt, though his conclusion agrees in a loose way with the observation that rowdiness of a crowd grows more rapidly than the simple addition of individuals would indicate. Models that are far more sophisticated, from a mathematical standpoint, sometimes make assumptions that are nearly as simple as those of Sidis. In all cases, caution must be exercised in assessing the value of microscopic psychological assumptions on the basis of the success or failure of macroscopic predictions.

Contagion

Processes of contagion have been a favorite topic for mathematical treatment. Contagion, as we have seen, means that a state present in one crowd participant may come to infect another. Social contagion is treated by mathematical theorists as formally similar to the diffusion process in physical science. Rapoport (1963) stated: "The occasional explosive spreads of rumors, fads, and panics attest to the underlying similarity between social diffusion and other diffusion and chain reaction processes, such as epidemics, the spread of solvents through solutes, crystalization,...etc." (p. 497). Social contagion may be treated in terms of models of a similar mathematical type.

Consider a crowd of men at a political rally in which a fight has broken out and appears to be spreading. What features of the situation need to be represented before mathematical analysis of contagions can proceed?

First we must start with a specifiable *population*, a group of persons for whom the analysis is relevant. Each member of the population may be in a number of *states*. For example, a member of the crowd may be violent or peaceful; or he may be somewhere in between, if more than two states are possible. To build a model, we must know whether the population is of constant size or not. Are newcomers being added to the population (a population *source*)? Are some participants leaving (a population *sink*)? We must also know whether the states are *reversible* or *irreversible*. Once a peaceful man becomes violent, does he remain in that state or can he revert to his originally peaceful condition? The infected states may be considered irreversible if the individuals are not expected to recover during the time under consideration. However, in some cases, a participant may recover with immunity; that is, once a man has passed through the violent state, he may recover in such a manner that he cannot again be infected. Some states may be absorbing states which, once entered, will persist for the duration. For example, a participant in a fracas may be knocked out cold. It is necessary to spell out these details before a mathematical representation of the diffusion of violence can be given, but in the very act of specification, attention becomes focused on aspects of crowd behavior that are of general import. Such thinking immediately points to the lack of detail in current formulations of contagion: none of them specifies whether contagion is reversible or irreversible, the variety of states into which members may pass, what types of immunity develop, or the effects of sinks and sources. Yet each of these features, whether treated in a specifically mathematical vein or not, is important to an understanding of the spread of behavior in a crowd. Rapoport, whom we have followed in this analysis, writes (1963, p. 498):

> To construct a general model of contagion process, it is necessary to list all the relevant states in which the members of the population may be and also to indicate the transition probabilities from one state to another. The event contributing to the probability of such a transition, typical for a contagion process, is contact between two individuals as a result of which one or both individuals pass into another state. However, it is possible to imagine also "spontaneous" changes of state, for example, from one stage of a disease to the next. Also when two individuals come into contact this may contribute to an increment of a state to which neither of the individuals belongs.

Rashevsky's theory of contagion. Rashevsky (1939, 1951) proposed two parallel models of mass contagion based on imitation. His simpler model assumes two classes of individuals exhibiting mutually exclusive behaviors. Within each class are a group of "actives," defined as those whose probability of engaging in the competing behavior is arbitrarily small, and a group of "passives," whose behavior is determined principally by their propensity to imitate others. Rashevsky notes that, although his model follows an assumption of passive imitation, the same formal relations would hold if the actives were to try to persuade or coerce the passives into a given activity (1951, p. 116).

Rashevsky assumes that the number of actives of each type is constant at values X_0 and Y_0. The number of passives engaging in each behavior varies with the preponderance of that behavior already existing in the population. Specifically, the time rate of change in the number of passives exhibiting X-type behavior, dX/dt, is directly proportional to the existing number of X's and negatively proportional to the existing number of Y's:

$$\frac{dX}{dt} = a_0 X_0 + aX - c_0 Y_0 - cY.$$

It follows from this model that stable configurations of behavior exist only when all the passives have moved to one behavior pattern, X or Y. The behavior of the system is completely determined by its initial condition: if the initial ratio of X to Y exceeds a critical value, the entire passive population become X-converts; if not, they turn to Y.

Once at equilibrium, the system will move only under the influence of outside forces. However, the system is extremely sensitive to such exogenous pressures. For example, a small autonomous change in the number of actives of either type, say, a rise of 100,000 in X_0, can cause an entire population of 10,000,000 to reverse its predominant attitude or behavior.

In a later, more sophisticated model, Rashevsky assumed a net internal tendency, θ, to exhibit behavior X or Y, positive θ indicating a net tendency to show X, negative θ indicating Y. He assumed θ to be distributed in Laplacean form, symmetrically about 0. That is, he assumed the average tendency of the population to be neutral. The dispersion constant, σ, of the distribution measures the homogeneity of the group, that is, the degree to which individual tendencies cluster around the neutral point. Similarly, Rashevsky assumed that an individual's tendency to engage in X or Y fluctuates over time, again having a Laplacean distribution, with dispersion constant k. Thus, k measures the stability of behavior of individuals over time. Finally, Rashevsky assumed the existence of a tendency to imitate, ψ, which grows as one or another form of behavior gains predominance, but which also "decays" as it grows. That is,

$$\frac{d\psi}{dt} = A(X - Y) - a\psi.$$

Working from these assumptions, Rashevsky obtained a complex differential equation which, though capable of explicit solution, is, as Rapoport (1963) pointed out, probably not capable of empirical verification.

However, the model does yield a set of instructive, and perhaps verifiable, equilibrium conditions. An equilibrium condition is one in which there is no spontaneous tendency for the population to move one way or the other. An equilibrium exists at $X = Y$, $\psi = 0$ (that is, the population exhibits both behaviors in equal proportions, and the net tendency to imitate is 0). This equilibrium can be unsettled by fluctuations in proportions of X or Y, or by external forces on the system. For small deviations, the system returns to neutral equilibrium; however, if a certain inequality holds, one form of behavior will become predominant and a new, stable equilibrium will be created. This inequality is

$$N_0 > \frac{a(\sigma + k)}{A\sigma k},$$

where a and A are constants and N_0 is the population size.

Thus, given the individual parameters a, A, σ, and k, N_0 is the smallest crowd which can be swayed to exhibit a predominance of one of the two behaviors in question. A smaller crowd will continue to show both in equal proportions. The margin by which N_0 exceeds $a(\sigma + k)/(A + k)$ reflects the degree of predominance of one behavior over the other. In short, the formula implies that large crowds may be more easily and completely swayed than small ones.

From the same formula, we see that less initial uniformity of the crowd (small σ) requires larger numbers for contagion to occur. We may also deduce the counter-intuitive proposition that the more stable individual behavior is over time (large k), the more readily contagion can occur. (It will be remembered that Rashevsky assumed that the population showed no net tendency toward X or Y; hence, "homogeneity" and "stability" refer to a tendency toward neutrality. If this restriction is removed, and we hypothesize an asymmetry in the distribution of θ, that is, a net proclivity for one behavior or the other, the above results do not follow. In such a case, as we would expect, equilibrium is most easily attained in the direction of the favored behavior.)

Types of Models

Bailey (1957) makes an important distinction between deterministic and stochastic, or probabilistic, models. Deterministic theories attempt to predict the *specific values* which dependent quantities will assume as a result of changes in independent variables, for example, the range of spread of information as a function of time. Stochastic models deal with the *probabilities* that systems will be in given states under given conditions, such as the probability that an item of information will have reached half the population in a certain amount of time.

Among all the phenomena of interest in the social sciences, mass behavior seems most amenable to classical, that is, deterministic, mathematical treatment.

This assertion proceeds mainly from the mechanical operation of certain mathematical facts:

  1. For sufficiently large groups, the proportions of members involved in particular behaviors can legitimately be approximated by continuous variables. This permits representation of their rates of change in the form of differential equations, for which an elaborate solution machinery exists.

  2. According to the "law of large numbers," the importance of statistical fluctuation is reduced as sample size or number of trials grows. Individual deviation from expected behavior patterns may therefore cancel in a large group. Thus, for mass phenomena, deterministic theory may produce satisfactory approximations to reality. Moreover, even for small-number cases where deterministic theories cannot generate predictions correct in every detail, they may serve a heuristic purpose as a starting point for more sophisticated, stochastic treatment.

The introduction of probabilistic considerations permits prediction of the degree to which contagion will affect small subgroups of the population. As Bailey points out, the assumption of homogeneous mixing, necessary for mathematical manageability, is likely to be true only for such small groups. Our attention is naturally brought to such units, and hence, to stochastic processes.

Bailey's principal example of the superiority of probabilistic models concerns the cyclical nature of epidemics over time. Bailey refers quite specifically to the spread of disease, but we may think in terms of the diffusion of a particular form of behavior—say, the adoption of a fad, spread of the dancing mania (Hecker, 1885), the widening enthusiasm for the Beatles, or the dissemination of hula hoops. Early deterministic work by Soper (1929) attempted to take account of epidemic cycles. However, Soper's model predicted damped oscillation, that is, predicted that recurrent epidemics would become progressively less severe until they died out entirely. Since this prediction is contradicted by fact, it remained for stochastic theory to develop a more accurate model. Bartlett (1957) used "Monte Carlo" (random number) methods on a computer to simulate the epidemic process, successfully describing the cyclical nature of real measles epidemics. An interesting aspect of his model was the specification of a critical size for communities, below which epidemics could not recur. His predicted value of 200,000 tallies well with the observed value of 250,000. Whether valid social analogs to these epidemiological notions of periodic contagion and critical population exist remains to be seen. Such "wave" phenomena as applause or outbursts of anti-Semitism might be profitably explored in this connection.

Models of Group Size

In the study of mass phenomena, it is important to know how crowds coalesce out of unstructured collectivities. Mathematical models describing the formation and dissolution of small groups within larger aggregates may contribute to our understanding of the patterns along which larger crowds form.

John James (1951, 1953) set this work on empirical ground with his survey of large numbers of freely forming groups in a variety of social situations. James reported the frequencies of appearance of groups of various sizes as they formed spontaneously on streets, in stores, on playgrounds, in public recreation areas, and at work places. He found that groups ranged in size from two to seven, with a mean of about three. The distribution of sizes was J-shaped, with frequency falling as group size grew.

Noting the small size of most groups and the similarity of size distributions in different social settings, James concluded:

1. Groups formed via face-to-face interaction gravitate to the smallest possible size (two) and the smallest number of possible relationships (one).

2. Variables of perception, thinking, and motor ability are more important in determining group size than motivation, space, social situation, or age of participants.

James (1953) also pointed out that the data fit a negative binomial distribution function, though he had little comment on the theoretical significance of that fact.

Coleman and James (1961) were able to develop a mathematical model to fit James's observations. Theirs is a stochastic model in which group sizes are represented as "states" (a group is in state 2 if it has two members). They developed transition probabilities from one state to another based on the following assumptions:

1. Isolated individuals (in state 1) have a constant probability of joining some group. This probability is independent of group size; that is, the "contagion" assumption (that larger groups are more attractive than smaller ones) is explicitly denied. As a consequence of the preceding postulates, the net influx to any group depends solely on the number of isolated individuals in the system.

2. Individuals have a constant probability of leaving a group; hence, the rate of departure from a group depends only on the number of people in it.

This birth-and-death model predicts that, in equilibrium, the distribution of group sizes will follow a "truncated Poisson" form. The prediction was confirmed for 19 of the 23 surveys taken by James. The authors suggest that the equilibrium behavior of an aggregate is determined by the "parameter" na/b, where n is the total number of groups ultimately formed, a is the probability of an individual spontaneously joining a group, and b is the probability of an individual leaving a group. Coleman and James suggested that this model could account for the growth of crowds if a were assumed to be an increasing function of time. (It will be remembered that they denied the proposition that a might be an increasing function of group size.)

The seeming success of the Coleman–James model was shown by White (1962) to be misleading. White demonstrated that no less than seven different sets of assumptions could predict an equilibrium distribution of the truncated Poisson form. Interestingly, one of White's models incorporates a contagion assumption, along with some counterbalancing assumptions. White stated: "Coleman and James erred in inferring from the close fit of their one model to the data that a contagious joining process could be ruled out as a component of any model valid for those data" (p. 167). White suggested that the most parsimonious model which predicts the appropriate equilibrium distribution is one based on a single parameter, γ, which represents the fraction of persons who leave groups and then remain isolated. As γ approaches zero in this model, groups, on the average, become larger and larger, and aggregates approaching crowd proportions begin to form. White's paper thus touches, however briefly, on the problem of relating small-group formation models to models of mass behavior. More important, it illustrates again the pitfalls of basing inferences about the validity of a set of social-psychological assumptions on the success of the aggregate model which those assumptions generate.

SUMMING UP

Where does this review of theoretical approaches to the crowd leave us? What are the main ideas? Starting with Le Bon, there were two main questions. The first was how we are to explain the homogeneity of crowds; the second, how we explain the emergence of uncivilized behavior among crowd participants. Thus, Le Bon concentrated on the transformation of the solitary individual in the crowd toward a condition of being like others, and expressing brutality. Freud accepted Le Bon's descriptions of savagery and homogeneity, but probed more deeply into the underlying psychological processes. The answer, he felt, lay in the relationship between the crowd member and the leader. Turner and Killian (1957), and also Lang and Lang (1961), challenged certain descriptive features of the crowd. In place of the idea, of *homogeneity*, Turner observed *differential participation*. Le Bon and Sighele were more concerned with the end results of a person's participation in the crowd. Turner looked at the way crowd norms and common understandings *emerge* in a fluid, undefined field. Smelser raised rather different questions, concerning himself not with the change in the individual but with the conditions of society that give rise to distinguishable forms of collective episodes. Here the general notion is that of tension or strain that cannot find release through the regular channels of society, and thus erupts in collective outbursts. The particular kind of eruption depends on where people believe the strain exists, and on other conditions, such as the nature of social controls. Mathematical theorists, such as Rashevsky, take a different tack, abstracting macroscopic processes and attempting to fit an equation to account for them. The phenomenon of collective behavior admits of several theoretical foci, and there is no single set of questions that constitutes *the* proper set of questions about the crowd.

Irrationality

One question, deriving from Le Bon, Sighele, and Freud, that is still in the air concerns the assertion that crowds are irrational. It is an issue that requires analysis. First, one may ask, what is meant by rationality? There are at least three criteria: (1) that once a goal is decided on, intelligent and efficient means for its attainment are employed; (2) that the goal itself is an appropriate human goal; and (3) that the actor performs with internal consistency.

Before imputing irrationality, then, certain features of the crowd situation must be kept in mind:

1. The response possibilities open to the crowd, as an aggregate, are sharply limited. However subtly an individual may express himself in private discourse, the crowd as a whole has access to a limited language. It may support assertions with cheers or applause, or react to them with negative expressions (such as booing, jeers, or the absence of applause). (The only possibility for the collective expression of complex linguistic sentiments is to use a linguistic form already known to everyone, such as the "pledge of allegiance" or even a song. Otherwise the expression of the crowd must remain simple and restricted to a few positive or negative expressions. The pledge of allegiance is written for crowd communication. Ritual becomes important for the very reason that the sequence of action is known to all beforehand, and thus can be engaged in simultaneously.) Given only two fundamental modes of response (positive and negative), a person may quite rationally support statements which on closer analysis contain contradictory elements, because he more or less approves of the statements. A qualified response is not possible for an assembly of 30,000 persons.

2. When wholly contradictory assertions are "supported by the crowd," we must ask whether the same individuals in the crowd are responding. Or are different subgroups in the crowd supporting different statements? This hardly represents irrationality, but rather the normal spread of opinion in a group. As long as writers continue to state, "The crowd cheered statement X, and then irrationally supported contradictory statement Y"—without specifying which elements in the crowd lent support to the two statements, and whether they represent identical individuals—we cannot speak of inconsistency.

3. Because of the breakdown of conventional guidelines to behavior, and the resulting planless quality of crowd episodes, persons in a crowd do not find themselves able to act within the comfortable grooves of convention. Rather the person must often respond quickly to novel situations and contingencies never before encountered. In retrospect, with adequate time for analysis, some of his actions may appear erratic and inefficient, but the luxury of adequate time for planning behavior is not always available to the participant in the crowd.

The emotionality of the crowd has sometimes been taken as an index of its irrationality, but Turner and Killian (1957) correctly argued that emotion and reason are not necessarily mutually exclusive (p. 17):

> Emotion and reason are not today regarded as irreconcilables. Emotion may accompany the execution of a well-reasoned plan, and the inadequately reasoned plan may be accompanied by no arousal of emotions. The rational-irrational dichotomy seems to have two distinct kinds of meanings. Based on external criteria, behavior can be called rational when it is an efficient way of achieving some goal. By this definition much institutional behavior is irrational and much collective behavior is rational. Who can say that the occasional lynching was not for several decades a fairly efficient way of keeping the Negro in a subordinate place? Using internal criteria, behavior is irrational when the individual does not weigh all possible

alternatives of which he can be aware in deciding his course of action. By this definition most institutional behavior is irrational, since social norms narrow the range of alternatives which the individual can consider. While each of the major types of collective behavior has its own characteristic ways of so restricting attention within the range of potential alternatives, collective behavior is not different from other types of behavior in this respect.

Violence

In the minds of most early students of crowds, and in the opinion of some contemporary observers, crowds have an affinity for violence and destruction. The mention of crowds brings to mind such phenomena as lynching mobs, pogroms, massacres, brutal race riots, and stampeding panics. Historical records are studded with acts of cruelty against helpless persons at the hands of crowds. While there is no sense in denying that such events do happen, and with fair frequency, a few points of analysis ought to be made.

First, it is obvious that acts of cruelty that are fully equivalent to those resulting from crowds have often been carried out by organized institutions, while still others have been carried out by solitary agents. Institutions, rather than crowds, have destroyed entire cities with aerial bombardment and have put whole populations to death. At the other extreme, individual murders have carried out their depredations in solitude and secrecy. So the question is not whether violence is ever found in crowds, but rather, whether it is disproportionately represented in crowds, as compared to individual violence, on the one hand, and institutional violence, on the other. An answer to this question is not easy to come by. It would be necessary to define a universe of crowds and to note the proportion of instances in which violence is represented. This would be compared to the proportion of instances of some other social form—say, organized groups—in which violence occurs.

Furthermore, there may be instances in which crowds may inhibit destructiveness among their members. Unfortunately, there can be no record of acts of violence that are suppressed because of the presence of witnesses, or as a result of the moderating influence of peers. Violence suppressed is invisible; violence manifest provides dramatic data.

The Image of the Crowd

The stamp of irrationality and depravity which Le Bon fixed on the crowd had such an indelible quality that we sometimes forget that other social analysts saw the crowd as fulfilling constructive social functions. For example, Bagehot (1869), Wallas (1932), Cooley (1909), and Dewey (1930) stressed the liberation of mind that occurred in the collectivity. Karl Marx (1848), in his influential social interpretation, regarded collective uprising, rioting, and mobs in a positive light, and attributed constructive, rational functions to this behavior. The birth of a new society, he believed, depended on crowd activity as its agent of change. The crowd knows what it is doing in pillaging, attacking, and even killing. In enacting the behavior required by historical necessity, Marx saw the crowd as displaying profound rationality. Our own decade has seen collective behavior in the service of a civil rights movement, seeking the enactment of values many enlightened persons desire.

Extremes

Finally, the study of crowd behavior has been dominated by a concern for the more extreme forms of crowd activity—the panic, the hostile mob, the agitated throng. A concern with extreme manifestations is exciting and entertaining, but it yields an unnatural focus, a concern with pathology without a statement of the normal conditions from which to define a pathological condition. The crowd was first presented to psychology in its pathological forms, and this focus has remained fixed for historical rather than scientific reasons. Mass media reinforce this bias. The newspaper reports a rampaging river that overflows its banks, but is little interested in the normal river flow throughout the year. But can flooding be understood without a firm grasp of the most ordinary and normal features of the river's course? It is not possible to understand the full nature of panic unless that understanding is firmly rooted in an understanding of the normal movement of men and women on an ordinary day in the life of the city. The study of crowds will move away from journalism and toward a mature science to the degree that our vision incorporates the normal scene as well as the extraordinary.

METHODS IN THE STUDY OF CROWDS

Somewhere near the beginning of a chapter on collective behavior it is customary to issue a stern warning on the difficulties that the field presents for scientific study, and to account on these grounds for the relative scarcity of scientific inquiry on this topic. One difficulty is that episodes do not always occur at a convenient time and place, and this unpredictability of collective behavior makes systematic firsthand observation difficult. Nor is it easy to generate collective episodes in the laboratory or field for purposes of investigation. Often investigators must rely on newspaper reports, historical records, newsreels, videotapes, and personal narratives. Yet a number of approaches have evolved which, used in combination, ought to lead to a firm empirical grounding.

SURVEY RESEARCH

Survey techniques may be employed in the study of collective episodes. The most famous use of survey procedures was undertaken by Hadley Cantril (1940). His study focused on a major panic that engulfed the Eastern portion of the United States on October 30, 1938. The occasion for this hysteria was a dramatization of H. G. Wells's *War of the Worlds*, presented as a Halloween feature by the "Mercury Theater of the Air." The aim of Cantril's research was to determine why thousands of Americans had come to conclude that they were being invaded from outer space, and why other members of the same audience were protected from this error.

Cantril tells us that because the social phenomenon in question was so complex, several methods were used to seek out different answers and the results obtained by different methods were compared. Two types of surveys were included in the research program. One was a series of intensive, detailed retrospective interviews of 100 persons who had come to believe in a Martian conquest of earth and of 35 listeners who had identified the play as a play. Other surveys considered were public opinion polls that covered a nationwide adult sample (supplemented by a special report on the reaction of children). The study also relied on content analyses of news items and of mail received by radio stations.

Among the aspects of the panic covered in Cantril's study were the characteristics of the broadcast that enhanced its credibility, the contributing influences of the historical setting (such as listeners' experiences with the Great Depression, their perception of the state of science, and their awareness of the threat of war in Europe), and the reinforcing or calming effect of other listeners.

In line with the aims of the study, Cantril's principal findings related to the frame of mind and psychological strategy that created personal susceptibility to *panic*. Outstanding among the demographic factors that differentiated more suggestible persons from less vulnerable ones was their level of education. Relatively educated people were able to avoid error by resorting to relevant information, and by bringing to bear a salutary degree of skepticism (causing them to "check" their sources of information). Psychologically, the mechanism leading to acceptance of the invasion as real seemed to be a combination of an acute need to "make sense" of the situation and either (1) a rigid frame of reference that prestructured a panic-producing interpretation or (2) the absence of any frame of reference at all.

Objective survey technique, with its emphasis on specifiable sampling procedures, helps correct gross inaccuracies reported in the press. Thus, whereas a newspaper reported that in response to a severe London smog "one of the world's biggest cities experienced a near mass panic," a sample survey revealed that only one percent of the respondents reported themselves as having panicked (Killian, 1956, pp. 10–11).

SECONDARY SOURCES

Views on techniques for forming an energizing crowd are to be found in the writings of revolutionaries (Lenin, 1902; Mao, 1938) and others who have made extensive use of mass action as part of their social program. Recently, Oppenheimer and Lakey (1965) published a set of instructions for causing collective disturbance. One may also examine documents distributed by the agents of social control. Police and militia manuals (Bellows, 1920) are an important source of information about current beliefs and practices of those who deal most directly with crowds and mobs. Such documents preceded Le Bon. In 1884, E. L. Molineux wrote on "Riots and Their Suppression," stressing particularly that "in its incipient stage a riot can readily be quelled if met boldly and resisted at once with energy and determination."

The International Association of Chiefs of Police (1963) recommends the following procedures in the control of hostile crowds (in italics, we have added a few phrases pointing up the relevance of the techniques to issues discussed in the chapter):

1. If the crowd is still collecting, he [the police officer] can make a quick determination of the facts and take the involved parties into custody. This can sharply cut down the size of the crowd and prevent an incident from getting out of hand. [*crowd crystals, precipitating incident, rates of formation*]

2. If a mob has already formed, call for reinforcements. Here a show of force is necessary, but not the use of force. Tension in a mob is usually highest at a point front and center. Look for the troublemakers—the most excited individuals. Extricate these individuals. [*salience of agencies of social control, structural features of the crowd, differential participation*]

3. A public address system can be a great help in dispersing a mob. The blare of the speaker, reinforced by a tone of authority, will catch and hold individual attention and turn it away from the excitable influences in the mob. [*disrupting polarization on leader, salience of agencies of social control, competing suggestions*]

4. A police cordon around a dangerous area will keep curiosity seekers out and thus prevent them from being infected by mob psychosis. [*spatial character of the crowd, restricting contagion by physical separation of crowd from others*]

Further suggestions (International Association..., 1963) include "fragmentizing the crowd into small isolated groups," on the grounds that this will impede the effects of contagion within the assemblage, and infusing the crowd with plainclothesmen who introduce competing slogans and moods, thus preventing the development of crowd unity (Trivers, 1965).

Westley (1957) examined police manuals and interviewed law enforcement officers, drawing conclusions relevant to theories of crowd formation and control. He pointed out that police are taught (1) to prevent crowds from polarizing on a leader or on any other focus of attention, (2) to remove the leaders of the crowd, and (3) to destroy the sense of anonymity and unanimity among members of the crowd. Such tactics highlight the importance of leadership and a sense of shared opposition in the development of hostile crowds.

PROJECTIVE DEVICES

Killian (1956) has suggested that the use of projective techniques may be a valuable method of learning the motives, feelings, and perceptions evoked by crowds. An informal study was performed at Harvard University using a projective format. Five photographs of crowds were interspersed with five TAT pictures of individuals, and subjects were given the standard TAT instructions for the set. Crowd features spontaneously mentioned by the subjects were size, density, movement, polarization, and how closely related the members of the crowd seemed. Subjects frequently pointed out subgroups in the crowd. Subjects tended to treat the crowd pictures as portraying actual historical occurrences, and were intent on placing the crowds in terms of time, space, nationality, and social class. They did not do this for TAT cards showing individuals. Projective devices constitute a convenient method for uncovering underlying attitudes which may, in the long run, be related to a subject's actual participation in mass events.

EXPERIMENTAL APPROACHES TO COLLECTIVE BEHAVIOR

Three distinct types of experimental research are relevant to the study of collective behavior. First, general experimental literature can be applied to the analysis of collective behavior. Second, crowd behavior can be simulated in the laboratory and subjected to experimental study. Third, field experiments can be conducted on natural crowd formations.

Application of General Experimental Literature

Experiments from many domains of social psychology can be brought to bear on the analysis of crowds. Typically, the findings are incidental to the study's main concern, but shed light obliquely on collective behavior. For example, Wallach, Kogan, and Bem (1962) noted that under specified conditions individuals in a group engaged in greater risk taking than they would have in isolation. The mechanism of diffusion of responsibility, cited as an important cause of risk taking, may help to account for the injudicious and riskful actions attributed to some crowds. Asch (1951), while mainly interested in the individual's conformity to group norms on a perceptual task, pointed out that background group support leads to the emergence of derision, badinage, and disdain for a lone individual deviating from the group. Apparently, group support lends the individual a sense of strength and a willingness to engage in attack. Further evidence for this comes from a study by Milgram (1964) in which subjects were induced by a group to inflict punishment on another person that was well beyond the level of punishment chosen by the individual in the absence of social pressure.

Obviously, it is impossible to list all experiments relevant to understanding collective behavior. Virtually any examination in the laboratory of processes of social influence or group action has at least a modicum of relevance to the behavior of those larger, unformed groups we term crowds. One final area of study should be mentioned because it is suggestive of basic processes operating in crowd behavior. Grosser, Polansky, and Lippit (1951) demonstrated that children could be led by imitation to perform antisocial behavior they would not otherwise perform. Recently, experimental work by Bandura and Walters (1963) has indicated the importance of a model in stimulating aggressive behavior in an individual. This suggests the possibility of one aggressive individual in a crowd serving as a model for other crowd participants, who come to imitate his behavior. Many other laboratory experiments could be devised in a way that would shed light on crowd behavior. For example, the consequences of *anonymity* for the release of aggression, risk taking, and the expression of anitsocial impulses can readily be studied by the use of masks, or by the study of social behavior that takes place in darkness.

Simulation of Crowd Behavior

The favorite haven of the social psychologist is the one-way observation room, where conditions can be controlled and effects noted and precisely observed. But it is not easy to fit a cheering multitude into a laboratory. Even if a sufficiently large number of persons could be assembled under one roof, it is not at all clear that they would represent a crowd truly worth studying. For the conditions that give rise to authentic collective episodes are not easily reproduced. They may depend on long years of frustration and deprivation that no experimenter would willingly inflict on his subjects. Moreover, certain forms of collective behavior, such as panic and riot, contain an element of danger to which subjects cannot legitimately be exposed. Finally, the subjects' knowledge that an experimental authority is directing events tends to run counter to the spontaneous and planless quality of much collective behavior.

Despite these limitations, several attempts to simulate crowd behavior in the laboratory have been made. In a well-known study, Meier, Mennenga, and Stoltz (1941) attempted to recreate the atmosphere of a mob under experimental conditions. Through a series of "news dispatches," students were informed that thousands of citizens were storming the local jail in order to take vengeance against an alleged kidnapper. The investigators wished to uncover the motives and composition of those who would join the mob. Questionnaires were distributed to students at the "height of excitement." Twelve percent indicated a desire to join the mob; 23 percent wished to observe the mob; 29 percent indicated they would have gone with the intention of deterring the mob from lynching victims; and 35 percent stated they would stay away entirely. Only the duller students, it was found, indicated a readiness to join the mob. Did the intelligent ones see through the experimenters' hoax? Is a written statement of intention equivalent to the actual mode of response under conditions of crowd excitement? Do real mobs fill out questionnaires en route to lynchings? What bearing do these highly irregular and artificial components have on our interpretation of the findings? All these questions need to be answered before the exact relevance of this study to crowd behavior can be assessed.

The study of panic is the one area of collective behavior in which a discernible experimental tradition has emerged. This is due not only to the inherently dramatic qualities of panic, but also to the fact that the conditions which give rise to it can be created instantaneously. Panic depends on a set of spatial conditions, but requires no long-standing events in time. In contrast to many other forms of collective behavior, panic is ahistorical, and thus can be accommodated to the experimenter's hourly appointment schedule.

In an early study, French (1944) created an artificial crisis situation for organized and unorganized groups. Groups were placed in a locked room and the subjects were led to believe the building was on fire (smoke poured under the door and fire-engine bells sounded). No panic developed, but the organized groups tended to react with greater uniformity than the unorganized ones.

There is a problem with this research, however, in that it is generally held that the essence of panic is competition for a scarce resource (Brown, 1954; Smelser, 1963). The resource may be the exit through a narrow corridor when the theater catches on fire, a lifeboat when a ship is sinking, or transforming unstable currency into gold as inflation eats away at the value of one's savings.

French's experiment could not be expected to lead to panic because there was no clear competition for a scarce resource.

Alexander Mintz's study (1951) comes closer to this requirement. A number of subjects stood around a bottle with a fairly narrow neck. Each subject held onto a string and each string was attached to an aluminum cone in the bottle. If one cone was withdrawn from the bottle at a time, there was no jamming at the narrow neck of the bottle. However, if more than one cone was withdrawn simultaneously, a jam occurred. Mintz varied a number of factors to study under what conditions jams would occur. The apparatus served as a analog for the classical jam at a theater exit when a fire breaks out. The structure of rewards and punishments (in the form of small fines and rewards) affected the number of jams, as did the cooperative or competitive sets of the subjects. In certain experimental conditions, water slowly rose in the bottles, and subjects paid fines and punishments according to the amount of their aluminum cone that got wet. Mintz concluded that the reward structure of the situation, and whether the subjects had a competitive or cooperative set, were more important than emotional contagion in determining whether or not jams occurred. He denied outright that intense fear or emotional excitement caused nonadaptive group behavior.

There is no really satisfactory experiment on collective behavior. The best is still that of Mintz, but it stands in relation to actual panic as the game of Monopoly does to high finance.

Deutsch (1949) labeled a situation of the type used by Mintz as one in which subjects are *contriently* interdependent. The use of an escape route by one person reduces the chance that the remaining persons will be able to escape. Moreover, simultaneous attempts to use the escape path reduce its effectiveness. Kelley *et al.* (1965) pointed out several other limitations of the Mintz experiments. The small monetary rewards used (ranging from 10 to 25 cents, and fines ranging from 1 to 10 cents) cannot be considered to test the effects of danger of the sort that occurs in a theater fire. To remedy this deficiency, Kelley *et al.* attempted to place subjects in a position of genuine fear by threatening them with electric shock.

Subjects were seated in separate booths with electrodes attached to two fingers. Before each subject were lights indicating his own position with regard to the danger situation and the position of the other subjects. By making a simple response (depressing a switch) the person could attempt to escape. This escape response was communicated to the other subjects by means of the signal lights. Only one subject could depress his escape switch at a time, but the escape mechanism required a full three seconds to operate. If more than one subject attempted to depress the escape switch, it failed to operate. Thus, a bottleneck situation comparable to that developed by Mintz was created. As the basic dependent variable, Kelley used the percentage of persons who succeeded in escaping during a standard time period.

Kelley and his associates studied the effect of a number of variables on this dependent measure, including the size of the escape crowd, the severity of the threat, and the availability of confidence responses. The percentage of successful escapes declined with the increasing severity of the threat, a result which makes good sense when compared to crises in the larger world. The availability of confidence responses, that is, a sign on the part of one or more member that he was willing to wait for others to escape, increased the number of successful escapes and reduced the number of traffic jams.

Kelley's situation differs from real-life panics in a number of important respects. The overall laboratory context assures the subject that a painful shock is the most severe consequence of not escaping. Further, jamming itself has no aversive quality, as it does in a real panic where frequently many people are killed by jamming and the accompanying body crush. Technically, Kelley's explanation deals with avoidance of a noxious stimulus rather than escape from one, while in real-life panics both avoidance and escape elements are often present.

The most significant contribution of Kelley's research is the theoretical notion of staggering of responses and the suggestion of techniques for creating a distribution of responses. Kelley argued that the distribution of attitudes toward the escape situation is the critical factor in the performance of a group of subjects. When all subjects have the same tendency to simultaneous escape (that is, when the distribution of responses is concentrated at the end of the attitude continuum that reflects high concern and feelings of urgency about escape), dire consequences may follow. One technique for creating a spread in the distribution of responses is the introduction of a confidence response by having one or a number of subjects indicate a willingness to wait for other to go first. This was found to have a dramatic effect in establishing an orderly escape procedure.

Field Experimentation

The artificial quality of laboratory studies can be eliminated by carrying out studies in natural settings. At the same time, one can retain the advantage of manipulating experimental variables. Sherif and Sherif (1953) report an unusual study that falls somewhere between the experimental study of small-group processes and the observation of spontaneously emerging collective behavior. Twenty previously unacquainted boys from homogeneous backgrounds were brought together at summer camp. The boys were divided into two groups and an effort was made to develop high *esprit de corps* within each of the groups. Once a sense of ingroup solidarity had developed, the groups engaged in competitive tasks. Intergroup animosity developed in the form of derogatory slogans, raids on rival camps, negative stereotypes, and even a desire for complete segregation. Finally, the investigators were able to remove intergroup tension by means of cooperative and functionally dependent tasks, such as fixing a damaged water tank that supplied the whole camp and raising funds for a favorite movie.

The implication of this study is that hostility between rival factions in society can be reduced if the groups can be brought together to work for common ends. Mere contact between groups does not suffice to produce social harmony. The contact situation must have four characteristics if hostility between groups is to be reduced: the groups must (1) possess equal status, (2) seek common goals, (3) cooperatively depend on each other, and (4) interact with the positive support of authorities, law, or customer (Allport, 1954). Each of these criteria was met in the Sherifs' study.

Other Techniques for Studying Crowd Formation and Functioning

Psychologists have been singularly unimaginative in devising methods to study collective behavior. In this regard, persons outside psychology have a good deal to offer (see p. 219). The classic argument against the possible study of collective episodes is that they occur unpredictably. But the investigator can go a long way toward overcoming this difficulty.

One possibility is to use the stimulus of a crowd itself as a springboard to the study of crowd formation. Here either natural crowds or synthetic ones could be observed, and from an aerial perspective one could note the effect of this stimulus on others who were not part of the crowd. A simple recording, of good quality, of crowd noise could be activated in a downtown area, and the rate of aggregation could be observed. One could note how many people are drawn to the crowd in a quickened pace, and how many turn away from the source of crowd stimulus. In all such observation, permanent photographic records, preferably obtained from an aerial perspective, are desirable.

Any suggestion of new methods in the study of collective behavior must mention the possibility of simulating crowds with computers, the application of advanced telemetric devices (both as a means of studying crowd movement and of studying physiological reactions of crowd participants), and the application of aerial photography and videotape recording. While past students of the crowd have had to rely on secondhand, verbal accounts of crowd episodes, news coverage of collective outbursts now provides an extensive file of primary data in the form of videotape recordings readily available to investigators and subject to systematic analysis.

Davis (1964) has suggested that, in view of the inherent difficulties of studying collective episodes, the next step ought to be the creation of a truly comparative file of personal recollection, historical accounts, and survey data on collective episodes, modeled after the Human Relations Area Files. Using a technique parallel to the cross-cultural method, one could formulate hypotheses about crowd episodes and, as far as possible, test them with reference to a large quantity of carefully categorized material.

Mock crowds have been used for training persons in the tactics of non-violent resistance (Oppenheimer and Lakey, 1965), and they may also serve some investigatory purposes.

In the end, there is no substitute for direct observation and measurement of authentic crowd behavior. A field that consists only of scholars contradicting each other from the armchair can easily degenerate into sterile scholasticism. The most important need in the study of crowds is to get the main questions off the debating rostrum and move them to a level at which measurement, controlled observation, and imaginative experiment can begin to play some part in choosing among competing views.

NOTE

1. The author wishes to acknowledge his indebtedness to Mr. Jeffrey Travers who prepared materials on mathematical theories of the crowd, to Eleanor Rosch for carrying out two empirical studies referred to in the text, and to Drs. Barry McLaughlin and Charles Thrall for editorial assistance. Mrs. Elinor White prepared the illustration on page 216. This chapter covers published material through 1965.

REFERENCES

ADORNO, T. W., ELSE FRENKEL-BRUNSWIK, D. J. LEVINSON, AND R. N. SANFORD (1950). *The Authoritarian Personality*. New York: Harper.

AKERS, E. R., AND V. FOX (1944). "The Detroit rioters and looters committed to prison." *J. Crim. Law Criminol.*, **35**, 105–110.

ALLPORT, F. H. (1924). *Social Psychology*. Boston: Houghton Mifflin.

ALLPORT, G. W. (1954). *The Nature of Prejudice*. Boston: Beacon Press.

ALLPORT, G. W., AND L. POSTMAN (1947). *The Psychology of Rumor*. New York: Holt.

ARENDT, H. (1954). *Origins of Totalitarianism*. New York: Harcourt, Brace.

ARGYLE, M. (1959). *Religious Behavior*. Glencoe, Ill.: Free Press.

ASCH, S. E. (1951). "Effects of group pressure upon the modification and distortion of judgement." In H. Guetzkow (ed.), *Groups, Leadership, and Men*. Pittsburgh: Carnegie Press, pp. 177–190.

BAGEHOT, W. (1869). *Lombard Street: A description of the Money Market*. Reprinted, London: Murray, 1931.

BAILEY, N. T. J. (1957). *The Mathematical Theory of Epidemics*. New York: Hafner.

BANDURA, A., AND R. H. WALTERS (1963). *Social Learning and Personality Development*. New York: Holt.

BARTLETT, M. S. (1957). "Measles periodicity and community size." *J. Roy. Statist. Soc.*, **120**, 48–59.

BELLOWS, H. A. (1920). *A Treatise on Riot Duty for the National Guard*. Washington, D.C.: Government Printing Office.

BETTELHEIM, B. (1943). "Individual and mass behavior in extreme situations." *J. Abnorm. Soc. Psychol.*, **38**, 417–452.

BLUMER, H. (1946). "Collective behavior." (First published 1939.) In A. M. Lee (ed.), *New Outline of the Principles of Sociology*. New York: Barnes and Noble, pp. 165–220.

———(1964). "Collective behavior." In J. Gould and W. L. Kolb (eds.), *Dictionary of the Social Sciences*. New York: Free Press, pp. 100–101.

BONDURANT, JOAN V. (1958). *Conquest of Violence: The Gandhian Philosophy of Conflict*. Princeton: Princeton Univ. Press.

BRINTON, C. (1958). *The Anatomy of Revolution*. New York: Vintage Books.

BROWN, R. W. (1954). "Mass phenomena." In G. Lindzey (ed.), *Handbook of Social Psychology*. Vol. 2. Cambridge, Mass.: Addison-Wesley, pp. 833–876.

———(1965). *Social Psychology*. New York: Free Press.

BRUCE, J. A. (1965). "The pedestrian." In J. Baerwald (ed.), *Traffic Engineering Handbook*. Washington, D.C.: Institute of Traffic Engineers.

CALHOUN, J. B. (1962). "Population density and social pathology." *Sci. Amer.*, **206**, 139–146.

CANETTI, E. (1962). *Crowds and Power* (transl. Carol Stewart). (German original published 1960.) London: Gollancz.

CANTRIL, H. (1940) (with the assistance of H. Gaudet and H. Herzog). *The Invasion from Mars*. Princeton: Princeton Univ. Press.

CHRISTIAN, J. J. (1960). "Factors in mass mortality of a herd of Sika deer (Cervus nippon)." *Chesapeake Sci.*, **1**, No. 2, 79–95.

CLARK, S. (1965). *All the Best in Japan and the Orient*. New York: Dodd, Mead.

COHEN, E. A. (1953). *Human Behavior in the Concentration Camp*. New York: Grosset and Dunlap.

COHEN, J., AND W. MURPHY (1966). *Burn, Baby, Burn*. New York: Dutton.

COLEMAN, J. S., AND J. JAMES (1961). "The equilibrium size distribution of freely-forming groups." *Sociometry*, **24**, 36–45.

COOLEY, C. H. (1909). *Social Organization: A Study of the Larger Mind*. New York: Scribner's.

COX, D. R., AND W. L. SMITH (1961). *Queues*, New York: Wiley.

CRAIK, G. L. (1837). *Sketches of Popular Tumults*. London: Knight.

DAVIS, K. (1964). "Something old, something new." *Contemp. Psychol.*, **9**, 222–223.

DEFLEUR, M. L. (1962). "Mass communication and the study of rumor." *Sociol. Inquiry*, **32**, 51–70.

DEUTSCH, M. (1949). "A theory of cooperation and competition." *Hum. Relat.*, **2**, 129–152.

DEWEY, J. (1930). *Human Nature and Social Conduct*. New York: Modern Library.

DOLLARD, J. (1937). *Caste and Class in a Southern Town*. New Haven: Yale Univ. Press.

DOLLARD, J., L. DOOB, N. E. MILLER, O. H. MOWRER, AND R. SEARS (1939). *Frustration and Aggression*. New Haven: Yale Univ. Press.

DOOB, L. (1952). *Social Psychology*. New York: Holt.

EDIE, L. C., R. S. FOOTE, R. HERMAN, AND R. W. ROTHERY (1963). *Traffic Engineering*, **33**, 21.

FESHBACH, S., AND N. FESHBACH (1963). "Influence of the stimulus object upon the complementary and supplementary projection of fear." *J. Abnorm. Soc. Psychol.*, **66**, 498–502.

FEUER, L. S. (1964). "Rebellion at Berkeley." *New Leader*, **47**, No. 26, 3–12.

FLUGEL, J. C. (1930). *The Psychology of Clothes*. London: Hogarth Press.

FRENCH, J. R. P. (1944). *Organized and Unorganized Groups under Fear and Frustration*. Iowa City: Univ. of Iowa Press.

FREUD, S. (1922). *Group Psychology and the Analysis of the Ego*. (German original published 1921.) London: Hogarth Press.

FROMM, E. (1941). *Escape from Freedom*. New York: Farrar and Rinehart.

GAZIS, D. C. (1967). "Mathematical theory of automobile traffic." *Science*, **157**, 273–281.

GILBERT, G. (1950). *The Psychology of Dictatorship*. New York: Ronald.

GLAZER, N. (1965). "What happened at Berkeley?" In S. M. Lipset and S. S. Wolin (eds.), *The Berkeley Student Revolt*. Garden City, N.Y.: Anchor, pp. 285–302.

GROSSER, D., N. POLANSKY, AND R. LIPPITT (1951). "A laboratory study of behavioral contagion." *Hum. Relat.*, **4**, 115–142.

HALL, E. T. (1966). *The Hidden Dimension*. Garden City, N. Y.: Doubleday.

HARLOW, F. H., AND J. E. FROOM (1965). "Computer experiments in fluid dynamics." *Sci. Amer.*, **209**, 104–110.

HECKER, J. F. K. (1885). *The Dancing Mania of the Middle Ages*. New York: Fitzgerald.

HOFFER, E. (1951). *The True Believer*. New York: Harper.

HOFSTÄTTER, P. R. (1957). *Gruppendynamik: Kritnik der Massenpsychologie*. Hamburg: Rowohlt Taschenbuch.

HOLINSHED, R. (1577). *Chronicles of England, Scotland, and Ireland*. London: Hunne.

HOVLAND, C. I., A. A. LUMSDAINE, AND F. D. SHEFFIELD (1949). *Experiments on Mass Communication*. Princeton: Princeton Univ. Press.

HOVLAND, C. I., AND R. R. SEARS (1940). "Minor studies of aggression: VI. Correlation of lynchings with economic indices." *J. Psychol.*, **9**, 301–210.

International Association of Chiefs of Police (1963). *With Justice for All: A Guide for Law Enforcement Officers*. Washington, DC., and New York: International Association of Chiefs of Police and the Anti-Defamation League of B'nai B'rith.

JACOBS, H. (1967). "How big was the crowd?—and a formula for estimates." University of California, Berkeley. (Mimeo)

JAMES, J. (1951). "A preliminary study of the size determinant in small group interaction." *Amer. Sociol. Rev.*, **16**,474–477.

———(1953). "The distribution of free-forming small group size." *Amer. Sociol. Rev.*, **18**, 569–570.

JANIS, I. L. (1963). "Group identification under conditions of external danger." *Brit. J. Med. Psychol.*, **36**, 227–238.

KELLEY, H. H., J. C. CONTRY, A. E. DAHLKE, AND A. H. HILL (1965). "Collective behavior in a simulated panic situation." *J. Exp. Soc. Psychol.*, **1**, 20–54.

KILLIAN, L. M. (1956). "An introduction to methodological problems of field studies in disasters." *Nat. Res. Council Publ. (Nat. Acad. Sci.)*, **5**, No. 465.

KÖNIG, R. (1958). "Masse." In R. König (ed.), *Soziologie*. Frankfurt and Hamburg: Fischer, p. 166–172.

LANG, K., AND G. E. LANG (1961). *Collective Dynamics*. New York: Crowell.

LE BON, G. (1895). *Psychologie des Foules*. Transl. *The Crowd*. London: Unwin, 1903.

LEDERER, E. (1940). *The State of the Masses*. New York: Norton.

LENIN, V. I. (1902). *What Is to Be Done?* Transl. S. V. Vtechin and Particia Vtechin, Oxford: Clarendon Press, 1963.

LEWIN, K. (1947). "Group decision and social change." In T. M. Newcomb and E. L. Hartley (eds.), *Readings in Social Psychology*. New York: Holt, p. 330–344.

LIEBERSON, S., AND A. R. SILVERMAN (1965). "The precipitants and underlying conditions of race riots." *Amer. Sociol. Rev.*, **30**, 887–898.

LORENZ, K. (1966). *On Aggression*. New York: Harcourt, Brace, and World.

LYONNS, G. (1965). "The police car demonstration: survey of participants." In S. M. Lipset and S. S. Wolin (eds.), *The Berkeley Student Revolt*. New York: Doubleday, p. 519–530.

McCONE, J. A., ed. (1966). *Violence in the City: An End or a Beginning?* Sacramento, Calif.: Governor's Commission on the Los Angeles Riots.

McDOUGALL W. (1908). *Introduction to Social Psychology*. London: Methuen.

———(1920). *The Group Mind*. Cambridge, Eng.: Cambridge Univ. Press.

McGUIRE, W. (1962). "Persistence of the resistance to persuasion induced by various types of prior belief defenses." *J. Abnorm. Soc. Psychol.*, **64**, 241–248.

MACKAY, C. (1841). *Extraordinary Popular Delusions and the Madness of Crowds*. Reprinted, Boston: L. C. Page, 1932.

MANNHEIM, H. (1965). *Comparative Criminology*. Boston: Houghton Mifflin.

MAO TSE-TUNG (1938). "On protracted war." Reprinted in *Selected Military Writings of Mao Tse-Tung*. Peking: Foreign Languages Press. 1961, p. 187–266.

MARTIN, E. D. (1920). *The Behavior of Crowds*. New York: Harper.

MARX, K. (1848). *Manifesto of the Communist Party*. Transl. Chicago: Charles H. Kerr, 1888.

MEIER, N. C., G. H. MENNENGA, AND H. Z. STOLTZ (1941). "An experimental approach to the study of mob behavior." *J. Abnorm. Soc. Psychol.*, **36**, 506–524.

MERTON, R. K. (1960). "The ambivalences of Le Bon's "The Crowd." Introduction to G. Le Bon, *The Crowd*. New York: Viking Press, p. v–xxxix.

METHVIN, E. H. (1961). "Mob violence and communist strategy." *Orbis*, **5**, 166–181.

MICHELET, J. (1848). *Historical View of the French Revolution* (transl. C. Cocks). (French original published 1847.) London: Bohn.

MILGRAM, S. (1964). "Group pressure and action against a person." *J. Abnorm. Soc. Psychol.*, **69**, 137–143.

———(1965). "Some conditions of obedience and disobedience to authority." *Hum. Relat.*, **18**, 57–76.

MILLARD, C. (1963). Photos (January 1963) in *Survey*, May 1963.

MINTZ, A. (1951). "Non-adaptive group behavior." *J. Abnorm. Soc. Psychol.*, **46**, 150–159.

MOLINEUX, E. L. (1884). *Riots and Their Suppression*. Boston: Headquarters First Brigade, M.V.M.

NEISSER, U. (1964). "Visual search." *Sci. Amer.*, **210**, 94–102.

NORTON, W. J. (1943). "The Detroit riots—and after." *Survey Graphic*, **32**, 317.

OPPENHEIMER, M., AND G. LAKEY (1965). *A Manual for Direct Action*. Chicago: Quadrangle.

ORTEGA Y GASSET, J. (1932). *Revolt of the Masses*. New York: Norton.

PARK, R. E., AND E. W. BURGESS (1921). *Introduction to the Science of Sociology*. Chicago: Univ. of Chicago Press.

PARKES, A. S., AND H. M. BRUCE (1961). "Olfactory stimuli in mammalian reproduction." *Science*, **134**, 1049–1054.

PARSONS, T. (1951). *The Social System*. Glencoe, Ill.: Free Press.

PENROSE, L. S. (1952). *On the Objective Study of Crowd Behavior*. London: H. K. Lewis.

PETERSON, W. A., AND N. P. GIST (1951). "Rumor and public opinion." *Amer. J. Sociol.*, **57**, 159–167.

PINKNEY, D. (1958). *Napoleon III and the Rebuilding of Paris*. Princeton: Princeton Univ. Press.

RAPOPORT, A. (1963). "Mathematical Models of Social Interaction." In R. D. Luce, R. R. Bush, and E. Galanter (eds.), *Handbook of Mathematical Psychology*. New York: Wiley, pp. 493–579.

RASHEVSKY, N. (1939). "Studies in mathematical theory of human relations." *Psychometrika*, **4**, 221–239.

———(1951). *Mathematical Biology of Social Relations*. Chicago: Univ. of Chicago Press.

REDL, F. (1942). "Group emotion and leadership." *Psychiatry*, **5**, 573–596.

REICH, W. (1946). *The Mass Psychology of Fascism*. (German original published 1933.) New York: Orgone Institute Press.

RITTER, P. (1964). *Planning for Man and Motor*. Frankfurt: Pergamon Press.

ROSS, E. A. (1908). *Social Psychology*. New York: Macmillan.

RUDÈ, G. (1959). *The Crowd in the French Revolution*. Oxford: Oxford Univ. Press.

———(1964). *The Crowd in History*. New York: Wiley.

SAPIR, E. (1935). "Fashion." In *Encyclopedia of Social Science*. Vol. 6. New York: Macmillan, pp. 139–144.

SCHMECK, H. M. (1966). "Traffic computerized." *New York Times*, January 16. Section 4, p. 7.

SCHULTZ, D. P. (1964). *Panic Behavior: Discussion and Readings*. New York: Random House.

SEARS, D. O., AND T. M. TOMLINSON (1966). *Riot Activity and Evaluation: An Overview of the Negro Survey*. Univ. of California, Los Angeles, Department of Psychology. (Mimeo)

SELZNICK, P. (1965). "Reply to Glazer." In S. M. Lipset and S. S. Wolin (eds.), *The Berkeley Student Revolt*. Garden City, N.Y.: Anchor, pp. 303–311.

SHELLOW, R., AND D. U. ROEMER (1966). "No heaven for hell's angels." *Transaction*, **3**, No. 5, 12–19.

SHERIF, M. (1936). *The Psychology of Social Norms*. New York: Harper.

SHERIF, M., AND C. W. SHERIF (1953). *Groups in Harmony and Tension: An Integration of Studies on Intergroup Relations*. New York: Harper.

SIDIS, B. (1895). "A study of the mob." *Atlantic Monthly*, **75**, 188–197.

———(1898). *The Psychology of Suggestion*. New York: Appleton.

SIGHELE, S. (1901). *La Foule Criminelle*. Paris: Alcan.

SIMMEL, G. (1964). *The Sociology of Georg Simmel* (transl. K. H. Wolff). London: Free Press.

SMELSER, N. J. (1963). *Theory of Collective Behavior*. New York: Free Press.

SOBOUL, A. (1964). *The Parisian Sans-Culottes and the French Revolution* 1793–4. (French original published 1958.) Oxford: Oxford Univ. Press.

SOPER, H. E. (1929). "Interpretation of periodicity in disease-prevalence." *J. Roy. Statist. Soc.*, **92**, 34–47.

TARDE, G. (1898). "Le public et la foule." *Revue de Paris*, **5**, 615–635.

———(1903). *The Laws of Imitation* (transl. Elsie Parsons). (French original published 1901.) New York: Holt.

TILLY, C., AND J. RULE (1964). "Measuring political upheaval." Unpublished manuscript, Joint Center for Urban Studies of MIT and Harvard University.

TOCH, H. (1965). *The Social Psychology of Social Movements*. New York: Bobbs-Merrill.

TRIVERS, R. (1965). "Riots in American history." Undergraduate honors thesis, Harvard College.

TURNER, R. H. (1964). "Collective behavior." In R. E. L. Faris (ed.), *Handbook of Modern Sociology*. Chicago: Rand McNally, pp. 382–425.

TURNER, R. H., AND L. M. KILLIAN (1957). *Collective Behavior*. Englewood Cliffs, N.J.: Prentice-Hall.

WADA, G., AND J. C. DAVIES (1957). "Riots and rioters." *West. Polit. Quart.*, **10**, 864–874.

WALLACH, M. A., N. KOGAN, AND D. J. BEM (1962). "Group influence on individual risk taking." *J. Abnorm. Soc. Psychol.*, **65**, 75–86.

WALLAS, G. (1932). *The Great Society*. New York: Macmillan.

WASKOW, A. I. (1966). *From Race-Riot to Sit-In: 1919 and the 1960's*. New York: Doubleday.

WESTLEY, W. A. (1957). "The nature and control of hostile crowds." *Canad. J. Econ. Polit. Sci.*, **23**, 33–41.

WHITE, H. (1962). "Chance models of systems of casual groups." *Sociometry*, **25**, 153–172.

WHITE, T. H. (1965). *The Making of a President, 1964*. New York: Atheneum.

WOOLBERT, C. H. (1916). "The audience." *Psychol. Monogr.*, **21**, 37–54.

THE INDIVIDUAL IN A COMMUNICATIVE WEB

Part 4

Introduction

If the world were drained of every individual and we were left only with the messages that passed between them, we would still be in possession of the information needed to construct our discipline. For every truly sociopsychological phenomenon is rooted in *communication*. If influence is to be exerted by one person on another, some message must pass from the influencing source to its target, whether it be an eloquently persuasive argument, a fleeting scowl, or the distal messages that modern technology allows. By this fact, social psychology acquires scientific potential, for what passes from one person to the next necessarily enters the public and thus measurable domain.

Several articles in this section began as personal experiences that were eventually transformed into an experimental inquiry. Perhaps an account of the diffusion trace-back study, which has not been previously published, best illustrates this interplay.

In 1954, I lived in a graduate dormitory at Harvard University. The dormitory rooms did not have private telephones, but there was a pay telephone in the hallway about 100 feet from my room. Students both made and received calls at the pay phone. The telephone often rang many times before a student bestirred himself to walk from his room to answer it, then summoned the person requested by the caller. The problem was that there was no norm or custom prescribing how often to perform this civic chore. When the telephone rang, no one in the dorm knew who it was for. Who then should answer it? As a possible solution I devised a formula, inscribed it on an index card, and posted it near the telephone. It stated: "To share equitably the burden of answering this phone, students should answer the phone two times for each call they receive. (This is to take account of those occasions when a call is received for you, and you are not in.)" The message served as a guideline in a previously normless situation.

Five years passed. I left the dormitory, spent a year in Norway and one in France, then in 1959 I returned to Harvard. While making use of a pay phone in a neighboring dormitory, I noticed near the telephone a card that stated: "To share in the burden of answering this telephone, it is traditional for students to answer the phone two times for each call he receives...etc." The notices were spread far and wide. This cultural item had become diffused. It was now a tradition, yet it had started as the act of a single person. That is how many items must work their way into the general culture. A person inscribes a bit of graffiti: "Kilroy was here," or, "Taki 183." It catches on, diffuses widely, and seems to be everywhere. But is it possible to trace the item back to its original source?

The problem of tracing cultural items to their origin was again revived in 1966 in a conversation with my colleague, Dr. Lane Conn. We had begun our discussion with the premise that many items of information, fads, and styles are spread in a community by person to person, word-of-mouth communication. Verbal crazes, such as the now defunct "swifties" or "Polish jokes," are one form which such communication can take, whereas rumors and the widespread diffusion of antiscientific attitudes represent another more significant level. We wondered whether we could start with some item of information then circulating in society and trace it backward to its point of origin by asking each individual to tell us where he or she had learned of the item of information, and to continuously move the inquiry one step backward until we found the true origin of such a fad. To avoid the contaminating problem of the mass media, we would work with items that were not likely to be communicated over the radio or through newspapers. Our underlying model was that information, jokes, or fads ultimately had a beginning in some human source, and we could trace it back to that source. We speculated, for example, that perhaps all "Polish jokes" which were then sweeping the country may have started with a single beer-drinking piano player somewhere in a Chicago bar. And through our systematic network search we would find him, much as the small world method zeros in on the target person.

As it turned out, we did not launch this society-wide study, but the following year my experimental social psychology class managed to examine the diffusion-traceback phenomenon on a more modest experimental scale.

The class initiated a message we hoped would diffuse throughout the community. Once the message had been circulated we would apply our trace-to-origin procedure. Since we knew the actual origin of the message, we would be able to assess the accuracy of the procedure, i.e., whether the procedure correctly brought us back to the known point of origin. First, we needed to create a message that could be passed along on a person-to-person basis. We did this by creating a little story, a joke, that anyone could hear by calling our telephone number. An automatic answering unit repeated the joke each time the number was called. (After some trial and error, we decided to use a moderately sexy joke for this purpose, one that seemed to appeal to Harvard freshmen! A sultry young voice at the other end of the line reminisced about a romantic evening, followed by the revelation that the caller was a father!)

To get the communication process going, we sent a postcard to each of five freshmen living in the Harvard Yard. The card stated: "Call this number, just for fun, 887-5532." Our assumption was that the joke was so funny, the freshmen would pass the number on to their roommates, and so on. And this indeed proved to be the case.

A few hours after the postcards arrived, the calls started to come in. And they increased in frequency until our telephone line was jammed with calls. After 320 calls had been received, our machinery was so overloaded it broke down. Still, the 320 calls gave us enough diffusion data to initiate the second part of the study: to trace the entire pattern of diffusion and see if we could trace it back to the five Harvard freshmen who had received the original postcards.

We located people who had heard the joke by interviewing students in the undergraduate dining rooms and by placing an ad in a local newspaper. We asked each person where he had learned of the telephone number, then followed up on this information much as an epidemiologist would follow up on people known to have been infected with a contagious disease. Through careful and systematic work, the class was able to trace the diffusion network back to the original five freshmen. Thus, on a small scale, the diffusion traceback procedure worked well.

Mr. John Fryer, one of the students in the course, gave a precise account of the diffusion patterns:

> ... the information (about the phone number) stayed largely within the Harvard freshman class. Of the 123 persons who learned about the telephone number, 103 were Harvard freshmen. The other 20 persons included 7 residents of the towns of Arlington, Brighton, and Lincoln, 2 Radcliffe freshmen, 5 Wellesley students, 3 Harvard upperclassmen, 1 freshman proctor, 1 Boston College student, and 1 student from Hiram College, Ohio... Within the freshman class, the channels of diffusion were largely determined by proximity. Beginning with about 0.5 percent of the freshman class in the first wave, the information spread to about 8 percent of the freshman class.

The appeal of the method used above is that it does not assume *a priori* categories of social structure, but allows such structures as are actually operative to be revealed through communicative processes. We have not applied this procedure to a society-wide process, but this remains an interesting prospect.

In the articles reprinted in this section, I have used communicative acts both as tools and as objects of sociopsychological inquiry.

Almost all of us have had the experience of encountering someone far from home who, to our surprise, turns out to share a mutual acquaintance with us. This kind of experience occurs with sufficient frequency so that our language even provides a cliché to be uttered at the appropriate moment of recognizing mutual acquaintances: We say, "My, it's a small world." "The Small World Problem" aims to elucidate this latent communication system, whose properties turn out to be interesting and more readily discerned through mathematical analysis than casual intuition.

What is the use of such a study? The criticism implied in this question has never bothered me, for any activity seems to me of value if it satisfies curiosity, stimulates ideas, and gives a new slant to our understanding of the social world. Nonetheless, I confess to being pleased when a medical investigator informed me that he found the small world method uniquely suited to his study of viral diffusion.

The use of a communication system as a tool is best illustrated in "The Lost Letter Technique." One attractive feature of the technique is that it uses a very ordinary event—coming across a lost letter—as the basis of measurement. And it moves away from an exclusively verbal study of attitudes, which, because of its convenience, comes so easily to social psychologists and other survey scientists. Indeed, what it seemed to do was allow us to survey deeds and use this as a sociological datum. True, how a person disposes of a letter addressed to "Friends of the Nazi Party" is not a very large deed (perhaps we should call it a "microdeed"), but when aggregated with the responses of many other people and compared with an experimental control, it does tell us something about how people act toward such an organization, and even whether they are willing to help or hinder it by their acts.

Society has never worried more about the effects of messages than it has about the messages transmitted on television. The concern arises because of the sustained exposure to television by the country's youth, and the high incidence of violent behavior depicted in this medium. Does viewing such violent behavior stimulate violence in the community? Social science could hardly formulate a question of greater significance for public policy. But the empirical question is not easily answered, as the excerpt from "Television and Antisocial Behavior" demonstrates.

Despite the negative character of the research findings, I am not yet willing to accept them as conclusive answers to the question of violence on television. Indeed, other investigators studying this issue have reported effects of television on the commission of antisocial acts. But in truth, the quality of the investigations is not compelling. In principle, it seems that repeated and sustained exposure to violence ought to have an effect on individuals, but experimentation has thus far failed to demonstrate it.

The final essay on photography attempts to explore the sociopsychological meaning of this "image freezing" medium. Since the analysis of photography is my current burning interest, let me say a little more about it. There is a special reason why photography deserves more attention by the psychologist than, say, the act of tying our shoelaces. Photography is a technology used to extend specifically psychological functions: perception and memory. It can thus teach us a good deal about how we see and how we remember. The challenge is to identify psychologically interesting components of photography and to deepen our understanding through analysis and experimentation.

Photography is not necessarily a social act. We may take pictures of inanimate objects and not even show the photographs to others. But most generally, the social context powerfully conditions our photographic behavior. This seems a useful working assumption. Photographic behavior, therefore, ought to be subject to sociopsychological analysis.

One may inquire, for example, into the effects of a camera's presence on social behavior. One reasonable hypothesis is that prosocial behavior is encouraged and antisocial behavior is inhibited when people are aware that they are being photographed. To study this, one of my students, Maya Heczey, recently compared the size of contributions to a medical charity by individuals who are photographed and those who are not as they make their donations. She found that in the presence of the camera, people give substantially larger donations to a medical charity. She also found that antisocial behavior is inhibited: Substantially more automobiles stop at an intersection (bearing a stop sign) when a person is present at the intersection taking pictures than when the person is present without the camera.

The experiment touches on the deeper issue of the degree to which people feel accountable for their actions, and how this affects their behavior. At one extreme, a person may perform an act unobserved by others. But even behavior performed in the presence of others has a transitory quality. It is enacted, then disappears. The camera carries the documentation of the act beyond the situation in which it was carried out. It thus alters levels of anonymity, responsibility, and deindividuation. The camera is the "individuating" device par excellence, always recording a *particular* person or thing. The photograph, by permanently documenting the action, implies the polar opposite of anonymity and accordingly enhances social control.

A host of interesting questions may be raised about photography as a human activity: How can we describe the social relationship between the photographer and the person photographed? What is the nature of the pose assumed by the person photographed? To what extent is the pose influenced by cultural factors? How does the nature of the photograph a person takes change from childhood to maturity? Who within the family takes photographs and who is photographed most often? What does this tell us about the inner emotional life of the family? To what extent does taking a photograph prevent a person from fully savoring the special qualities of the moment in exchange for a future record of it? When we photograph an event, do we necessarily become an impersonal spectator of it; does this diminish our ability to respond to the event in other ways? These questions chart experimental paths that remain to be explored.

18

The Small World Problem

The problem concerns the manner in which individuals are linked, through bonds of kinship and acquaintance, into complex networks, and the means of devising efficient paths connecting any two points within the network. For the sake of simplicity, let us call this "the small world problem," a phrase long current in our language, but first employed in the social sciences by Ithiel Pool (cited in Rand, 1964).

The simplest way of formulating the small world problem is: "Starting with any two people in the world, what is the probability that they will know one another?" A somewhat more complex formulation, however, takes account of the fact that while persons X and Z may not know each other directly, they may share a mutual acquaintance—that is, a person who knows both of them. One can then think of an acquaintance chain with X knowing Y and Y knowing Z. Moreover, one can imagine circumstances in which X is linked to Z not by a single link, but by a series of links, that is, X-a-b-c-d—y-Z. That is to say, person X knows person a who in turn knows person b, who knows c, ... who knows y, who knows Z.

Therefore, another question one may ask is: given any two people in the world, person X and person Z, how many intermediate acquaintance links are needed before X and Z are connected? There are two general philosophical views on the small world problem. Some people feel that any two people in the world, no matter how remote from each other, can be linked in terms of intermediate acquaintances, and that the number of such intermediate links is relatively small.

There is, however, a contrasting view that sees unbridgeable gaps between various groups. Given any two people in the world, they will never link up, because people have circles of acquaintances which will not necessarily intersect. A message will circulate in a particular cluster of acquaintances, but may never be able to make the jump to another cluster. This view sees the world in terms of isolated clusters of acquaintances. The earlier view sees acquaintances in terms of an infinitely intersecting arrangement that permits movement from any social grouping to another through a series of connecting links.

Concern with the small world problem is not new, nor is it limited to social psychologists like myself. Historians, political scientists, and even city planners

This paper was first published in *Psychology Today* magazine, Vol. 1, No. 1 (May 1967), pp. 60–67. Copyright © 1967 Ziff-Davis Publishing Company. All rights reserved. This paper later appeared in somewhat modified form in *Interdisciplinary Relationships in the Social Sciences*, M. Sherif and C. W. Sherif (eds.), Chicago: Aldine, 1969, pp. 103–120. Illustrations are from the Sherif volume. Reprinted by permission. Copyright © 1969 by Muzafer Sherif and Carolyn W. Sherif.

have spoken of the matter in quite unambiguous terms. Jane Jacobs (1961) who has written on city planning, expressed it in terms that many of us have entertained as children.

> When my sister and I first came to New York from a small city, we used to amuse ourselves with a game we called Messages. The idea was to pick two wildly dissimilar individuals—say a head hunter in the Solomon Islands and a cobbler in Rock Island, Illinois—and assume that one had to get a message to the other by word of mouth; then we would each silently figure out a plausible, or at least possible, chain of persons through which the message could go. The one who could make the shortest plausible chain of messengers won. The head hunter would speak to the head man of his village, who would speak to the trader who came to buy copra, who would speak to the Australian patrol officer when he came through, who would tell the man who was next slated to go to Melbourne on leave, etc. Down at the other end, the cobbler would hear from his priest, who got it from the mayor, who got it from a state senator, who got it from the governor, etc. We soon had these close-to-home messengers down to a routine for almost everybody we could conjure up (pp. 134–135).

The importance of the problem does not lie in these entertaining aspects, but in the fact that it brings under discussion a certain mathematical structure in society, a structure that often plays a part, whether recognized or not, in many discussions of history, sociology, and other disciplines. For example, Henri Pirenne (1925) and George Duby (1958), make the point that in the dark ages communication broke down between cities of western Europe. They became isolated and simply did not have contact with each other. The network of acquaintances of individuals became constricted. The disintegration of society was expressed in the growing isolation of communities, and the infrequent contact with those living outside a person's immediate place of residence.

THE UNDERLYING STRUCTURE

Sometimes it is useful to visualize the abstract properties of a scientific problem before studying it in detail; that is, we construct a model of the main features of the phenomenon as we understand them. Graph theory, which is concerned with the mathematical treatment of networks, provides a convenient way of representing the structure of acquaintanceships. (Harary, Norman, and Cartwright, 1965)

Let us represent all the people in the United States by a number of points. Each point represents a person, while lines connecting two points show that the two persons are acquainted. Each person has a certain number of firsthand acquaintances, which we shall represent by the letters a, b, c, ... n. Each acquaintance in turn has his own acquaintances, connected to still other points (see Figs. 18.1 and 18.2).

The exact number of lines radiating from any point depends on the size of a person's circle of acquaintances. The entire structure takes on the form of a

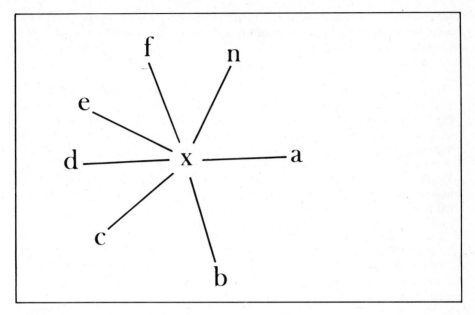

Fig. 18.1 *Acquaintances of X, a,..., n.*

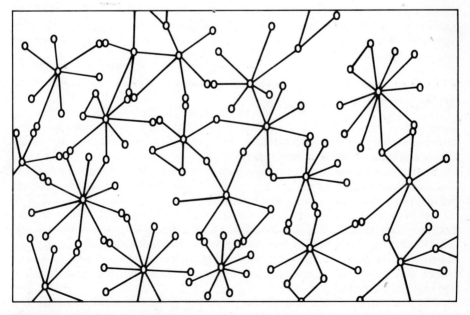

Fig. 18.2 *Network of acquaintances.*

complex network of 200,000,000 points, with complicated connections between them. One way of restating the small world problem in these terms is this: given any two of these points chosen at random from this universe, through how many intermediate points would we pass before they could be connected by the shortest possible path?

There are many ways to go about the study of the small world problem, and I shall soon present my own approach to it. But first, let us consider the contributions of a group of workers at MIT under the leadership of Ithiel de Sola Pool. Pool, working closely with Manfred Kochen of IBM, decided to build a theoretical model of the small world, and the model parallels closely the idea of points and lines shown in Figs. 18.1 and 18.2. To build such a model certain information needs to be known. First, you have to know how many acquaintances the average man has. Surprisingly, though this is a basic question, no reliable answers could be found in the social science literature. So the information had to be obtained, and Dr. Michael Gurevitch, then a graduate student at MIT, set about this task. Gurevitch (1961) asked a variety of men and women to keep a record of all the persons they came in contact with in the course of 100 days. It turned out that on the average, these people recorded names of roughly 500 persons, so that this figure could be used as the basis of the theoretical model. If every person knows 500 other people, what are the chances that any two people will know each other? Making a set of rather simple assumptions, it turns out that there is only about one chance in 200,000 that any two Americans chosen at random will know each other. However, the odds drop precipitously when you ask the chances of their having a mutual acquaintance. And there is better than a 50–50 chance that any two people can be linked up with two intermediate acquaintances.

Of course, the investigators were aware of the fact that even if a man has 500 acquaintances, there may be a lot of inbreeding. That is, many of the 500 friends of my friend may be actually among the people I know anyway, so that they do not really contribute to a widening net of acquaintances. Figure 18.3 illustrates the phenomenon of inbreeding by showing how the acquaintances of X feed back into his circle of acquaintances and do not bring any new contacts into the structure.

It is a fairly straightforward job to check up on the amount of inbreeding using one or two circles of acquaintances, but it becomes almost impossible when the acquaintance chain stretches far and wide. There are just too many people involved to make a count practical.

So the main obstacle in applying a model of this sort is the problem of social structure. Although poor people always have acquaintances, it probably turns out that they tend to be among other poor people, while the rich speak mostly to the rich. It is exceedingly difficult to assess the impact of social structure on a model of this sort. If you could think of the American population as only 200,000,000 points, each with 500 *random* connections, the model would work. But the contours of social structure make this a perilous assumption, for society is not built on random connections among persons, but tends toward fragmentation into social classes and cliques.

But could the problem admit of a more direct experimental solution? The Laboratory of Social Relations at Harvard gave me $680 to prove this was the

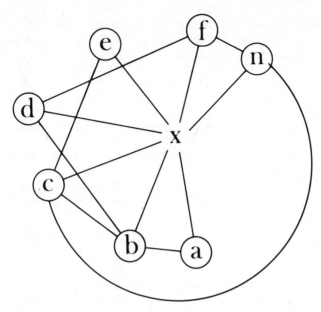

Fig. 18.3 *Inbreeding.*

case. My approach was to try to find an experimental method whereby if two persons were chosen at random, it would be possible to trace a line of acquaintances that linked the two.

Let us assume for the moment that the actual process of establishing the linkages between two persons runs only one way: from person *A* to person *Z*. Let us call person *A* the *starting* person, since he will initiate the process, and person *B* the *target* person. Then we would ask the starting person to try to establish contact with the target person using only a chain of friends and acquaintances. We could then see how long the chain was, and study many of its other properties. Of course, the starting person cannot, at the outset, know what the complete chain looks like: he cannot see beyond the circle of his immediate acquaintances, and the chance that anyone of his immediate acquaintances would know the target person is small. The starting person cannot see beyond the first link, he can only start the process on its way, by moving it one step toward the target.

The general procedure was to obtain a sample of men and women from varied walks of life. Each of these persons was given the name and address of "Target Person" (that is, an individual chosen at random living somewhere in the United States). Each of the participants was asked to move a message towards the target person using only a chain of friends and acquaintances. Each person could transmit the message to one friend or acquaintance who would be more likely to know the target person than he was. The friend would repeat the process until the message reached the target person. Messages may only move to persons who know each other on a first-name basis.

As a crude beginning, we thought it best to draw our starting people from some distant city such as Wichita, Kansas, or Omaha, Nebraska (from Cambridge, these cities seem vaguely "out there," on the Great Plains or some where). So letters of solicitation were sent to residents in these cities asking them to participate in a study of social contact in American society. (For certain purposes, residents of the Boston area were also used.) It was necessary to select a target person and the first individual to serve in this capacity was the wife of a Divinity School student living in Cambridge. In a second study, carried out in collaboration with Jeffrey Travers, the target person was a stock broker who worked in Boston and lived in Sharon, Massachusetts. To keep matters straight, I will refer to the first study as the Kansas study and the second study as the Nebraska study. These terms indicate merely where the starting persons were drawn from. Each person who volunteered to serve as a starting person was sent a document, which is the main tool of the investigation (see Fig. 18.4). I suggest that it be scrutinized to learn the flavor and details of the procedure, but let us quickly review its main contents. The document contains:

1. The name of the target person as well as certain information about him. This orients the participant toward a specific individual.

2. A set of rules for reaching the target person. Perhaps, the most important rule is stated in box 4; "*if you do not know the target person on a personal basis, do not try to contact him directly. Instead, mail this folder ... to a personal acquaintance who is more likely than you to know the target person ... it must be someone you know on a first-name basis.*" This rule sets the document into motion, moving it from one participant to the next, until it is sent to someone who knows the target person. Then, rule 3 takes over and the chain is completed.

3. A roster on which the subject affixes his name. This tells the person who receives the letter exactly who sent it to him. The roster also has another practical effect; it prevents endless looping of the document through a participant who has already been an earlier link in the chain. For each participant can see exactly what sequence of persons has led up to his own participation.

4. A stack of fifteen business reply cards.

Several other features of the procedure need to be emphasized. First, the subject operates under the restriction that he can send the folder on only to one other person. Thus, the efficiency with which the chain is completed depends in part on the wisdom of his choice in this matter. Second, by means of the business reply card, we have continuous feedback on the progress of each chain. The cards are coded so we know which chain it comes from and which link in the chain has been completed. The card also provides us with relevant sociological characteristics of the sender and receiver of the card. Thus, we know the characteristics of completed, as well as incomplete, chains. Third, the procedure permits experimental variation at many points.

In short, the device possesses some of the features of a chain letter, though it does not pyramid in any way; moreover it is oriented toward a specific target, zeros in on the target through the cooperation of a sequence of participants, and contains a tracer that allows us to keep track of its progress at all times.

The question that plagued us most in undertaking this study was simply: Would the procedure work? Would any chains started in Kansas actually reach our target person in Massachusetts? The answer came fairly quickly. Within a few days after initiating chains in Kansas, one of the documents was returned to the target person, the wife of a Divinity School student. The document had started with a wheat farmer in Kansas. He passed it on to an Episcopal minister in his home town, who sent it to a minister who taught in Cambridge, who gave it to the target person. Altogether the number of intermediate links between starting person and target person amounted to *two*!

As it turned out this was one of the shortest chains we were ever to receive, for as more tracers and documents came in, we learned that chains varied from 3–10 intermediate acquaintances, with the median at 5.5 Figure 18.5 shows what may be regarded as the main finding of the study; the distribution of 42 chain lengths from our Nebraska study, in which 160 persons started in an attempt to reach a stock broker who resided in Sharon, Massachusetts. The median number of intermediate persons is 5.5, which is, in certain ways, impressive, considering the distances traversed. Recently, I asked a person of intelligence how many steps he thought it would take, and he said it would require 100 intermediate persons, or more, to move from Nebraska to Sharon. Many people make somewhat similar approximations, and are surprised to learn that only 5.5 intermediaries will—on the average—suffice. Somehow it does not accord with intuition. Later, I shall try to explain the basis of the discrepancy between intuition and fact.

It is reasonable to assume that the theoretically pure number of links needed to complete the chains is even less than that shown by our findings. First, since our participants can only send the folder on to one of their 500 possible contacts, it is unlikely that even through careful selection they will necessarily, and at all times, select a contact best able to advance the chain to the target. On the whole they probably make pretty good guesses, but surely, from time to time, they overlook certain possibilities for shortcuts. The chains obtained in our empirical study are less efficient than those generated theoretically.

Secondly, the only basis for moving the folder to the target person is to work along certain highly rational lines. That is, a certain amount of information about the target person concerning his place of employment, place of residence, schooling, etc., is given to the starting subject, and it is on the basis of this information alone that he selects the next recipient of the folder. Yet, in real life, we sometimes know a person because we chance to meet him on an ocean liner, or we spend a summer in camp together as teenagers, yet these haphazard bases of acquaintanceship cannot be fully exploited by the participants.

There is one factor that could, conceivably, work in the opposite direction, that is, give us the illusion that the chains are shorter than they really are. There is a certain decay in the number of active chains over each remove even when they do not drop out because of reaching the target person. Of 160 chains that started in Nebraska, 42 were completed and 128 dropped out. These chains die before completion because a certain proportion of participants simply do not cooperate and fail to send on the folder on each remove. Thus, the results we obtained on the distribution of chain lengths occurred within the general drift of a decay curve. It is possible that some of the completed chains would have been longer than those that did get completed. To account for this possibility, Professor Harrison White of Harvard has constructed a mathematical model to show what the distribution of chain lengths would look like if all chains went

COMMUNICATIONS PROJECT

322 EMERSON HALL   HARVARD UNIVERSITY   CAMBRIDGE, MASSACHUSETTS 02138

We need your help in an unusual scientific study carried out at Harvard University. We are studying the nature of social contact in American society. Could you, as an active American, contact another American citizen regardless of his walk of life? If the name of an American citizen were picked out of a hat, could you get to know that person using only your network of friends and acquaintances? Just how open is our "open society"? To answer these questions, which are very important to our research, we ask for your help.

You will notice that this letter has come to you from a friend. He has aided this study by sending this folder on to you. He hopes that you will aid the study by forwarding this folder to someone else. The name of the person who sent you this folder is listed on the Roster at the bottom of this sheet.

In the box to the right you will find the name and address of an American citizen who has agreed to serve as the "target person" in this study. The idea of the study is to transmit this folder to the target person using only a chain of friends and acquaintances.

TARGET PERSON

Information about
the target person
is placed here.

HOW TO TAKE PART IN THIS STUDY

1 ADD YOUR NAME TO THE ROSTER AT THE BOTTOM OF THIS SHEET, so that the next person who receives this letter will know who it came from.

2 DETACH ONE POSTCARD. FILL IT OUT AND RETURN IT TO HARVARD UNIVERSITY. No stamp is needed. The postcard is very important. It allows us to keep track of the progress of the folder as it moves toward the target person.

3 IF YOU KNOW THE TARGET PERSON ON A PERSONAL BASIS, MAIL THIS FOLDER DIRECTLY TO HIM (HER). Do this only if you have previously met the target person and know each other on a first name basis.

4 IF YOU DO NOT KNOW THE TARGET PERSON ON A PERSONAL BASIS, DO NOT TRY TO CONTACT HIM DIRECTLY. INSTEAD, MAIL THIS FOLDER (POST CARDS AND ALL) TO A PERSONAL ACQUAINTANCE WHO IS MORE LIKELY THAN YOU TO KNOW THE TARGET PERSON. You may send the folder on to a friend, relative, or acquaintance, but it must be someone you know on a first name basis.

Remember, the aim is to move this folder toward the target person using only a chain of friends and acquaintances. On first thought you may feel you do not know anyone who is acquainted with the target person. This is natural, but at least you can start it moving in the right direction! Who among your acquaintances might conceivably move in the same social circles as the target person? The real challenge is to identify among your friends and acquaintances a person who can advance the folder toward the target person. It may take several steps beyond your friend to get to the target person, but what counts most is to start the folder on its way! The person who receives this folder will then repeat the process, until the folder is received by the target person. May we ask you to begin!

Every person who participates in this study and returns the post card to us will receive a certificate of appreciation from the Communications Project. All participants are entitled to a report describing the results of the study.

Please transmit this folder within 24 hours. Your help is greatly appreciated.

Yours sincerely,

Stanley Milgram, Ph. D.
Director, Communications Project

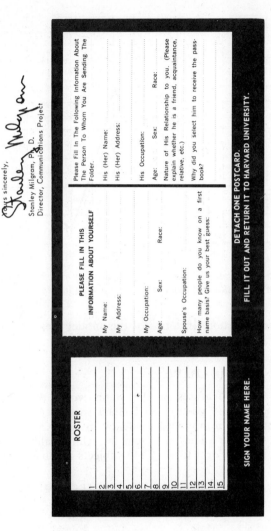

Fig. 18.4 *Document used in the small world problem.*

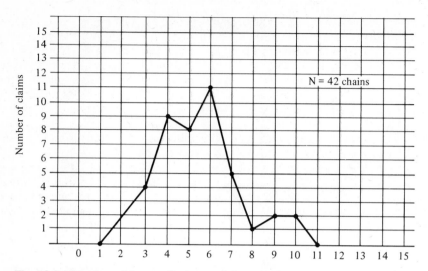

Fig. 18.5 *Number of intermediaries needed to reach target person. Each chain started in Nebraska and reached a target person in Massachusetts.*

through to completion. In terms of this model there is a transformation of the data, yielding longer chains.

EXAMINING THE CHAINS

There are several features of the chain worth examining, for they tell us something about the pattern of contact in American society. Consider, for example, the very pronounced tendency in our Kansas study for female participants to send the folder on to females, while males tended to send the folder on to other males. For a total of 145 subjects involved in the study, we find:

Female	→	Female	56
Male	→	Male	58
Female	→	Male	18
Male	→	Female	13

that is, subjects were three times as likely to send the folder on to someone of the same sex as someone of the opposite sex. This is true when the target person is female, less true when the target person is a male. Exactly why this is so is not easy to determine, but it suggests that certain kinds of communication are conditioned strongly by sex roles.

Subjects also indicated on the tracer cards whether they were sending the folder on to friends, relatives, or acquaintances. In this same series, 123 cards were sent to friends and acquaintances, while only 22 were sent to relatives. Cross-cultural comparison would seem useful here. It is quite likely that in societies which possess extended kinship systems, relatives will be more heavily represented in the communication network than is true in the United States. In

American society, where extended kinship links are not maintained, acquaintance and friendship links provide the preponderant basis for reaching the target person. I would guess, further, within certain ethnic groups in the United States, a higher proportion of familial links would be found in the data. Probably, if the study were limited to persons of Italian extraction, one would get a higher proportion of relatives in the chain. This illustrates, I hope, how the small world technique may usefully illuminate varied aspects of social structure, as well as cultural topics.

In Fig. 18.6 we show what kind of people were involved in some typical chains that stretched from Nebraska to Massachusetts.

Each of us is embedded in a potential small world structure. It is not enough to say, however, that each acquaintance constitutes an equally important basis of contact with the larger social world. For it is obvious that some acquaintances are more important in establishing contacts with broader social realms: some

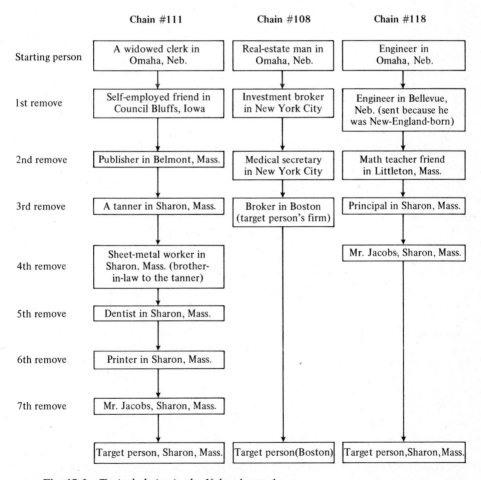

Fig. 18.6 *Typical chains in the Nebraska study.*

friends are relatively isolated; others possess a wide circle of acquaintances, and contact with them brings the individual into a far-ranging network of additonal persons.

Let us consider in detail the pattern of convergence crystallizing around the target person of our second target person, a stock broker living in Sharon, Massachusetts, and working in Boston. A total of 62 chains reached him,[1] 24 of these at his place of residence in a small town outside of Boston. Within Sharon, fully sixteen were given to the target person by Mr. Jacobs, a clothing merchant in town. He served as the principal point of mediation between the target person and the larger world, a fact that came as a considerable surprise, and even something of a shock for the target person. At his place of work in a Boston brokerage house, ten of the chains passed through Mr. Jones, and five through Mr. Brown, business colleagues of the target person. Indeed, 48 percent of the chains to reach the target person were moved on to him by three persons: Jacobs, Jones, and Brown. Between Jacobs and Jones there is an interesting division of labor. Jacobs mediates the chains advancing to the target person by virtue of his residence. Jones performs a similar function in the occupational domain, and moves 10 chains enmeshed in the investment-brokerage network to the target person (Fig. 18.7).

More detail thus comes to fill out the picture of the small world. First, we learn that the target is not surrounded by acquaintance points each equally likely to feed into an outside contact; rather, there appear to be highly popular channels for the transmission of the chain. Second, there is differentiation

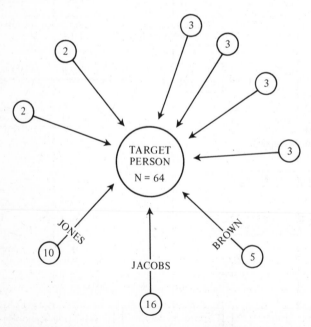

Fig. 18.7 *Convergence through common channels (includes 42 chains that started in Nebraska and 22 that started in the Boston area).*

among these commonly used channels, so that certain of them provide the chief points of transmission in regard to residential contact, while others have specialized contact possibilities in the occupational domain. For each possible realm of activity in which the target is active, there is likely to emerge a sociometric star with specialized contact possibilities.

GEOGRAPHIC MOVEMENT

Geographic movement from the state of Nebraska to Massachusetts is striking over the several links. Figure 18.8 shows the progressive closing in on the target area with each new person added to the chain. There are some cases, however, in which a chain moves all the way from Nebraska to the very neighborhood in which the target person resides, but never quite makes the necessary contact to complete the chain. Some chains have died only a few hundred feet from the target person's house, after a successful transmission of 1000 miles. Social communication is sometimes restricted less by physical distance than by social distance.

1305 miles	(starting position)
710 miles	first remove
356 miles	second remove
210 miles	third remove
79 miles	fourth remove
44 miles	fifth remove
20 miles	sixth remove
Target area	seventh remove

Fig. 18.8 *Geographic movement from Nebraska to Massachusetts. The chains progress toward the target area with each remove. The figure shows the number of miles from the target area with each remove averaged over all chains, completed as well as incompleted. For example, by the sixth remove, the average chain (assuming it is still active) is 20 miles from the target area. The target area is defined as any location less than 20 miles from Boston.*

The major research focus for future inquiry calls for changing the relationship between the starting person and the target person. If the two are drawn from different class backgrounds, does this decrease the probability of completing the chain? Does it increase the number of links?

In collaboration with Charles Korte, I am now applying the small world method to the study of communications in subgroups in American society; namely, Negro and white persons. We will have Negro starting persons and target persons, and white starting persons, and try to trace the lines of communication between them. We would first like to ask: In what degree are the racial lines surmounted? Can any sizeable fraction of the communications get through the racial barrier? If the answer is affirmative, what is the typical locus of transition? Does it occur at the neighborhood level? At the place of work? We are particularly interested in the persons who serve as links between Negro and white groups. In what way do they differ from others in the chain? Do they tend to occupy particular professional categories, such as minister, teacher, etc.? Is there any easier flow between Negroes and whites in Northern or Southern locales? Perhaps some new light can be cast on the structural relationships between Negro and white communities by probing with the small world method.

As stated previously, many people were surprised to learn that only 5.5 intermediaries will, on the average, suffice to link randomly chosen individuals, no matter where each lives in the United States. We ought to try to explain the discrepancy between intuition and fact.

The first point to remember is that although we deal directly with only 5.5 intermediaries, behind each of them stands a much larger group of from 500 to 2500 persons. That is, each participant selects from an acquaintance pool of 500 to 2500 persons the individual he thinks is in the best position to advance the chain, and we deal only with the end product of a radical screening procedure. Second, there is an element of geometric progression implicit in the search procedure, and there is nothing more alien to mathematically untutored intuition than this form of thinking. As youngsters, any of us were asked the question: If you earned a penny a day and the sum were doubled each day, how much would have earned by the end of a 30-day working period. Most frequently people give answers on the order of $1.87 or $6.45, when in fact the sum is more than $10,000,000 for one 30-day working period, the last day alone yielding $5,368,709.12 in wages. Elements of geometric progression with an increase rate far more powerful than mere doubling underlies the small world search procedure, and thus, with only a few removes, the search extends to an enormous number of persons.

Finally, when we state there are only 5.5 intermediate acquaintances, this connotes a closeness between the position of the starting person and the target persons, but this is in large measure misleading, a confusion of two entirely different frames of reference. If two persons are 5.5 removes apart, they are far apart indeed. Almost anyone in the United States is but a few removes from the President, or from Nelson Rockefeller, but this is only as seen from a particular mathematical slant and does not, in any practical sense, integrate our lives with that of Nelson Rockefeller. Thus, when we speak of five intermediaries we are talking about an enormous psychological distance between the starting and target points, a distance which only seems small because we customarily regard "5" as a small, manageable quantity. We should think of the two points as being not five persons apart, but five "circles of acquaintances" apart—five "structures" apart. This helps to set it in its proper perspective.

There is an interesting theorem based on the model of the small world. It states that if persons from two different populations cannot make contact, that no one within the entire population in which each is embedded can make contact with any person in the other population. Said differently, given person a embedded in population A (which consists of his circle of acquaintances), and person b embedded in population B, if a cannot make contact with b, then:

1. No other individual in A can make contact with b.

2. No other individual in A can make contact with any other individual in B.

3. In other words, the two subpopulations are completely isolated from each other.

Conceivably, this could happen if one of the populations were on an island never visited by the outside world. In principle, any person in the United States can be contacted by any other in relatively few steps, unless one of them is a complete and total hermit and then he could not be contacted at all.

In sum, perhaps the most important accomplishment of the research discribed here is that—although people have talked about small world connections, and have even theorized about it—these are, to my knowledge, the first empirically created connections between persons chosen at random from a major national population.

Although the study started with a specific set of questions arising from the small world problem, the procedure illuminates a far wider set of topics. It reveals a potential communication structure whose characteristics have yet to be exposed. When we understand the structure of this potential communication net, we shall understand a good deal more about the integration of society in general. While many studies in social science show how the individual is alienated and cut off from the rest of society, from the perspective of this study a different view emerges: in some sense, at least, we are all bound together in a tightly knit social fabric.

NOTE

1. This includes the 42 originating in Nebraska and 20 additional chains originating in the Boston area.

REFERENCES

DUBY, G. AND MANDROU, R., *Histoire de la Civilisation Française*. Paris: Colin, 1958.

GUREVITCH, M., "The social structure of acquaintanceship networks." Unpublished doctoral dissertation, Massachusetts Institute of Technology, 1961.

HARARY, F., NORMAN, R. Z., AND CARTWRIGHT, D., *Structural Models: An Introduction to the Theory of Directed Graphs*. New York: Wiley, 1965.

JACOBS, J., *The Death and Life of Great American Cities*. New York: Random House, 1961.

KORTE, C., AND MILGRAM, S., "Acquaintance networks between racial groups: Application of the small world method." *Journal of Personality and Social Psychology*, **15** (2), 1970, 101–108.

PIRENNE, H., *Medieval Cities: Their Origins and the Revival of Trade*. Princeton, N.J.: Princeton University Press, 1925.

POOL, I. DES., Unpublished memorandum, Massachusetts Institute of Technology.

RAND, C., *Cambridge, U.S.A.: Hub of a New World*. New York: Oxford University Press, 1964.

TRAVERS, J., AND MILGRAM, S., "An experimental study of the small world problem." *Sociometry*, **32** (4), 1969, 425–443.

The Lost Letter Technique

19

Throughout the summer and fall of 1967, the Communists staged a series of strikes, terrorist attacks and civil disorders in the British Crown Colony of Hong Kong. The aim was to apply pressure to the British and, some experts said, to dislodge them. The political sympathies of the 4,000,000 people in Hong Kong, an active, vibrant city precariously perched on Red China's doorstep were largely unknown. Harrison Salisbury of the *New York Times* noted that pictures of Chiang Kai-shek were displayed in shop windows of the overseas Chinese merchants, but wondered whether portraits of Mao Tse-tung hung in the back rooms. What exactly were the political loyalties of the overseas Chinese?

In 1967, the populace of Hong Kong stood firm. Despite the disorder, they did not join the Communist cause. The outcome was an unexpected relief to many Westerners, but it came as no surprise to our small research team. A few months earlier, we had obtained evidence that the majority of Chinese in Hong Kong favored Taiwan over Peking, and that they would act on their political loyalties.

The evidence consisted of several hundred letters, identical in content but differently addressed. They constituted the most recent application of an experimental method for assessing community orientations toward political institutions: the Lost-Letter Technique.

We shall return to the study in Hong Kong, but first, let me tell you how a lost-letter study is conducted—and why.

At the root, the technique is a simple one. An investigator distributes—drops —throughout a city a large number of letters, addressed and stamped but unposted. A person who comes across one of these "lost" letters on the street must decide what to do: mail it? disregard it? destroy it?

There is a widespread feeling among people that one *ought* to mail such a letter. This behavior is so widely acknowledged as proper that an item on the Wechsler Adult Intelligence Scale is based on it. This feeling also prevails in Chinese-speaking communities. In some circumstances, however—when the letter is addressed to an organization the finder thinks highly objectionable—he may *not* mail it. Thus, by varing the addresses on the letters and calculating the proportion returned for each address, one can measure sentiment toward an organization.

The technique gets around certain problems inherent in the survey interview

This paper was first published in *Psychology Today* magazine, Vol. 3, No. 3 (June 1969), pp. 30–33, 66, 68. The technique was first described in the article, "The Lost-Letter Technique: A Tool of Social Research," by S. Milgram, L. Mann, and S. Harter, *Public Opinion Quarterly*, Vol. 29 (Fall 1965), 437–438. Copyright © 1969 Ziff-Davis Publishing Company. All rights reserved.

—the usual method of assessing attitudes. When a research team wants to test public sentiment on a social issue, it ordinarily chooses a representative group of persons from the community, and questions them. The methods for selecting a representative sample have been worked out in very careful fashion, and are so effective that a sample of only 1200 persons can be used to predict national trends with great accuracy. But it remains true that once the person is selected for questioning, the information must come through a structured conversation. The resulting measurements measure only what the person *says*. This exclusive focus on verbal accounts, though of great utility, seems an unwise fixation in any scientific social psychology. It ought to be possible to measure *deeds* on a large scale and in a way that permits experimental variation.

In the lost-letter method, the respondent is not asked to speak; instead he is presented with a chance to act in regard to an object with political and social attributes. The basic premise of the technique is that his action will tell us something of how he relates to that object. By mailing the lost letter, he aids the organization in question; by disregarding or destroying the letter he hinders it. And he has defined his relationship toward the organization by the quality of his actions.

People confronted with interviews and questionnaires know they are in a special situation. They know that they have been chosen for study and that their behavior will be scrutinized. As Milton Rosenberg of the University of Chicago has shown, their concern with the way their responses will be evaluated can have a strong effect on what they say.

This problem is particularly acute in research concerning politically sensitive issues. A Chinese merchant in Kowloon is unlikely to tell an interviewer that he is willing to take actions to advance the fortunes of Peking.

Several years ago, in my graduate research seminar at Yale, I, along with Leon Mann and Susan Harter, developed a technique that avoided these problems—one that would measure attitudes without people's knowledge, through their actions instead of their words. The lost-letter technique was one solution. Lost letters have been used to inflame a populace and to study personal honesty, but we were interested in using the returns as a clue to how people felt and—more important—how they would act toward different political organizations. The information we gained would be sociological, not psychological. We would not know about the individuals who returned the letters, but we would have a return rate specific to each organization, and thus useful for certain purposes. The nature of the procedure guaranteed the anonymity of those who took part.

NAZIS AND COMMUNISTS

The first study, carried out in New Haven, was intended not to tell us something new about the world, but to show whether the technique would work at all. Members of the seminar addressed 100 envelopes each to two organizations that would doubtless prove unpopular with New Havenites, *Friends of the Nazi Party* and *Friends of the Communist Party*. As a control, we addressed 100 more to an organization about which we expected people to feel positively, *Medical Research Associates,* and 100 to a private person, *Mr. Walter Carnap* (see Fig. 19.1).

M. Thuringer

Medical Research Associates
P.O. Box 7147
304 Columbus Avenue
New Haven 11, Connecticut

Attention: Mr. Walter Carnap

M. Thuringer

Friends of the Communist Party
P.O. Box 7147
304 Columbus Avenue
New Haven 11, Connecticut

Attention: Mr. Walter Carnap

Fig. 19.1   *Sample envelopes in the lost letter study.*

The envelopes, all addressed to the same post office box in New Haven, contained identical letters. The letter was straightforward but, we felt, could interact suggestively with each address (see Fig. 19.2).

We distributed the letters in 10 preselected districts in New Haven—on sidewalks, in outdoor phone booths, in shops, and under automobile windshield wipers (with a penciled note saying "found near car"). Each letter had been unobtrusively coded for placement and section of city and, in a final bit of cloak-and-daggermanship, each envelope was sealed in a way that would show us later whether or not it had been opened. Then we waited. In a few days the letters came in, and as we had predicted—in unequal numbers. Whereas 72 percent of the Medical Research letters and 71 percent of the personal letters came back, just one-quarter of the Nazi and Communist letters were returned (see Table 19.1).

A considerable number of the envelopes had been opened: 40 percent of the Communist letters, 32 percent of the Nazi ones, and 25 percent of the Medical Research letters. Apparently people were more reluctant to tamper with a personal letter, for Mr. Carnap's mail came through 90 percent intact. The least returned letters were also the most opened. The trend held not only from letter to letter, but from location to location.

```
                                                    4/3/63


    Dear Walter,

          Just a note to tell you that the plans have been changed.

    The speaker can't be in New Haven in time for next week's

    meeting, so bring the two reels of film instead.  My guess is

    the film will have a very good effect on the group, particu-

    larly the new members.  I'll try to get a few recent

    acquaintances to show up.

          Grace and I are flying to Chicago as usual, but we'll

    be back in time for the meeting.  Regards from my brother, and

    keep up the good work.


                                         Best,
                                              Max
```

Fig. 19.2 *Letter for all seasons. The wording of lost letter in New Haven test is ambiguous enough to be "sent" to a variety of addresses.*

Table 19.1

	Placement				
Address	Shops	Cars	Streets	Phone booths	Percent return
Medical Research Associates	23	19	18	12	72
Personal letter	21	21	16	13	71
Friends of the Communist Party	6	9	6	4	25
Friends of the Nazi Party	7	6	6	6	25
Total	57	55	46	35	48

The initial results and the discrepant return rates showed that the basic premise of the technique held up: the probability of lost letters being returned depends on the political and social attributes of the organization to which they are addressed. Having established this, we could then apply the lost-letter technique to other circumstances where the answers were hard to obtain by conventional means.

In the realm of imagination the lost-letter technique seemed like a lazy man's social psychology, consisting of nothing more than dropping envelopes here and there, and waiting for the returns. But in actual practice, the physical distribution of letters to predesignated locations is a difficult and exhausting chore. Aching feet were common. We tried distributing the letters from a moving car, but this had to be done in darkness. The envelopes tended not to fall where we meant them to; also, as often as not, they landed wrong-side up.

Later, we tried an air drop over Worcester, Massachusetts (after requesting and receiving an official exemption from the city's littering ordinances). This did not work well either. Many letters, of course, came to rest on rooftops, in trees and in ponds. Worse still, many were swept directly into the aileron structure of the Piper Colt, endangering not only the results but the safety of the plane, pilot and distributor. In the end, we never did find a substitute for legwork.

To facilitate the research, some legal spadework seemed useful. We obtained permission of the Post Office Department to use the names of fictitious organizations. And a week before the New Haven study began, I told the FBI of our work, hoping to save our Government the expense of pursuing an illusory conspiracy. The agent I spoke with seemed appreciative and even offered to let me know how many reports his office received from the citizenry. As things turned out, however, when I phoned again, the agent said he had forgotten my earlier call. Half the force, he hinted, was out on the case. The number of reports that had come in was now classified and unavailable to me.

ON RACE

The New Haven study showed that the technique could work. We next wanted to see if it could be applied to a current social issue. In 1963, tensions over racial integration in the Southern states were at a peak. Newspaper headlines reported dramatic confrontations at motels and resturants. A Yale graduate student, Mr. Taketo Murata, drove south from New Haven with a batch of letters addressed to pro-civil rights groups and anti-civil rights groups. He dispersed them in black and in white neighborhoods in North Carolina tobacco towns. Inside, as before, was the same letter. The returns showed a neat reversal across neighborhoods. In black neighborhoods, the pro-civil rights letters were returned in greater numbers, while from Caucasian residential areas the "Council for White Neighborhoods" came in more strongly. Thus the technique seemed applicable to a real social issue and was also responsive to a demographic variable. Mann and Murata repeated the study in a Connecticut industrial town, where the results, though tending in the same direction, were less clear, reflecting the more moderate sentiments on racial integration in the North at that time. The growth of militant Northern civil rights activity in the past six years could conceivably lead to stronger differentials in response. In general the more divisive a society, the more likely the differences in return rates of letters relevant to social issues. In an extreme case, when a country has polarized into hostile camps, neither side will mail any letters for the other.

AN ELECTION

The technique had one serious shortcoming: we had no objective evidence of its validity. True, the Medical-Research letters had come in more strongly than the political-extremist letters, and the civil-rights letters reflected the neighborhoods in which they were dropped in a way that made sense, but we needed an exact criterion against which the results could be assessed. The 1964 Presidential election provided the opportunity. Working closely with Dr. Rhea Diamond, I distributed the following letters in several election wards of Boston: Committee to Elect Goldwater, Committee to Defeat Goldwater, Committee to Elect Johnson, and Committee to Defeat Johnson.

The results were summarized by the *Harvard Crimson* a few days before the election: "SOC REL FINDS PRO-LBJ BOSTONIANS WON'T MAIL LETTERS TO ELECT BARRY." And the historical record shows that the lost-letter technique correctly predicted the outcome of the election in each of the wards. But, although the technique identified the trend, it badly underestimated the strength of Johnson support. Overall, it gave Johnson a scant 10 percent lead over Goldwater when the actual lead in these wards was closer to 60 percent. This suggests that *the difference in return rates of letters will always be weaker than the extent of actual difference of community opinion.* Even if a person plans to vote for Johnson he may still be a good enough fellow to mail a pro-Goldwater letter. And some letters are always picked up and mailed by children, illiterates, and street-cleaners. There is a good deal of unwanted variance in the returns.

In this election study the letters placed on car windshields provided the best results (see Table 19.2).

Table 19.2

	Johnson	Goldwater
Committee to elect	25	9
Committee to defeat	13	27

Thirty-seven letters for each one of the four committees were dropped. There seemed to be two reasons for the superior predictive power of windshield letters. First, it is more likely that adults, and therefore voters, will encounter them. Second, a letter found on a car windshield, as opposed to one found on the street, seems more in one's personal possession and is more likely to be disposed of according to personal whim.

MAO VERSUS CHIANG

The lost-letter technique really showed us things we already knew, or soon would know. It was not so much that the technique confirmed the *events* as the fact that *events* confirmed the technique. Could the lost-letter technique be applied to a situation where the answers were not clearly known and would be difficult to get? The situation of the 17 million overseas Chinese provided an interesting case in point. How would they respond to an extension of Red Chinese power? Were they pro-Mao or pro-Nationalists? These are questions difficult to investigate with ordinary survey methods, but perhaps they would yield to the lost-letter technique. I wanted to disperse throughout Hong Kong, Singapore, and Bangkok letters addressed as follows: Committee for the Taiwan Government, Committee for the Peking Government, Committee to Overthrow Mao Tse-Tung, Committee to Overthrow Chiang Kai-shek and (replacing Medical Research Associates) Committee to Encourage Education.

Almost at once problems arose. Riots between the Malays and the Chinese began in Singapore just before our experimenter arrived. And in spite of written consent from the Malaysian Government, he was put back onto the plane almost as soon as he arrived at the airport. We postponed the Singapore study. The following year our experimenter in Hong Kong, a journalist from that city who had offered to distribute the letters and had been paid in advance, disappeared. After many months a Chinese colleague of mine reached him by telephone. The would-be experimenter said that in China research takes a *very long time.* In truth, he had absconded with the research funds. I decided to go to Hong Kong myself, stopping only in Tokyo to confer with Robert Frager, who was to assist me in this study. Informants warned us that distributing "overthrow" letters in the Crown Colony would be unwise.

In the end we used all five addresses in Bangkok and Singapore but only the pro-Mao, pro-Chiang, and Education letters in Hong Kong. The letters themselves were a Chinese equivalent of the straightforward earlier letter (see Fig. 19.3). All were addressed to a post office box in Tokyo, where many political organizations are located. One serious problem was the possibility of post office interference in the mailing of the letters. Even if the letters were returned to our Tokyo headquarters in unequal numbers, how could we be certain that post office policy was not producing the result? Perhaps postal officials systematically removed pro-Communist letters while sorting mail. We therefore introduced an experimental control by personally dropping several coded letters of each type directly into mailboxes served by various post offices in each city. The controls arrived in Tokyo intact, assuring us that differences in response rates were not due to postal policies but to the different response of the man in the street to the political attributes of the letters.

We employed groups of Chinese students as distributors. The students prepared written reports, some of which captured the ambiance of the Chinese study. Typical is this one:

"This is the first job which I think most embarrassing for I have to drop 100 letters on streets and roads as I walk along in Kowloon side. The Colony is always crowded and the pedestrians seem to stare at me when I have the intention of dropping a letter which has been addressed and stamped. In order to carry out my job efficiently I went to several bus stops and knelt down, pretending to deal with my shoes. By doing so I left the letter on the road as I stood up and proceeded on my way.

"The dropping of letters became difficult as I came to Kowloon Isai Village,

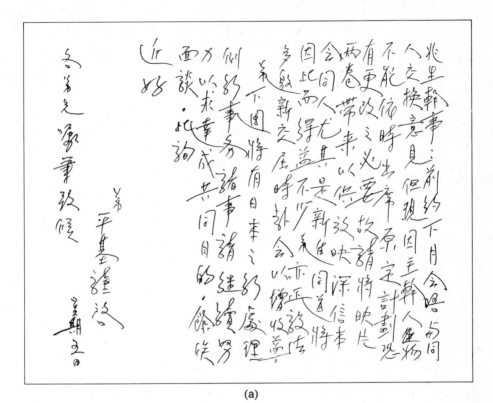

(a)

Executive Secretary Shiu Sang:
     We have previously arranged for a gathering of our
friends sometime next month for the exchange of views.
But I'm afraid that the plan has to be revised, since the
central figure will not be able to be present in time. Will
you please, therefore, bring with you the two reels of film
to the meeting for the purpose of showing. I'm confident that
these will be highly useful to our members, particularly
those new members. I am also trying to get as many new
acquantances as possible to come.
     I shall be going to Japan next week for the purpose of
handling some routine official business, and shall be back
as soon as it is through in order to be present at the
meeting.
     May I remind you to continue with your greatest effort
for our common cause so as to ensure its accomplishment.
     Best regards. All the brothers ask me to say "Hello"
to you.
                    Your younger brother,

                    Ping Kai

(b)

Fig. 19.3 *(a) Chinese letter used in the Hong Kong study. (b) Translation from the Chinese.*

the re-settlement. Here the dwellers are very mixed. There are people even on the staircase which is dirty and moisty. However the letters must be dropped and so I just dropped the letters on the sidewalk casually and carefully. If some people stare at me, I just gave them a smile.... It is a delight for me to observe in some areas where I have dropped the letters, the letters disappeared (as I came back the second time). Obviously they have been picked up by somebody else."

We found that substantially more pro-Chiang than pro-Mao letters were picked up and mailed. The returns were consistent, and taken together, the findings from the three cities showed a statistically significant pro-Taiwan feeling on the part of the overseas Chinese.

While I would hardly offer the superior return rate of pro-Chiang letters as definitive proof of the sentiment of overseas Chinese toward Peking and Taiwan, it is certainly evidence worth feeding into the total equation of political assessment. And it makes sense too. In Hong Kong, thousands of residents are political escapees from mainland China; and in Bangkok and Singapore many are engaged in small family business and would be hurt seriously by an extension of Communist power and influence.

Other investigators now have used the lost-letter technique to study attitudes toward Vietnam, and the McCarthy-Johnson primary in Wisconsin, with varying results. While the technique seems to reflect gross differences of opinion, it fails to reflect the subtle differences that are more typical of social disagreement. Yet when the study starts with an interesting idea, interesting results sometimes follow. For example, William and Melissa Bowerman, graduate students at Harvard, distributed anti-Nazi letters in Munich, and found a depression in the return of anti-Nazi letters in specific neighborhoods of that city. Thus, they pinpointed the areas of strongest neo-Nazi sentiment.

Some advice to persons who wish to employ the lost-letter technique:

1. In order to get significant differences between control and experimental letters, they must be distributed in sufficiently large numbers. No fewer than 100 and preferably as many as 200 letters should be assigned to each cell of the experimental design. There is much uncontrolled variance and it can only be transcended by using large numbers.

2. The lost-letter technique is not very good for subtle issues, or in connection with issues that do not arouse very strong feelings. It only works for issues in which there is clear-cut polarization, and which arouse a high level of emotional involvement.

3. There is no simple way to estimate population parameters from the differential response rates. On the whole, the procedure should not be used where sample survey technique is equally convenient or applicable, but primarily when the respondents' knowledge that he is involved in a study seriously distorts his response.

REFERENCES

MERRITT, C., and FOWLER, R., "The pecuniary honesty of the public at large." *Journal of Abnormal and Social Psychology*, **43**, 1948, 90–93.

MILGRAM, S., Comment on "A failure to validate the lost-letter technique." *Public Opinion Quarterly*, **33** (2), 1969, 263–264.

MILGRAM, S., MANN, L., and HARTER, S., "The lost-letter technique: a tool of social research." *Public Opinion Quarterly*, **29**, 1965, 437–438.

WEBB, E., CAMPBELL, D., SCHWARTZ, R., and SECHREST, L., *Unobtrusive Measures: Nonreactive Research in the Social Sciences*. New York: Rand McNally, 1966.

WILLIAMS, L.E., *The Future of the Overseas Chinese in Southeast Asia*. New York: McGraw-Hill, 1966.

Television and Antisocial Behavior: Field Experiments

20

INTRODUCTION

This is a report of research designed to test whether the content of television programs has a measurable effect on behavior. It aims more specifically at discovering the extent to which an antisocial act depicted on television stimulates imitation among its viewers. We hope that in addition to its substantive findings the report will contribute to the methods by which such studies are pursued.

Excellent reviews of relevant theory and research have recently appeared (Singer, 1971; Feshbach & Singer, 1971); and though it would be superflous to deal with them at length, we shall touch on some highlights:

1. The prevalence of violent acts on commercial television in the United States is undisputed. Gerbner (1971), defining violence as the use of physical force against others or one's self, either voluntarily or under compulsion, found that during prime television time in 1968–1969 violent incidents were depicted on the three networks at the rate of eight times an hour.

Barcus (1971), examining Saturday morning children's programming, reported that three of ten dramatic segments were "saturated with violence, [and] that 71 percent had at least one instance of human violence with or without the use of weapons..."

2. Investigations into the effects of violence have been of two general types: surveys and experimental laboratory studies. In typical laboratory studies, such as that of Bandura, Ross, and Ross (1963), children are exposed to film models of aggressive behavior, and are then observed in their play with toys, such as the Bobo doll.

Hartley (1964), clearly stated the limitation of this type of study:

> When we consider what constituted "aggression" and what behavior was referred to as indicating "violence" in the view of the investigators originally quoted, we are faced with a problem in communication. If a child pummels a toy that is primarily created to be pummeled, or chooses to play with one rather than another mechanical toy, or even bangs his toys about—are these the kinds of "aggressive" acts that cause parental or social concern? Is it valid to bracket these behaviors with the murderous

Excerpted from the book, *Television and Antisocial Behavior: Field Experiments*, written in collaboration with Lance Shotland, New York: Academic Press, 1973. The research was supported by a grant from the Office of Social Research, CBS, Inc. Reprinted by permission of Academic Press.

knife-fights of unstable adolescents and to refer to them by the same rubric, as Bandura (1963) and Berkowitz (1962) do, both directly and by implication?

Survey studies, such as that conducted by Himmelweit, Oppenheim, and Vance (1958), go beyond the laboratory in scope. But they suffer from the purely correlational nature of their findings. For example, if known criminals prove to have watched more violence on television than normal persons, we still do not know if exposure to television violence caused their criminal acts, or whether their addiction to television violence reflects a general preoccupation with violence.

3. A study by Feshbach and Singer (1971) broke new ground by introducing more natural circumstances for experimentally testing the effects of television. The investigators exposed several groups of boys in a camp to violence-rich or violence-poor television diets over a period of 6 weeks. They then studied the degree of aggressive play among the youngsters and found that the violence-rich group displayed less aggressive behavior in real life than the group exposed to violence-poor television fare.

An additional group of studies, sponsored by the United States Public Health Service (1972), was undertaken after the present research was underway: it did not influence our investigation and so will not be discussed here.

The Present Inquiry

Two main principles shape the present inquiry. The first is that we study the effects of television under natural circumstances. This applies both to the viewing situation and to the setting in which the potential influence of the program is assessed. Laboratory studies typically create an aura in which the act of "aggression" loses all socially signifigant meaning.

The second principle is that logically compelling results can be obtained only by using an experimental design, one in which the investigator varies value of the suspected cause and notes whether that leads to corresponding variations in the suspected effect. In this investigation, the content of a television program is subjected to controlled variation.

We expose the viewer, under a naturalistic set of circumstances, to a television program depicting antisocial behavior. The viewer is then presented with temptations in real life similar to those faced by the television character. The question is whether the television character's depicted actions influence the real life behavior of the viewers. And, of course, we run a control, a parallel condition featuring a television drama in which antisocial behavior was not an element.

What antisocial act should be used? It must be nontrivial, and hence constitute a meaningful antisocial act by the subject; it must be specific, so that the subject's commission of it can be clearly linked to its television enactment; but it must not be so grave an act that, should it be imitated outside the laboratory, the community would actually suffer serious consequences. And finally, it had to be embedded in a proper dramatic context.

The interplay of these requirements led us to settle upon an act in which the protagonist of a drama destroys a medical-charity collection-box and steals its contents. The act was well suited to our purposes: devoid of personal violence, it yet had real antisocial significance—destruction, theft and, moreover, theft from a beneficent social institution.

The next step was to embed the act in a proper dramatic context. We considered creating a special television program, with new characters, and presenting it as a television "special."[1] But this entailed two major problems: First, it is very hard to generate large audiences for special dramatic programs, and the larger the audience we could obtain for the purpose of our study, the better. Second, we did not wish to alert the audience to the fact that something was afoot; we wanted the antisocial act to appear in as natural a context as possible. These factors convinced us that it would be better to embed the act in an existing television series, which for practical reasons had to be a CBS program.

We rejected such programs as *Mission Impossible* and *Mannix* because they regularly depict such a degree of violence that our experimental act would appear trivial by comparison. We also rejected such a situation comedy as *My Three Sons,* which lacks the serious tone needed for the study.

In the end, we selected *Medical Center,* a typical hospital drama whose many episodes were entirely independent of one another, connected only by Dr. Gannon and a few other abiding characters. It would be feasible to write an episode around our planned incident without affecting the overall series, and the show, rated among the top 15, could deliver the sizable audience our experiment demanded. *Medical Center* seemed optimal for our purposes.

The Scenario

The scenario, created for the purposes of this experiment, was to have at its core the smashing of medical charity boxes.

The program centers around Tom Desmond, a young, white attendant at the Center, a recent father and owner of a small boat, with which he earns some extra money. At the beginning of the program, Tom quits his job, then changes his mind and asks Dr. Gannon to rehire him, but the job is no longer available. Tom's need for money grows desperate; his wife has fallen ill and he has defaulted in payments on the boat.

Meanwhile, Dr. Gannon, participating in a drive to raise funds for a community clinic, appears on a telethon and informs viewers that collection boxes for the charity have been distributed throughout the city. (The boxes, in fact, have been in evidence at the hospital during the opening sequences of the episode.)

As the critical sequence approaches, we find the dispirited Tom in a bar; one of the collection boxes appears unobtrusively in a corner. The television set is tuned to Gannon, who is asking viewers to call in pledges. Frustrated and angry, Tom dials the telethon but instead of making a pledge he pours abuse into the telephone. He calls in again, and is again abusive. Finally, he picks up a bludgeon, smashes the collection box, pockets the contents, and runs into the street.

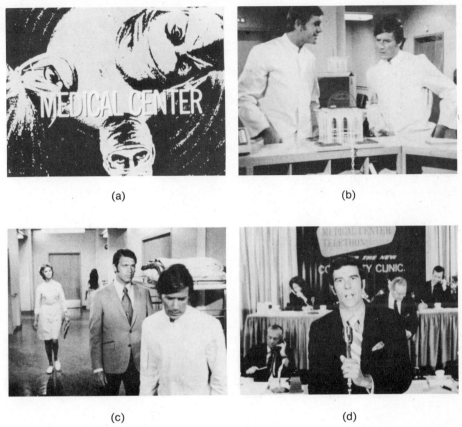

(a)

(b)

(c)

(d)

Fig. 20.1   *The basic scenario. (a)   The stimulus program is a popular medical series. (b)   Tom Desmond (right) works as an attendant at Medical Center. Collection banks for a Community Clinic are seen. (c)   Tom is scolded by Dr. Joe Gannon for poor work habits, and subsequently loses his job. (d)   A Medical Center Telethon is held to support the charity drive. (All photos copyright © Metro-Goldwyn-Mayer, Inc.)*

An exciting sequence ensues: to a pulsating jazz accompaniment and with quick camera work, Tom roams the streets searching out more collection boxes. He finds one and smashes into it, pockets the money, and runs on to another and another. He finds five in all, and he smashes and pilfers all of them.

There is little question that this antisocial sequence, which occurs in the last quarter of the program, constitutes the dramatic highpoint of the episode.

Four Stimulus Programs

In order to provide stimulus material for experimental comparisons, the story was written and filmed in three separate versions. Two of the versions use the outline above and differ only in the consequences to Tom. The third version omits the antisocial sequence.

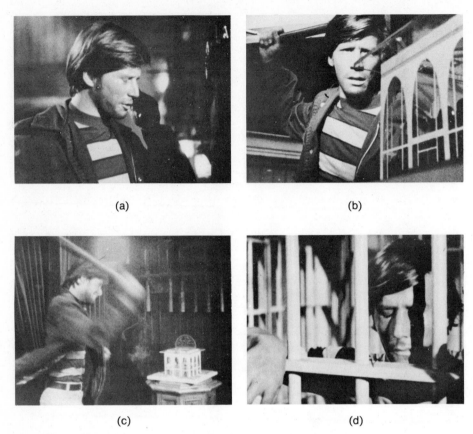

(a)   (b)

(c)   (d)

Fig. 20.2 *Antisocial version with punishment. (a) Tom makes an abusive telephone call to the Telethon. (b) Tom on the brink of smashing into the charity bank. (c) The antisocial act. (d) Tom is punished for his action. (All photos copyright © Metro-Goldwyn-Mayer, Inc.)*

Version 1: antisocial behavior with resulting punishment (WP). After Tom smashes the last charity box, he is apprehended by the police and jailed. He learns that it was unnecessary for him to break into the charity banks, for Dr. Gannon was willing to lend him the money needed to retrieve his boat. His marriage also appears to have broken up. This is a conventional ending, in that broadcast code requirements state that crime must not go unpunished.

Version 2: antisocial behavior, no punishment (NP). After the crime is commited, Tom is chased by the police. But he eventually escapes to Mexico, where his wife will join him. Since the culprit gets away with the crime, this program would not ordinarily be shown on television.

Version 3: prosocial behavior (PRO). In the prosocial version, Tom never breaks into the charity displays, although he seriously considers it, nor does he make any abusive telephone calls. He gets to the point of raising a bludgeon to

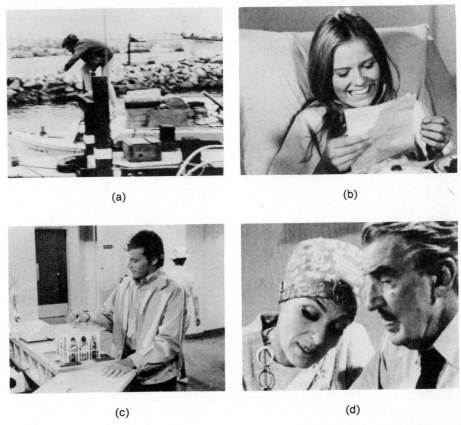

(a)   (b)

(c)   (d)

Fig. 20.3 *The other stimulus programs. (a) In the Antisocial version without punishment, Tom escapes arrest. (b) His wife receives word that he is safe, and in Mexico, where she will join him. (c) In the Prosocial version, Tom does not break into the charity banks, but contributes money to them. (d) The Neutral Program centers on the love affair of a career diplomat. It is completely devoid of violence. (All photos copyright © Metro-Goldwyn-Mayer, Inc.)*

break the boxes, then he thinks of his wife and child, and refrains from doing so. Finally, he drops a coin into one of the charity displays.

Neutral story. It is possible, of course, that the mere suggestion of an antisocial act on television is sufficient to provoke its imitation, whether or not the act is actually carried out. For example, a group of TV conspirators might talk about blowing up the Empire State Building without actually doing so, and this could conceivably be sufficient to instill this idea in someone. Therefore, we thought it best to use an unrelated episode of *Medical Center* as part of the experiment. For this purpose, we employed a sequence centering on a love affair between a foreign service officer and his long-suffering lady friend. This episode is romantic, sentimental, and entirely devoid of any violence or antisocial behavior.

Thus, four stimulus programs were used through the course of the experiment:

1. Antisocial behavior with punishment (WP)
2. Antisocial behavior with no punishment (NP)
3. Prosocial program (PRO)
4. Neutral program

Version 1 would test whether the depiction of an antisocial act engenders imitation. But because viewers of that version might be inhibited from imitation because the protagonist was punished, we would test another group with Version 2, in which he is not punished. Version 3 would indicate whether the mere contemplation of an antisocial act might motivate one in the same situation to commit the act, or whether Desmond's restraint and charitable contribution would induce prosocial imitation. And finally, the neutral program would provide a base line: the incidence of antisocial behavior among subjects who had not seen any of the experimental programs.

Assessing the Effects of the Program: General Idea

The next step in the logic of the design is to assess the effects on viewers of the several versions of the stimulus program. Toward this end, groups which have seen different versions of the program need to be exposed to an authentic charity display, and a comparison of the destruction rates of the several groups would constitute the principal experimental datum.

We recruited our subjects and exposed them to our stimulus program in a preview theater, over the air, or via simulated broadcasts on closed circuit television. And we promised all subjects a prize for their participation—a General Electric transistor radio.

The promise served several functions. It served, first, to attract our audiences. It served also to get our subjects to the laboratory, which in the guise of one or another gift-distribution company, presented our subjects with the opportunity to emulate Desmond's antisocial behavior. And finally, by properly scheduling the dates on which our subjects could pick up their radios, we could assure a smooth flow of traffic, with neither too few nor too many arrivals on any one date.

The gift-distribution center was on the 23rd floor of 130 West 42nd Street, an office building of somewhat faded distinction surrounded by a motley assortment of shops and banks, and pornographic bookstores, and movie houses. It is a busy and informal thoroughfare, where our subjects feel no necessity to dress up to make an appearance, which meant one less impediment to their participation.

Upon arriving on the 23rd floor, our subject could consult a directory, which directed him to the office of *Bartel World Wide* or one of the five other dummy gift-distribution firms we had set up for the study. The furnishings of all were virtually identical and entirely conventional: draped windows, pictures and advertising posters, a few chairs, a scattering of ashtrays and artificial flowers, a coat rack and telephone, and dominating the room, a formica counter. But no office personnel were to be seen.

Two other elements, critical to our experiment, were in each office: a handwritten note taped to the counter that, in the first experiment, said:

NOTICE

We have no more transistor radios to distribute. This distribution center is closed until further notice.

—wording designed to dash the subject's hope that he would get the prize he was promised. We intended, too, that the brusque notice would suggest that no one was present; that the subject was alone in an office where he had anticipated a pleasant experience rather than the frustrating one he was now undergoing.

It was upon the other critical element of furnishings that the subject could, if he were inclined, imitate Tom Desmond's antisocial behavior: a display mounted on one of the walls bearing a poster that showed a surgeon treating a little girl, a picture of a hospital ship, and the words, "Where There Is Hope There Is Life. Project Hope. A people-to-people program of medical education and treatment for developing nations." And mounted on the display, a clear plastic container with some change, a ten-dollar bill and four singles, one of which (dubbed The Dangling Dollar) stuck slightly out of the container.

This was the focus of our experiment: would the subject emulate the antisocial behavior he had seen in the television drama? Had that experience increased the likelihood of his behaving in a similar way? Concealed television cameras enabled us to watch.

In a few minutes the subject would leave the office and retrace his steps to the door that had admitted him to the corridor, only to find it locked. Arrows direct him to the exit; following them, he finds himself not at the elevators, but in a small room. A clerk appears at a teller's window and politely asks, "Are you here for your radio, sir? Sorry about the inconvenience, but we're distributing the radios here, since the *Bartel* people are ill. Do you have a gift certificate?"

Upon countersigning the certificate (so that we could later check whether the recipient of the radio had indeed seen the stimulus program), he received his prize neatly boxed, was thanked for coming, and left, his contribution to socio-psychological research at an end.

EXPERIMENT 1: THE FIRST PREVIEW SCREENING

At the outset, we did not wish to broadcast the stimulus material on regular television channels; we needed to develop and refine our assessment techniques without "wasting" the program on several million viewers. The problem was to expose a sufficient, but not excessive, audience to the program. Our approach was to bring several hundred participants together in a midtown auditorium and show them a version of the stimulus program on film. Then we assessed the effect of the film on their behavior.

Recruiting the Audience

We wanted a large but not unwieldy audience, a cross section of the population with a good proportion of young men and disadvantaged minorities, federal statistics (Uniform Crime Reports, 1970) having shown that most thefts other than shoplifting are committed by those segments of the population.

We used two recruitment methods. In the first, we advertised in the *New York Daily News, The Amsterdam News,* and *El Diario,* the New York Spanish-language daily, asking readers to send in a coupon if they cared to receive a transistor radio in return for giving us their reaction to a TV program they would see.

We also recruited participants from the streets, distributing business reply cards at subway stations in both black and white neighborhoods during rush hours, and at high schools at the end of the school day. The postcard (Fig. 20.4) bore the same copy as the newspaper ad except for the addition of a line restricting the participants' age to 16 to 40.

We received 1018 responses, which we divided into four groups (one for each of our experimental programs and the fourth, neutral one), balancing the groups for age and, through random assignment, for other characteristics.

In a few days we sent our respondents invitations on a *Television Previews* letterhead, informing them that they could bring a friend if they wished but that the friend would not be eligible for a prize. And we instructed the four groups to appear at one of four specified screenings (on consecutive Thursdays, at 6 and 8 P.M.) at the Network Television Preview Theater. (This theater had, in fact, been used to gauge audience reaction to TV programs and commercials for marketing and advertising concerns for several years; we could capitalize on the theater's authenticity to enhance our credibility.)

Of the 1018 persons who were sent invitations, a total of 607, constituting groups of between 137 and 162, actually reported to the theater.

Presentation of Stimulus Programs

At the Network Television Preview Theater, participants found a comfortable auditorium, manned by a staff of professional ushers, who collected their letters of invitation, led them to their seats, and distributed questionnaires and writing instruments. Five minutes after the scheduled hour, a master of ceremonies welcomed the participants, and discussed the need that people in television have for the opinions of viewers. He informed the subjects they would see a preview of *Medical Center,* and that we would be interested in their opinions of the program. Participants filled out some preliminary questions on age, sex, and television viewing habits. Then, the lights dimmed, and subjects were exposed to a one-hour episode of the stimulus program, projected in color on the theater's professional-size movie screen. No commercials were shown.

After the screening, the emcee led the audience through the rest of the questionnaire, reading the questions and pausing while they wrote their answers, turning at last to the gift certificate, which they were to sign. He then instructed the audience to take their certificates to *Bartel World Wide* or one of the other companies specified on the certificate, at the time also specified there (M, Tu, W, F 11–7; Sat 9–5), where, he said, they would countersign and surrender the

We'll give you a G.E transistor radio free.
If you'll spend an hour watching a new TV program.

If you're a man with an hour to spare, just fill in the coupon and mail it to us. If you're selected, you'll come to our studio, see an exciting TV program—and give us your opinion of it. And you'll receive the G.E. transistor radio free. Nothing to buy. No cost to you. And that's the truth.

(Restricted to ages 16–40.)

I'd like to watch your program:

_____
Name (print)

_____
Street

_____
Borough   State   Zip-

_____
Age   Occupation   Sex

Can you come: Weekdays ( )   Evenings ( )   Weekends ( )

_____
Hour you prefer   Telephone Number

Fig. 20.4.

certificates in exchange for their radios. Subjects were then thanked for coming and dismissed.

The gift certificate procedure enabled us to solve a major technical problem: we had to assess the behavior of several hundred subjects at the gift-distribution center, but we could not have them all arrive simultaneously, for we wanted them exposed individually to the charity display. It would not be realistic to schedule each subject for a specific hour and minute to pick up the transistor radio. The solution was to stagger the pick-up dates over a one-week period, and also over six gift companies. In this way we hoped to keep subject collisions to an acceptable level. To minimize effects idiosyncratic to any of the six laboratory testing rooms, half of each audience was directed to a different testing room on different days.

Subjects

Three-hundred and forty-two, or 70 percent of those who received gift certificates came to the laboratory for their radios. Fifty-three of these subjects were eliminated from our analysis because they were interrupted just before or during the test by other arrivals, encounters which we felt might have affected the spontaneity of their behavior.[2] Of the remaining 289 subjects, 89 percent were male, 12 percent had not completed high school, 14 percent had completed graduate or professional schools, 17 percent were between 15 and 19, 14 percent were over 50, 25 percent were nonwhite.

Assessment Procedure

From the time the subject reached the 23rd floor and stepped off the elevator to the time he left, he was observed via concealed television cameras. Working at monitors in the control room, we coded descriptions of the subject and his behavior. We noted whether the premium office was empty when he entered it and whether he entered alone; whether he stole from the collection box or donated to it; whether he took other items from the office, or whether his behavior was entirely neutral (see Fig. 20.5).

Additionally, fractional behavior that could lead to antisocial or prosocial behavior was noted. Thus, we noted whether the subject attempted to pry open the donation box, and whether or not he was successful in doing so. These fractional behaviors were coded because the stimulus material may lead to the initiation of an antisocial act that is not consummated. Moreover, we considered this detail pertinent to our study because an unfilled antisocial action is, before the law, nonetheless culpable; witness such legally defined crimes as *attempted* murder, *attempted* robbery, and so on.

Upon entering any of the unoccupied offices, our subjects looked about and discovered the notice taped to the counter. Their reaction was typically one of annoyance: they would pace the room, walk behind the counter, sometimes scrawl obscenities on the notice. Subjects invariably focused their attention on the charity display, with its pictures of the surgeon and child, the medical ship, and the attached collection box. This was the critical juncture. In nearly all cases, the subject left the room within a minute or two of his arrival.

Results

Before examining the effects of specific viewing conditions, we need to ask whether any antisocial behavior occurred at all, irrespective of viewing condition. For the total absence of such behavior in any subjects would indicate that there was really no temptation present, or that there were features of the testing

CODING SHEET
TELEVISION PROJECT

Experimental series _____   Subject #_____   Room_____

Treatment condition_____   Date _____   Loc:

Investigator coding behavior_____   Time _____

Brief description   Male   White   Age Estimate_____
of subject:
          Female   Black   Other _____

PRELIMINARY   Check box only if
          specific behavior occurs

1. Room is empty at time subject enters. (if not, specify)   ( )

2. Subject enters alone (i.e. not accompanied by others, whether he knows them or not.) If accompanied, specify.   ( )

3. Subject reads sign indicating no radios to be distributed (indicate reactions, if any).   ( )

4. Subject appears to notice, look at, or study donation box.   ( )

PRO-SOCIAL SEQUENCE

5. Takes money from pocket or wallet as if he were about to donate it to box.   ( )

6. Donates money.   ( )* Specify amount.

ANTI-SOCIAL SEQUENCE

7. Handles donation box without placing money in it.   ( )

8. Picks up instrument that could be used to damage or detach donation box.   ( )

9. Attempts to pry donation box open, or free from mounting, or attempts to pry mounting from wall.   ( )

10. Attempts to smash donation box.   ( )*

11. Takes the money or entire donation box.   ( )*

12. Damages or steals other items in room.   ( )

13. Enters more than one room (code behavior on additional coding sheet, attach to this one).   ( )

NEUTRAL BEHAVIOR SEQUENCE

14. Leaves room without any of above anti-social or prosocial actions.   ( )*

15. Subject interrupted in room by entry of another person (specify at what point in sequence).   ( )*

16. Subject surrenders gift certificate (if not, why not).   ( ) Certificate Number:

Did certificate number agree with treatment condition inferred from room or date: Yes   No   S's Name _____

Comments, anomalies   Full or emergency scoring (circle one)
          * = abridged emergency coding.

Fig. 20.5.

Fig. 20.6 *Assessing the effects of the program. (a) The Field Laboratory was located in this commercial building. (b) Interior of Lancelot Products, one of the dummy gift companies. (c) Interior of Interfax, another gift company. (d) A participant breaks into the charity bank (dramatized here). (e) Behavior was observed and coded in the control room. (f) Before departure, each subject receives a gift radio.*

Table 20.1 Proportion of subjects performing antisocial acts in Experiment 1 (all versions of program).*

Broke into bank and stole money	5.2%	(15)	
Removed Dangling Dollar only	3.5%	(10)	
Unsuccessfully attempted to break into bank	6.9%	(20)	
Stole other items from room	10.7%	(31)	$N = 289$

*The first four categories of antisocial behavior are not mutually exclusive. A single individual would have been scored for three acts if (a) he unsuccessfully attempts to break into bank, (b) removes the Dangling Dollar, and (c) steals other items from the room. A final convention: If a subject breaks into the charity bank and steals the money, he was scored for the first category (broke into bank and stole money), but was not scored for the second category (removed Dangling Dollar only), since in breaking into the bank, the Dangling Dollar becomes part of the general loot. The percentages reported in the tables are the percentages of subjects performing each specific antisocial act. This system is employed throughout, unless otherwise specified.

situation that completely inhibited antisocial action. Table 20.1 shows that this is not the case.

The fact that subjects engage in some antisocial action establishes the technical adequacy of the assessment situation, but it does not yet address the main experimental question: what is the effect of different viewing conditions on the rate of antisocial behavior? The results are shown in Table 20.2.

The three experimental programs (prosocial, antisocial with punishment, antisocial without punishment) do not differ among themselves by any statistical test in the breakage or theft rates they produced. However, the breakage rate in the neutral program (2.8 percent) appears lower than that produced in the antisocial WP condition (8.5 percent), though this trend does not reach statistical significance ($p = 0.14$, one-tailed.) Yet, it is the lowest breakage rate of any of the four programs, so perhaps the depiction of Tom Desmond's antisocial act did influence behavior. But the numbers are small, and the finding inconclusive; we need replication to strengthen the case.

EXPERIMENT 2: THE FRUSTRATION STUDY *(with Herman Staudenmayer)*

Our first experiment yielded some slight evidence that an antisocial drama might engender imitation. We wanted now to strengthen the case and, at least as important, to study the conditions under which imitation obtains. More specifically, we wanted to see if frustration was a necessary condition for imitation of the antisocial act seen in the stimulus program. Or would a program lead to imitation, even without frustrating circumstances?

Second, we were aware of the fact that the reaction to the frustrating note was quite strong, and came to dominate the mood of the participant. Perhaps differences due to the stimulus programs would be brought more sharply into

Table 20.2 Proportion of subjects performing antisocial acts according to stimulus program in Experiment 1.

| | Stimulus programs | | | | | |
	Neutral (n=72)	Prosocial (n=67)	Antisocial WP (n=71)	Antisocial NP (n=79)	All versions (N=289)	Significance of difference* (df=3)
Broke into bank and stole money	2.8% (2)	4.5% (3)	8.5% (6)	5.1% (4)	5.2% (15)	$\chi^2=2.49$, n.s.
Removed Dangling Dollar only	4.2% (3)	6.0% (4)	4.2% (3)	0.0% (0)	3.5% (10)	$\chi^2=4.33$, n.s.
Unsuccessfully attempted to break into bank	4.2% (3)	11.9% (8)	8.5% (6)	3.8% (3)	6.9% (20)	$\chi^2=4.92$, n.s.
Stole other items from room	13.9% (10)	13.4% (9)	8.5% (6)	7.6% (6)	10.7% (31)	$\chi^2=2.46$, n.s.

*Two tests of significance were used throughout, chi square and the Fischer exact test. Chi square was used when the expected frequencies per cell were six or greater, with one degree of freedom. All chi square values are corrected for continuity when df is equal to 1.

The Fischer exact test was used when expected frequencies per cell were less than six. The Fischer exact test yields probabilities directly (i.e., significance levels), and the absence of a χ^2 value in our reporting of significance indicates the Fischer exact test was employed. Significance levels are reported up to $p=0.30$. Beyond 0.30, we simply designate n.s. (nonsignificant). All reported significance levels are two tailed, unless otherwise specified.

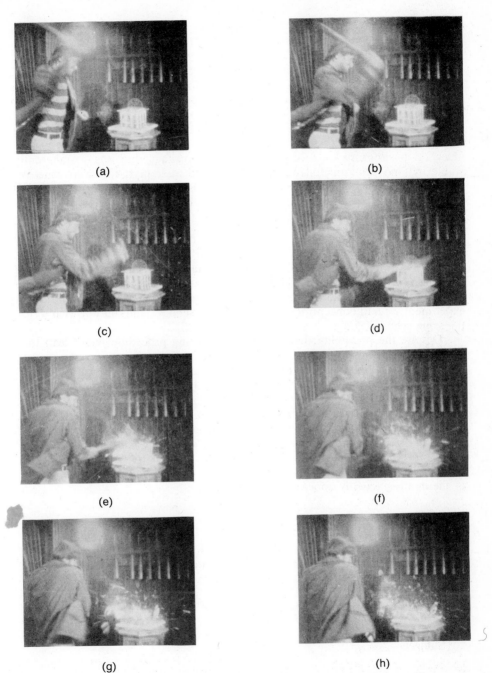

Fig. 20.7 *The antisocial act: Tom smashes his first of five donation boxes. (All photos copyright © Metro-Goldwyn-Mayer, Inc.)*

relief without frustration; perhaps, the reaction to frustration was so strong that it masked the effects of some of the treatment conditions.

Third, there is a well-known theory in social-psychology that frustration leads to aggression (Dollard, Doob, Miller, Mowrer & Sears, 1939), yet there have been few tests of this notion in naturalistic circumstances. The experiment would give us insight into the general proposition.

Fourth, we wanted some assurance that our dependent variable—breaking into the collection box—was a responsive variable, one that really moved if acted on by appropriate forces. Perhaps the breakage rate was so inherently stable that no experimental manipulation could alter it. If this were true, we could never show the effect of different stimulus programs. The present experiment, therefore, constitutes a test of the sensitivity of our dependent measure.

Recruiting the Audience

Our earlier procedure—newspaper ads and handbills—was cumbersome and costly, and though it netted us a good cross section of the New York City populace, it did not yield the sizable audience the study needed. Also, in the first experiment we had concentrated on public high schools, and did not wish to use the same schools again.

Despite the possibility that a shift in recruiting procedure might lead to a shift in our subject population, we changed recruiting tactics, resorting now to direct mail, lists for which are relatively cheap and easily obtained.

We used two lists: people who had made installment purchases, and high school seniors. Teenagers, according to Federal studies (Uniform Crime Report, 1970), constitute a high crime-risk group, which, we reasoned, would be responsive to our stimulus materials. Installment buyers would appear, on the face of it, to need money, and thus seemed potentially susceptible to temptation.

We printed our invitations, as before, on *Television Previews* letterheads: 13,468 letters went out, 30 percent of them to the high school list, and 7 percent of the invitees actually appeared at the screening.

Presentation of Stimulus Programs

We followed the procedure of our first experiment except for a single detail. Having encountered a total of only four prosocial acts in that earlier test, we decided to drop the prosocial version from the present experiment and concentrate on the versions most likely to elicit antisocial behavior—the WP and NP versions—and, also, the neutral program.

Subjects

About 75 percent of our theater audiences reported to the gift center/laboratory and, as before, collisions among the subjects disqualified a substantial number. Our final test population was thus 488. Of those, 82 percent were male; 70 percent, white; roughly 23 percent, over 50; some 20 percent were white collar or professionals; roughly 22 percent, blue collar.

How Frustration Was Reduced

The point at which frustration was strongly aroused occurred when the participant came to pick up the transistor radio and encountered the terse message in the empty distribution office. And this was the point where frustration could be markedly reduced. The technical problem was to expose the participant to the empty office, while at the same time reducing his disappointment. This was done, quite simply, by substituting a new message for the old, one that was considerably more polite, and which informed him that he was about to receive his transistor radio. The new notice read:

NOTICE

Sorry to inconvenience you, but this office
is temporarily closed because of illness.
Kindly pick up your radio in Room 1800 of
this building, where an office will be
kept open until 7 p.m.
Thank you for your cooperation.
—The Management

Results

The data presented in Table 20.3 show that neither antisocial version of our program elicited significantly greater rates of antisocial behavior than did the neutral program; no significantly greater incidence of breakage and theft is associated with the WP version (3.0 percent) than with the neutral program (8.2 percent); nor did the NP version (7.6 percent) fare better. Our other indices yield similar results; theft of the Dangling Dollar did not occur significantly more often with either the WP or NP group (4.0 percent and 7.6 percent) than with the neutral program group (5.9 percent).

Similarly, thefts of other items by the WP and NP audiences (6.9 percent and 9.8 percent) were no greater than by viewers of the neutral program (8.2 percent). Nor did the WP or NP audiences make significantly more attempts at prying into the collection box than did the neutral program audience (1.0 percent and 4.4 percent versus 3.5 percent).

Thus, we did not replicate the trend of the first experiment and that finding is now in grave doubt. The data also show that the high frustration level we induced does not, in fact, mask other behavioral effects, for when we reduced frustration, we still failed to get effects attributable to differences in the stimulus programs.

But quite aside from the effect of the stimulus programs, the presence of frustration proved to be an extremely powerful determinant of antisocial behavior. We can see this most clearly by comparing the percentage of subjects who committed any antisocial acts in the frustration (18.7 percent) and no frustration (2.9 percent) conditions; as shown in Table 20.4.

Six times as many subjects commit antisocial behavior when frustrated. Moreover the greater frequency of antisocial behavior holds over all categories, and in each of the three stimulus groups. For example, theft from the bank

Table 20.3 Proportion of subjects performing antisocial acts according to level of frustration and stimulus program.

| | Stimulus program | | | | | | Significance of differences $(df=2)$ | |
| | Neutral | | Antisocial WP | | Antisocial NP | | | |
	High frus. (n=85)	Low frus. (n=85)	High frus. (n=101)	Low frus. (n=89)	High frus. (n=92)	Low frus. (n=36)	Among high frus. conditions (n=278)	Among low frus. conditions (n=210)
Broke into bank and stole money	8.2% (7)	2.4% (2)	3.0% (3)	0 (0)	7.6% (7)	0 (0)	$\chi^2=2.76$, n.s.	$\chi^2=2.97$, n.s.
Removed Dangling Dollar only	5.9% (5)	2.4% (2)	4.0% (4)	0 (0)	7.6% (7)	0 (0)	$\chi^2=1.19$, n.s.	$\chi^2=2.97$, n.s.
Unsuccessfully attempted to break into bank	3.5% (3)	1.2% (1)	1.0% (1)	1.1% (1)	4.4% (4)	0 (0)	$\chi^2=2.13$, n.s.	$\chi^2=.42$, n.s.
Stole other items from room	8.2% (7)	1.2% (1)	6.9% (7)	0 (0)	9.8% (9)	0 (0)	$\chi^2=.52$, n.s.	$\chi^2=1.48$, n.s.

Table 20.4 Effects of frustration on commission of antisocial acts.*

Stimulus program	High frus- tration	n	Low frus- tration	n	Significance of differ- ence between high and low frustration conditions ($df = 1$)
Neutral	21.2%	85	5.9%	85	$\chi^2 = 7.24, p < 0.008$
Antisocial WP	13.9%	101	1.1%	89	$\chi^2 = 8.88, p < 0.003$
Antisocial NP	21.7%	92	0	36	$\chi^2 = 7.70, p < 0.006$
All versions	18.7%	278	2.9%	210	$\chi^2 = 27.20, p < 0.001$

$$N = 488$$

*Includes any antisocial act: 21.2 percent indicates that this percentage of the 85 subjects in the High frustration Neutral condition performed an antisocial act.

(breakage plus Dangling Dollar) is 11.9 percent when subjects are frustrated and 1.9 percent when subjects are not frustrated ($\chi^2 = 15.56, df = 1, p < 0.001$).

Our results show, therefore, that the theft rate is, in principle, a responsive dependent variable. Manipulations of level of frustration substantially boost the theft rate; but our manipulation of stimulus programs in contrast, did not affect the theft rate in any clear-cut way.[3]

EXPERIMENTS 3–6: GENERAL DISCUSSION

An additional series of four experiments (reported fully in "Television and Antisocial Behavior: Field Experiments") pursued the matter further.

Experiment 3 dealt with the effects of a model. We embedded a reminder of the antisocial behavior in the testing situation (a smashed bank) that we thought might interact with the stimulus program and add impetus to the antisocial response.

Experiment 4 dealt with eliminating the time gap between seeing the antisocial programing, and having the opportunity to imittate it. We arranged that our subjects could imitate the antisocial act even as they watched the program.

In Experiments 5 and 6, the stimulus programs were broadcast on network television, and home viewers tested for an imitative response.

While the antisocial behavior of breaking into the charity bank was manifested in all of the above experiments, it occurred with the same frequency for those who saw the antisocial version of the program and those who saw a neutral control.

We return to a detailed account of further experiments.

EXPERIMENT 7: THE TELEPHONE STUDY

There is a serious limitation in the experimental model we have worked with thus far. To understand it, we must consider the nature of the mass media. Stimulus content is transmitted to a very large number of people from an emitting source. Several million people across the country watched the *Medical Center* episode used in this study. Influence on only a very small fraction of the viewers could constitute an important *social* fact, but it would not emerge as a statistical fact in the experiment just outlined. For the assessment procedure by its very nature could test only a relatively small sample of those millions.

Let us say, for example, that the antisocial program influenced only one-tenth of 1 percent of the viewers—one person in a thousand; then fully a thousand of each million who saw it would be affected— a number of obvious social significance. Yet, our methods would not detect this fact because each of our experiments, necessarily limited in the numbers it can deal with, is based upon at most 500 subjects. And although that number is unusually large in terms of social-psychological experimentation, it would not tell the story, for one-tenth of 1 percent of 500 is *less than a single subject*.

It appears, then, that our method can disclose only much larger effects, those on the order of, say, 10 percent of the entire viewing audience. On that scale, if a million New Yorkers saw our WP-version, and 100,000 of them imitated the antisocial act, we could with our present methods detect the program's influence. But what if we are dealing with a phenomenon involving only one-hundredth of that number?

To overcome this limitation (1) we could employ extremely large numbers of subjects in the assessment situation, or (2) attempt to locate and use a subject population that was considerably more prone to influence by the media than the general population. A possible third course is to have very good information on *all* the antisocial imitation that occurs after our broadcast, not only in the laboratory but in the community at large. We did, in fact, seek precisely that data from several charity drives that were using collection boxes at the time of our broadcast; but all of them, reluctant to disclose the extent to which their efforts were vitiated by theft, declined to cooperate.

We can summarize the problem by stating that while the stimulus is transmitted to millions, the assessment procedures are geared to several hundred. We need to devise an assessment procedure that is sensitive to the fact that only a small fraction of those exposed to the program may be influenced by it. We need to show on television an antisocial act that anyone viewing in his own home could imitate with impunity, and which, if imitated, would be signaled to us. Toward this end, a second antisocial act was designed into the *Medical Center* episode. Namely, Tom Desmond makes two abusive telephone calls to a medical charity.

Desmond's antisocial use of the phone occurs when he responds to Dr. Gannon's telethon plea for pledges. In the first call, Tom says:

> Hello, Telethon. I wanna talk to Gannon, Dr. Joseph Gannon...I got a message for him. Tell him I think his clinic stinks. Tell him it's nothing but a crummy monument to his crummy ego. It...
> (*Click at the other end of the line.*)

In Tom's second call:

> **Tom:**   Hello, is Gannon still busy? I wanna talk to him.
>
> **Operator:**   He's busy, sir: do you wish to make a contribution?
>
> **Tom:**   No, I'm not making any contribution to your stinkin' clinic! How much money you got so far?

Operator: I don't have that figure, but if you wish to add to...

Tom: Well, instead of ADDING money, you can start subtracting. You're gonna start LOSING money any minute now!

(*Tom hangs up.*)

The next task, from a technical standpoint, was to provide the viewer with a convenient opportunity to imitate the abusive calls. This was done in the following way: immediately following the *Medical Center* episode, a public service commercial appeared, in which viewers were asked to call in pledges to an authentic medical charity, Project Hope.

The 30-second public service spot, which was sandwiched between commercial messages, featured an attractive Eurasian girl, seated alongside a model of the hospital ship HOPE, and requesting viewers to call in telephone pledges for this charity. Meanwhile, a local telephone number was overlayed on the screen, so that viewers would know what number to call. The girl said:

> My name is Kalen
> And I want to talk to you about the good ship HOPE.
> It's a floating medical center that trains doctors and nurses all
> over the world.
> And it saves lives—thousands of lives.
> Project HOPE has special programs in America, too!
> But it needs your help.
> Call this number and pledge some money.
> Call this number and with your pledge,
> Bring the world more HOPE.

A bank of telephone operators was trained to receive pledges and to write down all comments made by the callers. The calls were also recorded, a fact that the operators acknowledged by saying:

> Thank you for your call, which we will record to insure accuracy. Do you wish to make a pledge to Project Hope?

With the stimulus and appeal broadcast, the opportunity and means for imitation were at hand. If only one-tenth of 1% of the estimated 1,235,000 homes in New York tuned in to *Medical Center* imitated Tom, more than a thousand abusive calls would be forthcoming. We could compare that figure to the response of a control group–a similar audience that saw the public-service message immediately following a neutral *Medical Center* episode the week before. Would the proportion of abusive calls be greater following Tom's example?

(We were aware, of course, that there would be a limitation in our data: the basic unit would be the received telephone call, but we could not know whether a single individual would call a number of times, or whether every call would come from a different person. But since the same possibilities would inhere in the calls following both the stimulus and neutral programs, we would assume that the number of repeat calls is the same in both cases and so cancel each other.)

First Test

To provide a first test of the procedure, the Project Hope television spot was presented in Chicago and Detroit following *Medical Center* episodes on February 10 (Neutral Episode) and February 17 (Antisocial WP).

We considered the possibility that a person might imitate the antisocial behavior at some point after the commercial was shown. Perhaps there would be a sleeper effect, whereby the influence is not manifested until a period of time elapsed between the showing of the commerical and release of the behavior. To take account of this, two steps were taken.

First, we made certain that some telephone operators would remain on duty for the project for several days after the commercial was shown. Second, in order to stimulate additional calls, advertisements for Project Hope, asking people to call in pledges, were placed in Detroit and Chicago newspapers for several days just prior to each program and for several days after the program (February 7, 9, 12, 14, 16, 19, and 21). However, in order to distinguish between those persons calling in response to the newspaper advertisement, and those calling in response to the television spot, different telephone numbers were used in the newspaper and on the television spot. The experimental program shown in Chicago was the *Prosocial Version*, while the program shown in Detroit was the *Antisocial Version with Punishment*. The prosocial version did not contain any of the telephone sequences. The results are shown in Table 20.5.

As Table 20.5 shows, the main problem is that the Project Hope appeals did not create a sufficient number of calls for any meaningful analysis. Of the calls received, only two were ambiguously antisocial, and they followed presentation of the neutral program.

Table 20.5 Number of telephone responses to Project Hope appeals following Neutral, Prosocial and Antisocial WP programs (Chicago and Detroit).

	Chicago		Detroit	
	Feb. 10 *Neutral* $n=19$	*Feb.* 17 *Prosocial* $n=10$	*Feb.* 10 *Neutral* $n=12$	*Feb.* 17 *Antisocial* $n=31$
Clearly antisocial	—	—	—	—
Possibly antisocial	2	—	—	—
Pledge of funds	3	2	3	8
Wants further information	—	—	2	3
Hang up without responding	10	6	3	9
Miscellaneous (wrong number)	1	2	1	3
Child	3	—	3	8
Totals	19	10	12	31

New York Test

The test was repeated in New York City, but the procedures were altered in the following way. First, in order to increase the total number of calls that could be analyzed, the Project Hope television spot was repeated several times after the program was shown. Second, in the Chicago and Detroit test, the telephone number appeared on the screen only during the last 10 seconds of the 30-second spot. In New York, we would have the telephone number appear for 25 seconds, and thus give viewers greater opportunity to write down the New York number. Third, in Chicago and Detroit, the telephone calls were recorded, and the callers were informed of this in the operators' introductory remark: "Thank you for your call, which we will record to insure accuracy. Do you wish to make a pledge to Project Hope?" By checking the operators' written accounts in Chicago and Detroit with the recordings, we were satisfied that they had been accurate in recording the telephone comments. We thought that perhaps the announcement of recording the message would inhibit abusive calls. So, in the New York study, we eliminated the announcement and relied exclusively on the written report of the operators.

Finally, to generate more calls, we repeated the Project Hope spot several times after the program had been shown. We broadcast the neutral program on Wednesday, April 14; the antisocial WP-version, the following week, April 21. The Project Hope appeal appeared at the end of *Medical Center* just before 10 P.M.; an hour later, at the end of the following program, *Hawaii Five-O*; again during the 11 o'clock news; and twice more during the *Merv Griffin Show*, a night talk show. We repeated them again on each of the following Fridays, two days after the *Medical Center* presentations: at the end of *The Interns*, during the 11 o'clock news, and twice during *Merv Griffin*— for a grand total of 18 times, enough, we hoped, to generate a sufficient number of calls for statistical analysis.

There remains the question, of course, of how many persons who saw the original *Medical Center* episode were also likely to see the spots. According to the A. C. Nielson Company, 23.7 percent of the 5,200,000 television homes in the New York area were tuned in to *Medical Center* (at least during its last quarter-hour) on April 21, when the antisocial WP-version and the first set of Project Hope appeals appeared. And between 70 and 90 percent of those who saw the subsequent spots had also seen the program; e.g., 85 percent of those who saw the spot during the 11 o'clock news had also seen the critical *Medical Center* segment.[4]

Results

A total of 193 telephone calls were received in response to the Project Hope spots in New York, 124 in the week in which the neutral version of the program was presented, and 69 in the week in which the antisocial version was presented. The data are shown in Table 20.6.

More calls came in during the first week, when the neutral program was shown. What seems likely is that many of the same persons watch the program from one week to the next, and those primed to call in to a Project Hope

Table 20.6 Telephone responses to Project Hope appeals following Neutral and Antisocial WP programs in New York.

	Stimulus program		Significance of $df = 1$
	Neutral ($n = 124$)	Antisocial WP ($n = 69$)	
Clearly antisocial	6 (4.8%)	4 (5.8%)	$x^2 = 0.00$ n.s.
Possibly antisocial	14 (11.3%)	4 (5.8%)	$x^2 = 1.00$ n.s.
Pledge of funds	15 (12.1%)	14 (20.3%)	$x^2 = 1.73$ n.s.
Wants further information	14 (11.3%)	10 (14.5%)	$x^2 = 0.18$ n.s.
Hang up without response	60 (48.4%)	34 (49.3%)	$x^2 = 0.00$ n.s.
Miscellaneous (includes children, but not antisocial)	15 (12.1%)	3 (4.4%)	$x^2 = 2.30\ p < 0.13$
Totals	124	69	

commercial do so when the first appeal is presented. Thus, the control program siphoned off some of those who, had there been no control, would have called in response to the second program.

The clearly antisocial calls for the neutral program were:

1. I'll make a pledge if you tell me how many hairs you have on your cunt.
2. I'll make a pledge in your vagina.
3. Pussy!
4. Would you like to see my dick?
5. You're ugly.
6. You can't spell, what are you, stupid? (said to operator when asked for name).

The clearly antisocial calls for the antisocial program were:

1. That chink is ugly.
2. Up yours.
3. Lousy commercial.
4. What size tits?

We did not find an increase in percentage of abusive calls resulting from the program. Indeed, as we analyze the language of those calls that did come in, we see that not one of them actually imitates Tom Desmond's language. There is no use of the words "stinkin' crummy ego," nor does any caller threaten to diminish the money of Project Hope. Rather, we find a small array of sexually abusive comments that in no way seems to have been increased by the program.[5]

It is possible, of course, that a more interesting or stimulating antisocial action by Desmond would have inspired more imitation. If, for example—and this is purely speculative—we had shown him dialing a number that released the money in a pay phone, thousands of viewers might have dialed that number. It is also possible that the call he did make did not integrate into the motives of potentially antisocial viewers. The motives for breaking into a charity box seem clear enough if one is poor and needs money; the motives for making an abusive call are less so.

Of course, telephone calls reported in the mass media sometimes do appear to inspire imitation. The announcement on a television newscast of a few bomb threats seems to be dismayingly fruitful: as many as 4000 calls have clogged the New York City Police Department's switchboard on such occasions.

The differences between such perversely inspiring stimuli and those of our experiment are not entirely clear, though two points are worth noting. First, newscasts of bomb threats refer to real events, not to theatrical fictions, and may for that reason be more potent; and second, the gratification for calling in a bomb threat may not reside in the verbal delivery of the message, but in viewing its consequences, that is, the arrival of the police, clearing of the building, etc.

It is possible, also, that the abusive calls stimulated by the program were deflected to some other organization, and that somewhere in the city, a charity drive was receiving many antisocial comments stimulated by the program. But this is speculation, and in any case, we ought to have received at least a portion of those calls. We certainly made it easy enough for the stimulated subject to direct his abusive comments at Project Hope.

So far as the method used here is concerned, we believe that it is a promising one. It is potentially a very sensitive procedure and, possibly with some change in the stimulus material, could demonstrate imitative effects. In any case, it is clear from the experiment that not just any antisocial action shown on a single television program is likely to produce imitation. If this were so, we would have received hundreds of abusive calls in imitation of Tom Desmond's action on television. More than a million people saw the program in the New York City area, but our data show that the program had no effect in stimulating imitation of his action.

EXPERIMENT 8: THE EVENING NEWS STUDY

The subjects of our foregoing experiments had seen our models of antisocial behavior in theaters, at home, and on simulated, closed circuit broadcasts. But however varied the viewing circumstances, the programs themselves were presented as dramatized fiction. Perhaps real-life events are more likely to be imitated than dramatized ones. We set out now to test this possibility, by presenting the antisocial act as if it were an actual rather than a fictional event. Our site was, again, New York City; our medium, a closed circuit television newscast.

Recruiting the Audience

Using *Television Research Associates* stationary, we sent 7500 direct-mail invitations to a list of recent high school graduates (the lists exhausted in our previous experiments having been by this time reconstituted), promising a transistor radio if they would appear at the Statler-Hilton hotel and tell us what they thought of a news program and some commercials they would see. We netted 619 subjects.

All our subjects were high school seniors: male 556 (89.8 percent), female 63 (10.2 percent); black 158 (25.5 percent), white 453 (73.2 percent), other 8 (1.3 percent).

After arriving at the Statler-Hilton office of *Television Research Associates*, subjects were individually assigned to one or another of 16 guest rooms. The room was entirely conventional, with a convertible couch, tables, television set, and wall paintings. In one corner of the room, resting on a table, was a small charity display for the March of Dimes, including a clear plastic collection box containing 40 pennies, a $5 bill, and a protruding single—the Dangling Dollar. (We eliminated the latter after 25 sessions—half the total number—because conversations among the subjects indicated that some thought our procedure was a test of their honesty.)

A message flickering on each room's television screen stated:

PLEASE BE SEATED. PROGRAM TO APPEAR SOON.

(This message, like the news program he would see, was carried to the set by closed circuit cables.)

Soon, an announcer's voice was heard over the television set:

> This is Robert Lance speaking for Television Research Associates. Thank you for coming and offering to give us your opinion of a television news program and some of the commercials that go along with the program.
>
> As you know, the people connected with TV are very interested in audience reaction to their programs. Often, they will bring large audiences together in an auditorium to find out audience opinion. Today, Television Research Associates is trying to check out your opinion in a setting that is more natural than an auditorium, more natural for viewing television.
>
> In a few minutes you will see a fifteen-minute segment of the evening news. We are interested in your reaction to the program, and to the commercials, too. So sit back and enjoy the program. One further point. You were told you would be awarded a radio for coming here. Some of you may wonder if you will receive the radio today. The answer is "no." We do not have the radios here for you. If you follow the instructions carefully, the radio will be sent to you sometime within the next two months.
>
> The program will appear shortly.

The message was designed to communicate information about the ostensible purpose of the experiment, and introduce an element of frustration, which we had found necessary to obtain a measurable incidence of theft.

The News Program

The following news story, filmed for the purpose of the experiment, was inserted into a videotape of a local news program, and transmitted to our subjects on closed circuit television:

> A reporter, microphone in hand, appears beside a badly smashed Project Hope display. The reporter states that displays of this sort have been placed around the city, and have been smashed and rifled in alarming degree.
> The reporter then interviews a Project Hope official, who states that thefts of the banks are so widespread that receipts have declined in relation to those of last year.
> To investigate the problem first hand, the reporter states, the "action news team" placed one of the displays on a busy midtown street, and filmed what happened with a hidden camera. There follows a film clip in which, out of a throng of passersby, one man approaches the charity display, removes a tool from his pocket, and begins to pry it open. In a few seconds, he removes the dollar bill, and vanishes into the crowd.
> "They say that charity begins at home," the reporter sums up, "but not, apparently, if your home is New York City." A commercial follows, and the news program continues with other items of local news.

Thus, the subject is now presented with a model of antisocial behavior which is treated as having actually occurred, rather than a dramatized fiction. Moreover, he learns from the news story that the antisocial behavior in question is widespread.

The subjects were divided into experimental and control groups, 306 subjects seeing the critical news episode, and 313 subjects seeing the news program without the critical episode.

The data presented in Table 20.7 reveal conflicting trends. They show, on the one hand, that those who saw the neutral program commited more thefts of all money than those who saw the televised thievery ($\chi^2 = 3.22, df = 1, p < 0.08$). On the other hand, they also suggest that more of those who saw the antisocial version stole Dangling Dollars than those who saw the neutral program ($\chi^2 = 2.54, df = 1, p < 0.12$). We thus have conflicting evidence on the effect of the newscast.

Table 20.7 Proportion of subjects performing antisocial acts in the Evening News Study according to stimulus program.

| | Antisocial program | | | Neutral program | | |
	Stole all money	Stole Dangling Dollar	n	Stole all money	Stole Dangling Dollar	n
Tested with Dangling Dollar	6.5% (10)	9.7% (15)	154	12.1% (19)	4.5% (7)	157
Tested without Dangling Dollar	8.6% (13)	not applicable	152	12.2% (19)	not applicable	156
All subjects	7.5% (23)	not applicable	306	12.1% (38)	not applicable	313

$$N = 619$$

Of course, the Dangling Dollar and "stole all money" categories are not logically independent. A person who has stolen all the money has also taken the Dangling Dollar, although we have not counted him as doing so. Thus, the apparent higher influence of Dangling Dollar thefts in the experimental program may be a purely residual effect. There is a certain pool of potential thieves: if they are used up through taking all the money, they are no longer available to steal the Dangling Dollar.

How can we explain the lessened breakage in the neutral program? Are we dealing with catharsis? We doubt it, but think the explanation represents a possible artifact. The very fact that a person believes he is being tested for honesty is likely to inhibit antisocial behavior. And the presence of a news story showing theft from a charity box, combined with the actual presence of a charity box in the hotel room, was likely to engender a higher degree of suspicion in the experimental than the control subjects. This may have accounted for the lesser amount of breakage in the experimental group.

Indeed, informal interviews with subjects in the last 25 sessions reveal that about twice as many subjects in the experimental group thought the study had something to do with honesty—compared to those not exposed to the television depicted theft.

There is, furthermore, a feature of the stimulus material that may also have reduced its effectiveness as a model. We thought it would be well to show an actual incident of a person breaking into a charity display, an action model, which we achieved through the hidden camera story. However, the effect of mentioning the "hidden camera" may have been to arouse anxiety in subjects that their own behavior was surreptitiously under scrutiny. After all, the television depicted theft was "exposed," and fear of exposure may function in a powerfully inhibitory manner. It should be noted that this effect need not be limited to behavior in an experiment; knowledge of the fact that some banks have continuous photographic records of customer transactions, may serve to inhibit potential bank robbers, quite outside an experimental context.

The Evening News Study yielded contradictory findings, and the results are, at best, equivocal.

CONCLUSIONS

This research started with the idea that viewers imitate some of the antisocial action they see on television. We set out to measure actual imitation of a television depicted act. We created a program in which the act—breaking into a charity bank—is shown repeatedly, and with considerable dramatic impact. We created an assessment situation in which antisocial acts and imitation could easily occur.

In a first experiment, subjects saw one of four stimulus programs in a preview theater, and were then tested at a gift-distribution center. Result: a trend, though not statistically significant, that one of the anti-social programs engendered imitation. We wondered whether the high level of frustration experienced by the subjects obscured the effects of the stimulus program; we eliminated frustration in Experiment 2. Result: no evidence of imitation. We thought a model or booster placed in the assessment situation might interact with the stimulus program and produce an effect. Result: negative. We reduced the time delay between seeing the television act and the occasion for imitating it, by embedding both in the same situation. Result: negative. We broadcast the stimulus material in New York and St. Louis and again sought to measure imitation, but there was none. We changed the material from dramatized fiction to real life incidents presented on the news. Result: no imitation. We adopted a new paradigm of investigation in the telephone study, by giving an opportunity to any viewer to immediately imitate the act by calling in an abusive message. We hoped this would be a very sensitive measure that could pick up even slight effects. But again, we found no evidence that the antisocial program engendered imitation. We looked for effects in subpopulations, and here the results were equivocal. We did our best to find imitative effects, but all told, our search yielded negative results.

Two quite different interpretations of the results are possible: First, the programs did, in reality, stimulate a tendency in our subjects to perform antisocial acts, but our measurement procedures were deficient. Second, there was no imitative tendency induced by the program.

Let us consider the first possibility: The program had a potential for inducing imitation. Why might we have missed it?

First, the imitative response may occur in the subject at another point in time or space, and not within the assessment situation we had set up. Perhaps, a year from now, a subject on the threshold of breaking into a charity bank will be influenced by the program.

Second, perhaps we did not test the right subject population. Conceivably, people below the minimum age for this study would have been measurably influenced by the program. We chose to limit our subject population out of practical considerations and because we did not want to provoke mere children into imitating antisocial behavior. (Of course, we did study teenagers, but conceivably, television affects even younger children.)

Or, perhaps in the very process of recruiting subjects for our study, we eliminated those most likely to have been influenced by the program. It requires a certain discipline to come to a preview theater, fill out a certificate, and then show up at the gift-distribution center. Perhaps some delinquents in the population were excluded by this procedure. However, the fact that we did get considerable antisocial behavior in the laboratory does, somewhat, weaken this argument.

Fourth, it is possible that the program stimulates imitation in only a very small fraction of the viewing audience, and we could not pick this up with the numbers used in our assessment procedures. However, we did introduce the telephone procedure to get around this, though using a quite different antisocial act. Perhaps if we could combine the sensitivity of the telephone measure with the motivational properties of the theft measure, an effect might have been discovered.

And, of course, we can go on endlessly. For when an experiment yields no differences between the experimental and control conditions, there is an infinitude of factors that may account for this. However, these are merely speculations, and do not have the status of evidence until they are themselves converted to tested operations. Often we ourselves thought we had figured out why we were not getting imitative effects, converted this notion into an experiment, only to fail again in our search for an effect.

Let us assume now that our measuring procedure is completely adequate and that, in fact, the stimulus material does not induce imitation. This would still not mean, however, that television does not stimulate antisocial behavior. Let us consider the factors not treated by the experiments described here.

1. It is possible that the television depiction of a different antisocial action would have engendered imitation. Perhaps, an antisocial act that contains the germ of a new criminal technique is more likely to be imitated. Note the series of parachute hijacks that appears to have been, in part, due to the dissemination of this technique by the mass media.

2. Perhaps it is not so much the depiction of one antisocial act, as the cumulative impact of numerous violent actions shown on television, from childhood onward, that predisposes a person to commit antisocial behavior. Conceivably, our subjects have been so sated with the depiction of crime on television, that they are already maximally stimulated, and our program can add no further to it.

3. Or a more indirect mechanism may be at work, namely, that the norms and attitudes of society are changed by the frequent depiction of violence, so that even a person who has not viewed television, will be influenced by it through his absorption of general societal attitudes.

4. Perhaps the manner in which Desmond breaks into the charity banks did not stimulate imitation, because his actions were depicted dramatically rather than casually.

All of these possibilities exist, but are outside the scope of the present investigation. We can only urge that other investigators apply themselves to the study of these variables.

What then is the contribution of the present study? First, the evidence it has generated must be taken seriously, and serve as a constraint on discussion of television's effects. For the results of the present experiment are not that we obtained *no findings,* but rather that we obtained *no differences* in those exposed to our different stimulus programs. The research thus consistently supports the null hypothesis.

It is possible that people have been entirely too glib in discussing the negative social consequences of the depiction of television violence. Personally, the investigators find the constant depiction of violence on television repugnant. But that is quite different from saying it leads to antisocial behavior among its viewers. We have not been able to find evidence for this; for if television is on trial, the judgment of this investigation must be the Scottish verdict: Not proven.

Second, we hope the study has cleared the way methodologically for much new research. We believe that the general experimental paradigms presented here are by no means exhausted in the present investigation. The use of new stimulus material, younger populations, and modified assessment procedures can only further our knowledge of television's effects. The telephone study, though yielding no evidence of imitation in the present investigation, does point to the kind of experimental paradigm needed for further inquiry.

Not that the present paradigm is the only useful approach. Far from it. We carried it out because it seemed to us logical to start with a single program; if we could have demonstrated imitative effects in this single program, we could without equivocation have concluded that television stimulates antisocial behavior. That we did not find an effect does not exclude this possibility. We believe that future inquiry should direct itself to the long range effects of television, of many programs, over time.

Finally, in this research, a major television network extended its resources to social scientists wishing to study the possible effects of television depicted antisocial behavior. We regard this, not as the fulfillment of television obligations to society, but as a firm precedent, on which future investigation shall move ahead.

NOTES

1. Actually, a special program was written, incorporating the antisocial act. But it was a poor program dramatically, and we deemed it unacceptable for the purposes of the experiment.

2. Inclusion of these "excluded" subjects in the analysis of results does not alter the outcome of any experiment reported in this book.

3. In interpreting the meaning of the findings, two factors should be noted. First, the specific type of frustration is one in which the subject feels cheated, in that he does not get the reward he expected and feels he deserves. It is frustration centering on a breach of contract. One may therefore find his stealing items from the store to be somewhat "justified," in that in removing ashtrays, artificial flowers, and pictures from the company office he is "getting his due from them." However, the theft from a national charity can in no way be justified, since the money does not belong to the gift company in question. It has nothing to do with the fact that the company did not come forth with the promised radio. Thus, it is a case of the displaced effect of frustration.

4. Data based on the Nielson Station Index New York Instantaneous Audimeter, April 21, 1971. Data subject to qualifications.

5. The identical analysis was performed on the calls that came in response to the Project Hope spot immediately following the neutral and experimental programs. Since these were closest in time to the program, we thought they might be more likely to show imitation. But this was not the case. Twenty-four calls came in immediately after the neutral episode, with one clearly antisocial, and two possibly antisocial messages. Thirty-six calls immediately followed the antisocial *Medical Center* broadcast, with one antisocial message.

REFERENCES

Asch, S. E., "Studies of independence and conformity: A minority of one against a unanimous majority." *Psychological Monographs*, **70** (9), 1956.

Baker, R. K. and Ball, S. J., *Violence and the Media*. Washington, D.C., National Commision on the Causes and Prevention of Violence, 1969.

Bandura, A., "What TV violence can do to your child." *Look*, October 22, 1963, 46–52.

Bandura, A., Ross, D., and Ross, S., "Imitation of film-mediated aggressive models." *Journal of Abnormal and Social Psychology*, **67**, 1963, 601–607.

BARCUS, F. E., 1971. Cited in United States Public Health Service. Report to the Surgeon General. *Television and Growing Up: The Impact of Televised Violence.* (Superintendent of Documents, U.S. Government Printing Office, 1972.)

BERKOWITZ, L., "Violence in the mass media." In Berkowitz, L. (ed.), *Agression.* New York: McGraw-Hill, 1962.

DOLLARD, J., DOOB, I. W., MILLER, N. E., MOWRER, O. H., AND SEARS, R. R., *Frustration and Aggression.* New Haven: Yale Univ. Press, 1939.

FESHBACH, S., AND SINGER, R. D., *Television and Aggression.* San Francisco: Josey-Bass, 1971.

GERBNER, G., 1971. Cited in United States Public Health Service Report to the Surgeon General. *Television and Growing Up: The Impact of Televised Violence.* (Superintendent of Documents, U.S. Government Printing Office, 1972.)

HARTLEY, R. E., "A review and evaluation of recent studies on the impact of violence." Office of Social Research, C.B.S., June 24, 1964. Mimeo.

HIMMELWEIT, H., OPPENHEIM, A. N., AND VANCE, P., *Television and the Child: An Empirical Study of Television Viewing on the Young.* New York: Oxford Univ. Press, 1958.

LATANÉ, B. AND DARLEY, J. M., *The Unresponsive Bystander: Why Doesn't He Help?* New York: Appleton, 1970.

MILGRAM, S., "Some conditions of obedience and disobedience to authority." *Human Relations.* **18**(1), 1965, 57–176.

SINGER, J. I., (ed.), *The Control of Aggression and Violence: Cognitive and Physiological Factors.* New York: Academic Press, 1971.

UNIFORM CRIME REPORTS 1970., *Federal Bureau of Investigation, United States Department of Justice,* Washington, D.C. (Superintendent of Documents, U.S. Government Printing Office.)

UNITED STATES PUBLIC HEALTH SERVICE., *Television and Social Behavior: An Annotated Bibliography of Research Focusing on Television's Impact on Children.* National Institute of Mental Health, 1971.

UNITED STATES PUBLIC HEALTH SERVICE., Report to the Surgeon General., *Television and Growing Up: The Impact of Television Violence.* (Superintendent of Documents, U.S. Government Printing Office, 1972.)

21 The Image Freezing Machine

I

The habit of taking pictures is now so widespread, we forget how recent it is. At the beginning of the nineteenth century only a talent for drawing or painting would allow a person to visually record what he saw. At the end of the century anyone could do it with the aid of a simple rectangular box. He looked into a small ground glass window, framed the picture he wanted, then pushed the shutter. Kodak did the rest.

The best way to grasp the human significance of photography is not to think of camera, film, and tripod as something external to human nature, but as evolutionary developments as much a part of human nature as his opposable thumb. A deficiency existed, of sorts, in the way our sensory and information storing capacities functioned. They had limits, and photography was one way to overcome those limits. The limit in human functioning is simply this: Although we can see things very well, we cannot store what we see so that we can reliably bring up the image for repeated viewing. Instead, visual images are incompletely stored in memory, often in a highly schematized form, and subject to decay and distortion.

Moreover, memory is private. It resides in the neutral structure of the individual, and does not directly take the form of an external object that others can see. And when the person dies, all of the images stored in his brain vanish, along with all the other information he possesses.

It is the perishability of our visual experience that led men to seek to fix it by externalizing it: by placing it on something more permanent, and more available to public scrutiny than the brain. A first solution to this problem came about through the development of skills in painting and drawing. Man had the capacity to depict what he saw by representing those forms and colors on an external surface, such as the wall of a cave, or papyrus, silk, or canvas. But it required a special talent to do this, which only a fraction of men possessed.

An optochemical means for recording of visual images was achieved in the nineteenth century: Photography allowed anyone to freeze a moment of visual experience, and thus to augment his memory, to preserve it beyond his own lifetime, and to show others what he saw. To a psychologist this new capacity to fix and externalize visual experience is intriguing, for it immediately raises the question: what did people choose to render into permanent photographic images?

This paper originally appeared as a series of three articles for the *ASMP Journal of Photography in Communications, Bulletin 75*, (a magazine for professional photographers) in April, June, and August 1975. Reprinted by permission of the author.

In principle, the camera could be used to record any visual event: stars, lakes, garbage, loaves of bread, anything. But the fact is that, overwhelmingly, what people wanted to record was images of themselves. The growth of portrait photography in the nineteenth century is astonishing, even by today's standards of rapid technological exploitation. The nineteenth century absorbed photography with a voracious thirst that revealed the extraordinary need for an image freezing machine. The process was scarcely known before 1839; within twenty years commercial studios had sprung up in New York, London, Paris, and Basel. A hundred thousand daguerreotype portraits were made in Paris in 1849. By 1860 New York City claimed more than fifty photo-portrait studios. It is true that some photographers could make a living taking pictures of far away places and selling them. But overwhelmingly the business end of the enterprise rested on photo-portraiture. That is what people wanted most of all.

To understand how special this fact is, consider that when later in the century, the technical means for recording not visual but auditory events became possible, there was no such rush to get oneself recorded. Indeed, while people wanted pictures of themselves, they wanted sound recordings not of their own voices, but of impersonal cultural objects—above all, music.

So the recording of the visual aspect of experience, and the auditory aspect, are skewed in enormously different ways. Even today, there are hundreds of record stores in which we shop for sound recordings of musical groups. But picture stores, in which we shop for recorded images, are not to be found on anything like this scale.

We need to go a little deeper into the contrasts between visual and auditory recording. There is a scene in the film *Edison: The Man* that is revealing. Spencer Tracy, having just invented the phonograph, tries to persuade his infant son to say something into it, so that he can have a recording. But the infant refuses to say anything; and this vignette serves as a running gag through the film. The scene reminds us that the recording of sound depends on a performance, while visual recording does not. The photographed person may remain passive, and still be recorded. This contrast between the passivity of photography and activity of sound recording reaches down to the very origin of the physical energies underlying the two processes: the energy for a voice recording originates in the activity of the speaker, but the energy for a photograph of him is external in origin, merely light that has bounced off him. You can photograph a corpse but not record him on a casette. The potentially passive nature of the object photographed colors the entire process. It means the camera captures what one is, a state of being. One doesn't have to do anything for it. It merely soaks you in. Perhaps that is why voice recording studios, which require performance, have never developed on anything like the scale of photographic studios.

The phenomenon of photographic portraiture is even more revealing when we consider the sterotyped nature of portraiture. After all, even if a man wants a visual record of himself, he may want a record of himself doing something worthwhile, such as giving money to a poor beggar, helping a lame animal, or lending a tool to a neighbor. Instead, we find men and women seated before cameras, in general not doing anything, just looking, at most aided by a prop of a book or surrounded by other family members. People did not want so much a photographic rendering of themselves performing a specific action, as they wanted a general statement of their character. The sources of this attitude are not hard to find. To some extent they derive from traditional oil portraiture, and the camera was merely a cheap way to get the equivalent of an oil painting. Then, too, the early technology of photography did not permit action shots, and it was to the photographic entrepreneur's advantage to do all his work in the studio. But most of all, it was a desire to have not specific actions, but one's general likeness recorded for posterity. Although the subject knew that he had nothing to do but sit and be photographed, he realized that the full burden of a multitude of moods and moments would come to be represented by that single exposure of the camera. The burden placed on that moment was very substantial, and motivated the subject to work for an optimal image: he posed.

We all make some adjustment as we take account of the person we are dealing with. Our facial muscles, poses, and posture are subtly altered as we speak to a child, a lover, or a judge. Even half-consciously we are able to adjust ourselves to act in a manner appropriate to the specific situation. But the problem of a photograph is that, although it is taken in one situation, it may be seen by many people and in many situations. How then are we to adjust to the camera? How can we create a facial expression that is of generic usefulness, and not useful merely for a narrowly defined occasion?

The most typical strategy, particularly when photography was first coming into general use, was to use a socially conventional face, and express as much civic virtue as possible in the exposed moment, an attitude that, together with the technical necessity of holding a stationary position for a matter of minutes, led to the bland, stilted photographs which was the typical product of the nineteenth century Daguerrian studios.

There was one human experience which all human beings had known in the nineteenth century, which led them to underestimate the truthfulness of the camera. I am not speaking of portraits by artists, which were limited to the well-to-do, but a more mundane experience: the mirror. If you had never had a photograph taken of yourself, the best clue to what it would look like was based on what you had seen in the mirror. And that is where the surprise came in. For individuals almost never reject what they see in the mirror, but hundreds of Daguerretypes were angrily denounced by men and women who knew they were more comely than the photograph showed. What they should have learned is that the psychological preparations made before looking into a mirror are such that we do not affront our own self-image. Even today, individuals are constantly rejecting unflattering snapshots, firmly believing that they could never look as bad as the photograph showed. But such reactions rarely come upon looking into a mirror. Perhaps the old, "a mirror offers us a thousand faces; we only accept one," contains the relevant wisdom. The camera, by freezing our faces at a particular moment, from a particular viewpoint, often gives us one of those faces which we would prefer not to accept. But, unlike the mirror, we cannot make those instantaneous adjustments, turns of the head, lowering of the eyelids, search for the exact angle, that defuses the offending image. Rather we count on the photographer to function as a kind of ego supporter and photograph us as we would like to be presented to that generic constituency which is the audience of all photographs.

II

Photography is a way of recording, for further scrutiny, the visual aspect of things. Only one other sensory modality, hearing, has been similarly susceptible of recording. We do not as yet have adequate technologies for recording experiences of smell, touch, or taste. And we do not seem to feel much need for developing them. But of the need to have a visual record, there can be no doubt, as the growth of a vast photographic industry attests.

But it is not just the fact of capturing a likeness that is the essence of photography. We know that life masks can be made which depict the person's physiognomy in three dimensions, or at least in bas-relief. Yet such techniques never acquired the popularity of photography. Of course, there is the matter of the greater convenience of photography. But beyond that, the reduction of the image to the two dimensional plane is the crucial element.

Consider that steroscopic photographs were available as early as the mid-nineteenth century, yet only play a minor part in photography. Color film, though of high technical excellence, has found a secure place in photography, but it has not supplanted black and white, which continues to exert an attraction to millions of photographers, particularly those of artistic bent. It is the abstract-ing quality of the black and white two-dimensional photograph that appeals to many over the greater verisimilitude of stereoscopy and color. It remains to be seen whether the recently discovered hologram, with its uncanny shifting paral-lax, will force a fundamental change in emphasis. History suggests that though holograms may develop a significant niche of their own, they will not supplant the ordinary black and white print.

The viewer is part of the process of photography. As we look at photo-graphs, Rudolph Arnheim has pointed out, we see them through a special attitude which conditions our response to them. Unlike painting, in which we know that every detail is created by the effort of the painter, the photograph is interpreted as the product of a mechanical process. As soon as the camera is clicked, images within its view are encoded without further human effort onto the film. Details may be recorded without any necessary intention on the part of the photographer. Indeed, he may discover things in his picture he was not aware of at the time he took it. For the camera provides a mechanical and exhaustive rendering of visual surfaces, within the range of its technical capaci-ties. This directness and infinite inclusiveness confer on photographs a high degree of credibility. We are more likely to believe that an object depicted in a photograph really existed than, say, an object depicted in a painting. The truthfulness of the camera is not, of course, guaranteed by this fact. Photographs may be faked, or they may be unrepresentative of what they purport to depict. But even here, if we examine the photographs carefully enough, some detail in the photograph itself may belie the photographer's claim.

People possess a photographic urge, an enormous desire to fix the image of things in a form they can later consult. And it is, for many people, an urge to fix the image through their own efforts. The pictures one cay buy outside a famous landmark are no substitute for the pictures one has taken, even if the quality of the commercial product is superior to one's own. It is seizing the image through one's own act that seems uniquely satisfying.

The act of taking a picture, like the act of seeing itself, takes place in a broad range of human situations. When we are alone or with others, whether we are taking a picture of a rock or a lover, it always involves some sort of exchange, whose terms we may now explore.

First, there is the trade-off between the passive enjoyment of a unique moment, and the active process of photographing it. The man who sees a beautiful scene, and has his camera, stops to take a picture; but the photographic act may interfere with his fully savoring the experience. There is not only the minor inconvenience of carrying a few pounds of camera equipment, but the interruption of a fully spontaneous set of activities by the need to stop to take pictures, and divide one's attention between enjoyment of the scene and the mental set needed to photograph it. The photographic act devalues the moment, as one trades the full value of the present instant for a future record of it.

The very meaning of human activities, such as travel, comes to be transformed by photographic possibilities. We seek out places not only for their beauty, but because they are suitable backgrounds for our pictures. A group of tourists, Nikons hanging about their necks, sees its arrival at the Eiffel Tower as the consummation of a photographic quest. The place comes to be subordinate to its photographic potential. The value of our vacation will depend not only on what we experience at the moment, but on how it all comes out in the pictures. It is the contamination of the pleasurable present, by the photographic urge, that prompts growing numbers of vacationers to leave the camera home.

But if the photographing act is best seen as an exchange, this is most clearly present when we photograph other people. What kind of exchange is it? The English language is quite blunt about it. A photographer takes a picture. He does not create a picture or borrow one, he takes it. A camera bug travels to a foreign country, sees a peasant in the field, and takes a picture of him. Now why does the photographer think he has the right to snatch the image of the peasant? It is true the photographer invests time, film, and effort, into taking the picture, but I find it hard to understand wherein he derives the right to keep for his own purposes the image of the peasant's face. "Give it back, give it back," the peasant might cry, "It's my face, not yours."

Photography is an exchange, obviously unfair, and the native who once allowed himself to be photographed, just to be pleasant, in time may realize he is giving away something for nothing: his image. There is, of course, the pride he may feel of having been deemed worthy as a subject of a photograph, but in the long run this type of glory wears thin, and the native may decide to charge the photographer, as boys in the Caribbean do with increasing frequency. The relationship becomes a professional one.

Naturally, it is convenient for photographers to carry on their activities with the assumption that individuals, tacitly at least, give their assent to being photographed. (I am referring now not to the use of the photograph, which is bound by legal constraints, but to the act of photographing others, which is considerably less controlled by law.) But just how do people feel about giving away their image? How many people would actually agree to have their picture taken by a stranger for some unspecified purpose?

To study this, my students and I recently went into the streets of mid-town

Manhattan and, camera in hand, each of us asked a stranger: "May I take your picture?" If asked to explain his motives, the student answered simply, "I'm interested in photography." We posed the question to more than one hundred people in Bryant Park and on 40th and 42nd Streets.

In the street 35 percent allowed us to take their picture, while 65 percent refused. Hands went up over the face, people scowled, or walked hurriedly—reminding us that the act of photographing has given rise to a whole set of gestures which never existed before the camera. Gestures of the photographer, gestures of the subject allowing or refusing to be photographed. (Presumably, before the press photographer came on the scene, criminals rarely held their hands over their faces or dug their faces into contortional positions when arraigned.) Photography has created an entirely new choreography of human body movement.

In Bryant Park itself, the population divided evenly into those who assented and those who refused. Females were less willing than males to have their picture taken (but we need more data to confirm this). The willingness of people to have their picture taken interacts subtly with mood temperament and the exact pose and circumstance of the potential subject. Of the six people lounging on the grass whom we approached, five agreed to have their picture taken, an astonishingly high proportion. We have just begun this socio-psychological inquiry into the act of photographing, but one thing is already clear. The culture of photography is so widespread, and the normality of taking pictures so deeply rooted, that everyone understood what it meant to be photographed, and took the request in stride.

The importance of this fact can only be understood in comparison with other requests one might make. For example, a few years ago our class went into the New York subway. Each student stood in front of a seated passenger, and asked: "May I have your seat?" However trivial the request may seem, it is extremely difficult to utter, and for some impossible. (My own experience was one in which I was paralyzed, virtually unable to carry out the subway assignment; and after having carried it out I felt an enormous need to justify my request by appearing sick or faint.) But the act of asking if one might take someone's picture had none of these qualities—it flows naturally and is self-justifying. It is part of a shared culture. Perhaps in our culture we are profligate with our image because we feel the photographer does not really take it from us, but simply reproduces it, a form of visual cloning in which the original is not diminished, even while multiples of itself are created.

Every culture varies in the degree to which it is camera shy. The photographer can feel it in the reluctance he may have of taking pictures of the natives in any particular locale. Sometimes it seems an intrusion, an aggressive act. One solution, a friend once suggested, would be to have a camera deliver up to two pictures each time the shutter was snapped, one for the photographer and one for the subject. I suppose an SX–70 could be rigged up easily enough to do just that.

As I say, it is a cultural matter, and who knows where wisdom resides? In Peru, the Indian women run away when you aim the camera at them, and they look at you suspiciously even if you finger the camera. Maybe they are right, and the custom of letting strangers take our pictures bespeaks an inexcusable indifference to our own image. Who knows what the tourist with the Nikon will do with our image. Maybe he will laugh at it when he gets back home, use it for darts, or as a stimulus for bizarre sexual experiments.

But now we are slipping into insubstantial fantasies when a far more significant question remains in the relationship between the photographer and his subject. The question concerns the capacity of some photographers to render portraits of greater artistic depth than others. Some attribute this to the superior selectivity of the master photographer: he seeks out faces of potential interest, then selects the right moment to snap the shutter. No doubt this is part of the process. But when we examine photographs of, let us say Diane Arbus, we begin to understand that the psychological consistency in the faces of many diverse individuals must in part be due to the photographer's capacity to induce a certain attitude or expression in the subject, that a subtle psychological relationship exists between photographer and subject, in which the photographer—or at least some photographers—play a part in creating the faces they photograph.

But even the most mundane occasion for taking a snapshot involves us in a relationship, and moreover it is a relationship that others perceive and in some degree respect. For the photographic act occurs within a normative field, i.e., we don't just take photographs. The activity is circumscribed by certain social rules that are widely shared, even if they are implicit. People will exert some effort, for example, to avoid interference with the relationship. But how can this be measured?

We start with the idea of a "privileged space" between the photographer and his subject. There is a line of sight and it possesses a certain degree of inviolability. But just how much inviolability? The reluctance of bystanders to violate the line of sight is a measure of the strength and legitimation which they ascribe to the photographic act.

Our initial experiments on this topic were carried out on a major New York City thoroughfare (42nd street between 5th and 6th Avenues). The street is characterized by heavy pedestrian flow, and the pavement is conveniently divided into four lanes by pavement scratch lines (see Fig. 21.1).

The subject to be photographed posed along the inner wall of the street, the Bryant Park gate. Another student stepped back to the half width of the sidewalk, and held a camera to her eye as if to take a picture. The photographer held the camera for a five-minute period; observers counted how many people interrupted the line of sight between camera and subject, and how many people deviated to walk around it. In the first condition, the photographer stood at the point midway between the wall and the gutter. In the second condition, the photographer moved back to the 3/4 position (so that pedestrians only could squeeze through by using the remaining quarter of the sidewalk) and again held the camera to her eye for a five minute period. And finally, the photographer moved all the way back to the curb so that there was no way a pedestrian could pass without breaking the line of sight, except by ducking, waiting, or walking into the street.

The results speak well for the respect shown the photographic relationship: 90 percent respected the line of sight in the first condition, 69 percent in the

Fig. 21.1 *Illustration of the arrangement for the line-of-sight study. The photographer is shown taking a picture at the 3/4 mark.*

second, and 37 percent even when the entire sidewalk was blocked. It should give photographers heart to note that to avoid breaking the line of sight, a third of the New Yorkers detoured into the street, waited, or ducked very low.

To what extent is the special subject-photographer relationship being respected and to what extent is it the act of taking a picture being respected? A further experiment allowed us to check this. We substituted an inanimate object for the human subject, and performed the same line of sight variations. There are a far greater number of penetrations of the line of sight when the photographer is taking a picture of an object, rather than of another person. So the social relationship definitely plays a part in strengthening the inviolability of the line of sight.

We might ask whether any activity involving two people, and not only photography, would generate a similar deference. In another experimental condition our two experimenters abandoned the camera, and started playing ball from the 1/2, 3/4, and 4/4 positions on the 42nd street sidewalk, lobbing and rolling the ball to each other. Here there was far less respect for the relationship, and 91 percent of the pedestrians walked through (in the 3/4 position) compared to 31 percent when a photograph was being taken.

And people muttered that the pair had no right to play ball on the midtown sidewalks. But this remark was never made for the act of photographing. This suggests an important point: many activities, such as playing ball, are confined to a definable locus: in a school yard, in a park, etc. But there is no such definition for the act of taking a picture. Indeed, we work the other way: any place is considered appropriate for taking a picture, unless it is specifically excluded by violating sanctity or privacy, as in funeral parlors and brothels.

III

The job of the photographer and that of the psychologist interested in photography are very different. The photographer seeks to capture a particular moment on film; the psychologist tries to explain why the photographer is taking the picture, and how motives, perceptual processes, and emotional factors come into play. He tries to do this through research, conducting experiments, and formulating questions open to inquiry. It is odd that Eastman Kodak spends vast sums on research in film chemistry, but so little research has been carried out on the larger social and psychological processes of photography.

Consider, for a moment, not the history of psychology, but its history within a single individual. An important set of psychological questions concerns the way in which a person learns to take photographs. Although children, for example, are reported to have a clear, naive vision of things—imbued with wonder and freshness—the fact is that there are no great child photographers. Perhaps we have simply not placed the camera in the child's hands at a sufficiently early age, but I am skeptical of this argument, having seen large numbers of photographs taken by my own children. On the whole, the freshness, and even artistry we often find in children's drawings do not translate into their photographic view. Psychologists have studied children's drawings for many years now, and find that the drawings change systematically with age, and can often tell us a good deal about the mental processes of the child. But can photography be used in this way? What if we gave every two-year old a camera, and studied the pictures he took over the span of a lifetime. What would we learn about the child, and about the growth of photographic skill as he matures? Perhaps there are Piagetian stages of development that will be revealed through a study of children's photographs. Is there a systematic shift in what he photographs, and how he photographs it, comparable to systematic stages in the use of language and thought? The matter is worth looking into.

There is another side to the relationship of photography and human development. The individual learns not only how to take pictures, but also how to appear in them, that is, to pose. Infants, we know, are not self-conscious about cameras. They do not know what the camera is for, and this innocence allows us to capture their naive actions. But the child learns very quickly, and by five or six may not be able to stand in front of a camera without grimacing, and feeling ill at ease. In most individuals, this awkward feeling is gradually brought under control of an adjustive response: a pose. Studying how poses change over time, in different social classes, in different cultures, and through the growth and maturation of the individual, is a first-class problem for research.

The photographic process itself may help in the analysis of this aspect of photography. Eadweard Muybridge used the camera to obtain a sequence of pictures of humans and animals in action, so that he could better analyze the components of locomotion. We could do well to apply Muybridge's technique to the act of photography itself, as a way of better understanding it. How might it be used to study, for example, the pose?

Here is one possible scenario: A person comes to a portrait studio to have his picture taken. From the moment he enters the studio, a camera covertly takes a series of pictures of the person, perhaps one every ten seconds or so. The photographer performs his normal functions, poses the subject as he usually does, and snaps a series of portraits. By examining the portraits in the longer sequence taken by the hidden camera, it becomes easy to see how the official pose differs from the unposed pictures. It will help us to understand the adjustments the individual makes to the camera. The method would be particularly instructive when a master portrait photographer is at work, for we would then be able to trace photographically the means by which he brings his subject to the desired appearance for the portrait.

This technique is easy, but some questions are hard to answer even through ingenious experiments. Why, for example, are some people photogenic and others are not? Is it a matter of the perceptual effects in that certain three dimensional forms translate more flatteringly into flat photographs than others; or do some people come alive before a camera, and relate to it with a radiance and warmth elicited by no other stimulus, while others twist their faces into anxious masks? Probably both factors are at work, but a little research into the matter wouldn't hurt.

One of the most challenging areas for research deals with the psychological characteristics of the professional photographer. Certainly, some kind of visual intelligence is needed for this type of work. But beyond that, the forms of activity are so varied that different constellations of motives and abilities are probably at work in different domains of the photographic profession.

As to why people become photographers, the answers are probably as dependent on chance and circumstance as in any other occupation. But are there any "hidden" motives underlying the practice of the photographer's craft?

Freudian psychology might say that the profession of photography is a subliminated form of voyeurism, and underlying every lifelong commitment to photography is some remnant of the desire to catch a glimpse of the primal scene, i.e., sexual intercourse between parents. Like the little boy peeking at that special scene, the photographer positions himself to view an event, not to intervene in it, but to passively register it.

We need not take this interpretation seriously in order to acknowledge that a good photographer does require an extraordinary balance of passive and aggressive tendencies. He needs the agressiveness to intrude himself into situations where he is often irrelevent, and sometimes unwanted. Photographs of funerals, accidents, and grief-stricken moments are not generally offered up to the photographer; they are taken by him, as a thief snatches diamonds. At the same time, there is a passive component to photography, for the photographer must keep himself receptive to the images presented by the environment, and let them enter his camera.

Without overstating the case, we note how easily photography was presented as a highly sexualized activity in Antonioni's *Blow-Up*. Generally, to the working photographer, none of these factors will seem particularly important, since he is preoccupied with making a living, trying to please the client and turn a profit, worrying about competition and his integrity, wondering whether to fake a news photo, or whether to lend a hand to a suffering accident victim rather than simply photograph him. These conscious conflicts are no less important than so-called subconscious ones.

Photographs can constitute an important psychological document about an individual. Robert Akaret's sensitive book, *Photoanalysis*, shows how far one can go in interpreting the psychological meaning of individual snapshots. But one can also use the aggregate of photographs in an individual's possession as an index of his psychic life. First, people ordinarily photograph only what interests them. If we examine the photographs a person has taken during his lifetime, we will be able to discern the things that were important to him, and those that were not. It is probably as good a measure as we have of his enduring lifetime cathexes. One friend I know concentrated on hundreds of nature scenes, and very few of his wife, an indication of where his true passions resided—a fact also confirmed by his recent divorce.

My colleague, Dr. Stuart Albert, has suggested that we examine the entire content of family photo albums to see which events are recorded, and which are not. He believes that we photograph mostly during periods of rapid change and growth, thus explaining the preponderence of photographs of children in their period of rapid maturation.

Through the family photo album, the family constructs a type of fairy tale. Only the happy moments tend to be shown: birthdays, bar mitzvahs, weddings and vacations. Families construct a pseudo-narrative which highlights all that was life-affirming and pleasurable, with a systematic suppresion of life's pains. (At least, I have not yet seen a family album in which funerals and suicides are depicted.) However imperfect, the album is for most contemporary families the only narrative available of its history, having supplanted the family Bible, where, in earlier times, a record of births, deaths, and marriages was maintained.

Photography, I am convinced, is ready for an invasion of psychologists, experimentalists, who will not be satisfied to hear there is something called the "decisive movement"; they'll want to show just how long it is, and find out what would happen if Cartier-Bresson were saddled with a camera whose shutter snapped unpredictably from five to thirty seconds after depressing the release button. Would he miss all the good shots? The psychologists will want to know whether the immediate feed-back of a Polaroid system facilitates the learning of photographic skills, and whether certain personality types among photographers prefer color to black and white. The psychologist will want to probe into the enormous credibility of photographs (viewers tend to believe the things they show really happened). They will want to know who in the family takes the photographs, and examine the patterns of photographs a person takes over a lifetime.

But perhaps the most interesting set of questions concerns the photographs themselves, and the socio-imagistic reality they create. Let me explain. We start with the fact that photographs are often treated as compelling and incontrovertible evidence that the events depicted in them actually happened. This is overlayed by the fact that the photograph constitutes a reality, valued in and of itself. We all know the joke about the grandmother traveling with her grandchildren. A fellow passenger remarks on how attractive the children are. The grandmother rejoins: "That's nothing, let me show you their pictures." The pictures constitute a reality of their own, and evoke emotions, attitudes, and convictions. Photographs, therefore, not only depict realities, they create a new plane of reality to which people respond.

There is a universe of events that we smell, a universe that we hear, and there is also a universe of events whose existence is embodied in photographs.

Thus, each year we eagerly await the official Chinese Communist May Day photograph to see who is photographed alongside the Chairman, and who has been displaced. The official photograph is not only a reflection of the political reality, but itself solidifies that reality, becomes an element in it.

The question that arises for purposes of research, therefore, is: to what degree will events that exist in photographs exert an effect outside the photograph? For example, if we stop two strangers on the street, ask them to pose momentarily, and take a picture, have we thereby created through the photograph a bond that previously did not exist? If the photograph is circulated to others, will the two individuals, fortuitously brought together in the photograph, tend to be treated as a pair? Does the photograph act back on the real world, and begin to shape that world?

Events happen, not only in the real world, but in photographs as well, and this new focus of action may exert a devastating power. House detectives have known this for years. A photograph showing a political candidate shaking hands with a Communist Party Official can kill his chances for re-election, even when the photograph is faked.

Or, consider a more typical case. An aspiring young lawyer gets to see President Carter for five minutes. A photograph is taken of the two men chatting. The lawyer proudly hangs it behind his desk. The image freezing machine has done its work. Clients see the photograph, are impressed, draw inferences. The lawyer need never mention the photograph. It resoundingly speaks for itself, a powerful new element in the lawyer's career. The lawyer has learned through personal experience what prophets of photography have long suspected: a photograph does not only record events. It creates them.

NOTE

1. The sketch on page 346 is by Judith Waters.

REFERENCES

AKERET, R. U., *Photoanalysis: How to Interpret the Hidden Psychological Meaning of Personal and Public Photographs*. New York: Wyden, 1973.

ARNHEIM, R., "On the Nature of Photography." *Critical Inquiry*, Sept. 1974, **I**, 149–161.

BECKER H., Photography and Sociology. *Studies in the Anthropology of Visual Communication*, 1974, **5**, 3–26.

NEWHALL, B., *The History of Photography*. New York: Museum of Modern Art. 1964.

SONTAG, S., "Photography." *New York Review of Books*, October 18, 1973; November 13, 1973; and April 18, 1974.

INDEX

Index

Abraham, 102
Acceleration, crowd, 217, 218
vehicular, 37
Accident crowd, 219
Accretion in crowds, 210
Acquaintance, 281, 282, 284, 285, 292, 294
chain, 282, 284, 285, 286, 287, 290, 292
circles, 282, 284
links, 281, 287, 294
see also Familiar stranger
Acquiescence, 43
to group, 94
see also Authority
Acquisition of crowd members, 200, 204
Act, antisocial, 279, 306–337
communicative, 278
of cruelty, 260
of disobedience, 139
induction of, 178, 179
morally significant, 92
photographic, 344–350
Action, against a person, 178–187
collective, 247
conformity, 153, 178
of a crowd, 201–204, 221, 236
measure of, 297–304
mob, 226
mobilization for, 245–249
social, components of, 245, 248, 249
violent, 232
Activity, city and town, 30
crowd, 212, 218–220, 223, 225, 243, 261
human, photography as a, 280
states of, 201
Adaptations to city life, 29, 33, 35, 38
Adolescent perceptions of city, 39
Adorno, T. W., 239
Aggregate, vs. crowd, 212
individuals in an, 230
man-vehicle, 218, 219
and panic, 215

Aggregation, in crowds, 206
rate of, 206, 268
shape of, 206
in mental maps, 56
Aggression, 109, 117, 118, 121, 122
amount of, 238
displaced, 239
effects of exposure to, 306, 307
and frustration, 238, 239
stimulating, 264
target of, 239
Aggressive, crowd, 243
drives, 237
Akaret, R., 348
Akers, E. R., 225
Albert, S., 349
Alcohol, use of in Norway, 172–173
Alienated, influencing the, 153
Alienation, 30
Allport, F. H., 223, 229, 234, 239, 242, 244
Allport, G., 9, 171, 227, 228, 243, 267
Altman, D., 28
Altruism, 92, 99
in cities (social responsibility), 26
Ambience, measurement of, 3, 16
in New York, 34
in Paris, 34, 37–39
sources of, 37, 38
Ambiguity, and crowds, 243
in rumor, 227
American, analysis of mob psychology, 231
civil rights movement, 249
culture, 225
democracy, 13
experimenters in Paris, Athens, Boston, 36
internment camp, 13, 225
preconceptions, 36
psychology, 146
reaction to Genovese case, 43
society, 121, 159, 249, 286, 290, 291, 293

study of mobs, 231
tolerance for crowds, 216
see also Boston; Chicago; New York;
    United States
American Psychologist, 139
American Scientist, 54
Amsterdam News, The, 314
Analyses, content, 34, 262
Anecdote, 17, 130, 131, 134, 135
    use of in science, 231, 234
Animals, effects of crowding on, 217
Anonymity, benefits of, 30
    consequences of, 30, 117, 264
    in crowds, 223, 224, 230, 233, 242, 244
    level of, 279
    loss of responsibility through, 226
    in lost letter procedure, 297
    urban, 30, 51–53
    see also Familiar stranger
"Anonymity of the Flock" (K. Lorenz),
    224
Anonymous strangers, 31
Antonioni, 348
Anxiety, in groups, 237
    inhibitory, 5
    in obedience experiment, 6
    separation, 237
    in subway experiment, 6
    in TV study, 334
    see also Tension
Apathy, 99
    noninvolvement, 26, 27
    see also Social responsibility
Arbus, D., 345
Ardrey, R., 50
Arendt, H., 231
Argyle, M., 223
Arnheim, R., 342
Aronson, E., 134
Arrondissements, 68–70, 83–85, 90
Asch, S. E., 10, 12, 92, 94–96, 152–154,
    162, 178–179, 185–186, 188, 195,
    203, 222, 242, 264
ASMP Journal of Photography in
    Communications, 339
Assimilation in rumor transmission, 227
Associations of Paris, mental, 77
    verbal, 78
Athens, helpfulness in, 36
Attention in crowds, 212, 232
Atmosphere, urban, 33–35, 39
Attitude, assessing, 297
    change, 234

of crowd member, 240
in crowd study, 264
measure of, through actions, 297–304
toward escape situation, 267
toward importance of experiment, 166
toward McCarthy-Johnson primary,
    304
toward Paris, 89
toward Vietnam, 304
urbanite, 33
Auditory variation of Asch experiment,
    153
    see also Noise
Authoritarian character, 238
Authority, 92
    background, 114–116
    closeness of, 109–110
    desire for, 238
    diminished, 196
    disobedience to, 93, 102–123
    doctrinaire, 154
    experimenter as, 94, 104, 122, 130,
        131, 139, 145, 196
    and the group, 154
    of leader, 235
    legitimate, 144, 147
    medical, 96
    obedience to, 93, 102–123
    pressure of, 96
    rejection of, 2
    structure of, 13
    submission to, 12, 14, 145, 238

Bagehot, W., 239, 260
Bailey, N. T. J., 255, 256
Bandura, A., 264, 306, 307
Barcus, F. E., 306
Barriers, between familiar strangers, 3
    in mental maps, 57
Bartel World Wide, 312–314
Bartlett, M., 256
Baseline, home city as, 35
    in obedience studies, 123
    urban, 35
Baumrind, D., 93, 125, 139, 140, 142–146
Beatles, the, 241, 256
Behavior, acquired, 108
    antisocial, and television, 279, 306–337
    bystander, 20
    city, 31–36
    collective, 225, 264–268
    common standards of, 242
    contravalent, 186

crowd, 200–268
  effects of group on, 152–156, 179–198
  fractional, 316
  homogenization of, 96
  legitimized, 131
  photographic, 279
  prosocial, 279, 310, 319, 328
  role, 31–33
  social, 6, 12, 13, 20
  town, 31–33
"Behavioral Study of Obedience"
  (S. Milgram), 99, 140
Belief, in Smelser's theory, 245, 247,
  249, 251
  of subjects in obedience study,
  126–135
  systems, 234
  uniformity of, 242
Bellows, H., 262
Bem, D. J., 198, 264
Bengen, B., 41
Berkeley, 213, 215, 225, 246–248, 251
Berkowitz, L., 200, 307
Berkowitz, W., 36
Bettleheim, B., 44
Bickman, L., 27, 200
Birth order, of experimental subjects,
  183
  of war resisters, 148
Black, box conformity, 154
  Muslim, 249
  neighborhoods in South, 300
  telephone callers, 27
  see also Negro
Blacks, enslavement of, 13
Blake, R., 162, 188
Blumenfield, H., 38
Blumer, H., 207, 232, 239, 240, 244
Boston, 295
  Civil Rights Rally, 210, 212, 221
  election study, 301
  helpfulness in, 36
  lost child experiment in, 17
  target persons in, 286, 292
  walking speeds in, 36
Boundaries, of behavior, 244
  of crowd, 206–211
  in mental maps, 57
  national, 170
  neighborhood, 47
  in obedience study, 120
  and overload, 25
  permeability of, 209

  psychological, of city, 38, 58
  of Paris, 73, 83–84
  sharpness of, 210
Bowerman, M., 304
Bowerman, W., 304
Brandt, W., 149
Brattle Theatre breakdown of norms,
  215, 216
Brehm, J. W., 162, 188
Bridgeport, obedience experiment in,
  103, 115–116, 133
Bronowski, J., 186, 186
Bronx, the, 30, 47, 59–67
Brooklyn, 47, 53, 59–65
Brown, R. W., 10, 213, 215, 222, 226,
  230, 265
Bruce, H. M., 217
Bruce, J. A., 217
Bruner, J. S., 10
Burgess, E. W., 50, 232
Buss, A. H., 122
Bystander, apathy, 99
  in crowd, 240, 243
  experiments, 11, 20, 27, 153
  intervention, 20, 27
  at rally, 221
  research, 12
  urban, 42–46

Calhoun, J. B., 217
Canetti, E., 209, 220
Cantril, H., 209, 241, 261, 262
Carmichael, S., 216
Cartier-Bresson, H., 349
Cartwright, D., 198, 282
CBS, 308
Centrality and landmark recognition, 66
Chains of acquaintances, 282, 287–293
  see also Links
Chanowitz, B. Z., 90
Characteristics, of broadcast, 262
  of cities, 34
  of contact situation, 267
  crowd, 232–234
  of demonstrators, 225
  of experimental subjects, 183
  of members of mob, 226
  national, studies of, 159–170
  of rioters and nonrioters, 225
Charity, collection box, medical, 9,
  308–325, 332–337
  contributions to, 279

pledges to medical, 327–330
and pro-social conformity, 152
Chiang Kai-shek, 296, 302, 304
Chicago, 57
  atmosphere, 38
  helpfulness in, 31
  pro-social television program, 328, 329
  riots, 228
  University of, 297
Children, aggression in, 306, 307
  lost, 7, 17
  reactions of, to Martian program, 262
    to rejection, 160
  television programs for, 306
Chinese, cities, 7
  in Paris, 84
  reactions to lost letters, 296, 302–304
Christian, J. J., 217
City, behavior in, 28–38
  as a collective representation, 72
  icons of, 80
  and the individual, 16–23
  living in, 2, 7, 24–39, 99
  lost child in, 7
  mental maps of, 7–8
  perceptions of, 35
  psychological maps of, 38–39, 54–90
  reciprocated handshaking in, 17–18
  see also Maps; individual names of
    cities
City University of New York, 27–28, 31,
    51, 204
Civil rights groups, 300
Civilities, 29
Clark, S., 216
Class differences in mental maps, 82–85
Closeness, in obedience study, 123
  see also Immediacy; Proximity;
    Salience
Cognitive, core of city, 38
  element, 245
  field, narrowing of, 107
  processes, 33, 127
Cognitive map, of Boston, 38
  of childhood, 47
  multidimensional approach to, 21
  of New York City, 39, 55–67
  of Paris, 68–90
  technique, 55, 59
  see also Mental map; New York;
    Paris; Psychological map
Cohen, J., 228
Coleman, J. S., 200, 204, 257

Collective, action, 200
  behavior, 200–268
  decision-making, 227
  mind, 232, 234
  outbursts, 241
  paralysis, 27, 44
  psychology, 231
  representation of Paris, 72
  see also Crowd; Group
Commercials on TV, 9
Communication, in Berkeley protest, 247
  in crowds, 227, 228, 244
  lack of, 44
  systems, 276–278
  see also Lost letter; Photography;
    Rumor; Small world; Telephone;
    Television
Communist, 350
  Party, Friends of the, 297–299
  see also Lost letter
Community, control, 49
  critical size for, 256
  distortion in, 228
  orientations toward political
    institutions, 296
  urban, 48, 50
"Community of limited liability," 49
Commuters, 3, 51–53
  see also Familiar stranger
Compliance, see Conformity; Group
    pressure; Obedience; Pressure;
    Submission
Components of social action, 245,
    248–250
Computer simulation of, crowd flow, 217
  crowds, 268
  epidemic process, 256
Confederate, 94, 152, 153, 162, 179–182,
    187, 189, 202
  behavior of, 193
  reaction to, 195
  see also Experiment; Subjects
Conflict, of conscience and authority,
    154
  dissolving, 237
  experimental studies of, 92
  in group pressure experiment, 162
  among Norwegian subjects, 172
  in obedience experiment, 13, 104, 113,
    122, 125, 129, 131, 139, 141, 192
  and tension, 113, 139, 162
Conformity, 122
  action, 153, 178

beyond the laboratory, 153, 168
black box, 154
constructive, 153, 188
experiments, 12, 92, 94, 95, 153,
    160–177
in France, 156, 160–170
as a function of group size, 203
of inaction, 153
index of, 178
level of, 154, 168, 174, 177
measuring, 160
in national cultures, 154
in Norway, 156, 160–173
vs. obedience, 186
pro-social, 152
and reaction to ethics of experiment,
    174–177
signal, 178
and social control, 96
verbal, 154, 178
Conformity in Norway and France (S.
    Milgram), 156
Confusions in mental maps, 82
Congress of Racial Equality (CORE),
    211
Congressional Record, 42
Conn, Lane, 276
Connecticut industrial town, 300
Contact, pattern of social, 290
    see also Small world problem
Contagion, in crowds, 200, 232, 233, 234,
    239, 240, 242–244, 263
    process, 253
    social, 253
    theory, 240, 244, 254
Context, related to obedience, 115, 143
    university, 136
Contract, subject-experimenter, 186
Control of hostile crowds, 263
    see also Social control
Convergence, pattern of, 292
    theory of, 234, 239–242
Cooley, C., 260
Cooperation, 122
Core, of crowd, 207, 209
    of psychological maps, 38, 66
Corey, M., 137
Cox. D. R., 217
Craik, G. L., 225, 230, 231
Craze, 249
Crime, areas in mental maps of Paris, 84,
    85
    response to, 42–46

risk group, 322
    on television, 336
Criminal-act experiments, 131
Criminals, in crowds, 224–225
    war resisters as, 147–149
Critical trials, 165, 182, 183
Criticism, of laboratory experiments on
    rumor, 228
    of Le Bon, 233, 234
    of obedience experiment, 7, 93, 98,
        124–146
    overt social, 167
    of Smelser, 251
Cross-national research, 159–170
Crowds, 156, 200–268
    anonymity of, 223, 224
    Babel, 227
    boundaries, 207, 209, 210, 211, 224
    of cars, 219
    composition of, 224–226, 241
    crystals, 220, 263
    density, 215–218, 263
    dependence on physical-environmental
        conditions, 215
    formation of, 200–204, 211, 220, 241,
        262, 263, 264, 268
    vs. groups, 156
    image of, 260
    information flow in, 227–228
    irrationality of, 223, 226, 233, 259
    laminated, 211
    and language, 226, 230
    mental unity of, 212
    methods of study, 202, 206, 210, 213,
        216, 220, 261–268
        application of general experimental
            literature, 264
        computer simulation, 268
        experimental approaches, 264–268
        field experimentation, 267
        mock crowds, 268
        polarization quotient, 215
        projective devices, 263, 264
        secondary sources, 262, 263
        simulation of crowd behavior,
            265–267
        survey research, 261, 262
    models of, 255–258
    in motion, 217
    perception of, 229
    permeability, 209
    polarization, 210, 212, 213, 215, 263
    rationalizing the, 217

shape, 206, 222
size, 200–204, 220–223, 263
stimulus, 200–204
structure of, 206, 209, 211, 221
theories, 227, 230–261
    contagion, 239–244, 254
    convergence, 240–242
    emergent norm, 243–245
    Le Bon, 231–234
    mathematical, 252–258
    psychoanalytic, 235–238, 244
    Smelser, 227, 245–252
turnover, 114
violence in, 260
see also Aggregation; Collective
    behavior; Groups; Mob
Crutchfield, R. S., 178
Cue, in mental maps, 57
in Zimbardo study, 30
Cultural, core of city, 65
items, source of, 276
tolerance for crowds, 216
Culture, American, 225
conformity in national, 154, 159
French, 169
Japanese, 225
national, and cities, 38
norms, 217
Norwegian, 169, 171–173
and photography, 344
see also Cross-national research
Cycles, epidemic, 256

"The Dangers of Obedience" (H. J.
    Laski), 121
Dangling Dollar, 319, 320, 323, 324, 325,
    332, 333 f
Darley, J. M., 11, 27, 92, 99, 100
Davies, J. C., 225
Davis, K., 251, 268
Debriefing, in conformity experiments,
    167, 174–177
in obedience experiments, 97, 121,
    122, 140–143, 146, 182, 191
Decay curve, 287
Deception in experiments, 93, 126–128,
    136, 166, 167, 174, 176
see also Ethics
Deeds, elicitation of, 178
survey of, 278
vs. verbal behavior, 153, 178–187
see also Actions

Defiance, conditions of, 105
in obedience study, 193–198
see also Disobedience
DeFleur, M. L., 228
Demand characteristics, 93, 124, 129,
    134, 136
Denial, role of, 127
Density, animal, 217
crowd, 215–216
factor in computing crowd size, 222
population, 24, 25, 29, 37–39, 220
traffic, 218, 219
Desmond, Tom (television character),
    308–313, 319, 326, 327, 330, 331
Detroit, antisocial television program,
    328, 329
riots, 225
Deutsch, M., 266
Deviancy in cities, 31
Dewey, J., 260
Diamond, R., 198, 301
Differential participation in crowds, 212,
    258, 263
Differentiation among channels of
    transmission, 292
Diffusion traceback study, 277–278
Discrimination, of tones, 166
see also Black; Negro; Race
Disobedience, conditions of, 102–123,
    195–198
in experiments, 145
groups for, 192–197
of war resisters, 147–149
Dispositions, acquired behavior, 108
obedient, 117
Distillation effect in crowds, 221
Distinctiveness in psychological maps,
    66
Division 8 Newsletter, 51
Dollard, J., 238, 239, 322
Doob, I. W., 322
Downs, R. M., 68
Duby, G., 282
Dytell, R., 154

Ecological, factors, 207
validity, 134, 143
Ecology of crowds, 215–217
see also City; Environment; Rural;
    Urban
Edie, L. C., 219
Edison: The Man (film), 340

Ego, 237
El Diario, 314
Election, lost letter study of, 301
  Presidential, 213
  see also United States voting behavior
Elges, E., 121
Elms, A., 121
Embed antisocial act in television
  program, 308
Embeddedness in mental maps, 78
Emergent norm theory, 242–245
Emotion, crowd, 243, 244, 259
  in lost letter technique, 304
  sympathetic induction of, 239
  see also Anxiety; Frustration; Tension
Empathetic cues, 106–107
Encounters, meeting places to maximize,
  87, 89
Energy, mob, 252
England, national characteristics of, 160
  psychological maps of, 55
Environment, effect of on crowds, 215
  see also City; Ecology: Rural; Urban
Epidemic, 256
Equilibrium in crowds, 254, 255
Escape from Freedom (E. Fromm), 231,
  238
Estimate of crowd size, 221, 222
"Ethical Issues in the Study of
  Obedience" (S. Milgram), 93
Ethics, in conformity experiment,
  174–177
  experimental, 156
  inferred from behavior, 43
  of obedience studies, 93, 99, 139–146
Ethnic, allegiance, 27
  groups, in bystander research, 27
  in Paris, 84
  neighborhoods, 39, 48, 300
Evans, R., 93–100
Experiment, ethics of, 2, 174–177
  limits of, 99
  nature of, 1, 4, 11, 12
  source of, 12, 17
  uniqueness of psychological, 135
Experimental, approaches to collective
  behavior, 264–267
  comparisons of behavior, 36
  control, 12, 94
  design, 140, 179, 307
  manipulation, 194
  measures embedded in city life, 35, 36
  method, applied to field situations, 27

for assessing political orientations,
  296–304
  for tracing line of acquaintances, 285
paradigm, 92
techniques, 160, 189, 193
Experimenter, as authority, 139, 145,
  186–198
  degree of surveillance of, 110
  feelings toward, 141, 145
  group support for, 197
  motives of, 98
  in obedience study, 94–96, 103, 104,
    109, 110, 128
  obligation toward, 195
  orientation to, 109
  physical closeness of, 110
  power of, 131, 133, 196
  relationship with subject, 186
Experiments, auto vandalism, 30
  behavior toward compatriots and
    foreigners, 36
  Bridgeport replication, 126, 133
  bystander intervention, 20
  computer simulation, 217
  conflicting authority, 117
  criminal-act, 31
  on crowd formation, 220
  diffusion traceback, 277–278
  dual authority, 117
  effects of anonymity (homosexual
    tenants), 31
  effects of group forces in obedience
    group determines shock level, 117
    group follows orders, 117
    groups for disobedience, 117,
      192–196
    subjects in subsidiary role, 117
  entry to home, 28, 29
  Experiment I: baseline condition,
    188–192, 198
  Experiment II: groups for
    disobedience, 192–196, 198
  Experiment III: obedient groups,
    197–198
  experimenter absent, 110
  experimenter departs, 126
  experimenter present, 110
  familiar stranger, 3
  group pressure, 12, 92, 94, 152–154,
    162, 178–198, 264
  heart condition, 126
  help across ethnic lines, 27
  hospital nurses, 133–134

lost letter, 296, 304
moral judgment, 192
nitric acid, 129, 131, 137
noxious task, 133
on obedience, 2, 6, 11, 13, 93, 94, 97, 98, 102–123, 136, 139–143
painful noise, 137
of photographic process, 344–346
proximity, 106–109, 123, 126
reciprocated handshaking, 17, 18
remote feedback, 106–108, 126
Rosenhan, 127
self-image, 192
spontaneous shock levels, 191
study of national characteristics, 160–170
subway, 4, 344
telephone orders, 110
on television and antisocial behavior, 89, 313–337
  Experiment 1: first preview screening, 313–320
  Experiment 2: frustration study, 319–325
  Experiment 3: effects of a model, 325
  Experiment 4: eliminating time gap, 325
  Experiment 5: home viewers, 325
  Experiment 6: home viewers, 325
  Experiment 7: telephone study, 325–332
  Experiment 8: the Evening News study, 332–334
touch-proximity, 106, 120, 123, 126
town and city roles behavior, 34
traumatizing shock, 133
unsanctioned authority, 117
variations of Asch's experiment,
  action conformity, 153
  black box conformity, 154
  conformity of inaction, 153
  enduring aspects of yielding, 153
  forewarned subjects, 153
  group's response to pressure, 153
  influencing the alienated, 153
  pro-social conformity, 152
  repetition of stimulus, 153
  sequential influence, 153
voice feedback, 106–108, 126
walking speeds, 36
women as subjects, 117, 126
see also Methods

Exploring English Character (G. Gorer), 160

"Face block," 49
Facilities in Smelser's theory, 249
Familiar, areas of Paris, 83
  stranger, 3, 4, 51–53
Family, ties, 212
  photo album, 349
Fear, induction of, 207
Federal Bureau of Investigation, 248, 300
Feedback, to foster independence, 199
  remote, 106–108
  voice, 106, 122, 123, 127, 181
Feldman, R., 36
Ferri, E., 231
Feshbach, N., 163
Feshbach, S., 163, 306, 307
Feuer, L. S., 251
Field, experiments, 220, 228, 267
  situations, experimental methods applied to, 27
  structure, 197, 199
  study, of social intrusion, 11
  see also Experiments; Methods; Study; Survey
Flow, crowd, 217
  information, 227, 228
  traffic, 219
Foote, R. S., 219
Formula, Jacobs, for estimating crowd size, 215, 216, 222
  landmark recognition, 66
  mass contagion, 254, 255
  polarization, 213
  rumor intensity, 227
  staggered motion, 218
  synchronized motion, 218
Fox, V., 225
Frager, R., 302
France, conformity in, 160–170
  crowd behavior in, 225, 231
  national characteristics of, 160, 162–172
  taxi drivers in, 21, 23
Frank, J. D., 133, 179
Free Speech Movement, 246, 247
French, government, 21
  revolution, 249
  survey of organizations, 21
French, J. R. P., 179, 265, 266
Freud, S., 148, 232, 235–237, 242, 243, 258

Friends, of the Communist Party, 297
  of the Nazi Party, 278, 297
Friendship, ties, 212
  urban, 26
From, H., 51
Fromm, E., 231, 238
Froom, J. E., 217
"The Frozen World of the Familiar
    Stranger," 2
Frustration, aggression hypothesis, 238,
    239, 322
  study of antisocial behavior, 319–325
Fryer, J., 278

Gaertner, S., 27
Gaito, J., 202
Gallup, G., 160
Gannon, Dr. Joseph (television
    character), 308, 310, 326
Gasset, Ortega y, 231
Gaylin, W., 93, 147, 148
Gazis, D., 219
Genovese, K., 11, 12, 18, 20, 26, 27, 42,
    43, 44, 99
Gerbner, G., 306
Germany, anti-Nazi letters in Munich,
    304
  family in, 238
  national characteristics of, 170
  Nazi, 13, 96, 144, 149, 170, 238
  stage plays in, 159
Gerver, J., 23
Gestures in photography, 344
Ghetto, 39
Gilbert, G., 238
Gist, N. P., 228
Glazer, N., 251
Goffman, E., 50
Goldwater, B., 211, 301
Goodman, I., 5
Gorer, G., 160
Gould, P., 54, 55, 57
Gradient of asserted familiarity, 83
Graph theory, 282
"Great city" effect, 16
Greenwald, J., 54
Griffin, D. R., 57
Grosser, D., 264
Group, action, 44
  activity, 230
  in artificial crisis, 265
  cohesiveness, 171, 173

formation, 237, 256
  incipient, 108
  growth, 200, 204
  identification, 156, 169
  mind, 235
  norms, 173, 178, 264
  opinion, 167
  precipitating, in crowd formation, 220
  pressure, 12, 92–93, 152–154, 169, 173,
    178, 179, 182, 185–188, 194–198,
    222, 234
  response to emergency, 100
  response to presure, 153
  size, 203, 204, 256, 257
  sub-, 212
  support, 264
  synthetic, 162
  see also Crowds
Gurevitch, M., 284

Hall, E., 37, 206, 209, 216
Handbook of Social Psychology, 156
Handshake experiment, 17, 18
Harary, F., 282
Harlem, 224, 228, 230
  see also Ghetto
Harlow, F. H., 217
Harter, S., 296, 297
Hartley, R., 306
Hartley's test for homogeneity of
    variance, 183
Harvard Crimson, 34, 301
Harvard University, 9, 10, 33, 152, 162,
    263, 276, 277, 284, 287
Haussmann, E., 215
Hawaii Five-O, 329
Hecker, J., 256
Heczey, M., 279
Heider, E. R., 268
"Hell's Angels," 241
Help, withholding, 28
Helpfulness, 29, 31, 32, 36
Helplessness, 43
Heterogeneity, of city, 27
  of population, 24, 34, 39
Hierarchy, in authority, 122
  in mental maps, 57
  in roles, 132
  see also Authority
Himmelweit, H., 307
Hitler, A., 238
Hobbes, T., 9

Hofling, C. K., 134
Hofstätter, P. R., 233
Holland, C., 93, 124, 135, 136
Hollander, P., 20, 26, 42
Holocaust, 93
Homans, G. C., 196, 199
Homogeneity, of crowds, 232, 235, 241,
    242, 243, 255, 258
  illusion of, 243
Homogenization, of behavior, 96
  of crowd, 240
Homosexual, 31
Hong Kong, 296, 302, 304
Hooper, D., 38, 54, 55
Hostility, reduction of group, 267
Hovland, C. I., 234, 239
Human Relation Area Files, 268
Human Relations, 93, 102
Humphrey, N. D., 227
Hypnosis, 129, 130, 134, 135
Hypnotism model of crowd behavior,
    233, 236
Hypothesis, of arbitrary direction of
    group effects, 196
  of crowd structure, 207, 234
  frustration-aggression, 238
  of social behavior, 279

IBM, 284
Icons of the city, 80, 82
Identification, with disobedient
    confederates, 196
  with leader, 235
  with other members, 235
  object of, 237
Identity, group, 156
  and neighborhood, 48
Ik, the, 20
Illusion, in experiments, 97, 128, 132,
    133
  of homogeneity, 243
Image, of city, 20, 39, 57, 58
  of crowd, 260
  freezing machine, 279, 339–350
  self, 340, 341
  as social construction, 48
The Image of the City (K. Lynch), 7, 20,
    38, 57
Imitation, of antisocial behavior, 264
    306–337
  and mass contagion, 254
Immediacy of victim, 106, 123

In the Service of Their Country: War
    Resisters in Prison (W. Gaylin),
    93, 147
Inaction, conformity of, 153
  see also Bystander ⌐
Inbreeding in acquaintance nets, 284
Independence, in conformity
    experiments, 166, 168, 169
  among French, 168, 169, 170
  among Norwegians, 168, 169, 170
  in social life, 154
  see also Conformity
Index, of conformity, 178
  of irrationality, 259
  of mental unity of crowd, 212
  of psychic life, photographs as, 349
Individual, action and rumor, 227
  and communication, 276–280
  control of large populations, 223
  in crowds, 232, 233, 234
  differences, 182, 185
  effects of city on, 16
  effect of group on, 152–154, 182
  effects on, of exposure to violence,
    279
  in groups, 257
  judgment, 94
  in mobs, 226
  and photography, 347
  polarized, 213
  see also Conformity; Group pressure
Influence, and crowds, 234
  group, 185
  on perceptions of cities, 35
  see also Compliance; Conformity;
    Group pressure; Submission
Information, flow in crowd, 227, 228
  function of rumors, 227
  source of, 277
Informed consent, 97
Informed Heart, The (B. Bettelheim), 44
Inhibition, in obedience experiment, 114
  in subway experiment, 5
Institute for Advanced Study, 10
International Association of Chiefs of
    Police, 262, 263
Institution, behavior outside of, 245
  category of, 116
International Journal of Psychiatry, 93,
    124
Interns, The, 329
"Interpreting Obedience Error and
    Evidence" (S. Milgram), 93

Interstimulation in crowds, 239, 242
Interview, in conformity experiments, 166, 167
  in Evening News Study, 333
  in experiments, 135
  post-experimental, 123, 125, 127, 141, 182, 191
  psychoanalytic, 148
  of radio listeners, in panic study, 262
  survey, 296
  by C. Tavris, 2–14
  of war resisters, 148
Intuition, shared, 87
Invincibility, sense of, 242
Involvement, risks of, 45
  see also Bystander; Social intrusion
Irrationality of crowds, index of, 259
Italy, 231

Jacobs, H., 215, 216, 222
Jacobs, J., 282
James, J., 200, 204, 256, 257
Janis, I. L., 237
Janowitz, M., 49
Jante Laws, 172, 173
Janteloven, 172, 173
Japanese-Americans, 13, 225
Jewish quarter, 84
Jews, 44, 92, 239
Jodelet, D., 21, 68
John Birch Society, 242
Johnson, Lyndon, 301
Johnson, V. E., 137
Jones, E. E., 199
Journal of Abnormal and Social Psychology, 178
Journal of Personality and Social Psychology, 188, 200
Judgment, group, 195
  of lines, 162
  moral, 192
  reciprocal, 35
  of tones, 153, 162, 167
  verbal, 153, 154, 173
  see also Asch; Experiment; Group; Individual

Katz, I., 5
Kelley, H. H., 266
Kerr, C., 247
Kessler, S., 54
Kew Gardens, 20, 42–46
  see also Genovese, K.

Kierkegaard, S., 102
Killian, L. M., 212, 227, 232, 233, 242, 258, 259, 262, 263
Kochen, M., 284
Kogan, N., 198, 264
König, R., 231
Korte, C., 293
Kudirka, N. K., 133

Laboratory, approaches to bystander intervention, 27
  crowd behavior study, 265, 267
  procedure in obedience experiment, 103
  scientific, 116
  of Social Psychology, 21
  of Social Relations, 284
  see also Experiments
Lakey, G., 262, 268
Lamination effects in crowds, 211
Landmarks, Boston, 38, 55
  in mental maps, 55
  New York, 38, 39, 55
  Paris, 74–82
Lang, G. E., 212, 227, 232, 258
Lang, K., 210, 212, 227, 232, 258
Language and crowds, 226, 230
Laski, H. J., 121
Latané, B., 11, 27, 92, 99, 100
Law, of large numbers, 256
  of mental unity of crowds, 232, 243
Laws, Jante, 172, 173
Lazarus, R., 140
Le Bon, G., 219, 223, 224, 226, 228, 230–235, 239, 243, 244, 245, 251, 258, 260, 262
Leader, authority of, 235
  crowd, 232, 233, 235–238, 263
  see also Authority
Leadership, 243, 248
Learner, in group pressure experiment, 179–183, 186, 189, 193
  in obedience experiment, 103, 104, 126
Lederer, E., 231
Leveling, in crowds, 232
  in rumors, 227
Leventhal, H., 123
Levine, M., 28
Levinger, G., 179
Lewin, K., 242
Links, acquaintance, 281, 286, 287, 291, 294
  mental, 77

Lippit, R., 264
Lipset, M., 246, 248, 251
Locales, in Paris, 87, 88
  stimulus, 77
Locals vs. outsiders, 241
Locke, J., 9
London, 3, 49, 340
  atmosphere, 33, 37, 39
Lorenz, K., 206, 224
Loss of group members, 200
Lost, child, 7, 17
  letter, 1, 278, 296–304
"The Lost Letter Technique," 278, 296
Lucido, D., 17
Lumsdaine, A. A., 234
Lynch, K., 7, 20, 38, 50, 55, 57
Lyonns, G., 225

MacBride, P., 178
Manhattan, 24
  landmarks in, 38
  recognition study, 54–67
  trust of strangers in, 28, 29
Mann, L., 296, 297, 300
Mao Tse-Tung, 262, 296, 302, 304, 350
Maps, handdrawn, of Paris, 68–76
  mental, 7
  objective geographic, 56
  psychological, 38–39
  socioeconomic, 85
  see also Cognitive map; Mental map;
    Psychological map
March of Dimes, 332
Markman, P., 67
Martin, E. D., 226, 236, 237, 244
Marx, K., 260
Mass, action, 262
  demonstration, 211
  events, participation in, 238
  vs. people, 230
  phenomena, 256
  society, 231
Mass media, and crowd behavior, 228,
    261
  nature of, 325
The Mass Psychology of Fascism
    (W. Reich), 238
Masters, W. H., 137
Mathematical, analysis of small world
    problem, 278, 282, 287, 294
  theories of crowds, 252–258
McDonough, J. J., 121
McDougall, W., 232, 239, 242

McGranahan, D. V., 159
McGuire, W., 240
McKenna, W., 31, 32, 54
McLaughlin, B., 268
McWilliams, C., 18
Measure, of ambience, 3, 16
  of attitudes through actions, 297–304
  of conformity, 154
  of crowd, 210
  deficient, 335
  of friendliness, 17, 18
  lost letter as a, 297
  of mental maps, 21
  polarization, 212
  of urban atmosphere, 33–37
  see also Experiments
Mechanism, adaptive, 26
  of collective behavior, 239
  of contagion, 239
  of crowd behavior, 233
  defense, 237
  of displaced aggression, 239
"Medical Center," 308, 311, 314, 325,
    326, 327, 328, 329, 332
Medical Research Associates, 297, 299,
    301
Meier, N. C., 265
Meier, R. L., 26, 31
Memory, of city, 58
  and photography, 279, 339
  study of, 189, 193
Mennenga, G. H., 265
Mental, life, unconscious, 236
  patients, 226
  unity of crowds, 232
Mental map, 7, 8, 20, 21, 23, 50, 54, 55,
    57
  of Boston, 55
  of New York City, 21, 55, 57, 58
  of Paris, 7, 8, 21
  see also Cognitive map; Psychological
    map
"Mercury Theatre of the Air," 261
Merton, R. K., 233
Merv Griffin Show, 329
Message, 282, 285
Methods, anecdotal, 129
  comparative, 28
  computer simulation, 217
  of debriefing, 121, 140–143
  diffusion traceback, 277, 278
  estimated pain scale, 123
  experimental, 27

final itinerary, 86
free recall, 80
group pressure experiment, 179 ff
handdrawn maps, 68–76
of inquiry, 4
Monte Carlo, 256
obedience experiment, 103 ff
photographic recognition test, 80, 83
polarization quotient, 213, 215
post-experimental interview, 123
psychoanalytic interview, 148
psychological maps, 21, 55, 58 ff, 68 ff
questionnaire, 123, 174, 175, 177
recruitment, 314, 322, 332
self-report scale of maximum tension, 113
small world, 278, 285–293
of studying comparative behavior, 36
of studying crowds, 202, 210, 213, 215, 220–222, 260 ff
of studying effect of adaptation on perception of city, 35
of studying national characteristics, 159 ff
see also Anecdote; Crowds; Interview; Experiment; Measure; Motion picture; Photograph; Projective techniques; Questionnaire; Sampling; Scale; Survey
Methvin, E. H., 211
Middleclass, lower, in Germany, 238
in Paris, 84
reaction to violence, 44, 45
values, 241
Milgram, A., 90, 121
Millard, C., 206, 220
Miller, J., 121
Miller, N. E., 114, 322
Milling, 207, 240
Mintz, A., 266
MIT, 284
Mob, composition of, 225, 234
connotations of word, 230
energy theory, 252
hostile, 207, 233, 241, 261
see also Crowd
Mobilization in Smelser's Theory, 245 ff
Model, of antisocial behavior, 333
birth-and-death, 257
for comparative research, 36
of contagion process, 253, 254
convergence, 241
of crowds, 233

deterministic, 255
of group size, 200–204, 256–258
probabilistic, 255
of small world, 284
use of, in aggressive behavior, 264, 325
Mods, 241
Molecules in mental maps, 78
Molineux, E. L., 262
Moral, act, 149
involvement, 26
judgment, 20, 149, 192
obligations, 46
Morally significant act, 92
Morgenthau, S., 31, 32
Morris, D., 50
Morrison, H. W., 179
Moscovici, S. 21, 90
Motion, staggered, 218
synchronized, 218
Motion pictures, in crowd study, 202, 206, 220, 243
Motive, of antisocial viewers, 331
of crowd, 236
Motivation, mobilization of, 249
The Mountain People (C. Turnbull), 20
Movement, geographic, 293–295
Mowrer, O. H., 322
Murata, T., 121, 187, 300
Murphy, W., 228
Murray, H., 10
Muybridge, E., 347

Nadien, M., 28
The Nation, 18, 26, 42, 93
National, characteristics, 160 ff
differences, 159
see also names of countries, France, Norway, etc.
Nationality and conformity, 154, 159 ff
Naturalistic setting, 36, 134, 307
Nazi, anti-, 304
letters, 42
Party, Friends of the, 297–298
see also Germany
Negro, 39, 209, 216, 225, 230, 236, 239, 241, 250, 259, 293
see also Black; Ghetto
Neighborhood, black and white, 39, 300
concept of, 47 ff
defended, 49
ethnic, 84
New York, 26, 42, 43, 60 ff

in Paris, 8, 86
recognition of, 60 ff
Network Television Preview Theatre,
    314
New Haven, 103, 189, 297, 300
New York City, 25, 42, 340
    antisocial television programs, 314–334
    atmosphere, 16, 33–35, 37–39
    boundaries, 48
    cognitive map of, 38, 39, 59
    helpfulness in, 17, 28, 31, 46
    psychological map of, 21, 54–67
    tempo of, 37
    study of crowds in, 202–204, 220
    subway, 4
    walking speeds in, 36
    see also Bronx; Brooklyn; Harlem;
        Kew Gardens; Manhattan; Queens
New York Daily News, 314
New York Magazine, and mental map
    study, 60, 67
New York Times, 34, 42, 241, 296
New York University, 30
News program, in TV study, 332–334
Noise, crowd, 268
    painful, in obedience study, 137
Noninvolvement, 27, 29
    see also Alienation; Apathy; Social
        intrusion
Norm, 249, 250
    breakdown of, 215
    changing, 29, 336
    crowd, 258
    cultural, 217
    deviation from, 226
    moral, 7
    in Norway, 171
    -oriented social movement, 249
    and rumors, 227
    social, 5, 20
    theory, emergent, 239, 242–245
Norman, R. Z., 282
North Carolina, tobacco towns, 300
Norton, W. J., 227
Norway, conformity in, 160–170
    life in, 171–173
Numbers, absolute, 223
    effect on crowd formation, 220
    large, 24, 256
    of lost letters, 304
    significance of, 222
    see also Size
Nurses, study of, 133–134

Obedience, conditions of, 102–123
    vs. conformity, 186
    destructive, 139, 144, 188
    experiments, 6, 7, 92–99, 102–146, 154,
        197, 236
    see also Authority; Conformity;
        Submission
Observation, of city life, 24
    of crowds, 215, 229
    empirical, 220, 221
    of newcomer vs. long-time resident, 35
    room, one-way, 265
Onlooker, 210
    at accident scene, 219
    at demonstrations, 225
    response of, 44
    see also Bystander; Witness
Opinion, community, 301
    in France, 169
    see also Attitude
Oppenheim, A., 307
Oppenheimer, M., 262, 268
Organization for Comparative Social
    Research, 160
Orientation, community, toward political
    institutions, 296
    to experimenter, 109
    and mental maps, 57
    negative, toward group, 153
Origins of Totalitarianism (H. Arendt),
    231
Orne, M., 93, 124, 125, 128–137
Ortega y Gasset, 231
Oslo, 38, 172, 173, 176
    University of, 162
    see also Norway
Outsider vs. local, 241
Overload, 18, 25, 26, 30, 31, 33, 38, 39,
    53

Pailhous, J., 21, 23
Paired associate learning task, 103, 179
Palo Alto, 30
Panic, 215, 222, 248, 249, 261, 262,
    265–267
Paradigm, Asch's, 178
    experimental, 92, 337
    laboratory, 92
Paradoxical unknowns in mental maps,
    80, 82
Paris, 4, 16, 21, 23, 340
    atmosphere, 33–35, 37, 39
    as a collective representation, 72

crowds, 215, 224
  handdrawn maps of, 68–76
  helpfulness in, 36
  known and unknown, 83, 84
  mental maps of, 7, 8
  meeting places, 87, 89
  Piltzer Gallery, 21
  psychological maps of, 21, 38, 68–90
  recognition of scenes, 8, 78, 80
  secrets, 86–89
  social perceptions of, 84
  students in, 162, 166, 172
  urban renewal, 89
Park, R. E., 50, 232
Parkes, A. S., 217
Parsons, T., 248–249
Participant(s), in crowd, 229, 258, 259
  in mob, 226
  mobilization of, 248
  in obedience experiment, 93, 141–143
  reactions to being, 175, 176, 177
  see also Confederate; Partner; Subject
Partner in Asch's study, 195
Paths, commonly selected, 86
  in mental maps, 39, 57, 76
Pedestrians, in crowd studies, 201, 202,
    204, 220
  in photography experiments, 346
  walking speeds of, 36, 218
Peer pressure, 96, 193–198
  see also Confederate; Group pressure
Peking, 7
Penetration of crowd, 209
Penrose, L. S., 223
Perception(s), of cities, 35, 39
  of crowd, 229
  and group size, 257
  and photography, 279
  social, 84
Performance, effect of group on, 197
  measure of, 189
  prediction of, 6
Périphérique, 73
Permeability of crowd boundary, 209
Person, starting, vs. target person,
    285–293
Personal susceptibility to panic, 262
Personality, aggressive, 219
  conscious, 232, 233
  focal, 237
  unconscious, 232
Peterson, W. A., 228
Phenomenal unity of act, 108

Philadelphia, 17, 31, 36
Photoanalysis (R. Akaret), 348
Photographer, characteristics of, 348, 349
  subject relationship, 346
Photographic, act, 344–350
  aids, 221
  behavior, 279
  evidence, 224
Photographic Recognition Test, 78, 80,
    83
Photography, 279–280
  aerial, of crowds, 206, 215, 268
  of commuters, 3, 51
  of crowds, 212, 213, 220, 243, 263
  of death camps, 92
  of familiar stranger, 3, 51
  use of in psychological maps, 21, 39,
    58 ff, 80
  psychological processes of, 339–350
  see also Motion picture
Physical, conditions and crowd behavior,
    215
  contact in obedience experiment, 106
  layout of city, 37
  presence, of authority, 110
    of victim, 110
Pilot studies of obedience to authority,
    105
Pinkney, D., 215
Pirenne, H., 282
Plato, 9
Platoons, traffic, 219
Points, break-off in obedience study,
    118, 122, 189–193
  as feature of crowd, 206
  in graph theory, 282, 284
  in mental maps, 21, 39, 57
  of origin, 228, 277
  of rupture in obedience study,
    139
  of transmission, 228, 293
Polansky, N., 264
Polarization, 301, 304
  of crowd, 212, 213
  quotient, 215
Police, Berkeley, 246, 248
  car demonstration, 225
  contacting, 43–46, 100
  manuals, 262, 263
  Mississippi, 212
  New York City, 331
  reports, 221, 222
  and riots, 224, 228, 240, 244

Political, activity in Berkeley, 246–248
  boundaries of city, 58
  events, 223
  goals of war resisters, 149
Politics, assessing attitudes toward, 296,
    301–304
  in France, 169
  in Norway, 169, 172
  see also Lost letter
Polish jokes, 277
Pool, I., 281, 284
Population, 294, 295
  American, 284
  available, 200, 201
  crowd, 200, 222, 253–255
  density, 24, 29
  heterogeneity of, 24, 34, 39
  of Paris, 82, 84
  source of, 37
  see also Subject(s)
Pose, in photography, 347
Postman, L., 227, 243
Power, drawing, of crowds, 200–204, 220
  invincible, 233
Preconception about cities, 35
Prediction, of crowd size, 206
  of obedience, 6, 118
Prejudice, of Le Bon, 234
  and perception of crowds, 230
Pressure, authoritarian, 197
  group, 173, 178–198, 222, 223
  relief from, 172, 173
  social, 122
  see also Authority pressure; Group
      pressure; Peer pressure
Prison, records, 225
  reform, 99
  rioters sent to, 225
  war resisters in, 147 ff
Private vs. public action in conformity
    studies, 166, 167, 177
Privileged space, 345
Probabilistic models, 255, 256
Probability, 255
Project Hope, 313, 327–333
Projective techniques, 263, 264
  see also Rorshach, Thematic
      Apperception Test
Pro-social conformity, 152
  see also Helpfulness
Proximity, in diffusion study, 278
  in obedience experiment, 106–110, 123

physical, 26
  see also Crowds
Psychiatrist(s), use of in debriefing, 121,
    143
  predictions of obedience, 6, 118
Psychoanalytic view of collective
    behavior, 235–238, 244
Psychological, characteristics, 159 ff
  crowd, 232
  distance, 294
  document, photographs as, 348
  effects of city life, 16, 29 ff
  map, 21, 54
  of New York City, 21, 39, 54 ff
  of Paris, 21
  vulnerability, 29
"Psychological Maps of Paris," 21,
    68–90
Psychology, clinical, 160
  mob, 231
Psychology Today, 2, 281, 296
Public, conformity, 166
  opinion polls, 262
Public Opinion Quarterly, 296
Punishment, in antisocial program, 310,
    319, 323–325, 328
  and group pressure, 179 ff, 264
  in obedience study, 103 ff, 238
  rewards and, 266
  of war resisters, 147
Pusey, N. M., 10

Quartiers, 83–86
  see also Arrondissements
Queens, 59 ff
  see also Kew Gardens
Questionnaire, on English life, 160
  on familiar stranger, 51
  in mob study, 265
  open-ended, 174, 175
  reaction to ethics of conformity
      experiment, 174 ff
  in study of nurses, 134
  in study of urban atmosphere, 34
  used to create psychological map, 38

Race, and lost letter technique, 300
  see also Black; Negro
Rand, C., 281
Rapoport, A., 253, 255
Rashevsky, N., 223, 254, 255, 258
Raven, B. H., 179

Reaction, circular, 239, 244
Reciprocal fields, 108
Recognition, of New York scenes, 60 ff
   of Parisian scenes, 78 ff
   of scenes, 21
Recognizability, index of, 65
   relative, of scenes, 60 ff
Redl, F., 237
Rejection, reactions to, 160
Relationship, within crowd, 212, 235
   familiar stranger, 3, 53
   frozen, 3, 51
   in group, 257
   leader-follower, 236
   subject-photographer, 346
Reputation, neighborhood sources of, 48
Research, cross-national, 160 ff
   question, formulation of, 5
   technique, 178
Research Associates of Bridgeport, 115
Residence, effects of, on psychological
      map, 63 ff, 82, 84
Response bias, Queens, 65
Responsibility, abdication of, 100
   for actions, 96, 112, 144, 243
   diffusion of, 196, 264
   level of, 279
   loss of, 226, 233
   social, 26 ff, 44 ff, 156, 169, 171–173
Revolt, Hungarian, 226
   see also Riot(s)
Revolt of the Masses (Ortega y Gasset),
      231
Revue Scientifique, 231
Reward, effect of, 266
Ring, K., 137
Ring, in crowds, 207
Riot(s), 210, 211
   Berkeley, 225
   Birmingham, 231
   civil rights, 236
   control of, 262, 263
   Detroit, 225
   food, in England, 228
   in France, 224, 225
   Harlem, 224, 228, 230
   by Japanese-Americans, 225
   Los Angeles, 240, 244
   motorcycle, 219, 223, 241
   Naples, 231
   outsider, 241
   racial, 228

   and rumor, 227, 228
   Watts, 228
"Riots and their Suppression" (E. L.
      Molineux), 262
Ritter, P., 219
Rockefeller, N., 213, 215, 294
Rockers, 241
Roemer, D. U., 219, 223, 241
Role(s), behavior in cities and towns,
      31–33
   of crowds, 234
   of experimental subject, 128, 189
   of experimenter, 129
   of group, 154
   hierarchical, 132, 135
   of leader, 235–237
   of precipitating groups, 220
   in Smelser's theory, 249, 250
   teachers, 181
Roper, E., 160
Rorschach ink-blot test, 160
Rosenberg, M., 297
Rosenhan, D., obedience experiment,
      127, 132
Ross, D., 306
Ross, S., 306
Rudé, G., 224, 228
Rule, J., 224
Rumor, 227, 228, 243
Rural, urban differences, 17
   village, 48
Russell, R., Senator, 42

Saarinen, T., 54, 57
Salience of the victim, 106 ff, 123
Salisbury, H., 296
Samaritan impulse, 27, 46
Sample(s), of crowd locations, 222
   of crowd turnover, 222
   nationwide adult, 262
   in Paris map study, 21
   representative, of New Yorkers, 59 f
   selecting, 297
   in small world studies, 285 f
Sampling, of city incidents, 34, 38
   and psychological maps, 39, 59
Sandemose, A., 173
Savio, M., 248
Scale, estimated pain, 106, 123, 125
   maximum tension, 113, 114
Schachter, S., 160, 169
Schmeck, H. M., 219

Schultz, D. P., 215
Schuster, A., 45
Science, 24, 47
Scientific American, 159
Scott, J. P., 121
Sears, D. O., 239
Sears, R. R., 322
Seine, 8, 68, 73 f
Self-image, 192
Selznick, P., 251
Sequential influence, 153
Sex, roles and communication, 290
  of subjects in Paris study, 90
  as variable, in handshaking·
      experiment, 18
    in trust experiment, 28
  see also Women
Sharpening in rumor, 227
Sheffield, F. D., 234
Shellow, R., 219, 223, 241
Sherif, C. W., 267
Sherif, M., 242, 267
Shock(s), electric, 94 f, 103 ff, 126 ff,
    179 ff, 266 ff
Shor, R. E., 133
Shotland, L., 306
Sidis, B., 207, 209, 231, 252
Sigall, H., 134
Sighele, S., 231, 242, 245, 258
Signal vs. action, conformity, 178
Simmel, G., 25, 223
Simulation, of crowd behavior, 265
  of crowd flow, 217
  see also Computer simulation
Singer, J. I., 306
Singer, R. D., 306, 307
Situations, theory of, 119
Size (of crowds), 201 ff, 220 ff
  and anonymity, 223 f
  critical, 222, 256 f
  estimating, 221
"Sketches of Popular Tumults"
    (G. Craik), 230
Sleeper effect, 328
Slogan(s), in crowd behavior, 227, 232,
    236
  recall of, 229
Small world problem, 281–295
Smelser, N. J., 220, 227, 245–248,
    250–252, 265
Smith, W. L., 217
Smoke experiment, 100, 265
Smoking, 96

Soboul, A., 224
Social, class in Paris, 84 f
  classes, 284
  confirmation, 196
  conformity, 169 f
  constraints, 4, 6
  constructions, 47
  contact, 286
  control, 49, 96, 245, 249, 262
  criticism, 167
  devices to regulate crowds, 217
  disorganization, 217
  distance, 157
  function, constructive, 260
  identity, 244
  intrusion, 11
  involvement, 7
  matrix, 154
  movements, 249
  perceptions of Paris, 84
  responsibility, 26 ff, 156
Social psychologist, characteristics of, 10
Social psychology, 179
  contribution of, 92
  experimental, 1, 7, 11
  influence as central concept in, 275
  influence of Le Bon on, 234
  paradigms of, 92
Social screening devices, 25
  anonymity, 30
Social structure, 130 ff
  differentiation of, 96
Socioeconomic map of Paris, 85 f
Sociometric stars, 3
Solidarity in the community, 48
Solomon, H., 204
Solomon, R. L., 133
Solvency in crowds, 210
"Some Conditions of Obedience and
    Disobedience to Authority"
    (S. Milgram), 93
Sontag, S., 92
Soper, H. E., 256
Source(s), of ambience, 37 f
  of cultural items, 276 ff
  of information, 276 ff
  population, 37, 253
  secondary (in crowd), 262 ff
Span of sympathy, 27
Sport(s), events, riots in, 241
  in Norway, 172
Stanford University, 30
The State of the Masses (Lederer), 231

Staten Island, 59 ff
Staudenmayer, H., 319
Stea, D., 54, 57, 68
Steinberg, L., 67, 136
Stereotype(s), national, 159, 169
    of Paris, 68
    portraits, 341
    urban, 32, 36
Stigma, 16
Stimulus, crowd, 200 ff
    external, 186
    of individuals in a crowd, 229, 239
    repetition of, 153, 168
    television programs, 312 ff
Stochastic models, 255 f
Stoltz, H. Z., 265
Stranger, behavior toward, 28 f, 31
    familiar, 3, 51–53
Strecker, E. A., 226
Street(s), commonly selected, in Paris,
        86
    crowds, 232
    directions, asking for, 36 f
    patterns, 23, 37
    significance of the, 45
Stress, 97 f, 113 f, 140, 146
    see also Anxiety; Strain; Tension
Structural, conduciveness, 245 f
    strain, 245, 250
Structure, of acquaintanceships, 282
    of associations of Paris, 78
    of authority, 13
    crowd, 206 ff, 263
    field, 197 f
Student(s), Berkeley, 225, 246 ff
    Chinese, 303
    high school, 314, 322
    see also Subjects
Study, of behavior toward compatriots
        and foreigners, 36 f
    of Berkeley student demonstrators,
        225
    of boys in summer camp, 267
    of communications in subgroups, 293
    of cones jamming in bottle, 266
    diffusion traceback, 276 ff
    election by lost letter, 301
    of housewives' recall of slogan, 228
    Kansas, 285 f
    of mob under experimental conditions,
        265
    Nebraska, 285 f
    of panic in smoke filled room, 265 f

of panic by threatening subjects with
        electric shock, 266 f
    of Piazza del Palio, 220
    of profiles of London, Paris, and New
        York, 33 ff
    of revival meetings, 223
    of rioters in American internment
        camp, 225
    of rioters sent to prison, 225
    of television violence and aggressive
        play, 306
    using TAT and crowd photographs,
        263
    of walking speeds, 36 f
    see also Experiment(s)
Subject(s), cooperating, 134
    in crowd studies, 265 ff
    debriefing of, 121, 142 f, 167, 174 f
    disbelieving, 134
    experimenter contract, 186
    factory workers as, 168
    French, 162 ff
    Norwegian, 162 ff
    in Paris psychological map study, 21,
        68 ff, 90
    in psychological map study, 59 ff
    psychology undergraduates as, 137
    reactions to ethics of experiment,
        174 ff
    rights of, 97 f
    welfare of, 140 ff
    women as, 117
Submission, to authority, 12, 14, 105
    social, 187
    see also Obedience
Subway, crowds in Tokyo,
        216
    experience, 4 ff, 344
Suggestibility in crowds, 233
    see also Hypnosis
Survey(s), by Cantril, 261 f
    in crowd research, 262
    deficiencies of, 296 f
    organization, French, 21
    sample, 160, 304
    taken by James, 256 f
Suttles, G. D., 47–50, 84
Sutton, W., 45
Sweden, 49
Symbols, of the city, 39
    of Paris, 82, 87
Synthetic groups, 162
Szilard, L., 12

Taine, 224
Takooshian, H., 17
Tarde, G., 231, 239
Tape recording, in crowd studies, 268
  use of in experiments, 104, 162, 163,
    167, 177
Target person, 285 ff
TAT, *see* Thematic Apperception Test
Tavris, C., 14 ff
Taxicab drivers, in Athens and Boston,
    36
  in Paris, 21, 23, 36
Teacher, in group pressure experiment,
    179, 180, 189, 193
  in obedience experiment, 103
Telephone, calls, abusive, 309, 325 ff,
    335
  in diffusion traceback, 276–278
  use of to call police, 44
  use of in helpfulness studies, 27, 28,
    31, 32
  use of in obedience experiment, 110
  use of in nurse study, 134
Television, and antisocial behavior, 9,
    279, 306 ff
  auto accident on, 219
  effects of, 9
  form vs. contents, 9
  newscast, 332 ff
  Research Associates, 332
  and violence, 8, 9, 279
Tempo of city, 36, 37
Temporal dimension of crowd, 221
Tension, collective, 258
  in conformity experiments, 162, 168
  intergroup, 267
  in obedience experiments, 112–114,
    123, 125, 139
  scale, 113
  in subway experiment, 5
  see also Anxiety; Strain; Stress
Territoriality, 50
Thematic Apperception Test, 160, 263,
    264
Theory, Allport-Postman, 228
  contagion, 239 ff, 253
  convergence, 239 ff
  crowd, 212, 227, 230 ff
  emergent norm, 239, 242 ff
  frustration-aggression, 238, 239
  graph, 282
  mathematical, 252
  mental maps, 23

mob energy, 252
psychoanalytic, 235 ff
overload, 18, 25 ff
of situations, 119
Smelser's, 245 ff
sympathetic induction of emotion, 239
traffic, 219
urban, 24
validation, 160
see also Crowd; Model
Thrall, C., 268
Threat, reactions to, 160
Tilly, C., 224
Toch, H., 200, 206
Tocqueville, A. de, 159
Tokyo, crowds, 216
  lost letter study, 302
Tones, judgment of acoustic, 162 ff
Torgersen, U., 173
Torrey, R., 199
Town, Connecticut industrial, 300
  North Carolina tobacco, 300
  small, behavior in, 27 ff
    lost child in, 7, 17
    reciprocated handshaking in, 17, 18
Tracy, S., 340
Traffic, crowds of, 218 f
  flow, 219
  patterns, 37
Travel among Norwegians, 173
Travers, J., 268, 286
Trowbridge, C. C., 57
Tuddenham, R., 178
Turnbull, C., 20
Turner, L., 133
Turner, R., 212, 215, 221, 224, 227, 229,
    232, 233, 239, 241–245, 251, 258,
    259
Type(s), of central persons, 237
  of collective behavior, 248
  of crowd, 236
  of situations, 198

United States, 294
  Public Health Service, 307
  voting behavior, 169
  see also American
Universality, feeling of, 242
  impression of, 230
Urban, anonymity, 51–53
  atmosphere, measures of, 33–35
  differences, 17
  friendships, 42

imagibility, 20
life, 27
norms, 33
renewal in Paris, 89
setting, 2, 16, 156
theory and research, 24 ff

Validity of lost letter technique, 301
Value(s), -added determinants, 245, 251
ethical, and behavior, 43 ff
group, 154
in Norwegian society, 173
quantitative, of performance, 189
in Smelser's theory, 249 ff
specific, prediction of, 255
town, 33
Van Hoose, T., 134
Vance, P., 307
Vandalism, 30
Vehicles, crowds of, 218 f
Verbal, accounts, 35, 297
crazes, 276
judgment, 153, 154, 178
Victim, aiding, 43 ff
in group pressure experiments, 191
in obedience study, 102 ff, 142
responses of, 122, 185
subject as, 136
see also Feedback; Learner
Videotape, 268
Vienna, 38
Vietnam War, 13, 93, 148
Villena, J., 28
Violence, crowd, 235, 242, 260
effects of, 306
mob, 241
response to, 43 ff
and television, 8, 279, 306 f, 336 f
Visual components of cities, 37

Wada, G., 225
Wallach, M. A., 198, 264
Wallas, G., 260
Wallston, K., 137
Walters, R. H., 264
War, 102
resisters, 147 ff
see also Vietnam War; World War I;
World War II

War of the Worlds (H. G. Wells), 261
Waskow, A. I., 222, 236
Waters, J., 31, 54, 90
Waves of traffic, 219
Wechsler Adult Intelligence Scale, 296
Wells, H. G., 261
Wells, H. H., 199
White, E., 268
White, H., 257, 258, 287
Williams, J. T., 121
Winkel, G., 41
Wirth, L., 24, 25, 31
Witnesses, 11, 44 ff
see also Bystander; Onlooker
Wolin, S., 246, 248, 251
Woman, 29, 219, 230
Women, in crowds, 226
in helpfulness studies, 28, 29, 31
in mental map study, 60, 90
in obedience study, 117
and photography, 344
reciprocated handshaking by, 18
in sexual response study, 137
in small world study, 290
see also Sex
Woolbert, C. H., 213
Workers, agricultural, in France, 224
industrial, 168
on parade, 211
Parisian, 8
as rioters, 225
Working class in Paris, 84
World, small, 278, 281 ff
World War I, 121
World War II, 92, 149

Yale University, 238, 297
experiments in obedience to authority,
11, 102 ff
group pressure experiments, 162
Yielding, effects of, 153
in group pressure experiments, 183,
186
to a mob, 226
see also Conformity

Zalaznick, S., 67
Zander, A., 198
Zimbardo, P. G., 30, 98, 99